Technology
IN THE CLASSROOM
For Now and the Future

JANICE L. NATH
IRENE CHEN

Kendall Hunt
publishing company

Cover image © Shutterstock, Inc.

Kendall Hunt
publishing company

www.kendallhunt.com
Send all inquiries to:
4050 Westmark Drive
Dubuque, IA 52004-1840

Copyright © 2015 by Kendall Hunt Publishing Company

ISBN 978-1-4652-6658-3

Printed in the United States of America

Contents

Dedication

In the middle of this project, my husband, Anil Nath, was stricken with a massive stroke. He is a physician who worked hard throughout his life to save others. As a Cambridge and Oxford graduate, he studied hard all his life to know the latest techniques of getting patients through various difficult surgeries, including beating heart surgery. In addition, he has always been an excellent teacher as well. One of his surgery nurses reported that she learned more from him in a short time than she did in most of her nursing school. He is always a beacon to me of what it means to be a life-long learner and to many others with whom he has worked. He is having to live that now in a new way, but his grit and strength continue. I would like to dedicate my part of the book to him and all of the thousands of patients and their families for whom he made a difference. As a teacher, it is right that a book which encourages the best in teaching be dedicated to him.

Janice L. Nath

Introduction

When history looks back at our century, it will surely report that technology is a past and current "wonder of the world." There are few places where it does not touch our lives in this relatively new century—we can hardly imagine what there is to come. Yet, there are still many school and university classrooms that do not make full use of its power. There is so much to know, connect, and apply that is related to technology and learners.

When contemplating the creation of this book, we envisioned that all new teachers entering their first classroom will have the ability not only to use technology in exciting ways but to carefully consider all the ramifications—positive and negative—related to instructional technology. In other words, these should be skilled, creative, and reflective teachers who will prepare the next generation to do even more amazing work.

With that vision, we began to ask colleagues to carefully examine their content areas and construct chapters that would make a difference in the preparation of prospective teachers and for teachers who are already in the classroom. Each chapter offers classroom cases and thoughts for teaching and seamlessly integrating technology into EC-12 classrooms and for preservice growth and development in this electronic world in which we now live. We hope that these ideas will give the reader concrete examples and will also serve as a spark for them to create their own engaging ideas or to become excellent detectives to find just the right connection for instruction from the innumerable ideas and resources that are offered to those who search.

An analysis of the newly required technology competencies of a number of states reveals that more emphasis lies on "technology applications" rather than basic "computer literacy". In addition to their content knowledge, however, teachers of the twenty-first century also need to become familiar with American Disabilities Act and assistive technology, diverse learning, ESL (English as a Second Language) the digital divide, intellectual property, Internet security, and various ethical and social issues that involve the use of technology. Digital tools enhance the teacher capabilities to fulfill the many roles and responsibilities of teaching and using technology, but the reader should come away with a "bigger picture" of being a digital teacher.

We are still awed by the speed and magic that technology can bring to our lives, and we want our teachers to open that door for their students.

Organization of the Text

This text, written by university teacher preparation faculty and technology consultants, is designed to strengthen future teachers' understanding of the critical information in technology applications for K-12 teachers.

This text is organized in two parts: (1) Educational Technology Supporting the Content Areas, and (2) Using Educational Technology for Best Practices in Schools and for Teacher Education. In Section 1, the major content areas of technology combined with literacy, social studies, science, and mathematics classrooms are presented. This section also contains chapters on the use of technology with young children, special education, and ESL. In addition to teaching in the content areas, teachers also need to become competent with their work settings and maintain professional growth with professional development. The second section visits an array of topics on technology concerning other areas of the classroom: generic models of teaching, technology standards, legal and ethical use, and assessment. There are also chapters that discuss technology for help with certification testing, in creating a reflective practice, and governance issues in school systems.

Acknowledgments

First and foremost, the editors would like to offer a special thanks to the chapter contributors. Without their insights and contributions, this book may not have been possible. Tremendous effort goes into the creation of a book, and our authors should be given credit for their expertize, creativity, and research to bring this together. We also thank Kristin Anderson at Kendall Hunt for her vision and support in a project of this scope.

We would like to express gratitude to the many people who saw us through this book—to all those who provided support, talked things over, read, wrote, and offered comments. Drs. Tina Nixon and Libi Shen have helped to review, edit, and offer feedback on many of the chapters.

About the Authors

Sergei Abramovich, Ph.D. (mathematics), is Professor in the Department of Curriculum and Instruction at State University of New York at Potsdam. He is the author/editor of five books and numerous articles on the use of computers in mathematics education. His service to educational community includes membership on editorial boards of eight professional journals published in the United States and elsewhere.

Dr. EunJin Bang is an assistant professor in science education at Iowa State University. She has experience leading mentoring programs for elementary science teachers in Iowa that has incorporated both online and hybrid platforms. She also teaches both early childhood (K-3) and elementary (K-8) science methods classes that provide diverse technology experiences for teacher candidates.

Ronald S. Beebe is Associate Professor of Educational Research at the University of Houston-Downtown. He teaches courses on educational research, classroom-based research, assessment and evaluation, culture of the urban school, and statistics. His current research focuses on the impact of classroom-based research on teacher and student outcomes, as well as issues of equity and social justice. He has been awarded grants for work in student success, minority teacher recruitment, faculty professional development, and program evaluation. Additionally, his collaborative research includes investigating vocational outcomes, psychological practice, and online learning and assessment, with publications addressing career and vocational outcomes, professional development school practice, social justice, and online assessment. He currently serves as Interim Chair of the Department of Urban Education.

Katrina Borders (Master of Education in Administration and Supervision from the University of Houston-Main) has over 18 years of teaching and instructional coaching experience in K-12 schools. She currently serves as Director of the STAR Program, a \$3 million Title V student success initiative, at the University of Houston-Downtown. The Student Transition and Retention (STAR) Program is funded by the U.S. Department of Education. The program provides first-year students opportunities to acquire the knowledge and skills that will ensure their success in their initial year and their return to UHD in the second year. She is committed to assisting educators create collaborative and supportive learning environments in which all students will thrive.

Christal Gooding Burnett, Ed.D, is Associate Professor of Bilingual Education in the Department of Urban Education at the University of Houston-Downtown. She holds a Doctorate of Education in International Educational Development with an emphasis on bilingual/bicultural studies and family and community education from Teachers College, Columbia University. Dr. Burnett received her BA in Spanish from Carnegie Mellon and her MA in Language Learning and Policy from Stanford. She also has teaching experience as a bilingual elementary teacher. Her teaching and research interests include the education of emergent bilinguals, family involvement, and educational opportunities for underrepresented populations. Dr. Burnett currently serves as Interim Assistant Chair of the Department of Urban Education. She can be reached at burnettc@uhd.edu.

Irene Linlin Chen received her Doctor of Education in Instructional Technology. She previously served as an instructional technology specialist and computer programmer/analyst. As Professor of Educational Technology at University of Houston-Downtown, her current research interests are: instructional technology, assessment and evaluation, multicultural education, urban education, business education, and curriculum and instruction.

She has delivered K-12 inservice professional development activities for both faculty and staff and has given numerous state, national, and international presentations, most recently at Oxford, England. She is the co-author of *Technology Applications for K-12 Teachers* and a co-editor of *Wired for Learning: An Educator's Guide to Web 2.0.*

Myrna D. Cohen, Ed.D., is Professor of Education at the University of Houston-Downtown. Her teaching experience includes grades 2–12 as well as undergraduate and graduate classes in higher education. She has held leadership positions in several national and state organizations and has received state awards for her organizational work. She is coeditor of a number of books on teacher education. She served for eight years as the Chair of the Department of Urban Education and is currently serving as Associate Dean of the College of Public Service.

Michael L. Connell, Ph.D., is Professor of Mathematics Education at University of Houston-Downtown. Dr. Connell has over 30 years of mathematics education experience at both graduate and undergraduate levels working with students in field-based teacher certification programs. His research interests lie at the intersection between educational technology, learning theory, and mathematics education. He has written, presented, and published extensively in these areas.

Colin Dalton, Ed.D., is an assistant professor of literacy education and TESOL at the University of Houston-Downtown. His teaching and research interests include literacy development and practice utilizing alternate texts to develop life-long readers. He can be reached at daltonc@uhd.edu.

Viola M. García is a professor in the Department of Urban Education at the University of Houston-Downtown where she served as chair of the department. She was the recipient of the UH-D Faculty Award for Service in 2006. She has served the Southern Association of Colleges and Schools as a member of on-site and off-site review committees. Dr. Garcia joined the National School Boards Association board of directors in 2014, is immediate past president of the Texas Association of School Boards, and vice-president of the Aldine ISD school board where she has served since 1992. She also served on the Board of Directors of the Lone Star Investment Pool. Garcia is a fellow of the American Leadership Forum and participated in the Reform Governance in Action (RGA) program. She is a member of the National Association of Latino Elected and Appointed Officials and past president of the Mexican American School Board Members Association. She received a Doctor of Education from the University of Houston in Educational Leadership and Cultural Studies in Higher Education Administration.

Jose Maria Herrera is an assistant professor of elementary social studies methods at the University of Texas at El Paso and has taught courses in the fields of social studies education (K-8), critical pedagogy, and history. Dr. Herrera holds a BS in Applied Learning Development from the University of Texas at Austin, an MA in History from the University of Texas at El Paso, and a Ph.D. from Purdue University in American History. Dr. Herrera is certified in bilingual, Spanish, and secondary history education and has ten years' experience teaching in the public schools. Dr. Herrera's research interests in education are focused primarily on two issues: (1) developing effective and practical social studies instructional techniques for teachers, particularly critical reasoning skills; and (2) the status of social studies as a major subject at the elementary level.

Amelia Hewitt holds an Ed.D. in early childhood education. She is currently an associate professor at University of Houston-Downtown. Her primary area of interest is in addressing the needs of the whole child through developmentally appropriate teaching. Her current research as co-investigator focuses on the emotional and cognitive effects of collaborative partnerships between university faculty and university students, children, and teachers. She can be reached at hewitta@uhd.edu.

John Kelly, Ph.D., is an assistant professor in the Urban Education Department at the University of Houston-Downtown. He teaches a number of online/hybrid special education and classroom assessment courses that are designed to address the needs of the neo-millennial learning styles of future urban general educators. In addition, he provides instruction in graduate level educational research. He received his undergraduate degree from Rice University, his Masters from Prairie View A&M University, and a Ph.D. from the University of Texas at Austin where he focused on learning disabilities, behavior disorders, and developmental disabilities. His primary research interest is studying the impact of self-determination on LD/BD and PDD populations. In addition, he has a personal interest (a 26-year-old son and a 7-year-old grandson) in autism and developmental disabilities. Prior to entering the education field, he spent 30 years in the financial services industry.

Dr. Hsin-Hui Grace Lin is an associate professor in the Department of Teacher Leadership and New Literacies at University of Houston at Victoria. Dr. Lin received her B.S. degree from Fu-Jen Catholic University and her Ph.D. degree in Child and Family Studies from the University of Wisconsin-Madison in 1997. She began working as a principle investigator in the Center of Research and Policy on Basic Skills at Tennessee State University. Before coming to Houston, she worked as a manager of Data Management and Analysis under the Division of Policy, Planning and Research in the Department of Children's Services of State of Tennessee and as an assistant professor in the Department of Family and Consumer Sciences at Tennessee State University. Dr. Lin teaches developmental psychology courses. Her research focuses on students' academic achievements. Dr. Lin serves as a columnist for the Preschool Education Monthly in Taiwan and provides parenting and educational talks for the Texas Chinese Radio Station.

Dr. Sue Mahoney is an associate professor at the University of Houston-Downtown in the Department of Urban Education. She received her masters and doctorate from Texas A&M University. She teaches educational technology courses to undergraduate and graduate students. Dr. Mahoney has also served in the administration of UHD's Department of Urban Education as an assistant chair for undergraduate programs and as program director for the department's graduate and alternative certification programs. Her research interests include student buy-in to online classes, mentoring in the online environment, and effective teaching practices for the online environment.

Laura A. Mitchell, Ed.D., is an assistant professor in the Department of Urban Education at the University of Houston-Downtown. With her experience working in education as a bilingual teacher, ESL Specialist, and an assistant principal for the past 25 years, Laura combines her passions, by leading university students to discover their own passions for teaching.

Dr. Janice L. Nath, Professor at the University of Houston-Downtown, has coedited 12 previous books regarding teaching and teacher education and has served as editor of the *Texas Association of Teacher Educators' Forum*. She received the Howsam Award from the Texas Association of Colleges for Teacher Education (TACTE), the Booker Award from the Texas Association of Teacher Educators (TxATE) in recognition of significant contributions to the teacher educator preparation process, and, in addition, has received her university's Award for Excellence in Scholarly and Professional Activity. She has served as Associate Dean of the College of Public Service and has presented numerous times internationally, nationally, and at the state and local levels on various interests in teacher education, most recently at Oxford, England.

Dr. Tina Nixon has served students, parents, teachers, and administrators in the field of education for nine years. Throughout her years as an educator, she has served as a Project Grant Manager, District Trainer, and as a special and general education teacher. Dr. Nixon currently serves as a Technology Integration Facilitator for a school district in Northern Texas. She is very passionate about integrating technology into the classroom and planting seeds to grow life-long learners. She is the COO of the Jha'Kyric Nixon Scholarship, which was founded to provide scholarships to deserving graduating seniors who need financial assistance. The scholarship was founded in 2012 in memory of her brother.

Kim Pinkerton is an assistant professor at the University of Houston-Downtown. She earned a doctorate in reading and language arts from the University of Houston. She has previously taught as a public school teacher at the elementary level and as a developmental reading and writing instructor at the community college level. Her primary teaching and research interests include reading comprehension processes and practices, individualized literacy instruction methods, and past and present literacy histories of public school teachers.

Bernardo E. Pohl, Jr. (Doctorate of Education in Curriculum and Instruction from the University of Houston-Main) is Assistant Professor of Education in the Department of Urban Education at the University of Houston-Downtown. He currently lectures on education methodology, special education/disability studies, and social studies theory. He is the author of *The Moral Debate on Special Education* (Peter Lang Publishing), *The Moral Crisis in Special Education: Redefining the Social Model of Disability in Journeys in Social Education, and Voices of Empowerment* published in *The English Record*. His current areas of research interest are disability studies, social studies methods, and moral/ethical issues in public education.

Jacqueline J. Sack, Ed.D. and Assistant Professor of Mathematics Education at University of Houston-Downtown, has been in the education profession for almost 30 years, including 18 years teaching mathematics at middle and high school grades. Her research interests include visualization and characteristics of entry level activities that promote success for all kinds of learners. She has published and presented extensively in the area of visualization.

Libi Shen has a Ph.D. in Instruction and Learning from University of Pittsburgh, PA, and an outstanding dissertation award in the field of college reading and study skills from IRA. She started her college teaching career in 1989. Dr. Shen is a contributed author for the following IGI books: (1) *Educational, Behavioral, Psychological Considerations in Niche Online Communities*, (2) *Cases on Critical and Qualitative Perspectives in Online Higher Education*, (3) *Online Tutor 2.0: Methodologies and Case Studies for Successful Learning*, and (4) *Emerging Priorities and Trends in Distance Education: Communication, Pedagogy, and Technology*. Her research interests include reading skills, classroom management, curriculum design, and instructional technology.

Dr. Jane Thielemann-Downs is a professor at the University of Houston Downtown in the Department of Urban Education. During her career she has taught both graduate and undergraduate courses with specialization in Reading / Language Arts and Educational Psychology. Her research has focused on resiliency theory, the implementation of technology into teaching, and higher education administration. She is a children's book author (*Frederic Remington, Artist of the West* and *The Cursing Cure)* and has written numerous teacher preparation books and chapters for preservice teachers for teacher certification exam preparation. Her latest book in this area is *TExES Exam #231 English Language Arts & Reading 7–12 (3rd ed.) A Complete Content Review*.

Dr. Leigh Van Horn is Professor of Language and Literacy in the Department of Urban Education of the University of Houston-Downtown. She has received her university's faculty awards for both teaching and service. Her research interests include empathy in teaching and literacy experiences, literacy curriculum, and family literacy. She is currently serving as the Interim Dean for the College of Public Service.

Carolyn Wade holds an Ed.D. in early childhood education. She is currently an assistant professor at the University of Houston-Downtown. She earned a doctorate in early childhood from the University of Houston-Main. Her primary area of interest is in addressing the needs of the whole child through developmentally appropriate teaching. Her current research focuses on using music and the arts to enhance and expand developmentally appropriate teaching and assessment of young children. She can be reached at wadec@uhd.edu.

Dr. Stephen A. White has been in the field of education for 41 years. He has been a classroom teacher for grades 2–12. While in the classroom, Dr. White taught Spanish/ESL/Bilingual Education. After leaving the classroom, Dr. White worked in the publishing business as a National Consultant. As a National Consultant, Dr. White presented at local, state, national, and international conferences. Presently, Dr. White is an assistant professor at the University of Houston-Downtown.

Dr. Sissy S. Wong is an assistant professor in science education at the University of Houston. She teaches elementary and secondary science methods courses that incorporate technology to support and enhance science learning. Her research focuses on the professional development of beginning science teachers, specifically, in the areas of induction programs, mentoring, beliefs, and teacher knowledge.

Part I
Educational Technology Supporting the Content Areas

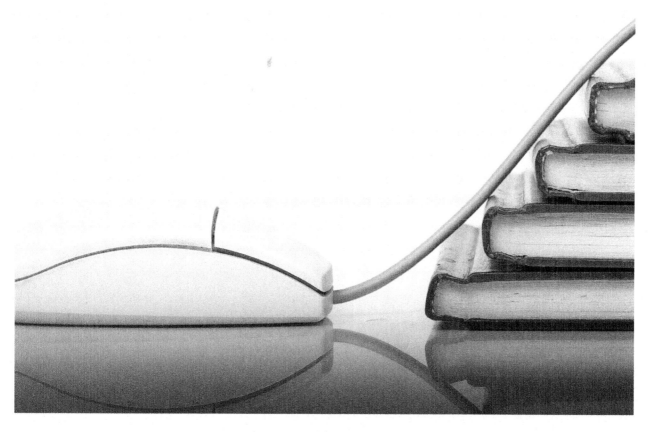

Chapter 1

Using Technology to Develop Literacy

Kim Pinkerton, Leigh Van Horn, Amelia Hewitt, and Colin Dalton

University of Houston-Downtown

Meet Sherry

Mr. Dalton has just finished reading *Catalina Magdalena Hoopensteiner Wallendiner Hogan Logan Bogan was Her Name* by Tedd Arnold (2004) to his first-grade class.

Mr. Dalton tells his class, "This story is special because of the character Catalina's name." Sherry excitedly expresses, "Yeah, her name is funny. It has a rhythm." Mr. Dalton explains the concept of rhyme in Catalina's name. He teaches the students about the rhyme in each name (first, middle, last).

Mr. Dalton encourages his students to create their own names. He shares his first: Colin Bolin Mark Bark Dalton Falton Salton. Each child then writes his or her name in rhyme and creates an audio file using hardware available in the classroom. Mr. Dalton then instructs students to create their own story to accompany their names through digital programs like iMovie. Students illustrate their story and narrate it through the digital program.

Sherry can't wait to share her creation. She volunteers to show her movie first to the class. She starts by saying, "This is the story of Sherry Berry, Lynn Bynn, Robinson Cobinson Tobinson."

Introduction

Technology is no longer a novel entity. Every teacher should be seen to be a reading teacher, integrating literacy skills and technology into curriculum in meaningful ways, rather than as a side note. Technology is a form of communication, and it brings with it different forms of understanding.

Reading encompasses a wide range of different pathways to communicate; so many things come together to make a reader. In this chapter, we focus on the most essential components of reading instruction and how to enhance these with technology. From the most elemental phonemic awareness to the complex aspect of reading comprehension, readers move through these components in a fluid and recursive way. We believe in an interactive approach to reading which provides readers with both the skills and the strategies they need to be successful. Therefore, even though the chapter is organized around the most powerful ways to use technology, when addressing phonemic awareness, phonics, vocabulary, fluency, and reading comprehension, teachers should always begin at the place where the individual student is on his or her path to reading.

Teachers should seriously consider how we are infusing technology into our reading instruction. It is not simply using technology because it is there; it is knowing first what one wants to teach and then making the decision that technology is going to help to enhance the experience and create a level of understanding. We need to think about questions such as what the students need, when they need it, and how best to help them develop a particular reading skill or strategy. In this chapter, we are offering authentic technology experiences to use at different phases in the development of students' reading progress. We want you to know that, just as we developed the ideas for this chapter based on what we saw as needs for pre-service teachers, every teacher can do the same for his/her students. We hope that these ideas will be used as a framework and that this framework will help begin the processes needed to develop learning experiences for students that use technology in the most powerful ways. We must learn to "read" students and then respond to what we have learned. We want to analyze them as we would study a character and try to predict what they would do next in literacy development.

Using Technology to Teach Phonological and Phonemic Awareness

Why is Teaching Phonological Awareness Critical to Reading?

Phonological awareness is one of the most basic, foundational components of literacy that promote reading and spelling success (Schuele & Boudreau, 2008; International Reading Association (IRA) & National Association for the Education of Young Children (NAEYC), 1998; Yopp & Yopp, 2009, 2000). This is an awareness of language that develops when parents, caregivers, and teachers expose children to talking, singing, and playing with language. The ability to discriminate sound and become aware of language sound patterns may even begin to develop before a child is born as mothers engage in talk with others and as they talk to, read to, and sing to their in-utero infants (Gerhardt & Abrams, 2000). The further development of phonological awareness should occur naturally when young children are given many opportunities to hear and play with language, and all of this can occur before children know anything about letters and phonics. This awareness can also be further developed through systematic, developmentally appropriate sound awareness instruction (Yopp & Yopp, 2009, 2000).

Phonological awareness includes awareness that our language is made of large chunks of sound (sentences), that our sentences are made of smaller chunks of sound (words), and that our words are made of even smaller parts (syllables, onset and rime, or individual sounds). A more complicated level of phonological awareness, known as phonemic awareness, involves the manipulation of phonemes, which are the smallest units of sound in language (Yopp & Yopp, 2009, 2000). Children can learn to manipulate individual sounds by segmenting (taking apart), blending (putting together), isolating (identifying a sound), deleting (taking away a sound), and substituting (removing a sound and adding a new one in its place).

While the concept of phonological awareness is the basis of literacy learning, it is also one of the most complicated concepts for parents and teachers to understand. Many children enter formal education settings with gaps. While some levels of phonological awareness (like phonemic awareness) are harder to learn than others, teaching phonological awareness does not necessarily have to occur in a linear manner (Yopp & Yopp, 2009).

Teaching phonological awareness is a natural part of the curriculum for most pre-kindergarten teachers, who offer learning opportunities for phonological awareness development through activities such as read-alouds, word play, rhyming activities, and so forth. When planning activities for children, teachers need to consider the idea that some children may enter school with certain gaps in their phonological development. This is an area where technology can make a difference. Technology can provide a link to assisting teachers in closing the gaps in phonological development by enhancing classroom-based lessons with phonological activities that are technology-infused. Investigations of the effectiveness of computer-aided instruction to develop phonological awareness skills in young children have been conducted. Some increases in skill level were found, but there were also indications that a multisensory approach may be of importance (Mitchell & Fox, 2001). Combining teacher instruction and engagement with various forms of technology may provide the right balance of seeing, hearing, saying, and doing to increase levels of phonological development.

Using Technology to Construct Ideas About Sounds

When teachers expose children to phonological awareness, they approach it in a very authentic, natural manner. Teachers can help children understand the complexity of sound in our language by engaging in the simplest activities. Songs, play, and many similar strategically planned learning experiences can build a foundation for sound awareness. Technology offers a wonderful place to begin.

The use of song in classrooms has been a part of learning for centuries. Parents have an awareness of the importance of song as well when they sing nursery rhymes with their children. For teachers who feel that they do not have an extensive musical repertoire, technology allows access to music through digital media devices like iPods and media sources like iTunes. Popular music collections and artists who have graced early childhood classes for years can now be found through these digital media devices and sources. For example, Raffi (1998) has a fun collection called *Singable Songs for the Very Young.* "Down by the Bay," "Willoughby Wallaby Woo," and "Baa Baa Black Sheep" are just a few of the selections available through this album. Even author Sandra Boyton (2013; 2004) can be found on iTunes in Sandra Boynton's *Philadelphia Chickens* and *Frog Trouble.* "Dinosaur, Dinosaur"

and "Busy, Busy, Busy" are very lively rhyming songs that are sure to get children in motion and playing with the sounds in the English language.

Technology also affords teachers the opportunity to find song lyrics at the click of a button. Songdrops.com and kids.niehs.nih.gov offer such lyrics for free. "Do Your Ears Hang Low," "Daisy Bell (Bicycle Built for Two)," and "Ten Little Monkeys," are just a few of the lyric texts that teachers can access. Teachers can print these lyrics and practice singing the songs before introducing them to the students. Songdrops.com even has the music available on iTunes with 60 free downloads for teachers. Other Internet Web sites and apps offer opportunities for music downloads such as Allmusic.com, iHeart Radio, and iTunes Radio.

In addition, a variety of Internet Web sites offer access to both song and visual media to accompany the tune. YouTube has a plethora of videos available for free. Dream English Kids offers song videos like "Good Morning Song for Children," "If You are Happy and You Know It," and many more. Children Love to Sing, also on YouTube, offers song videos like "We're Going to the Zoo" and "Animal Song." These include many animal pictures and videos to accompany the lyrics. Teachers and children can sing and move to the music—all while receiving the added benefit of sound awareness and development.

Using Technology to Introduce/Teach Sound Awareness

Encouraging children to listen to and contemplate sounds they hear is one way for them to formulate phonological ideas. Constructing ideas about sounds can be simply practiced through poems and read-alouds. Teachers can offer children opportunities to engage in games individually, with a partner, or in a small group setting. Through technology, teachers can provide students that extra practice necessary to help close phonological gaps.

Read-alouds should happen in classrooms daily. Read-alouds provide ample opportunity for discussion of language and sound and do not require large amounts of class time. Audio books from iTunes or related vendors and online storytelling Web sites allow the listener to enjoy the beauty of the story; teachers can also take time to teach students how to contemplate the sounds of our language. Children can hear the sound of language through audio books. Teachers can use Web sites like Barnes and Noble's Online Storytime to expose students to authors like Audrey Penn reading *The Kissing Hand* (1993) and to see images from the text. Readtomelv.com provides read-alouds of popular books shared by various entertainers such as *Chrysanthemum* (1991) by Kevin Henkes and *Fancy Nancy* (2005) by Jane O'Conner. Using online tools for read-alouds offers children the opportunity to hear varied vocal inflections, which heightens sensitivity to sound differences.

> **What's in My Name?**
> Chrysanthemum Sound Learning
> Poem Format
>
> **K/k/for Kasandra**
> First letter of first name   Sound of first letter   First Name
>
> **Catching, Kittens, Kangaroos**
> Word that starts with   Word that starts with   Word that starts with
> the same sound   the same sound   the same sound
>
> **Kites, Cats, & Kaleidoscopes**
> Word that starts with   Word that starts with   Word that starts with
> the same sound   the same sound   the same sound
>
> **K/k/for Kasandra**
> First letter of first name   Sound of first letter   First Name

Teachers can take this one step further and purposefully use sounds from the online books in lesson planning. For example, Mr. Phan, a kindergarten teacher plays with the sound in *Chrysanthemum* after hearing Henke's book. He then provides opportunities for students to engage in the same sound play with their own name.

Using Technology to Apply/Practice Using Sounds

Developmentally appropriate use of technology requires children to apply what they have learned through the use of hands-on application. Using technology to practice phonological skills can render developmentally appropriate, high impact sound encounters. In the development of these practical sound activities, teachers should consider cooperative learning through small group experiences such as in centers and through peer learning projects that are student-led.

Digital voice recorders allow students to capture their own phonological awareness understandings. Students can use voice memos to create rhyme, word approximation chants, and even more advanced phonemic awareness skills. For example, a small group of students can record a three-word rhyme that may include word approximations (nonsense words). A group of students in Mrs. Gray's class record "Bibbidi, Bobbidi, Boo" ("The Magic Song," 1948). Then, the next group listens to the created rhyme and records a new version by changing initial phonemes. They may choose "Zibbidi, Zobbidi, Zoo." After all small groups complete the recording, groups illustrate their rhyme; these can be transferred into a wordless digital book and read and re-read many times, as well as shared with parents and peers. For extension and challenge, each group can create a new rhyme pattern and start the process again.

The use of digital video allows students to practice phonological awareness in the most authentic method. Images, sound, and actions convey real-world use of sound and language. One possible use of video is the creation of a "Name Band" musical group. Initially, students practice with their own names by videoing themselves using musical instruments like tambourines and maracas to shake out the syllables in their first names. Students can be encouraged to create fun "Name Band" costumes to accompany their performances. Then, students form new "Name Bands" with their peers. Each group will create various musical rhythm patterns using the syllables in their names. For example, perhaps Amelia, Haley, Carolyn, Kendall, and Kim form a "Name Band." They create costumes, a musical pattern using their syllable rhythms, and their own instruments to accompany their sound rhythm. See example below.

A • mell ia, A • mel • ia (shake tambourines)

Kim (cymbals)

Ha • ley, Ha • ley, Ha • ley (rhythm sticks)

Kim (cymbals)

Car • o • lyn, Car • o • lyn (blocks)

Kim (cymbals)

Ken • dall, Ken • dall, Ken • dall (triangle)

Kim (cymbals)

Students can share their videos with peer and parents. These may also be included in the digital books mentioned above. As an extension, each "Name Band" member can rename themselves, choosing unique names, and they can start the video process once more.

Conclusion

Technology can clearly advance phonological awareness development. This tool lends itself to authentic practices that allow for many connections and creates opportunities for real-world application of language learning and development. Because sound is an essential component of language learning, phonological awareness and technology naturally complement each other. Teachers need to make deliberate choices in teaching. Integrating technology into phonological awareness development is no different. The integration needs to be chosen wisely to fit the needs of the students in order for learning to be developmentally appropriate.

Invitation to Consider This!

- Listen to Betty White read *Harry the Dirty Dog* (Gene Zion, 1956) on the storylineonline.net Web site.
  - What play with language could a teacher use to engage students in using this story?
  - Encourage students to create their own story using play with language.
- Give students a video recording device and challenge them to practice phonological awareness.
  - What kinds of things could they do?
  - What other devices could they use?
- Visit the Web sites in the Recommended Materials List insert and consider which are the most effective ones for phonological awareness connections.
  - How could students use these Web sites to deepen their phonological awareness knowledge?
  - How could teachers use these Web sites to deepen their phonological awareness instruction?

Using Technology to Teach Graphophonemic Awareness

Why is Teaching Graphophonemic Awareness Critical to Reading?

Graphophonemic awareness is the understanding of the smallest unit of written language (a letter) in combination with the smallest unit of spoken language (a sound). Graphophonemic awareness is commonly referred to as letter/sound correspondence, alphabetic principle, or phonics. This concept defines the idea that students, when they are learning language, move from an awareness of only sound in our language to an understanding that our language is made of symbols and that those symbols correspond directly to the particular sounds (Gillon, 2004; Yopp & Yopp, 2009). The ability to correspond letters and sounds and read a text "requires that children develop both awareness of the phonemes in spoken language, and knowledge of letter and sound patterns" (Mitchell & Fox, 2001, p. 316). In fact, Yopp and Yopp (2000) point out that, without phonological awareness, the letter systems are "arbitrary" (p. 131). It is important for children to make a connection between sounds and letters. Technology can aid in this letter/sound connection.

There are some basic concepts to consider when teaching graphophonemic awareness. First, teachers must be aware of the pureness of sounds in our language. In other words, teachers must be skilled in pronouncing the sounds appropriately and deliberately. For example, /p/ should involve a quick movement of the lips together and apart with an almost imperceptible breath sound that can be felt by holding one's hand in front of the lips. This is in opposition to pronouncing /p/ as /puh/.

Tyler Olson/Shutterstock, Inc.

Teachers should be purposeful in their development of graphophonemic activities. Children will enter early childhood classrooms with varying levels of graphophonemic knowledge. Some may not have any awareness of letter names and how those names correspond to the sounds that they know; others may know some of the letter names and sound correspondences, yet a few children may have knowledge of complex letter-sound relationships. Teachers should assess students while they are engaged in meaningful activities to determine where each one is in the process of learning the alphabetic principle. Activities should be constructed based on the needs of each individual child.

Finally, graphophonemic instruction should be developmentally appropriate and meet students at their levels of schematic knowledge (prior understandings children have stored in their brain). For example, most young children have an awareness of the sounds that are in their names. Teachers can use this knowledge as a springboard for teaching letter-sound correspondence related to their names. The focus on names can be extended to family members, classmates, and, finally, to the names of familiar objects in their environment. Graphophonemic learning can be so much more meaningful for students when they see how it applies to their daily lives.

Technology is a useful tool to customize graphophonemic instruction. It offers a vast array of ideas for practice and can be integrated easily into lessons and activities for students. Technology can assist teachers in making connections for students between schematic knowledge of spoken sound and print awareness. It essentially enhances and extends the teacher's lessons and improves the relationship children have with graphophonemic learning.

Using Technology to Construct Ideas About Graphophonics

When teachers engage students in graphophonemic activities, these experiences can be simple, but they should always be practical in nature so that students see how useful the knowledge can be in terms of their literacy learning. Every new letter–sound relationship taught should empower children to be readers. The purposeful planning of activities that allow for the integration of technology can ensure this outcome.

Early childhood educators can use songs and read-alouds in the classroom as natural ways to connect sounds and words to reading. Many sing-alongs found on the Internet display words on the screen to allow the singer to follow the lyrics and rhythm. On YouTube, Bob Zoom offers several videos of familiar tunes where each word is highlighted for students to practice one-to-one sound and word matching. Teachers can share songs like the "Itsy Bitsy Spider," "The Wheels on the Bus," and "Old MacDonald." In addition, teachers can find read-aloud apps through Apple, Google, and Android sources. As an example, the Read Me Stories app shares creative original stories and folklore read-aloud while words are highlighted on the screen. Finally, digital books can be read to students through apps like iBooks.

Students will hear the teacher reading, and children will watch and listen as the teacher points to the words on the screen. Teachers can show students how written language and sound work together by sharing these digital experiences.

Using Technology to Introduce/Teach Graphophonics

Once teachers have cultivated students' understanding of sounds through phonemic awareness instruction and exposed children to the written language through song, rhyme, and read-alouds, a natural bridge to the more distinct elements of graphophonics is built. Developmentally appropriate practice through whole-group interactions related to natural alphabetic principle activities encourages students to inquire about individual letter-sound relationships, which gives children the ability to begin to read and write simple words. For example, teachers need to consider differentiated instruction and student interest when teaching phonics, as opposed to only teaching letters by the week and other isolated, linear instructional approaches.

Extending on sound play with children's names (see phonological awareness), teachers can have students create a name collage through simple computer programs like PowerPoint or Keynote. In Mrs. Jimenez's first-grade classroom, each child uses a camera or searches the Internet to capture pictures that represent the initial sound in his/her name; these images are then uploaded to a computer to create the initial letter. As the child learns more sounds in his or her name, he or she uses the computer program to insert, crop, and arrange more images in the shape of each individual letter of his/her name.

As an extension, the student adds to his/her name collage by positioning the name in the center of the screen and then bordering the name collage with a draw tool that creates lines. Outside of this border, the

student then adds more pictures of images from the sound of his/her name and attempts spelling approximations for each image. Mrs. Jimenez then takes these striking name collages and combines them to create a digital class book of names for each student, serving as one of their first books for independent reading.

Using Technology to Apply/Practice Using Graphophonics

Once students understand how sounds and words connect and can create and read their own simple books, technology can be used to engage students in small group or peer learning activities that promote meaningful connections. These experiences encourage higher-level analyses, which lead to more finite studies of letter-sound correspondence. Touch screen digital technologies like iPads, new Windows programs, and Samsung Galaxy, afford opportunities for children to make practical applications by writing letters and words directly on a screen. Doodle Buddy and Kids Paint apps are two that are easy to use. Children can easily create, edit, save, and reword these written images infinitely. The new technology adds another dimension to sensory writing tools like shaving cream, sand, and rice. Tools such as these are much more developmentally appropriate in terms of learning to make the proper strokes for writing, rather than having them trace preprinted letters and words or write between the lines on paper.

Children as young as pre-kindergarten age can use digital dictation tools to record stories about their own drawings and illustrations. Students simply speak their story into the device, and the story is typed on the screen for students to read. Stories can then be downloaded, printed, and added to the illustrations. Dictation tools like Google Chrome's speech recognition engine and Notes on the iPad and/or iPhone provide these capabilities. For example, to use notes on the iPad and/or iPhone, go to notes, click on the microphone to the left of the space bar, then speak or say the story, and press done when finished. The student's dictation can be emailed directly to the teacher's email account, downloaded, and printed for the student to use. Other technology applications that are easily utilized by the students include SpeakText, which allows students to convert speech to text and share speech through social networks such as Facebook, Twitter, email, and SMS text messaging.

In the "Name Band" activity mentioned in the phonological awareness section, students used video technology to record themselves performing a name chant. To broaden this idea, teachers can urge students to use a dictation tool to record the performed chant. Students print the lyrics of the chant, add a photograph, or draw a picture of the "Name Band" players, and then share it with other students, peers, or parents. This encourages students to "show off" their creativity while extending sound, letter, and word knowledge.

Technology undoubtedly is a tool that can empower children to become readers in the classroom by offering opportunities to extend and increase graphophonemic awareness. It is essential for teachers to use technology in developmentally appropriate ways to integrate sound, letter, and word relation-ships in daily classroom activities. Assimilating technology requires that teachers contemplate best practices and tailor activities to meet the individual needs of the students. Teachers must offer meaningful, high-level exercises to prepare students for success as future readers.

Invitation to Consider This!

- Use a Smartboard to have students practice with letters or word learning. Try this game for younger students http://www.bemboszoo.com and this game http://teacher.scholastic.com/writewit/poetry/poetry_engine.htm# to learn about poetry for older students.
  - What could a teacher do to extend the learning and/or increase the connections for students?
  - How can students be encouraged to create their own game to enhance their graphophonic awareness?
- Have students extend digital dictation to Movie Maker or iMovie and challenge them to record their favorite stories. Once recorded have students add illustrations for each page.
  - What kinds of stories do they come up with?
  - What kinds of illustrations do they choose?
- Visit the Web sites and apps in the Recommended Materials List insert and consider which are the most effective for graphophonemic awareness connections.
  - How could students use these Web sites and/or apps to broaden their knowledge about letter, sound, and word connections?
  - How could teachers use these Web sites and/or apps to broaden their teaching about letter, sound, and word connections?

Using Technology to Teach Vocabulary

Why is Teaching Vocabulary Critical to Reading?

In this single sentence below from an award winning young adult trade book, there are nine words that could stop a reader without strong vocabulary knowledge.

> To move so large a body of troops, with all their necessary **appendages**, across a river a full mile wide with a **rapid current** in the face of a **victorious**, well-disciplined army nearly three times as **numerous** as his own, and a **fleet** capable of stopping the **navigation** so that not one boat could have passed over, seemed to present most **formidable obstacles**. (Meltzer, 1987, p. 98)

To understand a text, readers must understand the words that make up the text. To have a strong knowl-edge of vocabulary is to have a deep understanding of a large number of words; that is, to be able to read the words, write the words, think of the words, speak the words, view the words, and visually repre-sent the words with confidence. Brabham, Buskist, Henderson, Paleologos, and Baugh (2012) note that "children who begin school with limited vocabularies tend not to catch up with and instead fall farther behind more knowledgeable peers" (Chall, Jacobs, & Baldwin, 1990; Graves, 1986). Vocabulary learning takes place more commonly in vocabulary-rich environments where children have (a) multiple, varied, and interactive exposures to a large number of words, (b) opportunities to engage with vocabulary learn-ing strategies, and (c) the motivation to apply and practice what they have learned. In the subsections of this chapter devoted to vocabulary, teachers will learn about ways to use technology to help readers construct ideas about words, ways to use technology to introduce and teach word-learning strategies to readers, and ways for readers to use technology to apply and practice what they have learned about words. Information and communication technologies (ICTs) will continue to expand, and it will be im-portant for teachers to continue to search and develop ideas about powerful ways to engage students in vocabulary building.

Using Technology to Construct Ideas About Words

Teachers can use a free word "cloud tool," WordSift, to: (a) identify key words in a passage, (b) determine what words might need to be pre-taught to students before they read, and (c) to engage students in talking about word meanings.

To use WordSift, one downloads the free application, chooses and copies a printed text, and inserts the text in the WordSift text box. The application will generate a word cloud of the fifty most frequent words in the text in alphabetical order. The words will be of varying size, depending upon their frequency in the text. A user may click on any word in the cloud to see Google images of the word, to see a word wall displaying definitions for the word, and to see the sentences in the text that contain the word. A user may also sort the words in the cloud from the rarest to the most common to help decide the words that should be pre-taught before reading. Users can also click on the word cloud to highlight words related to a particular content of study, such as social studies. For example, Mr. Garza, a fourth-grade teacher, might engage students in talking about word meaning by displaying a word cloud, choosing a word, and then, examining the Google images together. Next, he might read the sentences from the text that contain the word and talk about the meaning of that particular word in the context of the writer's world. He could then invite students to work with a partner and choose a word or two to examine and discuss. Partners can share their investigations and discoveries in a whole class discussion. Students can add these words to their own personal electronic dictionaries. For a demonstration of WordSift using an excerpt from Martin Luther King's Letter from a Birmingham Jail, go to http://wordsift.com/site/video.

Figure 1.1 Word cloud on "Archeology" (showing relationship between archeology and other content areas).

Using Technology to Introduce/Teach Word Learning

Readers can integrate their growing knowledge of words by organizing related words into sets or language gestalts (Nilsen & Nilsen, 2005). This idea builds upon theory-based research about the usefulness of semantic mapping and features analysis as vocabulary acquisition strategies. Young readers may begin learning and collecting related words using *Montessori Crosswords*, an inexpensive application that allows them to drag and drop letters onto a grid to form words that correspond to images. When readers touch the letter they are able to hear the phonetic sound of the letter. There are a number of levels, including simple words with one sound, three sounds, consonant blends, and words related to a theme (language gestalts). Themes can include *house, animals, nature, food, clothes, colors, vehicles,* and others. After participating in the thematic experiences in *Montessori Crosswords,* young readers might work with the teacher to identify and map words related to a topic or concept found in a text or text set. For example, students might begin to organize words related to the zoo after a read-aloud and discussion of *Polar Bear, Polar Bear, What Do You Hear?* (Martin, 1991) and *Inside a Zoo in the City* (Capucilli, 2002), which contain words and illustrations for many animals to be found in a zoo. Brabham et al. (2012, p. 527) include a table of text sets for teaching concepts and semantically related words for *sizes, feelings, night/day, noises, speeds,* and *actions.*

Word mapping and feature analysis may be especially important for English language learners who can be confused about hypernyms (the general topic or superordinate) and hyponyms (specific items included in the general classification or subordinate) (Carlo et al., 2004). For example, readers of *One of Each* (Hoberman, 1997) learn about the hypernym, *house,* and many of the hyponyms that might be included in the larger topic of *house,* those being *window, door, staircase, floor, closet, bedroom, kitchen, fireplace,* and so on. Within this text there is also the hypernym, *furniture,* and the associated hyponyms, *clock, bookcase, cupboard, bed, table, chair, bureau,* and *footstool.* Readers may use electronic display boards to create visual representations of concept circles (Tompkins, 2001) that include the hypernym in the center of the circle with all of the hyponyms surrounding it. These concept circles can then be used to generate an electronic display of an interactive semantic feature analysis chart (Figure 2) that students can complete together while engaged in discussion.

Examples Hyponyms	Something you can open or pass through	Walls	Size	Purpose
Window				
Door				
Staircase				
Floor				
Closet				
Bedroom	yes	four	About '10' × '11'	a place to sleep, study, dress, etc.
Kitchen				
Fireplace				

Figure 1.2   An interactive semantic analysis chart.

Using Technology to Apply/Practice Word Learning

Readers can use media such as hyperlinked PowerPoint slides, wikis, or blogs to create multimedia glossaries that allow them to apply and practice their word learning. This strategy might be particularly helpful to readers who are learning content area vocabulary. Dalton and Grisham (2011) suggest that readers might create a PowerPoint slide that includes an image, a caption, a definition, a personal connection, an audible representation of the word, and a reference. These individual student-created "pages" could be linked to one another so that readers are creating and sharing a multimedia glossary that represents their study of an aspect of the content area (see Figure 3).

Word SLapPs is a customizable vocabulary application that can be used by teachers or students. Teachers can use the application to create learning experiences that are geared specifically to individual students or small groups. Students can use it to demonstrate their knowledge of content area vocabulary. Users can name a category, upload photographs from their personal library of images, record their voice asking questions, and/or provide information about the photographs. For example, students learning in a third-grade class who are learning about crocodilians, specifically the subgroups, alligator and crocodile might use Word SLapPs to demonstrate what they are learning. They might choose images that show the heads of the reptiles and ask viewers, "Which is the crocodile?" "Which is the alligator?" Those who respond would find that the answer is that the crocodile has a more pointed snout, while the alligator's snout is wide and rounded. Students could be asked to expand this experience by creating another set containing images of a fish, a turtle, and an Egyptian plover (a bird). The question could then be "Which of these are not eaten by crocodiles?" The answer is the Egyptian plover, a bird that actually goes inside the crocodile's mouth and cleans its teeth (Simon, 1999). The difficulty with the application is that students can only ask viewers questions. Viewers then tap on the image that "answers" the question. To see a demonstration of this application, search for "Word SLapPs demonstration video."

Research has shown us that "typically developing children learn 3,000 or more words each year which breaks down to about 10 per day and 50 to 70 words per week" (Brabham et al., 2012). Many of these words are first encountered indirectly through wide reading (Nagy & Herman, 1985), and for this reason teachers will want to encourage their students to read widely of both traditional books and e-books.

Reading electronic or e-books may be motivational to students because the experience is interactive and uses

Venomous Creatures

Venomous: Poisonous

Tetrodotoxin: The poison contained in the skin, blood, and organs of the puffer or blowfish.

I'll have the puffer fish!

The puffer or blowfish is the world's most dangerous food. Not all puffer fish are venomous, but most are. The fishes' skin, blood, and organs contain a poison called tetrodotoxin. An amount equal to what might be found on the head of a pin is enough to kill a human. There are chefs who are specially licensed to prepare puffer fish or fugu for restaurants. The poison in the puffer fish is also being tested for use as a non-addictive pain killer for patients with cancer. Each fish can provide six hundred doses of the puffer poison drug.

I have never eaten a blowfish and certainly do not think that I am brave enough to try one! I have seen dried blowfish hanging in a seafood restaurant for decoration. Some were even electrified and had little light bulbs inside of them. This is about as close as I want to get to the puffer fish, blowfish, or fugu!

Reference:

Singer, M. (2007). Venom. Plain City, OH: Darby Creek Publishing.

Image © Shutterstock, Inc.

Figure 1.3 A multimedia glossary entry.

specific means to invite readers to stop and think or do as they read. Schugar, Smith, and Schugar (2013) note the need for research that examines the features of e-books and their relationship to comprehension. This would help us fully understand how e-books may contribute to helping readers make meaning or understand what they read. Schugar et al. explain further, adding that some of the interactions within e-books may be distracting to readers. Teachers who want to suggest e-books as a motivator to encourage wide reading and vocabulary development should examine and review the e-books to ensure that the interactions help readers make text-based inferences and/or develop understanding of difficult vocabulary. However, in many e-books, the illustrations and surrounding text help readers infer meaning, just as they would in a traditional book. Additional features of e-books often include the ability for the reader to click on an unknown word and hear the word spoken and/or to listen to a definition of the word. Readers may also be able to highlight words or phrases of interest and take notes. The next section of the chapter will cover how e-books and digital stories can be used to enhance reader fluency.

Readers of traditional texts can go to Web sites such as Dictionary.com to hear the word pronounced and defined. They can also type the unknown word into a search engine such as Google and be confronted with a series of graphic, audio, and video definitions.

Ebner and Ehri (2013) conducted a study to determine the effectiveness of a structured think-aloud process for readers using the Internet to learn vocabulary. Readers were asked to read a text and access online resources when they encountered a word they did not know. Think-aloud participants were asked to remember that the goal was to learn the meaning of the listed terms and their relationship to the article being read and to read the text and think aloud to decide how a search would help them. During and after the search, they were asked to verbalize their thoughts about how the Internet search *was* helping and how it *did* help them reach their goal of learning the word. Their results revealed that students using the structured think-aloud process had significantly greater vocabulary gains over the students who were not asked to participate in the think-aloud.

Traditional texts might be used as the basis for an interactive audio recording that provides users with the opportunity to highlight or click on a word and hear it defined. Readers could begin with a reading of the picture book, *Miss Alaineus: A Vocabulary Disaster* (Frasier, 2000). Throughout the book, readers are treated to in-text definitions such as:

> Even my own mother laughed a little at the part about drawing for extra credit, but at least she stopped fast and said, "You know what I always say . . . There's gold in every mistake." **Gold?** *A bright yellow precious metal of great value?* **Mistake?** *Something done, said, or thought in the wrong way?* "Impossible," I told her. **Impossible:** *not capable of happening.*

(Note: As you read this excerpt from the book you may notice that the word "gold" is defined literally, rather than contextually as it might have been. If the word "gold" were defined contextually we would see a definition of "gold" as denoting something of value. That is part of the humor of this particular book). The in-text definition demonstrated in this picture book could be the inspiration for an interactive Readers Theater program. Following the reading, small groups of students in Ms. Allen's third-grade class might choose picture books, text excerpts from novels, informational books, excerpts from content area textbooks, or other texts. As they read the text together, they can select words that they feel users would need to have defined. They can then create a typed "script" of the text and included links on these words. Users of the text would be able to read the screen and, simultaneously, hear the Readers Theater performance by the makers. When the user encountered one of the linked words, he or she could click on the link and hear one of the makers reading a definition of the word.

Invitation to *Consider This!*

- Conduct an on-line search to identify potential sets of texts to address particular topics or concepts. Share with other teacher candidates.
- Create your own multimedia presentation for a word or concept to share with students.
- Examine digital stories on your own and/or look at review sites such as *Digital Storytime* www.digital-storytime.com and *Smart Apps for Kids* www.smartappsforkids.com to see reviews and information about interactive e-books that could motivate wide reading and vocabulary building.

Using Technology to Teach Reading Fluency

Why is Teaching Reading Fluency Critical to Reading?

> "His childhood, his friendships, his carefree sense of security—all of these things [seem] to be slipping away. With his new, heightened feelings, he was overwhelmed by sadness at the way the others had laughed and shouted, playing at war. But he knew that they could not understand why, without the memories. He felt such love for Asher and for Fiona. But they could not feel it back, without the memories. And he could not give them those." (Lowry, 1993, p. 135)

To adequately comprehend the stated and implied meaning of this passage from *The Giver* (Lowry, 1993), readers must be able to read accurately at a pace that allows for the timely completion of each sentence. In order to accomplish this, readers must possess a vast sight word vocabulary that allows them to comprehend words without having to pause to decode them. Additionally, fluent readers are able to identify logical groups of more than one word and read them with a single fixation. While accomplishing these tasks readers must recognize and replicate the author's intended expression. Finally, fluent readers connect content from the text to their existing background knowledge. As one can see, reading fluency is a multifaceted skill. It must be mastered and applied at the subconscious level in order for readers to concentrate on comprehension—the main purpose in reading. Therefore, fluency is the bridge to comprehension (the topic of the final section of this chapter).

Using Technology to Develop Reading Fluency

New teachers embarking on a career in education will witness children swapping their bulging backpacks full of textbooks for a sleek messenger bag containing an electronic device that holds all of their school related reading material. This single electronic device will hold all the student's textbooks, novels, class notes, assignments, projects, and even tests.

photo.ua/Shutterstock, Inc.

Reading material on different types of electronic devices requires dissimilar reading fluency skills. Reading a novel on an e-reader like the Nook or Kindle requires similar fluency skills used while reading traditional paper books. However, as noted, readers have the option to change the font size of the text and have immediate access to a thesaurus to determine the meaning of unfamiliar words. Reading textbooks on a tablet or a laptop/desktop computer requires students to view linked visual material (e.g., videos, maps, charts, tables, diagrams, and photos). However, clicking back and forth from the main text of the textbook to embedded links disrupts traditional fluency skills (Schugar, Smith & Schugar, 2014). Therefore, teachers must prepare students to read both types of texts with fluency. Ironically, due to students' increasing familiarity with multilayered material on their favorite Web sites and social media networks, it is the traditional reading fluency required to read traditional texts that involves the most focus. As teachers, we have all witnessed students focusing on their electronic devices for an hour or more and then struggling to maintain concentration on traditional reading tasks.

Utilizing Online e-Books for Children to Develop Reading Fluency

Electronic versions of children's picture books allow teachers to project large images of the books onto screens and electronic whiteboards. These huge electronic images of children's picture books make big books appear tiny by comparison. All of the students in a classroom can not only see the pictures but the text in electronic versions of these books. This provides teachers with an added dimension to the reading aloud of these illustrated books. Kindergarten and first-grade teachers can use a pointer to display directionality on the large projected images of these books. Students at higher grade levels can follow along, while utilizing the illustrations to enhance comprehension, as the teacher models fluent reading.

The International Children's Digital Library (http://en.childrenslibrary.org) provides teachers, parents, and children with free access to electronic versions of popular children's picture books from around the world. The books are displayed in their original format without animation, sound effects, or audio readings. The Tumble Book Library (http://www.tumblebooks.com/library/asp/home_tumblebooks.asp) is an online library of e-book versions of children's books, graphic novels, and videos.

The e-books come with the option of playing a professionally produced audio recording of each text. Additionally, most books include extension activities in the form of games and puzzles. Playing the audio accompaniments to the text allows children to follow along and hear well-paced, expressive readings that are perfect for children whether they are at home, in the car, or in other locales. For students to become fluent readers themselves, they need to hear fluent readers (Stahl & Heubach, 2005).

School districts often purchase branches of the Tumble Book Library for prices beginning at $599 per year for a deluxe branch and $799 per year, in 2014, for a premium branch, which includes extension activities and lessons targeting the Common Core (Tumble Book Library, 2014). However, free limited access to the Tumble Book Library is often available through the children's section of local public library Web sites.

Utilizing digital readers during Sustained Silent Reading (SSR), a well-recognized fluency development activity in schools, allows children to select books at their independent reading level. As an added benefit, they can easily change books at the click of a button without disturbing the rest of the class. Students disrupting SSR sessions with requests to go to the library and groans of "I don't like this book" will be a thing of the past.

Using Video Games to Develop Fluency

Teachers should encourage parents of video game players to purchase video games that contain the reading of directions, setting and character descriptions, and written narratives that establish the plot as a major component of playing the game. In addition to reading the onscreen narratives throughout the games, many games, especially those in the modern fantasy genre are linked to children's novels. Game titles read like a who's who of popular children's novels, including the *Harry Potter* series (Rowling, 1997–2007), *The Hunger Games* series (Collins, 2008–2010) and the *Twilight* series (Myer, 2005–2011). Simulation games like *SimCity, SimEarth*, and *SimLife* require vast amounts of reading and also build students' prior knowledge on a variety of social and political issues, resulting in more fluent future reading.

Patrick Foto/Shutterstock, Inc.

Utilizing Subtitled Foreign Films to Improve Reading Fluency

Reading subtitles while viewing foreign language films allows students to develop reading fluency skills, including: (a) reading endurance (concentration), (b) developing a broader sight word vocabulary, (c) expanding fixations to logically grouped words, and (d) building formal, linguistic, and content schema (Dalton, 2012). The pacing of the reading of subtitled foreign films also discourages fluency hindering mechanisms like voicing, lip movements, finger pointing, and head movements. Finally, viewing and reading age-appropriate subtitled foreign films provides students with another genre of fun reading material for free voluntary reading. Krashen (2004) contends that free voluntary reading encourages students to read extensively, resulting in improved reading fluency, comprehension, writing style, vocabulary, spelling, control of grammar, and oral/aural language skills. Teachers can assign the reading of subtitled foreign films for homework or place them on summer reading lists.

Utilizing Karaoke to Develop Reading Fluency

Besides offering students an enjoyable experience, singing well-known song lyrics with musical accompaniment can develop crucial reading skills (Gupta, 2006), such as the development of sight word vocabulary, reading fluency, and pronunciation. As mentioned earlier, teachers can download music lyrics from the Internet and create a handout containing the lyrics for each student. During class, the teacher can play the song on YouTube with only the audio component playing as the students sing along while reading the lyrics. The lyrics for The Beatles' song "Yellow Submarine", for example, contains numerous words that appear on common sight word lists of the most frequently used words in the English language. Frequent exposure to these sight words during karaoke performances of the song enables students to read the same words with better fluency when they reencounter them in other reading formats. A proper karaoke unit consisting of wireless speakers, composite video output, and recording capabilities can be purchased for less than $200.

Vadym/Zaitsev/Shutterstock, Inc.

Utilizing Podcasts to Develop Reading Fluency

Utilizing digital cameras, audio recording devices, and digital production programs like Microsoft Movie Maker and Apple iMovie provides teachers with a multitude of fluency development activities. Students can create digital stories, requiring them to create research questions, identify and evaluate information sources, interpret and use graphic sources of information, organize and record new information, and summarize and draw conclusions from information gathered from multiple sources (Common Core Standards, 2014). This multifaceted interaction with language develops reading fluency through the development of well-rounded literacy skills. Teachers can also record and post, using professional judgment, student performances of Readers Theater, a commonly utilized reading fluency and comprehension development activity, on social media Web sites, podcasts, video blogs, and video posting Web sites like YouTube, TeacherTube, and Vimeo, providing a far-reaching distribution of the students' work.

Invitation to Consider This!

- View YouTube postings of students participating in Readers' Theater.
- Watch a subtitled foreign film and monitor your own reading fluency and comprehension.
- View digital stories that are posted on TeacherTube.
- Sing several songs at the next karaoke night, paying attention to the reading skills involved.
- Play a simulation video game and recognize the reading skills involved and the schema development potential of the game's content.
- Read a novel on an e-reader, utilizing the font changing and thesaurus features.
- Read a textbook online and recognize the different fluency and comprehension skills involved when you access the embedded materials.

Using Technology to Teach Reading Comprehension

Why is Teaching Comprehension Critical to Reading?

A seventh-grade student recalls his elementary school reading, "When we were supposed to be reading in class, I would just lean up against the wall in the reading corner and look at the book and think about something else. When the teacher would come by, I would make my eyes move and pretend I was reading" (L. Van Horn, personal communication, 05/12/1998).

This student was not reading for comprehension; he was simply looking at the words. What does it mean to comprehend? To comprehend is to " . . . grasp the nature, significance, or meaning of" something, be it an act, an entity, or a text (Comprehend, 2014). In the field of literacy, we generally use the phrase "to make meaning" when we refer to the act of comprehending a text. We define a text as both printed text and visual text. In other words, a painting, a photograph, an advertisement, or a Web site; all of these could be texts, just as a news article, short story, comic, novel, or informational piece would also be considered texts. Theorist and educator, Louise Rosenblatt (2005) writes, that "A reader implies someone whose past experience enables him or her to make meaning in collaboration with a text. Even if the reader immediately rereads the same text, a new relationship exists, because the reader has changed, now bringing her memory of the first encounter with that text and perhaps new preoccupations" (p. x). Rosenblatt believed, as do the authors, that it is critical for readers to *actively engage* with texts. The way that we engage in reading a text may be different, depending upon the text and our purpose for reading. For example, we might read a short story and begin by calling up our prior knowledge and experiences. Then again, we might make personal connections to what we are reading. We might read the same short story at another time and focus on the author's use of the grammatical device of repetition. We teach reading comprehension in order to initiate readers into what Smith (1988) called "the literacy club," to define a place where we are "…participating in literate activities with people who know how and why to do these things," (p. 9), a place where people read and write with us.

Just as we are reaching to define text in a broader sense, we are also now defining literacy to include the digital world that encases us. Literacy is no longer about navigating the paper-based written word—nor is it even confined by just the written word. Literacy includes so much more, and according to Abrams and Gerber (2014), it is very complex. They propose that our definition of literacy should include everything from "traditional print to social media posts to video games" (p. 19). Therefore, as we invite our students to join Smith's "club," and, as we work to deepen their levels of comprehension, we must contemplate how to build a bridge across this vast chasm that is now literacy.

Web 2.0 and other advanced technology tools can help us engage our students in making meaning while reading. Here, teachers will learn about ways to use these new definitions of literacy to help readers construct ideas about comprehension, ways to use technology to introduce and teach comprehension strategies to readers, and ways for readers to use technology to apply what they have learned about comprehension. Information and communication technologies (ICTs) will continue to expand, and it will be vital for teachers to continue to search and develop ideas about meaningful ways to engage their students in comprehension building.

Using Technology to Construct Ideas About Comprehension

As readers engage with text, they are making continuous discoveries. They compare what they read with what they already know, what they want to know, and what they have learned. Creately is a free site containing K-12 graphic organizer templates. Students who are beginning to learn about the importance of activating prior knowledge before reading might use the interactive online KWL chart to document their thoughts before, during, and after reading. This can be done collaboratively or individually. Before reading, students will list what they know (K) that is related to the topic they are going to read about and what they want (W) to learn about as they read. After reading, students can list what they have learned (L). Because the act of reading and talking together about what we read often generates further questions, we suggest having students add a column documenting what they now (N) want to learn as a result of the initial reading, so the chart becomes a KWLN. Once students have a list of additional questions and wonderings, they can use a tool such as Wiki mindmap to begin their search. Wiki mindmap allows readers to enter a topic and link to Wikipedia research on the topic. This would be a starting point in a search for information. As students engage in these types of activities, they begin to construct ideas about how readers make meaning.

In addition to technology tools that help students activate schema before reading and organize information during reading, teachers can take an even bigger leap over the chasm and bring online games into the classroom. For traditional teachers of literacy, it seems a bit improbable, but "[video games] require players to be literate in ways that extend beyond the written word and often involve a level of critical thinking typically associated with school-based learning" (Abrams & Gerber, 2014, p. 18). These researchers tell us that online games require gamers to understand character and plot. These games require participants to pay attention to the details so that they can make inferences about where new paths will take them next. They must question motives of other characters; they must connect to previous gaming experiences. All of these are essential for understanding a text. What if teachers used online games to help students engage in metacognition about the reading comprehension processes? Could students learn how to better comprehend by analyzing the strategies they use for online games?

Using Technology to Introduce/Teach Comprehension

Digital book trailers have been shown to motivate students and expand their comprehension abilities. Working on digital book trailers provides students with the opportunity to read and talk with one another. Calkins (2001) notes that an important aspect of comprehension is the "social world of the classroom" stating that "When we teach comprehension, much of what we teach is a depth of listening, understanding, and response. Part of teaching comprehension, then, is making a place for astute and active listening." In addition, researchers have found that "…many [students] responded that they liked to read more and had learned to understand books better because the activity had helped them to better visualize the story" (Gunter & Kenny, 2012, p. 156). Research shows that students who lacked confidence in their writing abilities felt that they could express their understandings about the texts read by using digital book trailers. Students felt less hindered by a dependence on "first having to master vocabulary and sentence constructs—something they often struggle with" (p. 149).

Digital book trailers can promote practice with visualization and evidence-driven summarization. The premise behind this technology-based activity is that students can create an advertisement for their book, similar to a movie trailer. Digital Booktalk is an excellent Web site that includes many examples of book trailers created by students, teachers, and others with an interest in literacy education. These can be shared as models of what a book trailer can be.

natalia_maroz/Shutterstock, Inc.

After reading a text, students can design their book trailer using a storyboard. StoryboardThat provides an online storyboard generation platform. As part of the process of building a storyboard, students have to reflect on their visualizations and revisit the text in order to bring their imagined characters, settings, and scenes to life. In addition, they have to make decisions about the most important elements needed to convey the story without giving too much away. They want their viewers to know just enough about the book to want to read it— but not know so much that they *don't* have to read it. It is a delicate balance and requires close reading and honed summarization skills to create the perfect trailer that hooks viewers.

Once the storyboard has been created, student directors can begin transforming their ideas into a digital movie. Programs such as Movie Maker for Windows or iMovie for Mac provide enough tools to include music, images, movie clips, voiceovers, and so on. Animoto is an online tool similar to these two computer-based programs that can also provide devices for movie creation. If students feel that their creativity is stifled by these traditional movie making programs, perhaps teachers can allow students to create their own anime book trailer. Voki and Go Animate4Schools both allow users to select anime characters, scenes, and narration, which can easily be transformed into a book trailer. The final product, whether traditional or anime, is a short advertisement that brings a book to life and highlights the best of the plot. The ultimate goal for the director would be to entice others to read the book.

In addition to digital retellings, such as book trailers, teachers can utilize movie companions to books being read by their students. Book-based movies can be used to both assist and enhance reading comprehension. For students who struggle with visualization while reading, a movie clip can be shown before reading. The clip provides a visual foundation for characters and settings. Students can be taught to develop those initial visuals by adding their own interpretations as they read. Gunter and Kenny (2012) found that some students in their study just needed to "'get a visual'" first (p. 156). Teachers can guide students in the advantages of both, noting that the book or story often gives the reader deeper insight to thoughts after the movie shows the action.

Teachers can also engage students in comparative analysis to further this process. After reading a text, students can then watch the movie. Evaluations of similarities and differences can be conducted. They can analyze why directors make decisions to change characters, settings, and plots. Students can ultimately choose which they prefer—the book or the movie. The important component to this activity is that students must justify their examinations with evidence from both texts.

Using Technology to Apply/Practice Comprehension

We began this subsection about reading comprehension with the idea of initiating readers into the literacy club. Readers who are in the "club" will want to apply what they are learning by sharing their ideas about what they have been reading, planning future reading, joining a discussion group about a particular book or author, contacting an author, or even posting something they have written. Goodreads is a free Web site that accommodates all of these needs. Otis Chandler (2014), the co-founder of Goodreads, writes that "Knowledge is power, and power is best shared among readers" (https://www.goodreads.com/about/us). Coiro (2012) writes that " . . . emerging learning standards demand that online readers be personally productive, be socially responsible, and be able to collaborate with other members of a networked global community" (p. 646). Users join Goodreads by entering a name and an e-mail and creating a password. They may upload a photo and basic information and then begin posting. Users are provided with three shelves; read, currently reading, and to-read. Additional shelves can be created and labeled by the user to suit his or her personal interests. Readers can enter a book title and author, rate a book with stars, write a review for the book, and include information about the date the book was read. Books can be sorted by author, title, date read, and so on. A distinct feature of Goodreads is that readers can learn about the books their friends are reading. They can also create book discussion groups and talk about a book online. According to the Web site, (https://www.goodreads.com/about/us), "groups can be public, moderated, restricted by domain, or secret." Readers can have discussion groups with their classmates or even with people around the world! Key features of this particular aspect are the possibility for co-constructed meaning making and transformation of thought. Readers talking with one another about their own understanding of a text may develop a greater depth of knowledge. Readers grappling with the ideas of others may alter or further develop their thinking based upon insights gained through collaboration with others. We close this section with a thought about the growing importance of facilitating reader interactions with multiple texts and platforms:

> . . . becoming a fully literate text navigator includes more than the ability to interpret and critically construct meanings. A navigator effectively uses and creates all types of texts. In a world that offers almost infinite sources of information (and misinformation) and bombards us with all kinds of manipulative advertising and varieties of entertainment that exclude, ignore, and silence entire groups of people, a navigator takes charge, makes informed choices, intrepidly explores the sometimes "treacherous waters" found in the texts of our world, and, most important, feels prepared to deal with the seas of texts not yet present in our world. (Campbell & Parr, 2013, pp. 138–139)

Invitation to *Consider This!*

- Log on to Creately and explore the various graphic organizers platforms available. Create a graphic organizer depicting what is available and how you might use it in your classroom.
- Create your own Goodreads site and begin tracking your reading and that of some members of your literacy club of professional peers.
- Think of your favorite book and create a storyboard using StoryboardThat. Then transform your ideas into a book trailer.

Conclusion

Writing this chapter together has helped us think about and explore many ways to infuse technology with reading. We hope that you will use these ideas and your experiences in the *Invitation to Consider This!* activities as a beginning point for your own explorations during your internship and in your future classroom. It is our hope that you will find a way to share your discoveries with us so we can continue to consider how to make full use of the tools available to us to help our students become successful and fully engaged readers.

References

Abrams, S. S., & Gerber, H. R. (2014). Cross-literate digital connections: Contemporary frames for meaning making. *English Journal, 103*(4), 18–24.

Biemiller, A. (2001). Teaching vocabulary: Early, direct, sequential. *American Educator, 25*(1), 24–28.

Biemiller, A. (2004). Teaching vocabulary in the primary grades: Vocabulary instruction needed. In J. F. Baumann and E. J. Kame'enui (Eds.), *Vocabulary instruction: Research to practice* (pp. 28–40). New York: Guilford Press.

Brabham, E., Buskist, C., Henderson, S. C., Paleologos, T., & Baugh, N. (2012). Flooding vocabulary gaps to accelerate word learning. *The Reading Teacher, 65*(8), 523–533.

Calkins, L. (2001). *The art of teaching reading.* New York: Addison-Wesley Educational Publishers, Inc.

Campbell, T., & Parr, M. (2013). Mapping today's literacy landscapes: Navigational tools and practices for the journey. *Journal of Adolescent and Adult Literacy, 57*(2), 131–140.

Carlo, M., August, D., McLaughlin, B., Snow, C., Dressler, C., Lipman, D. et al. (2004). Closing the gap: Addressing the vocabulary needs of English-language learners in bilingual and mainstream classrooms. *Reading Research Quarterly, 39*(2), 188–215.

Chall, J. S., Jacobs, V. A., & Baldwin L. E. (1990). *The Reading Crisis: Why poor children fall behind.* Cambridge, MA: Harvard University Press.

Chandler, O. (2014). About Goodreads: A message from our CEO and Co-founder. Retrieved from http://www.goodreads.com/about/us

Coiro, J. (2012). Digital literacies. *Journal of Adolescent and Adult Literacy, 55*(7), 645–648.

Common Core Standards. (2014). Retrieved from http://www.corestandards.org/ELA-Literacy

Comprehend. (2014). In *Merriam-Webster's online dictionary.* Retrieved from http://www.merriam-webster.com/dictionary/comprehend

Cunningham, A. E., & Stanovich, K. E. (2003). Reading matters: How reading engagement influences cognition. In J. Flood, D. Lapp, J. Squire, & J. Jenson (Eds.), *Handbook of research on teaching in the English language arts* (Vol. 2, pp. 857–867). Mahwah, NJ: Lawrence Erlbaum.

Dalton, B., & Grisham, D. L. (2011). eVoc strategies: 10 ways to use technology to build vocabulary. *The Reading Teacher, 64*(5), 306–317.

Dalton, C. (2012). Subtitled foreign films as reading texts: *The Twilight Samurai. English in Texas, 42*(1), 31–34.

Ebner, R. J., & Ehri, L. C. (2013). Vocabulary learning on the Internet: Using a structured think-aloud procedure. *Journal of Adolescent and Adult Literacy, 56*(6), 480–489.

Gerhardt, K., & Abrams, R. (2000). Fetal exposures to sound and vibroacoustic stimulation. *Journal of Perinatology, 20*(8), S21.

Gillon, G. T. (2004). *Phonological awareness: From research to practice.* New York, NY: Guilford Press.

Graves, M. F. (1986). Vocabulary learning and instruction. In E. Z. Rothkopf (Ed.), *Review of Research in Education* (pp. 49–89). Washington, D.C: American Educational Research Association.

Gunter, G. A., & Kenny, R. F. (2012). UB the director: Utilizing digital book trailers to engage gifted and twice-exceptional students in reading. *Gifted Education International, 28*, 146. DOI: 10.1177/0261429412440378.

Gupta, A. (2006). Karaoke: A tool for promoting reading. *Reading Matrix, 6*(2), 80–89.

International Reading Association (IRA) & National Association for the Education of Young Children (NAEYC) (1998). *Learning to read and write: Developmentally appropriate practices for young children.* Newark, DE: International Reading Association; Washington, DC.

Krashen, S. (2004). *The power of reading: Insights from the research.* Englewood, CO: Libraries Unlimited.

Mitchell, M. J., & Fox, B. J. (2001) The effects of computer software for developing phonological awareness in low-progress readers. *Reading Research and Instruction, 40*(4), 315–332. DOI:10.1080/19388070109558353

Nagy, W., & Herman, P. A. (1985). Incidental vs. instructional approaches to increasing reading vocabulary. *Educational Perspectives, 23*(1), 16–21.

Nilson, A., & Nilson, D. (2005). Vocabulary development: Teaching vs. testing. In R. Robinson, (Ed.), *Readings in reading instruction* (pp. 196–204). New York: Pearson.

Rosenblatt, L. (2005). *Making meaning with texts: Selected essays.* Portsmouth, NH: Heinemann.

Schuele, C. M., & Boudreau, D. (2008). Phonological awareness intervention: Beyond the basics. *Language, Speech, and Hearing Services in Schools, 39*, 3–20. DOI: 10.1044/0161-1461(2008/002)

Schugar, H/R., Smith, C. A., & Schugar, J. T. (2013). Teaching with interactive picture e-books in grades K-6. *The Reading Teacher, 66*(8), 615–624.

Schugar, H., Smith, C., & Schugar, J. (2014). Teaching with interactive picture e-books in grades K–6. Reading Rockets. Retrieved from http://www.readingrockets.org/article/teaching- interactive-picture-e-books-grades-k-6

Smith, F. (1988). *Joining the literacy club: Further essays into education.* Portsmouth, NH: Heinemann.

Stahl, S. A., & Heubach, K. M. (2005). Fluency-oriented reading instruction. *Journal of Literacy Research, 37,* 25–60.

Sweeney, A. (2004). *Teaching the essentials of reading with picture books.* New York: Scholastic, Inc.

Tompkins, G. (2001). *Literacy for the 21st century. A balanced approach.* Upper Saddle River, NJ: Pearson.

Tumble Book Library. (2014). Pricing. Retrieved from http://www.tumblebooks.com/library/asp/pricing.asp

Yopp, H. K., & Yopp, R. H. (2000). Supporting phonemic awareness development in the classroom. *The Reading Teacher,* 54(2), 130–143.

Yopp, H. K., & Yopp, R. H. (2009). Phonological awareness is child's play. *Beyond the Journal: Young Children on the Web,* 1–9.

Recommended Materials Lists

Literature

Capucilli, A. (2002). *Inside a zoo in the city.* New York: Scholastic.
Collins, S. (2010). *The hunger games.* New York: Scholastic.
Collins, S. (2013). *Catching fire.* New York: Scholastic.
Collins, S. (2014). *Mockingjay.* New York: Scholastic.
Hoberman, M.A. (1997). *One of each.* New York: Scholastic.
Frasier, D. (2000). *Miss Alaineus: A vocabulary disaster.* New York: Harcourt.
Henkes, K. (2008). *Chrysanthemum.* New York: HarperCollins.
Lowery, L. (1993). *The giver.* Boston, MA: Houghton Mifflin.
O'Connor, J. (2005). *Fancy Nancy.* New York: HarperCollins.
Martin, B. Jr. (1991). *Polar bear, polar bear what do you hear?* New York: Henry Holt and Company.
Meltzer, M. (1987). *The American revolutionaries: A history in their own words 1750—1800.* New York: HarperTrophy.
Meyer, S. (2006). *Twilight.* New York: Little Brown Books for Young Readers.
Meyer, S. (2008). *New moon.* New York: Little Brown Books for Young Readers.
Meyer, S. (2009). *Eclipse.* New York: Little Brown Books for Young Readers.
Meyer. S. (2010). *Breaking dawn.* New York: Little Brown Books for Young Readers.
Rowling, J. K. (1998). *Harry Potter and the sorcerer's stone.* New York: Scholastic Press.
Rowling, J. K. (1999). *Harry Potter and the chamber of secrets.* New York: Scholastic Press.
Rowling, J. K. (1999). *Harry Potter and the prisoner of Azkaban.* New York: Scholastic Press.
Rowling, J. K. (2000). *Harry Potter and the goblet of fire.* New York: Scholastic Press.
Rowling, J. K. (2003). *Harry Potter and the order of the phoenix.* New York: Scholastic Press.
Rowling, J. K. (2005). *Harry Potter and the half-blood prince.* New York: Scholastic Press.
Rowling, J. K. (2007). *Harry Potter and the deathly hallows.* New York: Scholastic Press.
Simon, S. (1999). *Crocodiles and alligators.* New York: HarperCollins.
Singer, M. (2007). *Venom.* Plain City, OH: Darby Creek Publishing.

Films

Yamada, Y. (2002). *The twilight samurai.* Japan: Shochiku Co., Ltd.

YouTube Video

Bob Zoom example songs:
"Itsy Bitsy Spider" http://www.youtube.com/watch?v=h0K1Y-Rp1tY
"The Wheels on the Bus" http://www.youtube.com/watch?v=ag_sYU2PcBY
"Old MacDonald" http://www.youtube.com/watch?v=_YdG1LAfkXc
Children Love to Sing example songs:
"Animal Song" http://www.youtube.com/watch?v=KOwwaDh9W5E
"We're Going to the Zoo" http://www.youtube.com/watch?v=6xAqZJNrF2s

Dream English Kids example songs:

"Good Morning Song for Children," http://www.youtube.com/watch?v=U9Q7Y3t4m3g

"If You are Happy and You Know It," http://www.youtube.com/watch?v=Um5pNNtQK_k

Word SLaPs demonstration http://www.youtube.com/watch?v=19ag9oHgu1g

Music

The Beatles. (1966). "Yellow submarine." On *Revolver* [LP]. London: EMI.

Al Hoffman, Mack David, and Jerry Livingston "Bibbidy, Bobbidi, Boo." (The Magic Song, 1948).

Raffi (1998) *Singable Songs for the Very Young.*

Sandra Boynton (2013, 2004) *Philadelphia Chickens* and *Frog Trouble.*

Software

iMovie (Apple)

iTunes (Apple)

Keynote (Apple)

Movie Maker (Windows)

Notes (Apple)

PowerPoint (Windows)

SimCity

SimEarth

SimLife

Hardware

Digital Video Recorders

Digital Voice Recorders

iPad (Apple)

Kindle

Nook

Samsung Galaxy

Smartboard

Internet-based Programs

Google Chrome's speech recognition engine

WordSift

Web sites

Links to Songs—Use these songs to help practice phonological/phonemic or graphophonemic awareness development.

http://kids.niehs.nih.gov example songs:

"Do Your Ears Hang Low"

"Daisy Bell (Bicycle Built for Two)," 1892, by Harry Dacre

"Ten Little Monkeys"

http://pbskids.org/lions/videos

http://www.allmusic.com

http://www.songdrops.com

Phonological and Graphophonemic Awareness Links—Use these Web sites to practice sounds awareness or letter sound correspondence.

http://pbskids.org/lions/games/smartydoors.html

http://pbskids.org/lions/games

http://pbskids.org/lions/games/blending.html

http://pbskids.org/lions/games/monkeymatch.html

http://pbskids.org/sesame/home/alphabet-soup

http://pbskids.org/sesame/home/j-jump/#

http://pbskids.org/sesame/home/letters-big-bird

http://pbskids.org/sesame/home/play-inside-w/#

http://teacher.scholastic.com/clifford1/flash/concentration/index.htm

http://teacher.scholastic.com/writewit/poetry/poetry_engine.htm#

http://www.abcfastphonics.com/index.html

http://www.bbc.co.uk/bitesize/ks1/literacy/phonics/play/popup.shtml

http://www.bbc.co.uk/schools/wordsandpictures/index.shtml
http://www.letters-and-sounds.com/phase-2-initial-sound-game-1.html
http://www.professorgarfield.org/Phonemics/chickenCoop.html
http://www.professorgarfield.org/Phonemics/greenhouse/greenhouse.html
http://www.professorgarfield.org/Phonemics/hay_loft/hay_loft.html
http://www.professorgarfield.org/Phonemics/introCharacters.html
http://www.professorgarfield.org/Phonemics/pig_waller/pig_waller.html
http://www.professorgarfield.org/Phonemics/pumpkin_patch/pumpkin_patch.html
http://www.rif.org
http://www.starfall.com/n/level-k/letter-c/load.htm?f
http://www.teachyourmonstertoread.com/games/tm1/demo
Audio Story/Book Links—Use these links for read-alouds that promote phonological or
graphophonemic awareness.
Barnes and Noble's Online Storytime book example:
Kissing Hand by Audrey Penn, 1993
http://www.barnesandnoble.com/u/online-storytime-books-toys/379003588
http://www.readtomelv.com
http://www.sadlier-oxford.com/phonics/grade_k_1/longa.htm
http://www.sadlier-oxford.com/phonics/grade_k_1/zoo_a/zoo1x.htm
http://www.sadlier-oxford.com/phonics/student.cfm
http://storylineonline.com example books:
Harry the Dirty Dog (Gene Zion, 1956)

Other Links

http://animoto.com
http://creately./com/Free-K12-Education-Templates
http://dictionary.reference.com
http://www.digitalbooktalk.net
http://www.digital-storytime.com – a library of digital books to be purchased.
http://en.childrenslibrary.org
http://goanimate4schools.com/public_index
https://www.goodreads.com/about/how_it_works—information about the Goodreads program; a
free site where participants can share the books they are reading, participate in book discussions, create book lists for
    future reading and other inviting activities for readers.
https://www.goodreads.com/about/us—see above. Read this to learn about how the Goodreads program developed and
    about the philosophy of the program.
http://www.naturalreaders.com/download.htm
http://www.smartappsforkids.com—a searchable site with information about applications that are
free. Includes top lists, lists by age/subject, and links to view and purchase the apps.
http://www.storyboardthat.com
http://www.teachertube.com
http://www.vimeo.com
http://www.tumblebooks.com/library/asp/home_tumblebooks.asp
http://www.voki.com
http://www.wikimindmap.org
http://www.youtube.com

Apps

Phonological and Graphophonemic Awareness Links—Use these Web sites to practice sounds
awareness or letter–sound correspondence.
ABC Magic 5 Letter Sound Matching
ABC Pocket Phonics Letter Sounds & Writing
ABC Reading Magic 1 Short Vowel
Endless Alphabet
The Phonemix

Other Apps

Doodle Buddy
iBooks
iHeart Radio
iTunes Radio
Kids Paint
Montessori Crosswords
Read Me Stories
SpeakText
Word SLaPs

Glossary

Fluency—Fluency is the ability to read text quickly and accurately with comprehension and expression (Sweeney, 2004).

Graphophonemic Awareness/Alphabetic Principle/Graphophonics /Letter Sound Correspondence/Phonics—the ability to match letters and sounds; knowing the shapes of letters and names of letters; knowing about irregularities in letter/sound correspondence.

Phonemic Awareness—(a subset of phonological awareness)—recognition of individual phonemes; phoneme (smallest unit of sound).

Phonological Awareness—general awareness that our language is made of sound; concerned only with phonemes; sounds only; we are not looking at letters at all.

Reading Comprehension—To comprehend is to understand what is read. Reading without comprehension is simply word calling.

Vocabulary—a knowledge of word meaning. A well-developed vocabulary is an essential part of school success (Cunningham & Stanovich, 2003) and vocabulary instruction needs to be part of instruction for students at all ages (Biemiller, 2001, 2004).

Chapter 2

The Use of Technology and Social Studies

Jose Maria Herrera *University of Texas at El Paso*

Bernardo Pohl *University of Houston-Downtown*

Meet Stephen

Mr. Cotera was amazed at how much social studies education has changed since his days in elementary school. He fondly remembered the time when an ex-Peace Corps volunteer had been invited to his classroom to talk about his experiences serving in Botswana. He loved hearing about life in a different culture directly from a person who had lived, worked, and interacted with the people of that faraway land. That singular experience breathed life to the lessons that his sixth-grade teacher taught concerning Africa that year.

At the moment, Mr. Cotera's sixth graders were video conferencing directly with Mr. Albert, a Peace Corps volunteer who was still in the field. Students were talking with Mr. Albert and his students in Ecuador, and they were enjoying a lively interchange about life, school, and other aspects of each other's culture. Three more video conference calls were planned with other volunteers in Peru, Paraguay, and Colombia to allow students the opportunity to explore a wide variety of Latin American cultures. Mr. Cotera reflected on how technology not only increased the number of speakers he could bring into his classroom but how it turned a normally second-hand experience into a first-hand journey of discovery for his students. Indeed, technology had brought the world into Mr. Cotera's classroom.

Technological developments over the past years have revolutionized the instruction of social studies. The development of computers and the Internet have provided the modern-day teacher with a plethora of options to develop and enrich effective instruction. For example, various presentation and multimedia editing tools, whether computer-based or Web-based software like MS PowerPoint and MS MovieMaker, allow teachers and students to construct more sophisticated presentations that take advantage of students' varied learning styles. The digitization of books, newspapers, photographs, letters, and other archival materials by academic and government institutions provide a wealth of primary documents ("originals" from those people who actually "lived" the event in some way) available for use in the classroom that were not easily obtainable in the past. For example, if one wanted an image of the original United States Constitution, various sites provide a projectable image. As another example, letters from settlers, explorers or those participating in various wars throughout much of history can be obtained instantly. Notably, advances in online communication allow classrooms located in countries, states, cities, or schools apart to communicate, share ideas, and enrich our understanding of each other.

In this chapter, we discuss the common technology options available for the classroom teacher and provide examples of how to effectively integrate them into the instructional practices for social studies. First, we will review hardware and software that is commonly available in schools. Afterwards, we will examine Web resources and engage in discussions and strategies applicable to the four main strands in social studies (history, geography, government, and economics) with detailed activities and ideas.

Hardware

When considering the available hardware in the social studies classroom, a teacher must examine its use not only for themselves but also for their students. Many modern-day classrooms are equipped with an electronic whiteboard and a computer. Document cameras are steadily replacing the overhead projectors, staples of the last century's classrooms. In addition, many schools are equipped with digital projectors--either in the classroom or made available to check out from the school library or media centers.

Of all the pieces of hardware, certainly the most important tool available to teachers of social studies is the computer. A computer, with an Internet connection and its abundance of useful software, is an invaluable tool to help an instructor plan and organize lessons, conduct research, and engage students in innovative approaches to learning. The computer presents numerous opportunities and possibilities for the constructivist-minded social studies teacher. This is particularly true due to the abundance of primary material that is made available online by international, national, state, and local governmental agencies, universities, libraries, museums, and other archival sources, which can be accessed by teachers and students and used in multiple ways in the classroom. Items that would once have required special fieldtrips to the source of the material or official requests by the teacher can be accessed and employed instantaneously in the classroom. Coupled with a digital projector and a scanner, the computer can replace most of the image projection operations of older technologies.

Some pieces of hardware evolve from past technologies, replacing older features and improving upon their function. For instance, the digital document camera is superior to the overhead projector. Unlike the overhead, teachers do not need to make transparencies beforehand of the objects they want to project. The digital document camera can focus upon any object, image, or text and project a perfect reproduction on a screen or whiteboard. Color projections like maps (once prohibitively expensive to reproduce for use on overheads) are no longer a factor limiting a teacher's planning—when there is a document camera available. A teacher can project objects as he/she sees fit, without having to organize the images to make transparencies or be forced to limit the number of images because of potential costs. The ability to project 3-D images allows the teacher to place artifacts under the digital document camera so that students can examine them from their seats.

The electronic whiteboard is another example of new technology in many classrooms. Using an electronic whiteboard, the teacher is easily able to label and mark images to aid in instruction. This enhances the ability of the teacher and students to interact directly with technology, which gives the advantage of more student engagement. For example, this technology can provide a number of social studies games for students such as Place the State (a drag and drop state locator game).

Digital cameras and electronic whiteboards are not always found in every classroom, but they are usually available within a school for teachers' use. For example, a scanner is another piece of hardware that is not in every classroom but is very beneficial to

teachers. The most important use of a scanner is that it allows one to acquire material that does not already exist digitally or cannot be accessed online. For example, if multiple copies are needed, one can easily scan information on a printer. One can also use a scanner to upload hard copies of materials to Web sites and emails.

Digital cameras can be equipped to take both still pictures and video. These can be saved onto computers and can be manipulated using a number of programs such as MSPaint and movie making software.

Software

The real value in computers lies in their ability to access material over the Internet and the variety of software that is available to manipulate, organize, or employ the information a teacher can obtain online. Programs like PowerPoint allow teachers considerable flexibility in organizing seamless presentations. It is user friendly and can also be easily manipulated by children to create their own presentations. MS MovieMaker and other similar software programs create a platform for teachers and students to edit existing video recordings or to construct new ones from photo images. These programs provide for considerable manipulation of both video and audio effects. Adobe Photoshop, MSPaint, and animation software allow users to create their own images or manipulate existing images. Audio production and editing software, like Apple GarageBand, give students opportunities to create and record music, dialogue, and sound effects. Edmodo, a social learning platform targeted for K-12 students, serves a similar function to a BlackBoard page and allows teachers to set up discussions, post assignments, and deliver grades, and, in addition, the user can embed document, audio, and video files. These are only a sample of some of the most used software. Certainly, programs like Word, Excel, Publisher, and Visio have their own applications, and they will also be mentioned in the chapter.

The Web

As mentioned earlier, the most powerful instructional tool available to a teacher is a Web-connected computer. With an unrestricted Web connection, a teacher can obtain an abundance of information, primary documents, lesson plan ideas, videos, and audio files as well as acquire easy access to rapid communication with people around the world. Students can also access the Internet to conduct a variety of research. As illustrated in the opening story, the teacher used a simple Skype connection and a projector to set up a "classroom visit" from a person in another country. In terms of available informational sources, the Web can provide substantial research, lesson planning, and instructional material to enrich teaching. Combined with existing computer software, teachers and students can manipulate these sources into a variety of project ideas like digital timelines, artifact studies, remote conferences, blogs, and visual and audio productions. For instance, using MS Visio, students can draft a perfect timeline and easily attach text and/or images garnered from the Internet to create a clean and legible product. A teacher can also find multiple images of written and cultural artifacts and project them on the board for students to examine. As mentioned at the opening of the chapter, a teacher can set up a remote conference with a variety of guest speakers, multiplying the amount of opportunities available to tap into valuable human resources. Now teachers can use programs such as Skype, hosts Google Hangouts, and use Apple FaceTime to bring authors into the classroom and/or collaborate with teachers and students from afar.

Using digital cameras a teacher can set up and film a performance, and, using movie editing software, can professionally edit the film both for image and sound quality. Mrs. Kenton's third-grade class was studying the community, so she assigned learning groups to shoot a variety of short film clips on a segment of their area. One group took community helpers, another took mapping the main municipal areas, and so forth. All were put together to create the "our town" class project.

The greatest concern for teachers in dealing with the Web is in determining the quality and legitimacy of accessible sources. School and district policies can also erect considerable barriers to the free usage of the Internet. For instance, while one can normally access useful freeware on the Web, existing school policies and the variable reliability of sites limit the type of downloads permitted. This is especially frustrating when some school district "block" sites like YouTube, which do contain a fair number of valuable videos for social studies, due to the fear that inappropriate sites will be accessed. Some school districts have rectified the issue by writing scripts that allow different levels of filters for teachers and students. For example, some teachers have access to YouTube to find teaching material, but students can only view the sites if teachers copy and paste the YouTube link into online programs such as SafeShare and TeacherTube.

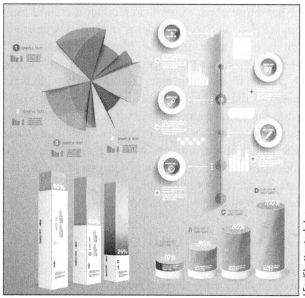

LFor/Shutterstock, Inc.

Visual representation: Data can be colorfully organized and displayed using a variety of software programs available, including easily accessible ones like MS PowerPoint, Word, and Excel.

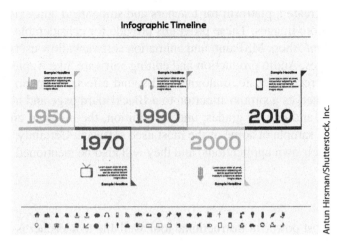

Infographic Timeline

Timeline: This image demonstrates the type of graphic possibilities in constructing a timeline.

In addition, some districts erect bandwidth barriers that can similarly restrict what can be downloaded. Such school and district policies have prompted some tech savvy teachers into downloading appropriate materials at home on a flash drive for use in their classroom. However, a teacher must always be sure that any material brought into the class is in line with school or district policies and restrictions and that it enhances instruction.

The remainder of the chapter will be divided into four sections dedicated to strategies dealing with each of the major strands in social studies: history, geography, economics, and government. Each strand section will examine the use of technology in four ways in the context of social studies education: (a) data collection, (b) sensory aids, (c) student production, and (d) research. In addition, detailed application examples will be included.

Teaching History with Technology

The instruction of history can benefit considerably from recent technological developments. At its most basic, computer resources and software can aid the instructor in presenting more effective information to his/her class. Document cameras can help a teacher seamlessly share an object, such as a seventeenth-century map, with his or her entire class, rather than passing it around individually to each child. Using video, the opening scene of *Saving Private Ryan* provides a visceral experience of the D-Day landings, unmatched by anything on the written page. An audio file of Dr. Martin Luther King's "I Have a Dream" speech can deliver the proper emotional tone of that moment in history. A copy of an authentic letter from a Union soldier can bring a personal touch to the daily reality of the Civil War. A historical "Fakebook" page can allow a student to assume the identity of a historical character, speak in his/her voice in conversation with others, and provide an alternative platform to the typical research report. In addition, some museums are digitizing their holdings and making them accessible online. In short, there are multiple ways in which teaching history can benefit from current technology tools.

Data Collection/Research

In terms of data collection, current technology can be employed in a variety of means. In the broadest terms, Internet sources provide a multitude of sites that teachers and students can visit to enrich their understanding of a particular historical era. One useful site, especially for those teaching and studying about Texas history, is the *Handbook of Texas Online*, an online site published by the Texas historical society

Mexican President Gustavo Diaz Ordaz greeting a leader of the Confederation of Mexican Workers (CTM).

(https://www.tshaonline.org/handbook). Through this site, students and teachers can access a detailed encyclopedia of significant people and events in the history of Texas. The site also gives access to most of the back issues of the society's journal, the *Southwestern Historical Quarterly* (https://www.tshaonline.org/shqonline/digital-content). If a search for Lorenzo de Zavala is launched, for example, the Webpage will provide a detailed account of his life and provide multiple links that connect to articles detailing events and people with whom he interacted. The *Portal of Texas History*, a site administered by the University of North Texas, contains digitized copies of important archival documents related to Texas (http://texashistory.unt.edu). Searchers can actually read and/or print copies of these documents, providing them an opportunity to examine important events in the history of Texas at a more intimate level. In the continued search for Lorenzo de Zavala, one can, for instance, find letters and other primary documents pertaining to his life. Through his letters, students can obtain a more intimate portrait of the man who was the first Vice President of the Texas Republic and his concerns and interests pertaining to the Lone Star State.

As an example, Ms. Wegner used this lesson for using primary resources with her seventh-grade Texas history class:

> She titled her lesson *Friend to Enemy.* The students were instructed to use *The Portal of Texas History* online site and to download copies of the documents (personal letters between Lorenzo de Zavala and Antonio Lopez de Santa Anna) listed below. Each document link comes with a function that permits the student to translate the original document. Ms. Wegner made sure that students used this function to translate each page and then instructed them to examine each of the documents as they detail different stages in de Zavala's relationship with Antonio Lopez de Santa Anna. Both of these men played key roles, on opposite sides, of the Texas Revolution, but they started out as friends. The breakdown of their friendship provides some insight into the political turmoil that played a key role in facilitating and fueling the Texas Revolution. Ms. Wegner asked her students to consider the following questions: How does their relationship change over the course of the letters? Do the letters provide any clues to why the relationship changed? What does this mean to the growing differences between Mexico and Texas?
>
> 1. texashistory.unt.edu/ark:/67531/metapth6015/m1/1/?q=de%20zavala%20santa%20anna
> 2. texashistory.unt.edu/ark:/67531/metapth5951/?q=de%20zavala%20santa%20anna
> 3. texashistory.unt.edu/ark:/67531/metapth6699/m1/1/?q=de%20zavala%20santa%20anna

In terms of national history, a teacher can find many primary documents by searching key words such as "Mayflower primary documents" (mayfowerhistory.com/primary-sources-and-books) or "Louis and Clark primary documents" (www.archives.gov/education/lesson/lewis-clark). One can even view the letter from Christopher Columbus to Ferdinand and Isabella from 1493 or other documents for world history.

Visual Aids

Programs like PowerPoint, Prezi, Keynote, or Google Slides can help teachers to seamlessly deliver visuals during a history lesson. The availability of online archival images and documents provides the teacher with the basic materials to enhance his or her oral instruction. A teacher can collect a series of images, including primary documents, photos, and maps and organize them into a Prezi presentation that will coordinate with the lecture and enrich students' experiences. Text can be included with the images or in separate slides. Video and photo clips can be imbedded into slides to further deepen the quality of the instruction. PowerPoint can also include a variety of extras to enhance the visual appeal of the slides. The ability to jump slides and return to a point of origin allows the presenter to avoid being forced into a linear presentation. Teachers can also upload their presentation into their Google Drive to make the slide available to students. Teachers can choose to share a link for students to view the material or allow the students to serve as collaborators by inserting additional videos, images, or materials they may be asked to gather. Unlike PowerPoint, Google Slides allow teachers to site resources such as Web sites and images directly within the slide using the "research tool" feature. This is especially helpful for both teachers and students. The student interest and level of engagement that can be created for social studies in exciting presentations should definitely replace "reading the chapter and answering the question in the back" of yesteryear.

The following discussion is intended to outline how Mr. Kahn used online archival resources and an MS PowerPoint slideshow to construct an effective historical presentation. He wanted to craft a project focused upon the Japanese attack on Pearl Harbor in1941. He began by visiting a site which belongs to the Naval History & Heritage Command (http://www.history.navy.mil/photos/events/wwii-pac/pearlhbr/pearlhbr.htm). In this Web site, Mr. Kahn obtained a concise overview of the event as well as a large selection of download-able images of the Pearl Harbor attack. These images, which included maps as well as photographs taken both by American and Japanese participants, not only provide visual contexts for students, but they also provided a way for Mr. Kahn to construct an effective narrative for his classes. A good lecture generally follows a "story pattern," and, using PowerPoint, Mr. Kahn organized the images effectively to tell the story in a way that coor-dinated with his talk. To make teaching more student-centered, each image was arranged in his presentation in such a way as to stimulate conversation with the students and help them explore the pertinent themes in a spe-cific order. To help provide students with a sense of American outrage in the aftermath of the attack, Mr. Kahn did a search for post-attack newspaper headlines and found a large sample of images that could be copied and pasted onto the presentation. Students accessed these images and provided examples of different newspapers to read. He asked students to consider: Do all the news reports cover the event in a similar tone? Are there variations between the ways the news is reported in different newspapers? Videos and audio files concerning Pearl Harbor were also imbedded in his PowerPoint presentation. The following Web site contains an audio clip announcing the attack upon Pearl Harbor (https://archive.org/details/PearlHarborAttackAnnouncement), which Mr. Kahn played later. Furthermore, the National Archives contain a series of pages that include docu-ments, audio files, and images that pertain to Pearl Harbor and can be downloaded by teachers to imbed into their presentation, including an audio clip of President Roosevelt delivering the day-of-infamy speech (http://www.archives.gov/education/lessons/day-of-infamy). In addition, these sites include lesson ideas and tips for more effective use of the primary documents that they provide. Finally, as a point of comparison, Mr. Kahn played a clip of the attack upon the World Trade Cen-ter and then played an audio recording of the speech President George W. Bush made afterwards.

Another way to employ visual aids is through ar-tifact studies. With today's technology, a teacher or student is able to collect a large variety of artifact im-ages that can be projected on screen and will allow learners to examine and explore the material culture of people in the past. For example, a teacher can make a search of the artifacts found upon the body of Otzi, the nearly intact cadaver of a prehistoric man found in the Alps. The image search will return a considerable number of detailed images that will allow students to examine and deduce information about the life of pre-historic people. An excellent Web site for obtaining images of actual archeological digs and artifacts is the Archeology Data Services site (http://archaeolo-gydataservice.ac.uk/learning). Although not designed with younger children in mind, the Archeology Image Bank section of the site provides a great deal of im-ages that can be downloaded and examined for older students after logging in. Another useful site is Ar-cheology for Kids (http://archaeology.mrdonn.org) with links for teaching learners how to conduct and organize their own archeological dig.

Monte Alban: A Pre-Columbian city located in Oaxaca, Mexico

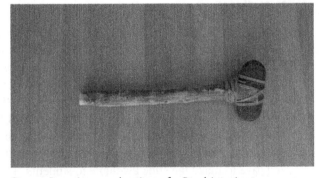

Stone Axe: A reproduction of a Pre-historic stone ax

Technology and Student Products

Naturally, every piece of technology that has been discussed so far can also be placed in the hands of the stu-dents to make their own products. At a time where there is great concern for authentic assessment of student learning, technology projects provide one of the best platforms to accurately gauge student performance and encourage them to take ownership of their education. One of the more exciting technological combinations is the pairing of movie-making software with the availability of affordable digital cameras. These two technology tools, coupled with downloadable digital audio/visual files (as well as a scanner), can bring to life the old school report!

The documentary report is one of the best ways to motivate students in order to get their best effort on the venerable book report. This type of technology report combines multiple literacy elements with social studies objectives and provides students an authentic platform upon which they can demonstrate such skills as understanding the main ideas, logical sequencing, summarization, and oral skills. In addition, the various elements that go into producing a documentary benefit different learning styles, making this approach perfect for group projects.

A teacher can start by downloading a documentary film from the PBS series *The American Experience* http://www.pbs.org/wgbh/americanexperience. These are some of the best examples of the art of documentary filmmaking and will provide students a quality visual example for their own project. The teacher should be sure to explain salient features of the art form—from the selection of images to the way in which narration, sound effects, and music affect the tone of the story. Teachers can have students select a subject relevant to what the class is currently studying. Teachers like Ms. Bhatiya, for example, in her integrated writing unit talked to students about how the director of the recent movie, *Pompeii*, took his fascination with ancient Roman history into making meticulous digital images that meshed with his story line. There were many artifacts

that were easily accessed online to recreate the images true to the science of the volcanic explosion of Mount Vesuvius along with the ash-covered actual city from those times. Some of his inspiration for characters came from the excavated body casts of those who had actually been killed in the explosion and from the beautifully preserved mosaics which are also available on the Web.

Let us assume that the American Civil War is another topic. A student-centered instructor generates a multitude of suitable documentary subjects from battles, campaigns, individual personalities, political issues, and events that form the basis of a documentary. The teacher then provides a list of these potential topics. A teacher should be sure to generate a robust list so that no student feels like he or she had to settle on an unwanted subject because of being the last to make a selection. After students have selected a topic, they are tasked with researching their subject and planning a documentary (or, in the case of Ms. Bhatiya, a historically correct drama/story). A teacher must be sure to adjust the expected length of time of the documentaries based upon the age of the students. The younger the students are, the more likely they will require direct help from the teacher to complete the project. Teachers can create a Symbaloo, which is a start page with multiple links that will reduce the time students use searching the Internet and allow them to focus more an the actual documentary. At the elementary level, the documentaries should probably be no more than 5 minutes in length. Students first develop the script for their presentation using available primary and secondary sources,

The Roman Coliseum. Other artifacts that can open up history.

and they time them. They download images, video, and music that they plan to incorporate into their documentaries. The following are a sampling of the available Web sites that provide either primary material or links that students could, for example, use for a Civil War project:

> The Civil War Trusts Primary Sources page:
> http://www.civilwar.org/education/history/primarysources
> Library of Congress Primary Documents Web site
> http://www.loc.gov/rr/program/bib/ourdocs/CivilWarRecon.html
> Cornell University Library Civil War Documents
> http://ebooks.library.cornell.edu/m/moawar/waro.html
> National Archives: Teaching with Documents
> http://www.archives.gov/education/lessons/civil-war-docs

Providing students with a large piece of butcher paper allows a backdrop so that they can construct a storyboard (which resembles comic book panels with notes matching dialogue, music, and images) to plan and construct their final product. Once this has been completed, teachers have the option to ensure that time should be apportioned at the school's computer lab or a schedule for the classroom computers made to facilitate the process of editing the movies. If a campus uses mobile devices, this can be done seamlessly by taking pictures using the device and uploading them into moviemaking programs. For example, pictures can be taken with the camera on a smart phone or pad and uploaded using the same device into the iMovie application (app). Movie-editing software lets students manipulate the individual panels, thus permitting placement and edited video and images to exact time frames. The software contains functions that allow the user to implement special effects like color tone and transitional breaks. Once the visual elements are in place, students are able to overlay the audio elements at their discretion. When completed, students can then burn the completed product on a video CD or other media formats. Students also have the option to upload the video into YouTube and then embed them on the teacher's Web site or within a learning management system (LMS) such as Moodle. This can also be an opportunity to teach copyrighting as an important responsibility in social studies.

Teaching Geography with Technology

Students today are encouraged to become information producers rather than passive information-takers. They are expected to synthesize, analyze, and conceptualize information that is important and crucial. Technology and the Internet have increased the availability of tools that enhance students' learning experience related to geography. As a result, geography teachers have ample availability of technology tools for the classroom for data collection, visual aids, student production, and research enrichment(Al-Bataineh, Anderson, Toledo, Y Wellinski, 2008; Dawson, 2008; Harris, Mishra, & Koehler, 2009; Wright & Wilson, 2009).

Data Collection: Geographic Information System (GIS)

At the forefront of geography and technology, there is the Geographic Information System (GIS). GIS has taken the geography world by storm, and it would be very hard to overlook its present value as a teaching tool (Baker, 2005; Benaivis, 2008; Demicri, 2011; Fitchett & Good, 2012; Henry & Semple, 2012; Kerski, Demicri, & Milson, 2013). GIS is an information system that stores, analyzes, manipulates, and presents geographic data. When addressing and utilizing data, the uses for GIS are infinite. For example, a class can analyze the historical tectonic movement of a country, visualize the shopping habits of a particular neighborhood or zip code, or track the monthly rainfall amount of a state or province. This could also be used for city planning, natural disaster rescues, and many more practical purposes.

Each day the use of data in the world increases, and more people are using economic, political, social, cultural, and geographic statistics to understand their world and daily lives. Benaivis (2008) points out that one area where he see this increase is in the use of geospatial data, which is information about regions and places. The pressing need to efficiently use and present such data has encouraged the creation of powerful and sophisticated hardware and software such as GIS to access and interpret this information through maps, charts, and tables. In one example of its use, Andersen (2011) explains how in the state of Utah, teachers, students, and community leaders are utilizing GIS in communities and neighborhoods to understand the local use of water reservoirs, using this information for the conservation of lakes, creeks, and rivers. Furthermore, GIS has extensively been used in several cities in the "Mapping Our City" project. In this project, students in Boston, for instance, used GIS to understand the historic physical changes of the Boston Harbor (Sanders, Kajs, & Crawford, 2001). The Yale Genocide Studies Program (http://www.yale.edu/gsp) and the U.S. National Holocaust Memorial Museum Mapping Initiative (http://www.ushmm.org/maps) are using GIS and digital mapping to explore historic and contemporary genocide activities around the world (Fitchett & Good, 2012). In the past, GIS has been used to understand areas of the world more susceptible to imperialism and colonization, patterns of regional and global economic development, and the concentration of children population in high- and low-income urban areas (Lloyd, 2001).

Scott Prokop/Shutterstock, Inc.

GIS is widely available as a stand-alone software or Web-based interface format, and it can be obtained commercially or as Open Source. Commercially, GIS is available through ESRI, Autodesk's MapGuide, Bentley Systems, ERDAS, InteGraph, and MapInfo, among others. As open source software, GIS is available through GRASS, QGIS, OSGeo, SAGA, ILWIS, and IDRISI.

http://data.geocomm.com

http://www.esri.com

http://www.top20sites.com/gis

In the classroom, GIS is becoming a very popular tool to use for understanding patterns of migration and urban sprawl. For example, GIS for History (http://www.gisforhistory.org), a project by the University of Illinois and The National Endowment for Humanities, uses statistical census data to provide ready-to-use lessons, maps, and statistical information regarding early immigration in this country. Teachers can use different lessons from this Web site to help students explore geographic factors in such topics as slavery and the Great Migration of the Early 1900s or to analyze the nation's first census of 1790.

http://www.gisforhistory.org/projects/slavery

http://www.gisforhistory.org/projects/greatmigration

http://www.gisforhistory.org/projects/firstcensus_st

Besides the full lessons, each section in this Web site provides full interactive GIS maps. For example, Mrs. Blakely uses the GIS maps in the Great Migration section (http://www.gisforhistory.org/projects/greatmigration) to research American urban migration patterns of minorities in industrial centers in the early 1900s. First, she introduces the subject to the class by identifying basic migration vocabulary, including the concepts of push and pull factors (what causes people to move away from or go to a particular location). Then, she uses primary sources such as letters, diaries entries, and city records to help the students understand migration motives for leaving a place and the life of the immigrants once they had arrived and became settled in a new city. Using visual primary sources, such as photographs, Mrs. Blakely adds a human context to the understanding of migration. By using photographs, students can visually explore the life of an immigrant. The following two web sites contain images and other documents pertaining to the migration of Southerners. The first site looks at overall Southern migration, while the other three specifically address the migration of Southern African Americans into the northern cities. The last Web site in particular has a large selection of visual images.

http://faculty.washington.edu/gregoryj/diaspora/photos

htmhttp://www.tahg.org/module_display.php?mod_id=89&review=yes

http://www.uic.edu/educ/bctpi/historyGIS/greatmigration/gmdocuments.html

http://www.inmotionaame.org/gallery/index.cfm?migration=8&topic=1&type=image

Once students have explored the online primary documents, they access the Web site GIS for history and use the "Great Migration" data map. Mrs. Blakely divides the class into groups, and each group explores urban migration pockets during different decades. Using the maps, students discover the areas the immigrants preferred to settle and the type of transportation used. Using primary sources, students identify the reasons for leaving. They can also explore the preferred cities and neighborhoods. Using GIS, students can investigate the population change of a particular neighborhood in a particular city as well as map migration patterns there. Mrs. Knight, the grade-level language arts teacher, follows this lesson by having students write an essay about where each student might like to live when he or she grows up and why (using some of the information they have gained in Mrs. Blakely's social studies class). A positive point about these Web sites and the information available is that it is free of charge, and teachers such as Mrs. Blakely and Mrs. Knight can create lessons such as the one mentioned at a very low cost.

Visual Aids: Google Earth®

Educators would be hard pressed to find a geography class in recent years where Google Earth® (GE) has not been employed. GE has become a regular staple for geography teachers due to the benefits of using its geospatial visual aids to promote a rich learning environment in schools (Baker, 2005); as such, GE has become the tool of choice in many social studies classrooms. GE is not precisely a true GIS but a virtual map, globe, and geographic information system. However, teachers have been using it as a substitute for GIS due to the geospatial qualities of the program and the ease of data manipulation.

As a geospatial visual tool, GE has many appealing features. It is a free, Web-based software that is easy to use and interface, making an attractive alternative to commercially available GISs (Demicri, Karaburun, & Kilar, 2013). The evolution of GE through the years is another reason why it is the favorite geographic tool of teachers. The days when GE only provided a zoomed view of a street or a 3D model of a major U.S. or Canadian city have passed. The latest versions of GE provide the most recent NASA satellites pictures, weather maps updated within the hour, up-to-the-minute oceanic and volcanic information, and instant traffic reports, among many other features. The possibilities for using GE in the classroom range from mapping current regional conflicts (Weidmann & Kuse, 2009) or exploring geological evolution (Parker, 2011) to create e-portfolios about the historical movement of music or virtual tours of Paris (Guertin, Stubbs, Millet, Lee, & Bodek, 2012).

http://www.google.com/earth

http://www.lessonplanet.com

http://www.gelessons.com/lessons

http://www.google.com/earth/educators

GE is an exceptional tool for virtual applications. For instance, students can use GE to understand the economic development of a country or region. Mr. Nguyen started his lesson by analyzing NASA's night satellite pictures of the world. By doing this, the students began to explore the areas of the world with highest and lowest economic activity by identifying the areas with the greatest and least energy consumption. Then, Mr. Nguyen divided his class into different groups, assigning each group a different city, country, or region of the world. Using other tools, students added captions, videos, and sounds to create a multimedia presentation. Students further enhanced this experience by comparing current Google street level pictures of an area with older pictures to analyze the economic changes throughout the area's history.

Student Production: Web 2.0: Social Network/ Digital Media/Blogosphere

Today, a teacher would most likely be surprised to find students who are not connected to Twitter®, Facebook®, Skype®, or Instagram®. Wikipedia, for example, lists well over 150 Web sites for social networking, including 18 Web sites that have more than 100 million registered users. Virtual communities are here to stay—and, increasingly, they are part of daily life. Educators can no longer ignore the fact that their students, the digital natives, socialize, take virtual/online classes, and conduct a great portion of their life in the virtual communities of the Internet.

For quite some time, educators have heard calls to incorporate social studies as a matter of course into the social network community (Green, 2001). As recent literature continues to highlight the benefits and need for constructivist student-centered learning (Beck, 2003; Britzman, 2003; Craig, 2005; Goldstein, 1995; Kincheloe, 1997; Sanacore, 2005), many scholars see social and virtual networks as the perfect pedagogical model for geography students (Dawson, 2008; Wang, Hsu, & Green, 2013; Zip, Parker, & Wyly, 2013). For the most part, social studies and geography teachers have used Web sites that are available to the general education community (e.g., Edmodo,

Sophia, Teacher 2.0, Edutopia, iTeach, edWeb), adapting these Web sites to their needs and to what they want to accomplish in the classroom. However, we are witnessing the appearance of some noteworthy social networks, which are specifically tailored for the geography teacher. Several of these areas are discussed below.

National Geographic (www.nationalgeographic.com) has, in reality, become the "one-stop shop" for almost everything related to geography, even offering a blog and social network section. Lately, however, My Wonderful World Web site has captivated the virtual community (http://www.mywonderfulworld.org). This is a collaborative project sponsored by National Geographic, Roper, and other institutions and has become a favorite site for schools. This Web site is extensive, providing comprehensive sections for both teachers and students alike, which are full of videos, maps, lessons, and school activities. It offers links to all other major geographic Web sites, such as the World Factbook, which is generated by the CIA (Central Intelligence Agency), providing opportunities for students and teachers to set up a virtual classroom, sign up for blogs and global collaborative activities, and join chats in the geographic community.

Geography U (http://cunegeog.blogspot.com) is another social network specific for geography lovers. Created as a class project by Joel Helmer and his students (Helmer & Bloch, 2010), the Web site has become very successful in promoting geography in the virtual community in the form of traditional blogs. The Web site is run by students so, unfortunately, activity slows down when schools are not in session.

Geography U and My Wonderful World currently seem to be the most popular geography Web sites capturing the attention of teachers and students. However, there are other geography noteworthy Web sites for social networking. If one wants to combine social activism and geography, then New Geography (http://www.new-geography.com) is available. This Web site offers news and reports about the latest policies, economic trends, and urban demographic issues. New Geography is specifically tailored for those living in urban areas, offering readers the chance to subscribe, submit written pieces, and join virtual conversations. If a teacher wants his/her class to explore how government policies affect the urban landscape, this is an excellent Web site.

Another Web site worth visiting is Supporting Geography Teachers (http://geographysupport .blogspot.com). This Web site is becoming much more than threads and comments. In recent years, this site has evolved into a true virtual community where many geography teachers share their lessons and ideas for the geography classroom. Other Web sites that merit attention are Dr. Laurie's GeoBlog, Digital Geographies (http://dlgb.wordpress.com), ICT Across the Curriculum (http://ictacrossthe curriculum.wordpress.com), and John Barlow's Blog (http://johnbarlow.wordpress.com), which are only a few of the countless of blogs that one can find on the World Wide Web.

Tupungato/Shutterstock, Inc.

psamtik/Shutterstock, Inc.

Radu Razvan/Shutterstock, Inc.

Blogging is an excellent way to engage students. Teachers can utilize blogs, for example, to encourage students to share their work. For instance, in the GIS immigration project discussed earlier, students can use blogs to share ideas, new tools, Web sites, and relevant information for the project. Teachers can require the students to post preliminary work so that their students can provide each other with feedback and suggestions for the final product. Furthermore, blogs can be used to showcase final presentations. In the case of geography, blogs can be used to explore different regions, summer travels, imaginary trips, and much more. For example, Mr. Dewey's class picks a city such as Rome to explore. Using Google Earth street view, each day the entire class explores a different street of the chosen city, each of which covers a specific time period in history. Then, using a blog, each student narrates how, as a tourist, he or she would spend a day in that part of the city.

An example of this can also be seen in Mrs. Mitchell's class. Mrs. Mitchell, who had lived in Japan, was excited to teach a unit on Kyoto. She wanted students to explore the country and its customs, so she first showed her young students some of her own pictures coupled with more professional images in a presentation. During center time, she allowed students to use the street views to visit some of the more famous sites along with neighborhoods (during cherry blossom time) and to use the *Hear Japanese Survival Phrases*. As children had a cup of green tea and used chopsticks for their snack, they watched a slide show of Japanese castles with a photo gallery of samurai artifacts and traditional Japanese clothing.

Mrs. Mitchell brought in her own futon quilt that she had used to sleep on while living there, showed pictures of an inn where she had stayed with pictures of a traditional sleeping arrangements (on the floor), and gave each student his/her name in Japanese to copy during art (japanesetranslator.co.uk/dictionaries/your-name-in-Japanese). She pulled up TripAdvisor for Kyoto ryokans (traditional inns) during math time and showed students how to look at the pictures and decide in which one they wanted to "virtually" stay, including the cost and its location on the map of Kyoto. The class elected Momijiya Annex. Mrs. Mitchell then pulled up some McDonald's, Burger King, and KFC menus from Japan to compare prices and types of food offered. Children noted that some different items included the Teriyaki Mac Burger and a Shrimp Filet-o. There was also a cup of ramen noodles with chopsticks on the menu. Students converted the yen to the dollar for several items using a currency converter on Mrs. Mitchell's phone app. Finally, children listened to traditional Japanese music from www.youtube.com/watch?v=IMxWA8Yuahc and compared it with the Top Japanese song of the year on YouTube as well. The combination of real and virtual experiences made this lesson a powerful cultural introduction to another country.

Research Enrichment: Web sites

Research has always been an important component of learning, and the Internet is increasingly becoming our main research tool. As such, when it comes to geography, research, and the Internet, the amount of resources and Web sites available to teachers and students is enormous, and it would be a titanic effort to enumerate all of them. With that said, it is worth mentioning some of the prominent names when it comes to geography research tools available on the Internet.

As mentioned, National Geographic (www.nationalgeographic.com) is at top of the list of resources for both teachers and students. Students can learn how to use historical maps, start conservation projects, and set up virtual classrooms. National Geographic offers one of the largest collections of digital maps that students and teachers can access via the Internet.

The National Aeronautics and Space Administration (www.nasa.gov) Web site offers a unique perspective for those who like to explore our planet from a different perspective. From watching a spacewalk in the International Space Station to the latest satellite images exploring cyclone patterns in the Pacific, it can be found at ww.nasa.gov. The Web site does require a certain amount of maneuvering, and it is not quite as user friendly as other more popular government Web sites. However, the Web site does offer resources that geography lovers, teachers, and students should consider. For example, in their Digital Learning Network (DLN) a list of events show the earth from space, the history of women in space, mapping the moon, and other topics that the social studies teacher might employ. In addition, NASA offers gaming through Moonbase Alpha, as one "steps into the role of an explorer in a futuristic lunar settlement." Other gaming opportunities exist in social studies in all areas, including community issues (SimCity; Civilization IV), history (The Oregon Trail; Roman Town), battle and economic strategies, and others.

The National Oceanic and Atmospheric Administration (www.noaa.gov) Web site is a helpful resource for those whose interests lie in meteorology, the environment, and geography. The agency is responsible for the National Hurricane Center, National Oceanographic Data Center, National Weather Service, and National Marine Fisheries Services, among other agencies. Moreover, each of these sub-agencies has its own Web site, offering a wealth of information and data to those who want to learn more about the environment. Studying wind patterns in the desert, analyzing the movement of the polar caps in the Artic, or observing the migration of mammals in the Pacific Ocean is only a mouse click away at www.noaa.gov.

Other notable government agencies with excellent geographic information on their Web sites are the CIA with its Fact Worldbook (https://www.cia.gov/library/publications/the-world-Wfactbook), United States Geological Survey (http://www.usgs.gov), Library of Congress (http://www.loc.gov), and the Smithsonian Institution (http://www.si.edu).

As noted, it would be impossible to list every Web site available to geography teachers on the Internet. However, in terms of data collection, the government Web sites often appear to offer the best resources. Other suitable places that geography teachers can visit in the Internet are: the Perry-Castañeda Map Collection at the University of Texas (http://www.lib.utexas.edu/maps), Maps of India (http://www.mapsofindia.com), the British Weather Service (http://www.metoffice.gov.uk), European Space Agency (http://www.esa.int/ESA), Yale University Genocide Project (http://www.yale.edu/gsp), United Nation's Food and Agriculture Organization (http://www.fao.org/home/en), and World Wildlife Fund (http://worldwildlife.org). All of these Web sites are easily accessible by doing a Google search.

The information gathered on these Web sites can be useful for the projects mentioned in these sections. As an example, as detailed in the following lesson plan from Lane Community College, students are using GIS to study ancestry patterns in the United States by gathering the information available in these Web sites. Then, students can use GIS software such as ArcView to create their own maps and investigate migration patterns of their own families. Furthermore, blogs can be used to share the information gathered, and Google Earth can be used to create a multimedia/simulation presentations of the data collected.

Lesson Plan

Teaching Guide
Lesson Title: Spatial Patterns of Ancestry in US Counties
Subject Area: Geography – Introduction to Human Geography
Grade Level: High School (9-12)
Goal: Students will learn about normalizing data and develop Boolean logic queries to explore correlations.

Lesson Description: Students will describe spatial data patterns representing ethnicity and ancestry. The data for this exercise is from the 2005 U.S. Census self-identified ancestry. Students will describe the spatial distribution as dispersed, clustered, or random. Students will explore the different minimums and maximums of data ranges and discuss how a lack of awareness of these differences can mislead a map reader.

ITSE National Technology Standards
1) Develop positive attitudes toward technology uses that support lifelong learning, collaboration, personal pursuits, and productivity.
2) Use technology tools to enhance learning, increase productivity, and promote creativity.

Geography Standards - Geography for Life 9–12th
1) Understand the distribution and complexity of Earth's cultural mosaics.
2) Understand how to use maps and other geographic representations, tools, and technologies to acquire, process, and report information from a spatial perspective.
3) Understand how to analyze the spatial organization of cultural features on Earth's surface.

Objectives:
1) Students will participate in a Think-Pair-Share activity on their own family's movements.
2) After reading the US 2000 Census PDF, students will describe the spatial patterns of ethnic and ancestry identity in the United States in a classroom discussion.
3) Students will evaluate data ranges of spatial data on their activity sheet.
4) Students will design five Boolean Logic queries on their activity sheet.
5) Students will evaluate correlations as positive, negative, or nonexistent on the activity sheet.

Prerequisites:
1) Students should have completed the GIS Tutorial activity and be familiar with geospatial skill such as viewing data layers, performing Boolean logic queries, and analyzing spatial patterns.
2) Students should be familiar with basic concepts of immigration and migration as discussed in an introduction human geography course.

Focus: Ask students, in Think-Pair-Share groups, to each share where his/her family has lived as far back as can be remembered. If the student knows his/her genealogy, have him/her share from where his/her family came originally. Ask if there is anyone who would like to share with the whole class.

Materials: Computer access with high-speed Internet; student activity sheets.

Geospatial Tools and Questions – Pattern, correlations, description – identify, query.

Lesson Estimated Time: Approximately 60 minutes outside of class, 30 minutes in class

Connections:

Prior/Future Knowledge: We already know that we are a country of mostly immigrants—mainly from "push/pull" factors. Many of those reasons were economical and/or had to do with conflict or other world events.
Cultural Connections: Given current world conflicts and events, from where do we see the most immigrants coming at this time to the United States? Why? Which states are seeing the most influx of new residents? Why do you think this is so?
Connections to the Community: How have these immigration and migration patterns changed our own ___ (city, state, country)?
Connections to Other Content: Why, historically, did most people come to this state? How can scientists use this kind of data (outbreaks of disease, etc.)? How has technology helped political scientists to get information?
Connections to Students Interests and Experiences: Many places in the world do not have the richness of various cultures as we do . . . especially in foods. What are some foods that you enjoy that are culturally different which have been brought in by various immigrants groups? What are some regional foods which may be different regionally in our country (e.g., cheese curds are a popular snack in the northern dairy states)? What are some things that are traditional for your family at holidays like Thanksgiving (these are often very regional)?
Lesson Procedure: After discussing migration and immigration, students will be given this activity as a homework assignment: they are asked to read the US 2000 Census PDF, which explains ancestry data. In class, following the completion of the assignment, the class will discuss the overall patterns and correlations they uncovered. Students are asked to reflect on the data quality and how this type of data and geospatial analysis is used.

Assessment: Students will be assessed on their activity sheet. Each student will have completed answers with at least 80% correctness.

Closure: Ask students, "If you could immigrate to another country, which one would it be and why? If you could move to a different area, where would it be and why?" Take several answers but have all students quickly fill out an Exit Ticket to leave before exiting the classroom.

Resource: Lynn Songer http://gis.lanecc.edu/arcserver-flex/ancestry_us/USancestry_TG_03082012.doc/at_download/file.

Teaching Economics with Technology

Current technology offers multiple options for hands-on learning in economics that will breathe life into what many students may consider a dry subject. When most students think about economics, they usually focus on the quantitative side (the numbers/statistics) of the discipline but ignore the equally important qualitative element (attempts to see reasons behind the numbers, using interviews, shadowing, etc.). The following lesson ideas provide multiple options for addressing both elements giving, students the tools to apply knowledge, collect data, and synthesize solutions to practical economics issues.

Data collection/Research

Data collection is an integral part of economics education. Both the qualitative and quantitative elements depend on accurate data to formulate strategies and make wise economic decisions. Both students and teachers can use Excel to program spreadsheets to organize information from surveys and studies. Easier to employ, in terms of both data collection and evaluation, are sites like SurveyMonkey. SurveyMonkey allows the user to make and launch surveys of 10 questions or less for free. The site will also categorize responses and provide visuals that can be customized and downloaded for presentations. Even elementary-aged students can design and launch simple surveys, allowing them to engage in "market research activities" that will help guide decision making.

The following project taken on by Mr. Avalos provides a practical example in his fourth-grade classroom that collects both quantitative and qualitative data and helps students plan their perfect end-of-school party. He has a brainstorming lesson with students. The class must decide (among other items) what food, decorations, and activities should be part of the celebration. Mr. Avalos sets up a simple survey that provides a variety of categories for each element on which students must decide. On the survey, students must not only select their preferred food, decorations, and activities (quantitative data), but they must also explain their choices (qualitative data). When all the students have taken the survey, Mr. Avalos demonstrates the final quantitative (numbers) results to the students. The qualitative data is then analyzed by the class so that students can understand the personal reasoning for each student's selection. Mr. Avalos is also able to have students view their comments through a word cloud (Moodle). In this manner, students can understand that in the world of economics, not everyone gets what they want, but there is a rational way to address and meet the needs and/or preferences of the majority of the members of a selected group. At higher levels, individual students can engage in their own market research projects using SurveyMonkey and employ the results for a variety of projects. One potential project would involve students creating a piece of print advertising to sell a particular product. Students could set up a survey that asks responders to identify certain preferences like color, text styles, graphics, and other elements and use the data to guide design decisions. When students present their finished product, they use the data to explain their design choices.

Consumer Survey: This image demonstrates how some businesses are able to use smartphone accessible polling software to obtain instant data on customer satisfaction.

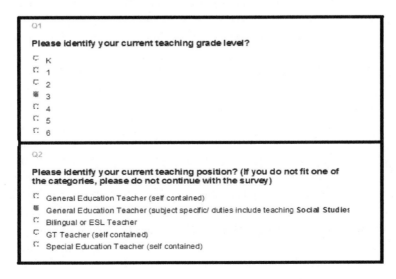

Students can also use programs such as Google Forms to create surveys and disaggregate data. Google Forms is a free Google app that allows an increased number of questions. Students and teachers can use tools similar to Survey Monkey within Google Sheets to breakdown data and create visuals.

Visual aids

There are a variety of electronic visual aids available for economics lessons. The aforementioned SurveyMonkey allows the user the option of turning data into a variety of charts that can be organized into a presentation tool and projected onto a projector screen or whiteboard. Sites like TargetMap (http://www.targetmap.com) provide existing maps with a variety of economic themes (from the practical, such as world unemployment rates, to the whimsical like the consumption rates of a particular company's products) that can be used in the classroom. This also allows the user to input data to create their own economic themed maps that can be shared in the classroom. In addition, sites like Vintage Ad Browser (http://www.vintageadbrowser.com), contain accessible databases full of different product ads (from the 1830s to the present day) that can be employed to compare consumer habits and interests as well as to chart the evolution of marketing trends for selected products.

Mrs. Krueger's lesson provides an example of how to use the Vintage Ad Browser site for charting the development of food advertising in America. She goes to the Vintage Ad Browser site to select and download samples of food ads throughout the decades (and if possible, find ads that sell a similar type of product). She downloads copies of the Poster Document Analysis Worksheet located in the National Archives Web site (http://www.archives.gov/education/lessons/worksheets) to help students analyze each advertisement. Her students then compare and chart the evolution of advertising trends. There are a variety of conclusions and economic lessons that can be derived from this exercise. For example, some questions might include: What do these observations say about people's consumption habits at different times in America's history? How have advertisers changed the way they present such products to the public? Do the ads target specific groups of people based on such elements as gender, race, or other demographic factors? Another teacher, Mr. Keithly, provides his students with menus from a restaurant from the last 3 years and asks groups of students to compare them. Students find that items have gone up considerably in price, but there is not a big change in items. He presents students with a generated list of prices from the grocery store needed to make some of the items, the wages that the restaurant pays, the rent, and the electric bill. Each group will then create its own food business with these issues in mind.

Developing Student Products

The best way to learn about economic principles is through constant testing and application. The mysteries of the market are not so opaque if one considers the role of information in promoting clarity. Certainly the Web has revolutionized the speed and availability of information that is available for application in economics-based projects. The real trick is in helping students discover how a certain piece of information can affect economic issues. Suppose Mr. Lang is conducting a class concerning commodities. Among the most important information the teacher must convey is to identify the location of those commodities. A dedicated search can provide students with information concerning the most important, or potentially most valuable, world commodities. One news story from 2012 suggests that 14 commodities (oil, natural gas, aluminum, copper, nickel, zinc, gold, silver, platinum, cotton, sugar cane, corn, wheat, and soybeans) presented the greatest potential for investment. Mr. Lang's students then use this information to chart the most valuable sources for those commodities. Various sites provide information identifying the top soybean producing countries, for example. A quick look would indicate to students that more than 80% of soybean production is dominated by just three countries—the United States, Brazil, and Argentina. Students can input the production statistics on an Excel spreadsheet and then use TargetMap (http://www.targetmap.com) to produce a visual representation of the major soybean producers (and duplicate similar maps for other important commodities). Using newspapers and other news sources, students can identify issues that can affect the production of these commodities (conflicts, weather events, political instability, new production opportunities, pest infestation, laws about land use, new technological developments, etc.) and, by extension, affect their price in the marketplace. Mr. Lang can then help students chart changes in commodities' prices to gauge how these types of events affect the value of commodities. For instance, he may help students to see what would happen to the price of soybeans if

Argentina suffered a drought or if China (the fourth largest producer) tripled their cultivation of the crop. A drop in production of soybeans would affect the cost of animal feed (soybeans are the most common and cheapest source of protein), thus affecting the price of animal products like meat and dairy. Soybeans are also used to make resins and other byproducts that can be used to make everything from crayons and makeup to plastics. In addition, soybeans are a major source of biodiesel fuel. In other words, this one simple crop and its various applications are thoroughly interconnected into the world economy. The long term goal is for students to develop the ability to predict the general trend in commodities' prices and to understand how prices are affected by global events. From a student standpoint, when groceries and other necessities are high, there is less family money for entertainment. While such a project could have certainly been done in the age before the Internet, the amount and speed of research as well as the accuracy and timeliness of the information obtained would have made it an impractical classroom project. Learning these economic principles will help students learn how to be wiser consumers, an invaluable skill in our market-based economy.

Finally, two useful Web sites deserve mention. The first is Numbeo (http://www.numbeo.com/common), which provides timely worldwide demographic information from cost of living to quality of life indices. The second Web site is the historical cost of living calculator sponsored by the American Institute for Economic Research (https://www.aier.org/article/48-cost-living-calculator), which will calculate the relative value of money from different American historical eras. Both can easily be used and incorporated to a variety of economics-based projects and lessons. Both provide excellent opportunities for instructing students on the relative value of money and costs in various contexts.

Students can use Numbeo to engage in a project that would allow them to compare the cost of living between two countries. Students could create a slide show demonstrating contrasting images of such items as housing, food, and entertainment while linking them with the information they obtained on such items from Numbeo. Students could then visually and statistically compare the relative meaning of cost of living. The historical cost of living calculator provides an easy tool for teaching young children relative value. A teacher could obtain supermarket circulars to have elementary age students plan "a dinner party." Using the information, students could then determine a total cost for the party and then, using the cost of living calculator, they could determine what they would actually spend to obtain the same items in a different era. For instance, a party that would cost $150.00 in 2013 would have only cost $5.72 in 1913. Using another site titled MeasuringWorth.com (http://www.measuringworth.com/datasets/uswage/result.php), students are able to compare the yearly salaries of unskilled workers in 1913 ($179.00) to those of 2013 ($17,827.44). By dividing the cost by the salary, the students would be able to determine that a worker in 1913 would be spending 3.2% of their salary to throw such a dinner party in comparison to a worker in 2013 who would only be expending 0.8%, or clearly one fourth of what his ancestor paid one hundred years earlier. Students could thus appreciate that the relative cost and value of items are an important component for understanding the historical cost of living and the difficulties people faced in the past. Using similar types of activities, they can begin to see economic trends in times of depression, inflation, and many others. Having an economically savvy population bodes well for individuals, their families, and the country.

Teaching Government with Technology

The traditional government class continues to focus its attention in equipping students with the basic knowledge of government structure, voting participation, and citizen rights. However, new curriculums demand that students do more than absorb knowledge; they must become active knowledge producers as well. While other areas of social studies have flourished in the use of technology, its use generally continues to be absent from the government classroom, aside from the common blog. Although the technological tools presented in the following lessons are more commonly used in other social studies subjects (such as geography), these tools can also enhance the civic experience of students.

Data collection

Although we discussed GIS in the context of geography education, it is equally as valuable for teaching government. Because GIS is an information system that stores, analyzes, manipulates, and presents geographic

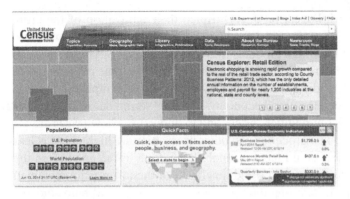

data, the same data can be explored for understanding potential political issues. For example, various forms of demographic data can be analyzed, such as the shopping habits of a particular neighborhood or zip code or the religious/ethnic concentrations found in certain geographical areas, to deduce certain commonalities or points of interests for a community. For instance, the amount of time people dedicate towards church attendance would give a person a reasonable idea of how influential religious concerns would be to a certain community. Thus, in a government class, GIS can be easily used to understand and predict voting patterns throughout specific districts.

Mrs. Hernandez employed GIS to help students understand voting patterns during critical election years. First, she introduced the subject with the class in identifying basic voting vocabulary, including the concepts of political participation, suffrage, and turnout. Then, she used primary sources (e.g., letters, campaign Web sites, and city records) to help the class understand both political motives and the crucial issues that were dominating local, state, and national elections. The Web site for the Gallup Company

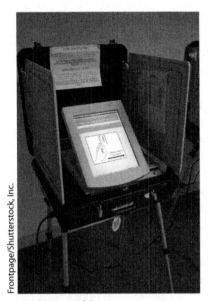

Voting machine – a computer

provides a great deal of current and historical statistical data concerning politics, the economy, and social issues that can be used to study trends (http://www.gallup.com/PopularTags.aspx). Visual aids, such as flyers, videos, and advertisements, add a visual context to the understanding of the political process. The frequencies with which certain issues are addressed provide students with an understanding of what issues are dominating the current conversation. Powerful questions emerge when students were asked to verbalize what they saw and how they saw it. Mrs. Hernandez then had her students use readily available voter data from databases such as the Census Bureau (http://www.census.gov) and other data sources. The class was divided into different groups, and, using the data, each group explored a congressional district. Using the data obtained, the students interpreted and analyzed the data with user friendly software such as ArcGIS for Windows or Canvas for Macintosh. With this information, there are multiple possibilities; for example, students can predict election outcomes, future trends, possible places where traditional election patterns can be reversed, and much more. Furthermore, using GIS, teachers and students can explore how a population change of a particular neighborhood or congressional district can alter voting results.

Visual aids: Google Earth®

In the government class, Google Earth can be a prime tool for virtual applications. For instance, in Mrs. Ahmad's government class, students can use Google Earth to further explore a candidate. She often starts her lesson by analyzing a candidate's road schedule during presidential or state elections. Then, she divides the class into different groups, assigning each group a different candidate. Using Google Earth, the student can select a number of stops their candidate makes. Using Google Earth Placemark, the students can add captions, videos, and sounds to create a multimedia presentation of their assigned candidate. In

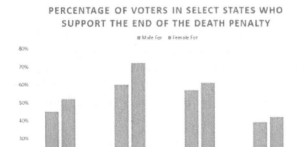

this way, students can create a Google Earth Tour of a political candidate. Information that can be gathered digitally from online editions of local newspapers can help students chart the issues that the candidates are addressing at each stop. Students can begin to discern whether candidates are consistent with the selection of issues that they address, and they can also see if a candidate changes their message based upon the community they are addressing. In doing so, students can also deduce what issues candidates perceive as being of importance to each of the communities they visit and/or if they are staying consistent in their overall messages. Furthermore, by visiting Web sites such as C-SPAN (http://www.c-span.org) or the White House (www.whitehouse.gov), students can keep themselves up to date with congressional hearings and government events, becoming more familiar with the candidate's position on certain issues. Students can visit an incumbent candidate's congressional Web site (www.house.gov) or the senate's Web site (www.senate.gov) and explore the candidate's past congressional attendance and voting record.

Student production: The Blogosphere

Virtual communities are here to stay; more and more, they are becoming a part of our daily lives. The result is that social networks are no longer exclusive novelties for the computer gurus. As noted, teachers can no longer ignore the fact that individuals socialize, take virtual/online classes, and conduct a great portion of their life in the virtual communities of the Internet for entertainment, for making connections, and for many other social issues. For example, during the tragic loss of Malaysia Flight 370 in 2014, social communities were used to call hundreds of international volunteers to help in the search of the downed plane.

arka38/Shutterstock, Inc.

As recent literature continues to highlight the benefits and need for constructivist, student-centered learning (Beck, 2003; Britzman, 2003; Craig, 2005; Goldstein, 1995; Kincheloe, 1997; Sanacore, 2005), many scholars see social and virtual networks as the perfect pedagogical model for geography students (Dawson, 2008; Wang et al., 2013; Zip et al., 2013). For the most part, social studies classes have used Web sites that are available to the general education community (e.g., Edmodo, Blackboard Learn, Sophia, Teacher 2.0, Edutopia, iTeach, edWeb), adapting these Web sites to their needs and to what they want to accomplish in the classroom. However, there are numerous blogs sites available for the government teacher and student.

Blogs are incredibly rich resources and places to share ideas and be engaged in meaningful discussions. Teachers can use the US Teacher Government Blog (http://usgovteducatorsblog.blogspot.com) to share their latest ideas and discussions about government in the high school classroom. Other similar sites are:

The American Class Government:
(http://ochsgovernment.blogspot.com),

Word Press Government:
(http://www.howto.gov/training/classes/wordpress-for-government-blogs-and-microsites),
Mr. Anderson's Government Class Blog:
(http://andersongovernmentclass.wordpress.com),
Abay's Government Blog:
(http://abay-gov.blogspot.com).

Blogging is an exciting way to have one's class become highly engaged. Teachers can utilize blogs (or wikis), for example, to encourage the students to share their work. For instance, in returning to Mrs. Ahmad's Google Earth Candidate Tour government lesson, students can use blogs to share ideas, new tools, Web sites, and relevant information for the project. Another social studies teacher, Mr. Dues, requires his students to post preliminary work so that they can provide each other with feedback and suggestions for a final product. In the blog, students can post the links to their candidate's latest speech or tour stop. Furthermore, blogs can be used to showcase a final presentation. In the case of government classes, blogs can be used to tap into the electoral pulse of different regions. Using Google Earth street view, each day an entire class can explore the geographic feature of a candidate's new stop, analyzing the economic, ethnic, and cultural background of the that region.

There is another opportunity to help students explore the dissemination of political ideas and opinions in addition to blogging—political cartoons. The United States has a fine tradition of political cartoonists—from Thomas Nast to Herb Block. Political cartoons are an innovative way to highlight complex political ideas or critiques and present them in a more accessible medium. Examining cartoons and producing them can help students distill the root of political issues. A teacher may start by visiting a selection of Web sites dedicated to prominent political cartoonists. One example is the Herb Block foundation Web site, which contains a sizeable selection of the influential cartoonist's best work (http://www.herbblockfoundation.org). Block's career spanned almost 70 years from the Great Depression to the election of George W. Bush, so that students are able to see the evolution of the cartoonist's work as well as to understand his political points of view. One can also select to view multiple cartoons written by different artists concerning a specific issue. If students were to conduct a Google images search like "Gun Control Political Cartoons," the search should return a large selection of cartoons. A cartoon analysis worksheet from the National Archives can be downloaded to help structure the activity (http://www.archives.gov/education/lessons/worksheets/cartoon_analysis_worksheet .pdf). Students can examine the cartoons and compare them to each other. By discussing how the cartoonist uses certain images and short text to get across a certain idea, Mrs. Dolche, a fifth-grade teacher, then provides students with an important political issue and asks them to produce a political cartoon of their own that illustrates their stance and views. There are three Web sites that can be easily used for students to construct their own political cartoons:

Makebeliefscomix one allows the user to make a simple three panel comic that it can be sent to oneself: http://www.makebeliefscomix.com/Comix
Bitstrip provides the user with considerable flexibility when it comes to making cartoons, like multiple panel designs and layering:
http://bitstrips.com/create/comic
Pixton is a pay site, but it is the most the flexible in terms of graphic manipulation and the company does offer reasonable pricing for teachers to use their product: http://www.pixton.com/schools/overview

Political cartoon created for a project.

The first two sites are free to use and are often sufficient to calm the concerns of less artistic students. The third site has reasonable bi-monthly rates for educators, which is charged per the student—about a dollar a student on average. The site is extremely flexible in design selections, allowing a great deal of options for making comic strips to comic books.

http://www.archives.gov

http://www.loc.gov

Research Enrichment: Web sites

Research has always been an important component of learning about the government and political issues, and the Internet is increasingly becoming the main research tool. As such, when it comes to government, research, and the Internet, a wealth of connections exist. With the amount of resources and Web sites available to teachers and students, it would be an overwhelming effort to enumerate all of them. With that said, it is worth mentioning a few of the more popular names for social studies research tools available on the Internet.

The U.S. government Web site (www.usa.gov) is at the top of the list, offering innumerable resources for education. The Web site offers a link to every government agency Web site made available to the public. In this Web site, students can find out how to contact their congressional representative, explore the White House, learn voting regulations, explore different laws, and even become involved in different blogs. For those looking for original pictures, audio, and other primary sources, the Library of Congress (www.loc.gov) or the National Archives (www.archives.gov) are excellent sources. In these Web sites, researchers can find unedited audios of early presidential speeches, unique pictures of the Great Depression, or drawings of a slave cabin.

Elementary teachers will be delighted to use Kids USA Gov (http://kids.usa.gov). This is the official US government Web site specifically for children. It is full of interactive games, lessons, quizzes, videos, tutorials, and much more. Universities, foundations, agencies such as the Library of Congress, Smithsonian Museums, the Census Bureau, FBI, CIA, NASA, NOA, the United Nations, and other countries' governments offer Web sites full of information, including sections for teachers and students. This site provides these resources free of charge as a public service.

The information gathered on these Web sites can be useful for the projects mentioned in these sections. For example, in her government classroom, Mrs. Barrera can have students use GIS to investigate the political process in the United States. The students can gather the information available in these Web sites and then use GIS software such as ArcView or Google Map Maker to create their own maps. Blogs can be used to share the information gathered and/or to present the students' multimedia presentations. In the end, the limitless possibilities of technology use will depend on the creativity that teachers use to design motivating and meaningful lessons. As mentioned earlier, there is no rationale for students to find their social studies lessons as simply "read the pages and do the questions at the end of the chapter." There is plenty of technology available that will allow the events and facts of the past and present to come vibrantly alive.

Conclusion

The Twenty-first Century Social Studies Classroom

Technology has, without a doubt, great potential in the teaching of social studies. Throughout this chapter, tools, applications, and uses, as well as some of the innovative ways for teaching and learning, have been presented. Technology, with its new advances, global interconnection, and networks has changed and revolutionized the social studies classroom, much as the printing press, the light bulb, or the television did decades ago. In the information age, we are just beginning to grasp the possibilities of the twenty-first century social studies classroom.

Notably, technology has allowed the modern teacher to have a plethora of informational sources available at the touch of a fingertip. It allows the creation of projects that help students apply the lessons of the classroom in new and innovative ways. Finally, it is an important tool for helping students form bridges between different regions and cultures. In an increasingly global society, ignorance of other people, other places, and other customs hampers our ability to construct a better nation and world. With the technological tools that are now available to teachers, we can increasingly prepare our students to become better global citizens.

References

Al-Bataineh, A., Anderson, S., Toledo, C., & Wellinski, S. (2008). A study of technology integration in the classroom. *International Journal of Instructional Media, 35*(4), 381–387.

Andersen, D. (2011). Community mapping: Putting the pieces together. *The Geography Teacher, 8*(1), 4–9.

Baker, T. (2005). Internet-based GIS mapping in support of K-12 education. *The Professional Geographer, 57*(1), 44–50.

Beck, U. (2003). Toward a new critical theory with a cosmopolitan intent. *Constellations, 10*(4), 453–468.

Benaivis, L. (2008). Applying the GIS in school education: The experience of Japanese geography teachers. *Geografija, 44*(2), 36–40.

Britzman, D. P. (2003). *Practice makes practice: A critical study of learning to teach.* Albany, NY: SUNY Press.

Craig, C. J. (2005). The epistemic role of novel metaphors in teachers' knowledge constructions of school reform. *Teachers and Teaching, 11*(2), 195–208.

Dawson, S. (2008). A Study of the relationship between student social networks and sense of community. *Educational Technology & Society, 11*(3), 224–238.

Demicri, A. (2011). Using Geographic Information Systems (GIS) at schools without a computer laboratory. *Journal of Geography, 110,* 49–59.

Demicri, A., Karaburun, A., & Kilar, H. (2013). Using Google Earth as an educational tool in secondary school geography lessons. *International Research in Geographical & Environmental Education, 22*(4), 277–290.

Fitchett, P. G., & Good, A. J. (2012). Teaching genocide through GIS: A transformative approach. *The Clearing House: A Journal of Educational Strategies, Issues and Ideas, 85*(3), 87–92.

Goldstein, B. S. (1995). Critical pedagogy in a bilingual special education classroom. *Journal of Learning Disabilities, 28*(8), 463–475.

Green, T. (2001). Tech talk for social studies teachers: Virtual expeditions: Taking your students around the world without leaving the classroom. *Social Studies, 92*(4), 177–179.

Guertin, L., Stubbs, C., Millet, C., Lee, T. K., & Bodek, M. (2012). Enhancing geographic and digital literacy with a student-generated course portfolio in Google Earth. *Journal of College Science Teaching, 42*(2), 32–37.

Harris, J., Mishra, P., & Koehler, M. J. (2009). Teachers' technological pedagogical content knowledge and learning activity types: Curriculum-based technology integration reframed. *Journal of Research on Technology in Education, 41*(4), 393–416.

Helmer, J. W., & Bloch, N. (2010). Teaching geography in the blogosphere. *The Geography Teacher, 7*(2), 73–76.

Henry, P., & Semple, H. (2012). Integrating online GIS into the K–12 curricula: Lessons from the development of a collaborative GIS in Michigan. *Journal of Geography, 111*(1), 3–14.

Kerski, J. J., Demirci, A., & Milson, A. J. (2013). The global landscape of GIS in secondary education. *Journal of Geography, 112*(6), 232–247.

Kincheloe, J. L. (1997). Fiction formulas: Critical constructivism and the representation of reality. In W. G. Tierney & Y. S. Lincoln (Eds.), *Representation and Text: Reframing the Narrative Voice* (pp. 57–80). Albany, NY: State University of New York.

Lloyd, W. (2001). Integrating GIS into the undergraduate learning environment. *Journal of Geography, 100*, 158–161.

Parker, J. D. (2011). Using Google Earth to teach the magnitude of deep time. *Journal of College Science Teaching, 40*(5), 23–27.

Sanacore, J. (2005). Increasing student participation in the language arts. *Intervention in School and Clinic, 41*(2), 99–104.

Sanders Jr., R. L., Kajs, L. T., & Crawford, C. M. (2001). Electronic mapping in education: The use of geographic information systems [Electronic version]. *Journal of Research on Technology, 34*(2), 121.

Wang, S.-K., Hsu, H.-Y., & Green, S. (2013). Using social networking sites to facilitate teaching and learning in the science classroom. *Science Scope, 36*(7), 74–80.

Weidmann, N. B., & Kuse, D. (2009). WarViews: Visualizing and animating geographic data on civil war. *International Studies Perspectives, 10*(1), 36–48.

Wright, V. H., & Wilson, E. K. (2009). Using technology in the social studies classroom: The journey of two teachers. *Journal of Social Studies Research, 33*(2), 133–154.

Zip, L., Parker, R., & Wyly, E. (2013). Facebook as a way of life: Louis Wirth in the social network. *Geographical Bulletin, 54*(2), 77–98.

Chapter 3

Teaching Science with Technology

Sissy S. Wong, EunJin Bang

University of Houston, Iowa State University

Meet Mrs. Calandar

Mrs. Calander, an elementary teacher, is preparing a science unit on life cycles of plants and animals. During the unit, students will be growing plants from seeds and raising mealworms (*Tenobrio molitor*) for the class project. She wants to integrate technology in the projects to increase her students' technology literacy. As she looks online, she is overwhelmed by the options of Web sites, lesson ideas, and tools she can use. Mrs. Calander starts to wonder how she can purposefully select what to integrate into her science class and what she should consider when integrating technology into her classroom.

How Can Technology Support Science Learning?

Incorporating technology into science instruction increases creativity, motivation, participation, and collaboration in classroom activities because it engages students in real world learning and promotes problem-solving skills (Lombardi, 2007). Teaching inquiry-based science using technology can provide many authentic experiences, which are experiences that reflect real-world situations and their solutions. According to Lombardi (2007), students who engage in authentic learning experiences are able to:

- *determine* reliable from unreliable information;
- exhibit *patience* during sustained learning experiences;
- *synthesize* patterns and trends in various settings;
- be *flexible* in considering different disciplines and cultural components in formulating problems and solutions.

Although these skills are important for learning in all content areas, they specifically align with those required to develop scientific literacy.

Science teachers have integrated technology in instruction for decades. For example, laboratory exercises have often included technology such as digital scales, microscopes, and graphing calculators. In fact, science teachers were the first to include hand-held devices such as probes and micro-computers to collect data in the 1980s (Wallace, 2002). Science teachers recognize that including technology is not only beneficial because it supports student learning of content, development of critical science skills, and increases engagement in science, but it also provides authentic learning experiences since real scientists utilize technology with similar problems and tools.

Teaching science with technology also acculturates students into the field of science and represents how science is conducted in our constantly changing world. Using technology supports the teaching of science content that students should learn and incorporates the nature of science, or how science happens, and how scientific knowledge develops (Lederman, 2007). Scientists often integrate various technologies in their work, and scientific accomplishments are often supported by cutting-edge applications of technology. A comprehensive science education experience, therefore, involves "a commitment to the inclusion of technology, both as a tool for learning science content and processes and as a topic of instruction in itself" (American Association for the Advancement of Science [AAAS], 1993: National Research Council [NRC], 1996, as cited by Flick & Bell, 2000, p. 39).

Integrating technology effectively is complex. To integrate technology effectively takes understanding of content, pedagogy, and the technologies themselves. The benefits, however, are important to student

learning of content, mastery of skills, and engagement in science. Teachers recognize the importance of integrating technology in the science classroom and know that when used purposefully, technology mediates authentic science learning experiences by providing access to data, scientific tools, and other resources. Due to the advantages of integrating technology in teaching and the prevalence of technology in science and our society today, there is now a major expectation for teachers to be proficient in incorporating educational technology into their instruction (Lyublinskaya & Zhou, 2008).

Considering Students When Incorporating Technology into the Science Classroom

When implementing technology as a meaningful tool in the science classroom, science teachers need to consider students' knowledge of and experiences with technology. While some students are technologically savvy, some may be novices. For example, the Digital Divide may be prevalent in low income areas with students from less affluent homes (and even other countries in which technology is not well advanced) and may create

learners who are not "digital natives." Students will have varied prior experiences and knowledge of scientific tools, such as microscopes, as well as more common forms of technology like digital cameras, MS Office applications, using Internet search engines, and so forth. It is important to be prepared to assist students so that all can access the benefits of using technology in science learning.

It is also important for science teachers to pay attention to students' learning styles. Teachers tend to implement technology tools that are aligned with their own learning styles—not necessarily with those of their students. Science teachers should be aware of the full spectrum of students' learning styles and provide alternative technology tools and electronic activities that are better aligned with their students' particular learning styles. Motivation may also be a factor with science and technology. Teachers may feel that *any* technology task may be motivating for today's science student. That may not necessarily be the case. Students must be well prepared for using the electronic science tools involved. Those students who have extensive technological experience will feel motivated to use them, but those who are not as comfortable may feel apprehensive of activities where technology is at the forefront. Using small learning groups is one excellent way of supporting learners who are less able with technology.

In addition, science teachers also need to be sensitive to culture, gender, and special needs of their students when implementing technology tools for teaching science. For instance, female students have been known to have poor self-concepts about science and may tend to avoid science tasks that are not familiar to them (Baker & Piburn, 2007). Providing the best technology tools may be able to help alleviate these types of debilitating traditional self-concepts in science.

Educational Technology as a Way to Mediate Access to Content

There are many ways to integrate technology for richer learning in science, and one common approach is to utilize the Internet as a way to access content information. With a wireless or wired connection, science students can access the Internet with desktop computers, laptop computers, tablet computers, smart phones, and other devices. Through the Internet, there are multiple avenues to access information, including Web pages, videos, podcasts, and games. The information can be invaluable for student learning in science, and it is crucial to be aware of the wide array of information that is available. Technology and digital resources evolve; therefore, it is difficult to include a comprehensive list of online resources for the science classroom. However, many online resources for science teachers help make current information available, and initiating a new search prior to teaching a lesson should reveal new discoveries or information on the science topic. The Internet helps to ensure that students (and teachers) receive the latest information on a topic throughout the rapid changes in science knowledge. The following are examples of some formats outlined by Martin (2012) for teachers to consider when planning inquiry-based science lessons incorporating the Internet (see Table 3.1).

Online resources can support learning, but the amount of information can also be overwhelming to both teachers and students. Without careful planning by the teacher, students can become unfocused and frustrated during online searches. To keep students focused on the topic under study, teachers must first make sound decisions on how to evaluate Web sites to ensure they are appropriate for students and decide how to make them accessible to students. According to Martin (2012), teachers should ask the following when evaluating Web sites for student use:

- Is the science content accurate and up to date?
- What are the qualifications of the author or organization that created the Web site?
- Is the Web site age-appropriate and user-friendly?
- Does the Web site provide links to other quality Web sites that are on the same topic or closely related to the same topic?
- Does the Web site suggest accommodations for diverse learners, such as English language learners and students with disabilities?

Once teachers have explored and bookmarked the many Internet options to support science content learning, it may be advisable to create Web sites by using Weebly, Wix, or Google Sites for their students to begin their exploration. On these Web sites, teachers can include content, assignments, and other resources. Some teachers may also digitally record and upload lessons that occurred in the class so that students can review them. Currently, some teachers are also incorporating the flipped classroom concept where lessons or materials are uploaded prior to the class. By having students review the material before class as an introduction, or after class for review, class time can be used for activities or discussions. This can be a particularly beneficial option for science teachers to consider since it would provide maximum laboratory time during school hours.

Table 3.1   Examples of Internet formats and resources

Type	Use
WebQuests	An inquiry-based activity that challenges students to complete a basic task that supports learning of science content. Typically, the process and guidance are provided by the teacher for the suggested Web sites. Ex: WebQuest.org
Wikis	Web sites that can be edited and involve a collaborative effort to construct and update. Teachers and students can include thoughts, ideas, and questions for feedback from other people. Ex: Wikipedia
Web applications	Web sites that provides a place for teachers and students to ask questions to experts in the field. Ex: Ask-A-Scientist, Ask-A-Biologist
Blogs	Web sites that contain text, audio, and videos on a topic. Students can use blogs to present a topic, review a topic, increase engagement in a topic, and initiate questions. Students can also initiate a blog as a means to communicate and collaborate with others. Ex: National Geographic Blogs, NASA Earth Observatory Blogs
Podcasts and vodcasts	Podcasts are digital audio files distributed over the Internet (i.e., Vodcasts are digital videos distributed over the Internet). Both are one-way and can be accessed to introduce, teach, or review topics. Ex: NOVA science NOW, EdTech Talk, DiscoveryNews, NOVA Vodcast
Glogs	Virtual posters that can include text, audio, photos, and music. Posters can be shared with others over time to show changes or process. Ex: Glogster
Communications software	Free or paid versions of software that mediate audio and video communication via the Internet. This software may be useful to foster collaboration in real-time between students and peers around the world. Ex: Skype, Google Hangouts, FaceTime
Presentation Tools	These are various tools that allow for integration of text, audio, and images in a single product. Students can create interactive slide shows or digital stories as products of their science learning. Ex: MS Office, Prezi, Brainshark

According to the National Science Teachers Association ([NSTA], 2005), teachers must be aware of the issues below when creating videos for public viewing:

- following the school and district policies for safety standards, handling of hazardous materials, and disposal of chemical and biological waste;
- reinforcing safety procedures such as wearing eye protection, aprons, and protective clothing;
- practicing safety procedures when handling chemicals, fire, and biohazards; and
- including safety concerns and rules with demonstrations in the video.

It is also pertinent to note that Internet safety should be a priority in and out of the classroom. Teachers need to be explicit in their instructions on Internet safety. School firewalls and filters are helpful in preventing access to inappropriate Web sites, but there should be other measures taken to ensure a safe and meaningful experience on the Internet. When preparing students to access the Internet, teachers should arrange all monitors so that they are visible during the activity (Martin, 2012). According to Craig (1999), students should be taught Internet etiquette, or Netiquette, in the classroom, which includes:

- obtaining permission for the topic before using the Internet;
- focusing only on the topic that was approved;
- checking for spelling in the search bar to ensure that searches are focused on topic;
- reading the description of Web sites before selecting it, and never opening a Web site that is flagged as possibly harmful;
- taking notes if appropriate and keeping track of addresses (URLs) of useful Web sites;
- never giving out personal information (even to those who are in the scientific community); and
- reporting cyberbullying to a trusted adult immediately.

"Netiquette" and technology guidelines that are specific for the science classroom include:

- being aware of science ideas of experiments that may be dangerous. Never replicate experiments (especially from Web sites) without proper approval, supervision, and guidance;
- laboratory safety that gives clear instructions for how to handle and care for laboratory technology (have students sign a laboratory safety contract to reinforce the importance of safety when working with laboratory and expensive and perhaps fragile technology equipment);
- ensuring technology is age appropriate for the students to maximize science learning;
- providing time and opportunity to learn about technology so that it can be used safely and effectively;
- making sure that students are aware of cords and other technology hazards that may obstruct walking paths and having them move about the classroom with caution; and
- being sure that students are accessing resources and Web sites that are equitable to all students.

Although these tips are important, they are not all inclusive. (Please refer to other chapters in this book for additional information on Internet safety for students.) As technology evolves and teachers see ways that Internet utilization advances, it is vital to be updated on methods and aspects of Internet safety, particularly in certain areas of science, and to practice them in and out of the classroom.

Technology as a Way to Collect Data

It is essential for students to learn how to collect electronic data with technology in the science classroom. Using technology to collect data supports the development of basic science skills such as measurement, as well as the "integrated process skills of interpreting data and formulating models" (Park, 2008, p. 33). Some technology, such as cellular phones and computing tablets, has become common place in our everyday lives. In the context of the science classroom, cell phones can also be useful tools to support the learning process. Most cell phones have calculator functions as well as digital cameras that can capture pictures and videos that may be used for data collection or for composition of student products. Many kinds of apps extend other cell phones features.

Cell phones, tablets, or other devices that can capture a digital image can be used when upper elementary students learn about the "big idea" of the interdependent relationships among ecosystems. For instance, students organized in collaborative learning groups can design a milkweed bug or mealworm habitat that consists of four essential elements—food, water, shelter, and space. Each team can come up with their own focus questions, or teachers and students can establish a focus question for the class such as, "How are milkweed bugs or mealworms related within food chains?" or "What are milkweed bugs' or mealworms' main food sources?"

Figure 3.1 Students following safety protocol when using science technology and equipment.

After a class makes a decision about their focus questions, each team can then proceed with pre-experimentation activities in order to explore and share their prior knowledge related to food webs by using a visual workspace such as Kidspiration or KidPix software in order to create associate words and symbols and to build concept maps related to their focus questions. It is also important at this stage for a teacher to engage students in building foundational skills needed to understand and properly use the targeted technology being used in each lesson.

Once each team builds their habitats, they can become involved in collecting data by taking still pictures and video clips of their milkweed bugs or mealworms throughout the project. As a long-term project, each group can keep a digital science jour-

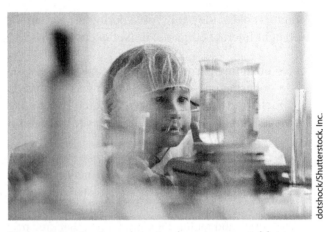

Figure 3.2   Students learning how to use a tablet to collect data.

nal by creating a Pinterest-style rolling-board at a social networking site that is safe for children and adolescents (e.g., Yoursphere). This will enable students to post and share daily or weekly digital imagery of changes in their milkweed bugs or mealworms. Later, students can engage in data analysis of their collection of images and address feedback made by the classmates posted on the social networking site they are using. After engaging in data analysis and creating knowledge statements related to their initial focus questions, families and friends may be invited to an open house day (or even a "digital open house") in which the students showcase their multimedia slide shows or digital stories. This is just one example of the many types of data collection activities and projects that students can do with technology.

Another form of technology that is often associated with science learning is probeware and sensors. These are devices used to make scientific measurements and typically consist of probes and software that are used in conjunction with microprocessors such as computers and calculators (Park, 2008). Probeware/sensors allow for collection of data in real-time and measurement of different variables. There are many types of probeware/sensors, and the information they can collect and analyze is diverse. For example, Vernier Software and Technology produces over 70 types of probeware/sensors, software, and microprocessors for K-12 science education including:

Selected Examples of Probes/Sensors	
Subject Area	**Probe/Sensor**
Biology	• Hand-Grip Heart Rate Monitor • Temperature Sensor • CO2 Gas Sensor • O2 Gas Sensor • SpectroVis Plus Spectrophotometer
Chemistry	• Gas Pressure Sensor • pH Sensor • Temperature Sensor • Conductivity Probe • SpectroVis Plus Spectrophotometer
Physical Science/ Physics	• Dual-range Force Sensor • Gas Pressure Sensor • Motion Detector • Temperature Sensor • Accelerometers

Figure 3.3   List of Vernier Software & Technology probeware.

Research supports the use of probeware for the simultaneous display of data collected in real-time. According to Thornton (2008), incorporating probeware to collect data in real-time resulted in the following benefits:

- Students were able to connect concrete measurements of physical phenomenon with "simultaneous production of the symbolic representation" (p. 6), which helps students learn abstract concepts.
- Real-time data collection fosters critical thinking skills by focusing on data analysis and conclusion formation over data collection and management.
- Real-time data collection promotes collaboration and learning between peers.
- When used purposefully, probeware use can increase students' spatial visualizations, which is an essential in the field of physics.
- Probeware is accessible to novice students as well as technologically sophisticated students.

Figure 3.4 Child using voltmeter to do experiments on electricity.

Probeware/sensors can also help students understand mathematical relationships between measured variables and build models of phenomenon (Park, 2008). Students who regularly used probeware/sensors during science activities scored significantly higher on assessments than those that did not use probeware/sensors (National Center for Education Statistics, 2002).

Considerations for integrating technology to collect electronic data:

- Ensure that lessons and activities are inquiry-based. Technology can be used in teacher-centered and student-centered ways. Consider how to integrate technology in a ways that support student-driven learning opportunities.
- Consider the best tool available for what it is that students need to measure. To understand what the best tool available may be, recognize what tools are capable of doing and how they might be modified to collect data about related topics.
- Learning how to use technology can be time consuming. If the tool will only be used for limited number of lessons or to teach limited number of objectives, consider whether the time required to teach how to use the tool is justified.
- Although there are many benefits to incorporating probeware/sensors in science teaching, they should be used purposefully. For example, a thermometer may be more efficient and easier to use when measuring temperature for a single occurrence. Probeware/sensors would be appropriate when measuring temperature over time because of the devices' capacity to create representations of the changes during the data collection period.

Technology as a Means to Access and Analyze Data

Technology in the science education classroom includes Web-based (online) sources that can increase access to resources and information. Educational researchers have concluded that authentic activities take place in real-life locations, and these authentic experiences can also occur through thorough Web-based learning opportunities (Herrington, Oliver, & Reeves,

Figure 3.5 Students using an oscilloscope to measure voltage over time.

2003). In fact, Web-based learning situations provide access to many of the same resources that scientists use in their work (Lomardi, 2007).

Inquiry-based learning using online data can increase students' interest in science, their use of inquiry skills, and their content knowledge (Trundle, 2008). With the immense amount of information available online, students should be able to explore and find a topic in which they find interest. This interest can make the topic more relevant and inspire student-driven questions and inquiry investigations (Windschitl, 1998). The personal investment in the topic and engagement in inquiry-based activities provide opportunities to apply inquiry skills to investigate and learn about the topic.

Figure 3.6   U.S. Geological Survey "Education Resources" Web page.

There are various Web sites that can provide access to scientific data. For example, the U.S. Geological Survey (USGS) provides data on topics such as water quality, climate, and land use, as well as natural hazards such as volcanic and earthquake activity. On the USGS Web site, there are data sets that can be utilized to create tables and graphs to develop data representations. The data can be compared and analyzed to understand patterns and trends of the changes on Earth. USGS also has resources for teachers and students in the teaching and learning of geological sciences (http://education.usgs.gov).

Another example is from the San Diego Zoo (http://zoo.sandiegozoo.org/video-more). Students may select animals to observe through San Diego Zoo's various animal cams. Possible animals they can observe include tigers, apes, koalas, pandas, polar bears, condors, and elephants. Student can be encouraged to ask questions like:

- What kind of animal is it?
- What are they doing, and why is it important to their species?
- What kinds of foods do they eat?
- How do they play?
- What do their habitats look like in the zoo versus in the wild?
- In what ways has the zoo matched this (or not)?

Students can use a graphic organizer, like a KWHL chart, to record their observations (see Table 3.2). A teacher can also use a KWHL chart to assess students' learning of scientific knowledge over time.

Students may also complete a digital animal journal to keep a record of observations. This will provide an opportunity for students to use inductive reasoning skills and analyze the data they collected over the period of time to answer questions they developed during the project.

Table 3.2   Example KWHL chart on animal observations

K	W	H	L
What I know	What I Want to Know	How will I find information?	What I learned
Animals live in the zoo and in the wild. Animals eat food. There are many types of animals. Many animals have fur. Many animals sleep a lot.	How long do pandas live? What does the panda eat? Why are pandas endangered? Where are pandas from?	Use the Internet. Read books. Observe pandas via the Webcam. Ask the teacher. Ask a scientist.	The panda eats bamboo. They are endangered because the bamboo forests are being cut down. Pandas are from China. Pandas live by themselves in the wild.

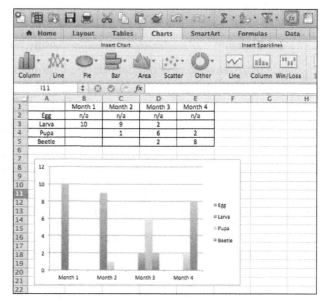

Figure 3.7   Screen capture of MS Excel spreadsheet and bar graph of mealworm data.

Analyzing and representing data is an important skill for science education. Graph literacy, which includes the ability to compose and interpret graphs, is critical for students to understand and communicate findings. Students can compose graphs by hand, but software, such as MS Excel, is a common tool that students can use to record their collected data and data transformations. In MS Excel, students can create various graphs, including column, line, pie, and bar graphs. For instance, a group of students who have been engaged in learning about the life cycle of mealworms can create a table using MS Excel to represent the rate of metamorphosis of their mealworms. This clustered column graph can be used to discuss the life cycle of mealworms.

This method can also be applied to the life cycles of plants. For instance, students who have been engaged in observing the growth of sweet pea flowers can measure the changes of roots and stems over time and then transform their data table to a line graph. This line graph can be used to discuss the primary and secondary growth of plants. Students can also learn to use common functions and formulas in Excel such as finding the sum, average, frequencies, and count of numbers.

Through Web sites such as those from USGS and the San Diego Zoo, students can investigate questions about our natural world. Like scientists, students will be able to create their own conclusions from data as well as consider incomplete and uncertain information, examine complex patterns, and encounter the complexity of real-life science. With technological tools, students have opportunities to use actual scientific data and engage in authentic science exploration and learning while analyzing and representing data using graphical representations.

Table 3.3 includes additional examples of Web sites with scientific data that students can access and analyze.

Although online sources can provide opportunities for data collection and analysis, there are aspects to consider for the science classroom (Trundle, 2008):

- Maintain focus on the topic by suggesting certain Web pages for students to explore. There is so much information available online that students may become overwhelmed or drift off-task if they begin their exploration without guidance. Rubrics and "gateways" (or interim deadlines) can often provide timelines and structure for completion as well as guidelines for quality.
- Consider what data is appropriate for the topic and grade level of students. There are many excellent Web sites with data, but teachers must consider what is cognitively appropriate for the age of the students in relation to the objectives and goals of the science lesson.
- Think about how to make relevant data accessible. Since schools and districts may have firewalls, there may be limits on what can be accessed. Being prepared with accessible sources of data lesson will help ensure that a lesson goes forth smoothly.

Table 3.3 Example Web sites with scientific data

Organization	Web Site	Suggestions
The United States Naval Observatory (USNO)	http://aa.usno.navy.mil/data/docs/RS_OneDay.php	Students can retrieve complete sun and moon data for one day.
National Oceanic and Atmospheric Administration (NOAA)	http://www.noaa.gov	Students can collect weather-related data.
The Cornell Lab of Ornithology	http://cams.allaboutbirds.org/all-cams	This is all about birds—students have recorded their live birds' cams.
Annenberg Learner Interactives	http://www.learner.org/interactives/parkphysics/index.html	Students can design a roller coaster.
Your Weight on other worlds	http://www.exploratorium.edu/ronh/weight	Students can collect data about their weights on different planets (e.g., Mercury, Venus, etc.).

Technology as a Means for Videos, Animations, Imagery, and Simulations

Technology can provide access to scientific phenomena via videos, models, simulations, images, and haptics (to be discussed later). These resources can help students learn abstract ideas and access visuals that may assist in the learning of scientific concepts.

Videos and Animations

There are many Internet resources that provide videos and animations of scientific phenomena (e.g., USGS). When used before a lesson, videos and animations can help introduce a topic or initiate discussion that reveals prior knowledge on a topic. When used after students explore a topic, videos and photos can help with concept development by providing greater explanations or elaboration on a topic. Video clips and animations can illustrate abstract ideas. For example, teachers can use Web-based video clips to support the ideas behind the processes of digestion (e.g., http://kidshealth.org) or how the Earth's land masses have changed as viewed from space (http://landsat.gsfc.nasa.gov). Teachers must, however, ensure that the videos they select model safety procedures when they provide online media and videos for student viewing (NSTA, 2005). Again, this includes making sure that persons who are featured in the video are wearing appropriate clothing and protective gear and that they demonstrate the best practices of safely handling chemicals, fire, and biohazards. Videos should also be explicit in the safety concerns that are related to their content.

Students can also create videos, digital stories, and animations to explain their understanding or elaborate on a topic. Software that students can use to create voiceover presentations, videos, or digital stories include Windows Movie Maker, iMovie, or Brainshark. Animation tools such as GoAnimate (http://goanimate.com), xtranormal (http://xtranormal.com), or PBS (http://pbskids.org/go/studio/animate) are free for students to use. Creating videos or animations not only helps teachers assess student understanding of a concept but supports student-centered instruction that encourages creativity, collaboration, and application of knowledge to new situations.

Simulations and Models

Teachers can use simulations and models for numerous science concepts (e.g., to explore how various forms of precipitation may impact erosion of a landscape). Students can build models of atoms and molecules to understand the interaction between charged particles and what occurs when bonds form or break between atoms. An

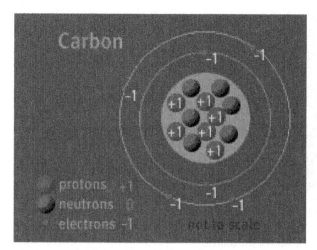

Figure 3.8 Screen capture from Atom Builder.

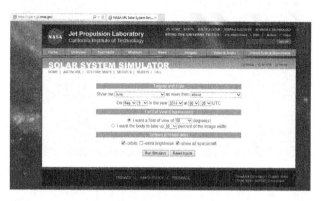

Figure 3.9 NASA Jet Propulsion Laboratory Home Page (http://space.jpl.nasa.gov).

example of an atomic simulator is the Atom Builder (http://www.pbs.org/wgbh/aso/tryit/atom). On this Web site, students are challenged to manipulate parts of an elemental atom to design a neutral atom.

Another Web-based simulator is the University of Colorado Boulder's Physics Education Technology Project (PhET). PhET provides multiple simulators on various science topics such as energy transformation, plate tectonics, and molecular structures (http://phet.colorado.edu/en/simulations/category/new). On PhET's simulators, students can explore simulations and practice creating molecules from atoms, which reinforces the meaning of subscripts and coefficients in molecular formulas. The simulators also help students connect molecular names with multiple visual representations of different molecules (http://phet.colorado.edu/en/simulation/build-a-molecule).

Imagery and simulation technology can even help students "travel in space." The National Aeronautics Space Administration (NASA) Web site (www.nasa.gov) is an excellent great resource for images and simulations. Specifically, collaboration between NASA and the Jet Propulsion Laboratory (JPL) has resulted in online simulation and modeling programs that students can access to learn and explore our solar system (e.g., http://space.jpl.nasa.gov). Through this online simulator, students can change their location in the solar system and show what they are viewing from that perspective. For example, students can simulate viewing the different moons of Jupiter from the planet Jupiter or "view" our sun from Mars by modifying the settings provided on the Web site.

Students can also modify the date and time of the simulations to view changes over time. For instance, an inquiry activity on phases of the moon may include opportunities for students to explore images of the moon over a period of one month. Students may be asked to observe the moon and note anything interesting in their science journals. By comparing images of the moon over time, students may better understand the cycle of the phases of the moon and how the phases change over time.

Apps and Games

Application software (apps) has become a common way for teachers and students to access information, tools, and games. Apps were initially created to increase productivity by making a specific task or information easily accessible. Apps can be downloaded on computers, smart phones, tablets, and other electronic devices. In science education, apps can provide teaching and content resources that may be useful in the designing and instruction of science lessons. Apps can also provide ways for students to access science information and interactive games.

Scientific games, either accessed through the Internet or apps, can help students in learning about science. Carefully selected games can introduce, reinforce, or elaborate on concepts as well as promote problem solving and critical thinking skills. For example, there are games that challenge students to use science to solve problems or puzzles that range from realistic to imaginary. Games can also be used to help students connect science with other subjects such as mathematics, technology, and engineering. Table 3.4 shows examples of apps and games that may be useful in science teaching and learning.

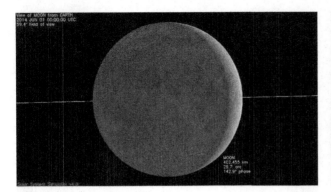

Figure 3.10   Screen capture of image of moon from Earth on June 1, 2014 from NASA Jet Propulsion Laboratory simulator.

Figure 3.11   Screen capture of image of moon from Earth on June 7, 2014 from NASA Jet Propulsion Laboratory simulator.

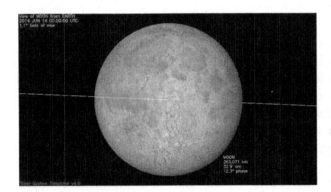

Figure 3.12   Screen capture of image of moon from Earth on June 14, 2014 from NASA Jet Propulsion Laboratory simulator.

Figure 3.13   Screen capture of image of moon from Earth on June 21, 2014 from NASA Jet Propulsion Laboratory simulator.

Haptic Technology

Technology can even help students feel and experience force, pressure, and temperature via haptic devices which are physical devices that students can hold or touch and are programmed to provide realistic reactions for choices or motions completed by the user. The physical movement involved in this type of technology may support learning of content (Paul, 2014) as well as increase engagement in the content. For example, haptic devices have been developed to allow students to control space shuttles in a simulation of our solar system. As the student maneuvers the virtual spaceship with a handheld device, he or she can feel an increase in temperature as the "ship" veers closer to the sun. When the student maneuvers the spaceship to land on a planet, the device will resist the user's hand, simulating the pull of gravitational force. Common haptic devices with which students may already be interacting include video gaming controls. For example, in car racing games, Nintendo's Wii handheld controls may vibrate when one car collides with another. There is an expectation that more of these types of devices will enter the science classroom in years to come. One can certainly see their potential for fostering student learning of science concepts.

Table 3.5 includes examples of Internet resources for images and visualizations:

Suggestions on how to meaningfully integrate images and visualizations include:

- Purposefully choosing images and videos that target the specific content and instructional goals to provide a view of what students may not normally see.
- Using images and visualizations to provide clarification or stimulate questions and interest.

Table 3.4 Example science apps and games

Type	Name	Description
App	The Elements	An interactive reference app that includes information on the elements through facts and high-quality images.
App	K12 Periodic Table of Elements	Engaging and informative app that provides key characteristics of the elements on the periodic table.
App	Video Science	Access lessons, demonstrations, and videos of science experiments that can be recreated in the classroom or at home.
App	Science Glossary	Glossary of science terms and short biographies of key science figures.
App	Skeletal Systems	Interactive app to explore the human skeletal system. Information about the various bones in the body is easily accessible in this app.
App	Earth-Now	App to access historical climate data from NASA satellites. Information is provided via an interactive 3D globe.
App	3D Brain	Explore the human brain via an interactive 3D image. Provides information on the functions of the various parts of the brain as well as relative cognitive disorders.
Scientific game	EcoKids http://www.ecokids.ca	Web site with eco-themed games and activities on various science topics such as wildlife, climate change, energy, water, and land use.
Scientific game	Immune Attack http://immuneattack.org	This game provides an opportunity to engage in an adventure to explore the human body. This game also includes technology, engineering, and mathematics concepts.
Scientific game	CSI Web Adventure http://forensics.rice.edu	Students learn about forensic science concepts and apply their knowledge to solve crimes and mysteries.
Scientific game	Animal Jam http://www.animaljam.com	Students engage in a mission to discover animals and plants. This game is adaptable to students of all skill levels as they follow a storyline to learn about our world.
Scientific game	Discovery Kids Games http://discoverykids.com/games	Discovery Kids has multiple games to explore science. Games include undersea adventure, mummy maker, and chopper lift.
Scientific game	Amusement Park Physics http://www.learner.org	Students learn about the physics behind amusement park rides and are challenged to design roller coasters that will pass a safety inspection.

- Including meaningful images or simulations that stimulate questioning and student inquiry. Ask questions such as:
  - What do you see?
  - What do you think the different colors represent?
  - What do you see when you compare these different images?
- Focusing on student-driven observations and conclusions and not on the teacher pointing out what should be noticed (Bell & Park, 2008).

Table 3.5 Example Internet resources for images and visualizations

Organization	Web Site	Suggestions
Mars student imaging project	http://mars.nasa.gov/msip	Students can take a picture of Mars using a camera on the NASA's Mars Odyssey orbiter.
Try Science	http://www.tryscience.org/fieldtrips/fieldtrip_home.html	Virtual field trips to science centers, experiments, etc.
Edheads	http://www.edheads.org	Students can engage in virtual activities that meet state and national standards (e.g., simple machines, virtual knee surgery, stem cell heart repair, etc.). Students can engage in interactive Web platforms designed for children.
InnerBody	http://www.innerbody.com	Students can learn about human body systems using a virtual human anatomy system.
Virtual Lab	http://www.mhhe.com/biosci/genbio/virtual_labs	Students can become virtually involved in frog dissections.
U.S. Environmental Protection Agency (EPA)	http://epa.gov/kidshometour	Students can learn about chemicals (including their basic uses and interactions) around their households.

- Supplementing instruction with simulations and not replacing it (Bell & Smetana, 2008). Consider what the simulation can do that another strategy cannot, the time it will take to implement the simulation, and how the simulation can be integrated in a student-centered way.
- Determining how the simulation can be incorporated so that focus remains on the content. As noted earlier, technology may become distracting due to the time required to learn how to use the tools. It can also become distracting because the interactive nature of some technology, and its application can sometimes be *overly* engaging for students. One way to help students maintain focus is to help students work through the initial set-up or manipulations so that they can utilize the simulation as intended.

Technology as a Means to Inquiry and Collaborate with the Scientific Community

Technology is important for authentic science learning experiences, but these experiences must also include collaboration and community participation (Lombardi, 2007) within the school or with others outside of the school setting. Collaboration is essential for students to share and construct knowledge through social interaction (Brooks & Brooks, 1999). Social networking tools can connect students with other students at a different location or experts in the field to share questions and ideas (See Table 3.6).

Students can use technology to synchronously (together in real-time) or asynchronously (at various times) share information and products within a group or across groups with blogs, e-portfolios, video-capture tools, and online platforms (Lombardi, 2007). For teachers, the opportunity to support student learning is enhanced with technology through means of providing immediate feedback and intelligent tutoring systems. Teachers can also promote learning and reflection through popular tools such as podcasting, flipped classroom, and other Web-based opportunities that provide access to instruction, information, or replay of recorded occurrences (Lombardi, 2007).

Connecting students with scientists can provide an engaging and authentic learning experience. For instance, communications software (e.g., Skype or Google Hangout) may be used to connect students with

Table 3.6 Internet resources for collaboration and interaction

Type	Use
Blogs	Web sites that contain text, audio, and videos on a topic. Students can use blogs to present or review topics, increase engagement in a topic, and initiate questions. Students can also initiate a blog as a means to communicate and collaborate with others.
Communications Software	Free and paid versions of software that mediate audio and video communication via the Internet. This type of software may be useful to foster collaboration in real-time between students and peers around the world. Ex: Skype, Google Hangouts, FaceTime
Collaboration Tools	There are various presentation tools that allow for collaboration as students compose a product. These tools can incorporate text, audio, and images in a single product. Ex: Google Drive

scientists from around the world. This could be an opportunity for scientists to share their work and current findings with students to support and enrich the ideas under study. Students should prepare questions to ask the scientist to gain insight into the topic as well as the science profession. The opportunity to see scientists in authentic contexts may also remind students that science is a diverse field. Scientists themselves are diverse, as well as their areas of study. Scientists can be either gender, any ethnicity, various ages and may work in various environments, including laboratories and many types of indoor and outdoor field sites, hospitals, businesses, in space, and so forth. Misconceptions about science can be confronted when students see that science does not always happen in a laboratory and that scientists can be from all areas of the world. Connecting students with a diverse array of scientists in various fields can help to reinforce that there are many areas in science that they can pursue.

Collaboration allows students to compare their own science processes and knowledge with others. Students also develop greater understanding of the nature of science when students compare how scientists in different cultures or settings address and explore scientific phenomena. Science is socially and culturally embedded. With technology, students can develop a more complex and authentic image of what science is and how scientists "do" science.

Next Generation Educational Technology for Science

Educators are constantly thinking of ways to integrate next generation technology in the science classroom. Although many tools are not necessarily generated for educational purposes, many have applications that can help students be more engaged and creative during the learning process (Luckerson, 2014). For example, three-dimensional imaging software, such as Maya or Blender, allows students to add details such as texture and shading to animations, models, and simulations. The following are examples of additional next generation technology that can be used to foster science learning (Luckerson, 2014):

- Three-dimensional (3-D) printers are becoming increasingly affordable and accessible. For example, MakerBot is a 3-D printer that can be found in over 5,000 schools in the United States. Students can use these printers to create models for educational purposes. Students can create cars to learn about physics or virtually dissect frogs (www.mhhe.com/biosci/genbio/virtual_labs/BL_16/BL_16.html) to learn about anatomy. Students have also used 3-D printers to create functional artificial limbs when tasked to address a current need in society.
- Next generation textbooks, such as the SmartBook by McGraw-Hill, will highlight important concepts and assess students at the end of chapters through online quizzes. Teachers can also access student test data from the SmartBook to gauge student progress.

- Chalkboards of tomorrow will be connected with student computers. For example, Hewlett-Packard is developing a touchscreen chalkboard that will allow students to duplicate notes and access multimedia through a wireless connection from the chalkboard to the students' individual computers or other devices.
- Classroom desks of tomorrow will be designed to be more adaptable to the changing needs during lessons. Currently, there are modular desks that convert from individual desks to a larger work surface to foster small group activities.
- Forward thinking toys are being developed to teach important topics such as compassion and empathy. The Empathy Toy, which was funded by Kickstarter, is a toy found in classrooms around the world that engages students in creating a building block structure while blindfolded. Having empathy for others is critical when working in collaborative groups during science activities and investigations, and, indeed, much of scientific research involves decisions for real people in critical situations such as the Ebola outbreak in 2014, the recall of vehicles for safety reasons, placement of tsunami warning equipment in beach areas, and so forth.

A Framework for Integrating Technology into the Science Classroom (TPACK)

The Technological Pedagogical Content Knowledge (TPACK) framework (Koehler & Mishra, 2009) can help explain the essential areas of knowledge needed to effectively integrate technology in schools (see Figure 3.14. According to the TPACK framework, learning-to-teach science with technology includes three essential knowledge fields: Content Knowledge (CK), Pedagogical Knowledge (PK) or knowledge of learning and teaching, and Technology Knowledge (TK). When the three knowledge fields of CK, PK, and TK are merged together, four new intersecting areas of knowledge emerge in the framework: Pedagogical Content Knowledge (PCK), Technological Content Knowledge (TCK), and Technological Pedagogical Knowledge (TPK). Ultimately, the intersection between CK, PK, and TK results in Technological Pedagogical Content Knowledge (TPACK). The following figure brings each of these areas forth so that the teacher can see the "big picture" and the details of what he or she should know when approaching a science/technology lesson. Please see Table 3.7 for descriptions and examples of the components and intersections of the TPACK framework.

The TPACK framework should be used as a thinking tool to consider important kinds of knowledge for effective teaching with technology. In this framework, the role of content, pedagogy, and technology are equally important as the combinations of the three forms of knowledge. Teachers-to-be can begin to learn about these areas of knowledge and skills as they begin their preservice education and continue as they move into their own classrooms. Knowing about children, instruction, science, and technology separately and together will determine the success of their students. According to Koehler & Mishra (2009) the individual and interrelated nature of content, pedagogy, and technology in the TPACK framework is complex. Teachers need to be flexible when negotiating each of these areas, and they should also know that each one also affects all of the others in various ways.

Understanding the different forms of technology and the insight that thinking deeply about one's teaching brings through the TPACK framework

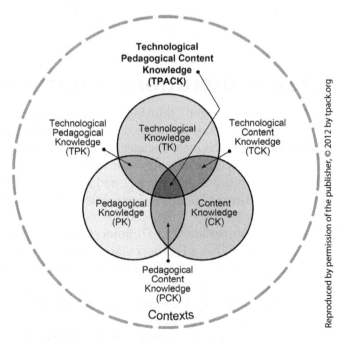

Figure 3.14   The Technological Pedagogical Content Knowledge (TPACK) Framework for learning-to-teach science with technology. Reproduced by permission of the publisher, © 2012 by tpack.org.

Table 3.7 Components of the TPACK framework

Knowledge Field	Description	Examples in the Context of Science Teaching:	Examples of Self-Generated questions	Examples of What I Currently Know
Content knowledge (CK)	Knowledge about the subject or content that is to be taught. Not only is the CK in science different than other subject areas like history or language arts, the CK is also different by age of the students and grade levels.	• Knowledge of science concepts and the nature of science • Scientific inquiry • Scientific facts, theories, methods, and evidence-based reasoning	Q) What are the content objectives of my lesson? Q) What are the major ideas I want to ensure my students of understanding about the lesson (for example, on food chains and food webs)?	• Food chains are linear sequences that show the energy transformation from one living organism to another via food. • Food webs show the interconnected pathways between different food chains in an ecosystem.
Pedagogical Knowledge (PK)	Knowledge about the general techniques, methods, and instructional practices of the act of teaching and teaching for understanding. PK includes educational goals and rationales as well as understanding of "how students learn, general classroom management skills, lesson planning, and student assessment" (Koehler & Mishra, 2009, p. 64).	• General strategies for teaching, learning, and assessment • Cooperative learning strategies • Knowledge of students and their lived experiences • Understanding of how students construct knowledge and learn skills • Knowledge of "cognitive, social, and developmental theories of learning and how they apply to students in the classroom" (Koehler & Mishra, 2009, p. 64).	Q) What would be the most effective teaching and learning methods for my upcoming lesson (e.g., classroom management, collaborative learning roles, teacher roles, and diagnostic, formative and summative assessments)?	• Student-centered Inquiry-based science learning and teaching • The 5E Model of Instruction (Engage-Explore-Explain-Elaborate-Evaluate)
Technological knowledge (TK)	Knowledge that is necessary to think about and work with technology and how to apply technology in and out of the classroom setting. TK includes the notion that technology can help or hinder objectives and also being able to recognize changes in technology and adapt to those changes.	• How to use a microscope, digital scale, graphing calculator, etc.	Q) In what ways may I apply available technology tools and resources that will work best to achieve the goals of my upcoming lesson?	• Web sites • Databases • Simulations • Tools for collaboration

(continued)

Table 3.7 Components of the TPACK framework (*Continued*)

Knowledge Field	Description	Examples in the Context of Science Teaching:	Examples of Self-Generated questions	Examples of What I Currently Know
Pedagogical Content Knowledge (PCK)	Knowledge of what pedagogy is appropriate and necessary to teach certain content and how to translate content for teaching. "PCK covers the core business of teaching, learning, curriculum, assessment and reporting, such as the conditions that promote learning and the links among curriculum, assessment, and pedagogy" (Koehler & Mishra, 2009, p. 64).	• How to teach science content, such as food chains and food webs • How to teach science content to students of specific grade levels, such as fourth grade, seventh grade, or eleventh grade	Q) In what ways may I interpret the targeting of big ideas, scientific practices, and crosscutting concepts? Q) In what manner can I find ways to represent these three dimensions above? Q) In what ways can I tailor the instructional materials to students' prior knowledge?	• Alignment among objectives, activities, and assessments • The best strategies to teach the content to the diverse student population
Technological Content Knowledge (TCK)	Knowledge of how content and technology interact, including benefits and constraints. Teachers need to recognize that content can be influenced by specific technology, and they should be able to purposefully select technology that will support content learning.	• How to select technology to teach the science content • How to use technology to teach the science content • Consider the time investment of teaching students to use the technology in comparison to the frequency of using the tool • What is the best tool to teach the concept?	Q) What do I know about the ways in which certain types of technology tools and resources either facilitate or hinder the learning of scientific concepts? Q) Based on these initial assessments, what are my choices of technologies for the scientific concepts?	• Class Web sites and blogs • Handheld digital devices (e.g., tablet computers and probeware/sensors) • Interactive Media • Laptops • Mobile devices (M-learning) (e.g., Piazza) • Online media (e.g., YouTube) • Data sets from Internet sources • Simulation and modeling programs

Table 3.7 Components of the TPACK framework (*Continued*)

Knowledge Field	Description	Examples in the Context of Science Teaching:	Examples of Self-Generated questions	Examples of What I Currently Know
Technological Pedagogical Knowledge (TPK)	Knowledge of how technology can impact teaching and learning. TPK is important since most technologies were not created for educational purposes. TPK allows teachers to be creative and open-minded in recognizing the limits and possibilities of technology and adapting the technology to support teaching and learning.	• Instead of having the whiteboard at the front of the room mainly for teacher use, consider how to make it accessible by all students to promote brainstorming and collaboration. • Software like Microsoft Office Suite was designed for business settings. Consider other options like Google Docs to support collaboration between students, teachers, and others outside of the classroom.	Q) What do I know about how certain types of technology tools and resources either facilitate or hinder teaching and learning? Q) Based on these initial assessments, what are the choices of technologies for my teaching and learning? Q) In what ways can these technologies be cross-examined in terms of how students learn and inquiry-based student-centered learning?	• Class Web sites and blogs • Handheld digital devices (e.g., tablet computers and probeware/sensors) • Interactive Media • Laptops • Mobile devices (M-learning) (e.g., Piazza) • Online media (e.g., YouTube) • Data sets from Internet sources • Simulation and modeling programs
Technological Pedagogical Content Knowledge (TPACK).	Knowledge of effective instruction integrating technology, pedagogy, and content. Teachers need to recognize that different circumstances and contexts impact how CK, PK, and TK is considered. Teachers must be flexible in how to negotiate the three forms of knowledge and highlight the complexitites of each.	• The combination of knowing the science content, how to teach the science content, and what technology is the most appropriate to teach the science content. • What are the strategies and technologies most appropriate for teaching various content (e.g., food chains and food webs).	Q) What are the elements of effective learning-to-teach science with technology?	• Incorporating simulation software in an inquiry-based lesson to teacher—food webs and food chains.

Note: Koehler, M. J., & Mishra, P. (2009). What is technological pedagogical content knowledge? *Contemporary Issues in Technology and Teacher Education, 9*(1), 60–70.

may help teachers integrate technology in effective and purposeful ways. TPACK also illuminates the highly complex field that is science teaching. Often, each component of TPACK is studied on an individual basis. The power of the TPACK framework is to consider how these domains interact to reveal the complex nature of knowledge and practice. Technology is a powerful tool that can enhance or hinder science teaching and learning. It should not be oversimplified or used without purpose.

Summary

Teachers must carefully consider the complexity of teaching science with technology. Technology can help students to access content, collect data, and analyze data. Technology can also provide images and simulations as well as connect students with the scientific community. The TPACK framework can also help to unpack the components of the complex task of science teaching. Although technology offers many benefits, teaching science with technology requires purposeful planning and meaningful integration of technology. It is not simply asking students to create a slideshow or assigning students to use the Internet to research a topic. Technology must be incorporated purposefully, intentionally, and equitably in the science classroom.

Mrs. Calander, whom we met in the beginning scenario, continues to think about the complexity of teaching science with technology. There are many resources to consider. Remembering the TPACK framework she had learned about in her science methods class helped her to bring together all of the components of the complex task of teaching science. Mrs. Calander also realizes that teaching science with technology is not simply showing students a video clip or movie, asking small groups use a digital tool to collect data without purpose, or simply showing pictures from the Internet. Incorporating technology in the science classroom requires a detailed plan with multiple goals, rationales, and thoughtful integration of the many tools available. She begins to think through the process of what students must know combined with what technology tools would best support them and how she will manage her classroom while the lesson progresses. The lesson begins to take shape and the TPACK framework reminds her of the many details that go into having students learn and be excited about science.

References

Baker, D. R., & Piburn, M. D. (2007). *Constructing science in middle and secondary school classrooms*. Needham Height, MA: Allyn and Bacon.

Bell, L., & Park, J. C. (2008). Digital images and video for teaching science. In R. L. Bell, J. Gess-Newsome, & J. Luft (Eds.), *Technology in the secondary science classroom* (pp. 9–22). Arlington, VA: NSTA press.

Bell, R. L., & Smetana, L. K. (2008). Using computer simulations to enhance science teaching and learning. In R. L. Bell, J. Gess-Newsome, & J. Luft (Eds.), *Technology in the secondary science classroom* (pp. 23–32). Arlington, VA: NSTA press.

Brooks, J., & Brooks, M. (1999). Chapter 9: Becoming a constructivist teacher. *In search of understanding: The case of constructivist classrooms* (pp. 101–118). VA: ASCD.

Craig, D. V. (1999). Science and technology: A great combination. *Science and Children, 36*(4), 28–32.

Flick, L., & Bell, R. (2000). Preparing tomorrow's science teachers to use technology: Guidelines for Science educators. *Contemporary Issues in Technology and Teacher Education, 1*(1), 39–60.

Herrington, J., Oliver R., & Reeves, T. C. (2003). Patterns of engagement in authentic online learning environments. *Australian Journal of Educational Technology, 19*(1), 59–71. Retrieved from http://www.ascilite.org.au/ajet/ajet19/herrington.html

Koehler, M. J., & Mishra, P. (2009). What is technological pedagogical content knowledge? *Contemporary Issues in Technology and Teacher Education, 9*(1), 60–70.

Lederman, N. G. (2007). Nature of science: Past, present, and future. In S. K. Abell & N. G. Lederman (Eds.), *Handbook of research on science education* (pp. 831–880). Mahwah, NJ: Lawrence Erlbaum Associates.

Lombardi, M. (2007). *Authentic learning for the 21st Century: An overview*. Educause Learning Initiative, ELI Paper 1/:2007. Retrieved from http://alicechristie.org/classes/530/EduCause.pdf

Luckerson, V. (2014, September 22). Too cool for school: Disruptive tech is changing how kids learn. *Time, 184*, 16.

Lyublinskaya, I., & Zhou, G. (2008). Integrating graphing calculators and probeware into science methods courses: Impacts on preservice elementary teachers' confidence and perspectives on technology for learning and teaching. *Journal of Computers in Mathematics & Science Teaching, 27*(2), 163–182.

Martin, D. J. (2012). *Elementary science methods: A constructivistic approach.* Independence, KY: Wadsworth.

National Center for Education Statistics. (2002). *Science highlights: The nation's report card 2000.* U.S. Department of Education Office of Educational Research and Improvement. NCES 2002-452. Retrieved from http://nces.ed.gov/nationsreportcard/pubs/main2000/2002452.asp

National Science Teachers Association. (2005). *Safety in the science classroom.* (Safety Issue Papers by NSTA's Safety Advisory Board). Washington, DC: Author.

Park, J. C. (2008). Probeware tools for science investigations. In R. L. Bell, J. Gess-Newsome, & J. Luft (Eds.), *Technology in the secondary science classroom* (pp. 33–42). Arlington, VA: NSTA press.

Paul, A. M. (July 9, 2014). Is the body the next breakthrough in education tech? *The Hechinger Report.* Retrieved from http://hechingerreport.org/content/body-next-breakthrough-education-tech_16629

Thornton, R. K. (2008). Effective learning environments for computer supported instruction in the physics classroom and laboratory. In M. Vicentini & E. Sassi (Eds.), *Connecting research in physics education with teacher education.* International Commission on Physics Education. Retrieved from http://web.phys.ksu.edu/icpe/Publications/teach2/Thornton.pdf

Trundle, K C. (2008). Acquiring online data for scientific analysis. In R. L. Bell, J. Gess-Newsome, & J. Luft (Eds.), *Technology in the secondary science classroom* (pp. 53–62). Arlington, VA: NSTA press.

Wallace, R. M. (2002, May). *Technology and science teaching: A new kind of knowledge.* Paper presented at the Technology and its Integration in Mathematics Education (TIME) Conference, Battle Creek, MI. Retrieved from https://www.msu.edu/course/cep/953/readings/WallaceTimeFinal.pdf

Windschitl, M. (1998). Independent student inquiry: Unlocking the resources of the World Wide Web. *NASSP Bulletin, 82,* 93–98.

Chapter 4

Teaching and Learning Mathematics in Technologically Intensive Classrooms

Michael L. Connell, Jacqueline Sack, *University of Houston-Downtown*

Sergei Abramovich, *State University of New York at Potsdam*

Meet Ms. Josephson

Ms. Josephson, the lead math teacher at River View Middle School, is concerned by her students' declining problem-solving scores. She is perplexed because these same students' *computation* scores have been going up. After sharing this concern with her principal, she has been asked to provide suggestions to update the software used in the school's computer lab. As she investigates further, she is amazed at the resources available to reinforce computation, but, unfortunately, that is not the problem her students are facing. There are also many resources to address problem solving; however, the problems do not relate to the curriculum she is responsible for teaching. How can she bridge between the skills her students have and the problems they need to solve?

Where Are We Now?

Mathematics instruction is currently undergoing significant shifts concerning the nature of content as well as the manner in which foundational understandings are to be developed. For example, the National Council of Teachers of Mathematics (NCTM), through their ongoing efforts to implement their Principles and Standards for School Mathematics (2000), has been changing the face of what constitutes mathematics and how we think about its teaching and learning. Of particular note for this chapter is that this new focus includes an increased emphasis upon the dual nature of mathematics itself, which must be understood if technology is to be used effectively. Basically, when viewed as a content area, mathematics has a "bit of a split personality." To use an example from language art, there are parts of mathematics that function very much like a noun (the concepts of mathematics), while others function much more like a verb (procedures, which many think of as "actually 'doing' math").

To expand on this notion, when a teacher uses the word *sphere*, most students will picture a rounded ball-like shape in their mind. This memory is very "noun-like" in that it may be described and its properties can be expanded. For example, a student could initially have thought about a baseball. This evokes a different set of properties than if they had thought of a tennis ball, a golf ball, or a table tennis ball. If we think of a "base-ball" as being a noun, then "seamed" is an adjective which may be used to describe it. Therefore, we see that a baseball has raised seams, a tennis ball is fuzzy, a golf ball is dimpled, and a table tennis ball is smooth. They also have different sizes, bounce differently, have different colors, and so on.

Despite these additional properties there is a "sphere-like" property common to each. As a more formal concept of "sphere" is developed, this core mathematical idea plays a noun-like role. The properties which a sphere can have, such as radius and location, play the role of adjectives. A sphere can have a radius of 5 centimeters in the same sense that a baseball can have seams. The seams are a property of the baseball (Figure 4.1), and the radius is a property of the sphere. Clearly, there are many "noun-like" portions of mathematics which play an important role in developing new ideas. This type of mathematical understanding gives us things to think ***about*** and forms the basis for later more formalized ***concepts***.

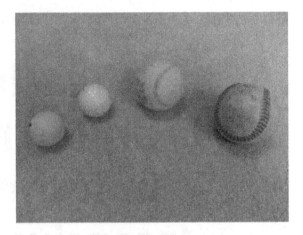

Figure 4.1   Different types of spheres.

Now, let us consider an alternate type of mathematical structure—a ***procedure***, or set of actions. If a student had earlier pictured a baseball when asked to visualize a *sphere,* it might be perfectly natural to have also pictured themselves or others throwing the ball. This is an action which can be performed ***on*** the ball. Other reasonable actions, or ***verbs***, might include catching the ball, hitting the ball, and scoring the winning home run!

In a very similar way, there are mathematical ***procedures***, or sets of actions, we can naturally perform on the sphere. For example, we can increase or decrease its radius (Figure 4.2),

rotate it around an axis (Figure 4.3),

or move it from one spatial location to another (Figure 4.4).

These actions are just as natural to perform on a sphere as throwing would be to a baseball. Like the actions performed on a baseball, they are "verb-like" in nature and describe what can be done with (or to) the "nouns." Such ideas form the basis for later, more formalized ***procedures***. The role technology can play in visualizing these ideas for learners should not be overlooked. The graph in Figure 4.5, for example, was created using a computer-based spreadsheet but could just as easily have been done using a smartphone app, an online graphics program, or a handheld calculator.

Things become a little more complicated, however, when the mathematics described has both noun and verb-like features (i.e., requiring understanding of both ***content*** and ***process*** components). For example, the number "2" can be a noun describing a position in a sequence or how many of something one might have. In this case, we are clearly using the noun-like features. In a different context, however, "2" can describe: how many times something appears (as in the case of filling a bowl of cereal "2" times); a base used by computers to represent other numbers (this is also called Binary); or the power to which a quantity is raised as shown in $X^2 + 3$.

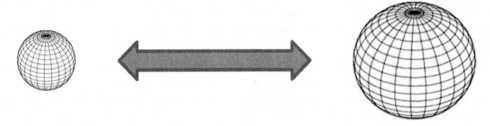

Figure 4.2   Changing a sphere's radius.

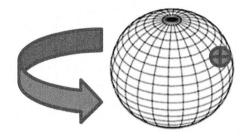

Figure 4.3   Rotating a sphere.

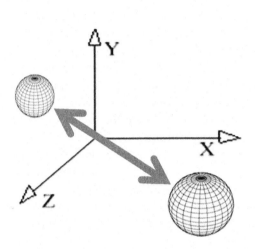

Figure 4.4   Different types of spheres.

X	Y
-5	-7
-4	-5
-3	-3
-2	-1
-1	1
0	3
1	5
2	7
3	9
4	11
5	13

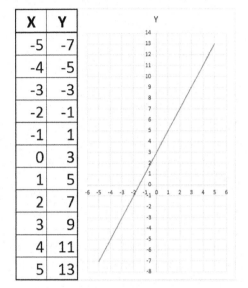

Figure 4.5   Graph of **Y = 2X + 3**.

Most students are familiar with situations like this in their daily lives. A baseball can be sitting on a table or undergoing motion in a game. It can even be placed atop a trophy to symbolize a major victory following that homerun mentioned earlier! Unfortunately, most students (and a few teachers) are less familiar with the dual nature of mathematics.

For students to develop meaningful mathematical understandings, they should have many rich experiences in mathematics from these two markedly different perspectives. Therefore, as we select appropriate technology, we need to allow learners to experience mathematical structures containing both concepts to think *about*—the "noun-like" content features and processes to think *with*—the "verb-like" procedural features. Once a teacher can see this "dualism" about mathematics, it has major impacts on potential roles of technology in the mathematic classroom.

This can be shown very clearly when considering multiplication strategies.[1] Multiplication is used to compute area, and area can be used to illustrate multiplication—so both the concept and procedure can be illustrated at once. The Algebra Tiles application from the National Library of Virtual Manipulatives (found at http://nlvm.usu.edu/en/nav/frames_asid_189_g_3_t_2.html?open = activities&from = category_g_3_t_2. html) was used in Figure 4.6 to model (X + 1) (Y + 2) (Figure 4.6).

In this figure, we see a rectangle being formed from placing representative tiles along two dimensions—X + 1 in the vertical direction and Y + 2 in the horizontal direction. The resulting algebraic product is shown by the area itself. To fill this rectangle, the student needs to use an XY piece, two X pieces, one Y piece, and two single squares of the Virtual Manipulatives. When this is written out in standard form, it shows that

---

1. Another application from this resource will be used later as an example of a high level interaction with technology.

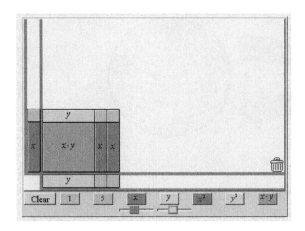

Figure 4.6   (X + 1) (Y + 2).

(X + 1)(Y + 2) = XY + 2X + Y + 2. In order to get to this point, however, students need to be able to utilize both the conceptual and procedural aspects of the representation created through interaction with this application. The rectangle is the noun, and "how it got there" is the verb.

As this example shows, thanks to technology, it is now possible for learners to experience both the conceptual (noun-like) and procedural (verb-like) aspects of mathematics using the same types of data and use of similar tools to those of practicing mathematicians.

It does not stop here! As technological tools in the classroom have become more sophisticated, the user interface has become much more amenable to direct student manipulation. For example, the National Library of Virtual Manipulatives mentioned above provides an extensive collection of applets (http://nlvm.usu.edu/en/nav/vlibrary.html), making it possible to use virtual manipulatives directly paralleling those traditionally used in mathematics classrooms (e.g., fraction bars, money, color chips, base blocks, tangrams, and many more). This site allows students to directly experience both the noun- and verb-like features of mathematics. If the students have had earlier experience with the more traditional physical manipulatives upon which the virtual is based—base ten blocks, for example—these can be highly effective tools and enable an entirely new set of student interactions with mathematics (Abramovich, 2012).

Starting with this type of technologically-enabled tools that are capable of embodying both concept and process, there is tremendous expansion of mathematical reasoning that may be brought into the classroom. For example, the computer can serve as a tool to record the information that has been generated by the students' activities, capture the essence of the activity by allowing the students to organize their work in powerful structures, and create formal records of action that may be shared or used in later problem-solving endeavors and shared globally via the Internet.

Object-Based Tools in Mathematics Teaching and Learning

Today, object-based tools can create multiple representations which, when implemented properly, can be a significant asset in developing mathematical power, flexibility, and applications. What is often missing, however, is meaningful data for these tools to work with. Technology comes to the rescue here as well. There are many sites containing real-world data for use in the classroom. Figure 4.7 shows some of these found at http://www.csss-science.org/classroom.shtml .

An important distinction should be made at this point. Effective technology use does not involve simply visiting a Web page that presents information or a step-by-step demonstration of a process. Such information is important on occasion, but this does not constitute a particularly powerful understanding and does not take full benefit of the potential interactions between the student and technology. As the examples in this chapter should serve to illustrate, such a use of technology is analogous to using a valuable painting to kill grass. While it is true that grass *can* be killed by blocking sunlight from reaching it for a long enough time and a painting could certainly be used in this fashion, this would certainly a poor use for such a valuable resource!

In the same way, when used together with a student-centered and meaning-driven approach to teaching, technology can do so much more than the mental equivalent of killing grass! It can lead to new levels of mathematics understanding and representations of concepts far more powerful than that generally experienced in today's classrooms. Perhaps in no other content area is it so important to see learning technology as a "means to an end."

An effective tool to think with in learning mathematics, as we have noted, should encompass both the **noun** and the **verb** (i.e., both the **conceptual** and the **procedural** aspects of mathematics). Let's see if this perspective can be shown more clearly by expanding upon the multiplication example shown earlier.

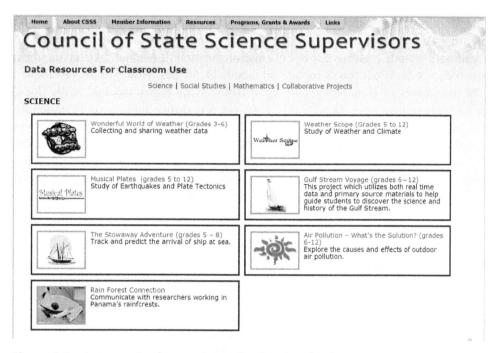

Figure 4.7   An example of a repository of online data for classroom use.

Multiplication Table

x	0	1	2	3	4	5	6	7	8	9	10	11	12
0	0	0	0	0	0	0	0	0	0	0	0	0	0
1	0	1	2	3	4	5	6	7	8	9	10	11	12
2	0	2	4	6	8	10	12	14	16	18	20	22	24
3	0	3	6	9	12	15	18	21	24	27	30	33	36
4	0	4	8	12	16	20	24	28	32	36	40	44	48
5	0	5	10	15	20	25	30	35	40	45	50	55	60
6	0	6	12	18	24	30	36	42	48	54	60	66	72
7	0	7	14	21	28	35	42	49	56	63	70	77	84
8	0	8	16	24	32	40	48	56	64	72	80	88	96
9	0	9	18	27	36	45	54	63	72	81	90	99	108
10	0	10	20	30	40	50	60	70	80	90	100	110	120
11	0	11	22	33	44	55	66	77	88	99	110	121	132
12	0	12	24	36	48	60	72	84	96	108	120	132	144

Figure 4.8   The Multiplication Table: An example
of a **Low Level Interaction**.

A common task in mathematics education is that of developing an understanding of basic multiplication. This task can be approached using three levels of technology-enabled objects. First, look at a very simple case where a technologically enabled *Object* simply presents static information—often in the form of facts to be memorized—to a student. An example of such a **Low Level Interaction** may be found at http://www.math2.org/math/general/multiplytable.htm and should be intimately familiar to most readers—the multiplication table (see Figure 4.8).

In this example, technology simply presents this object as information—as a Web page. Although it is excellent to have this as an informational chart, the level of interaction is low and the resulting understanding is primarily of promoting student awareness of existing information. It is much like having the multiplication chart taped to a student's desk, but this is mobile on handheld devices. However, this example does not take advantage of the true power of technology, and, apart from saving paper and ink, really does not have any advantage over a simple printed page. Despite this, however, it is surprising how often students encounter this type of model in technology use. In such cases, students are presented with a static text or information display which is presented in a static form which cannot be directly interacted with. Killing grass, anyone?

There is at least one time, however, when such a static representation works very well. When the students themselves create it! For example, a very common task in elementary school is developing a personal meaning for geometric concepts and definitions. PowerPoint is a natural tool to share the results of a geometry scavenger hunt, for example, and allows the students to practice taking, editing, and selecting digital photographs representing these ideas.

In finding examples, it is a good idea to encourage students to find two examples—one naturally occurring and one man-made—for each item from a list drawn from the grade level curriculum. Students then create a PowerPoint where each item comprises a single slide. Depending on their grade level, for each item they might: (1) give their definition, (2) describe their find, (3) provide a photograph(s), (4) identify why their example(s) should be considered accurate, and (5) show what a "textbook" example would look like. An example of such a slide for the term "Parallel Lines" is shown in Figure 4.9.

The ability to quickly share, comment, and edit upon their finds allows their ideas to be expanded. In this case, although the final product is a static representation, the process leading to its creation is a highly interactive and meaningful activity.

In a more powerful **Medium Level Interaction**, the student can act directly upon the technological object itself. In this case, the understandings which emerge are created by the student who acts upon the technologically enabled object (whose properties were both programmed and presented in a form allowing for easy manipulation by the student). At its most simply, the student chooses to press certain keys to try for a particular result, and the device reacts. When a student uses a calculator, for example, this is typically the level of interaction they experience. This is true whether using a traditional calculator or a computer emulated calculator such as that shown in Figure 4.10.

Along this line, a very rich set of useful calculators can be found online at Calculator Soup. Their very impressive listing of potential tools may be accessed at: http://www.calculatorsoup.com/calculators. Among other tools, they include calculators for loan, mortgage, time value of money, math, algebra, trigonometry,

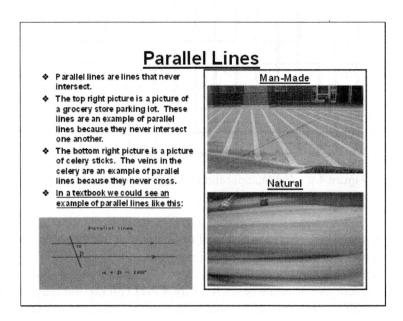

Figure 4.9   Geometry Scavenger Hunt.

fractions, physics, statistics, time and date, and conversions. Since many of the pages show work and/or equations, they can be quite helpful to the student trying to understand their calculations.

Such tools can be extremely powerful in allowing students to explore and apply number to parts of the universe that would otherwise be unavailable to them. For example, using the interactive tool at http://htwins.net/scale, it is possible to explore the relative sizes of objects in the universe ranging from the smallest units of space time to the largest cosmic structures (see Figure 4.11 below).

A multiplication-based example of this **Medium Level Interaction** may be found at: http://naturalmath.com/mult/mult2.html. This Web site provides an alternative view of our old friend the multiplication table. The following screenshot shows the display which is presented when the student uses this object to perform the action of $3 \times 4 = \square$.

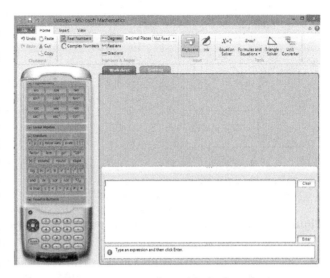

Figure 4.10 A computer-based "calculator."

In this more powerful example, the object does more than just provide an answer. In addition to a correct numerical answer, the object created an alternative representation (in yellow) which then was presented to the student. This ability of objects to interact with the student and with other objects provides for a tremendous leverage in their utility and power. In case of this second multiplication table example shown in Figure 4.12, the second level of object creation was fairly transparent to the student. This served primarily to provide an alternate representation that would hopefully be familiar to the student—in this case, modeling multiplication using an area model. Although relatively simple, in many ways this latter example exhibits some of the characteristics of a **High Level Interaction**

In a truly **High Level Interaction**, the direction of the interaction still originates with an action being performed by a student, generally in response to a problem situation or problem solving goal. As was the case with **Medium Level Interactions**, the student performs actions of their choice directly upon the object. The object may, depending upon the supporting programming or context, link to other conceptually related objects for additional processing or representational purposes. In other cases, the student may interact with intermediary objects to create specific representations and tools of their own design and choice.

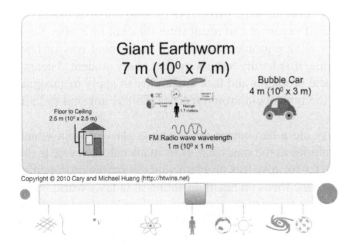

Figure 4.11 The scale of the universe.

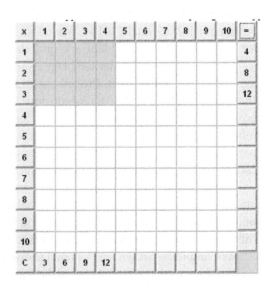

Figure 4.12 The Multiplication Table: An example of a **Medium Level Interaction**.

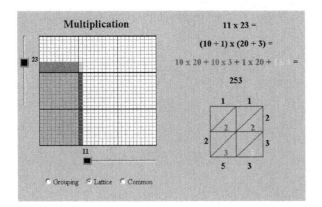
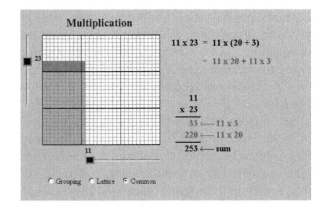

Figure 4.13   The Multiplication Table: An example of a **High Level Interaction**.

An example of such a **High Level** Interaction is shown in Figure 4.13, which was created using the applet at http://nlvm.usu.edu/en/nav/frames_asid_192_g_1_t_1.html?from = category_g_1_t_1.html.

This pair of screenshots shows a student's interaction with yet another multiplication object to model the multiplication problem 23 × 11. In this case, the object allows the student the ability to change a number of important aspects of the model. For example, it is possible to change from the *Lattice* representation shown in these diagrams, which should be familiar to Montessori teachers, to *Grouping* and *Common* models used in typical textbooks. Once a representation is chosen, the associated records of activity and problem setting automatically change. This allows the student to explore not just one but many different ways of representing the problem. As a tool offering **High Level Interaction**, it is important to spend some time actually interacting with it! Try modeling a few multiplication problems on your own prior to continuing.

Problems in Teaching and Learning in the Mathematics Classroom

Many of these instructional issues are also present in traditional mathematics classrooms—even in the absence of technology. In many mathematics classrooms, instruction typically emphasizes procedures, memorizing algorithms, and finding the "one right answer" at the fastest speed possible. Unfortunately, in such environments, reasoning, problem solving, and sensibility are rarely addressed—if at all. Mathematics, as it is often presented in these settings, is not a subject open for discussion, debate, or creative thinking—nor are students encouraged to find alternative ways to solve a problem or different procedures for carrying out an operation (Abramovich & Connell, 2014). When this happens students often become adept memorizers of procedures—but, they are typically unable to interpret their results or apply their findings.

To draw upon our earlier language example, students become verb-strong, but they do not understand the nouns they are acting upon! Procedural and computational expertise can result from this, but little else. Such students are able to follow the algorithms necessary to solve a problem but cannot understand why or how those algorithms answer the question at hand. Given this, it is hardly surprising that many students became imbued with rigid mental representations of mathematical problems and lack any ability to apply metacognitive strategies. The consequences of this often escape the typical classroom teacher. This is not said to fault teachers but to draw attention to this problem.

Consider this story problem as an example, "Harry ate a hamburger and drank a glass of milk which totaled 495 calories. The milk contained half as many calories as the sandwich. How many calories were in the sandwich and how many in the milk?" You may want to try to solve this problem yourself before proceeding! This type of problem is good for students to address with the focus on healthier eating in today's world.

As Campione, Brown, and Connell showed in 1988, this version of the problem is generally solved nicely by students. However, once one changes the supporting text slightly to include pricing information for the sandwich and milk, to update the calorie information, and to change the name of the store where Harry purchased the hamburger and milk, things go off the rails quickly. Especially if the name of the store happens to be Seven-Eleven!

In a follow-up study, students were given their choice of representations, computational processing, and checking. In nearly half of the students' work, the answers did not match with any of the previously used solution methods or answers from the earlier study (If you really must know. . . 165 calories, if you want to check your earlier work).

However, the answers did make an odd sort of sense—once the initial disbelief passed. Answers from this new set of students included 77, 18, 7, 11, 1 4/7, and so on. The students obviously had taken the two smallest numbers they saw in the problem and then simply applied operations—with no regard to meaning or reasonableness. The presence of extraneous information triggered a series of nearly automatic calculations which took the place of careful problem solving and reasoning. It should be noted that the students' calculations were done perfectly.

When the participating teachers looked at the results, they were understandably shocked. These were average students who had scored well on every test (of computation) they had taken in their class the year they had encountered *Harry and the Hamburger*. Their lack of ability to flexibly transfer their computational abilities (the procedural **verb**) to any meaningful problem situation (the underlying **noun**) brought a previously hidden problem into the open.

Using Technology for Solving *Harry and the Hamburger* Problem

When students understand the relationships presented in the problem setting, however, it is easy to use an appropriate technology, a spreadsheet for example, in solving the *Harry and the Hamburger* problem. Furthermore, once it is created, the same spreadsheet can be used for posing a multitude of similar problems with different data but sharing the same deep structure. The use of a spreadsheet in this case is particularly powerful, as it enables the distribution of calories between milk and the hamburger to be shown both numerically and geometrically. The latter case is shown in the bottom part of Figure 4.14, when calories in milk are shown to be one-third of the total calories. If you look carefully at Figure 4.14, you can see a slider attached to the cell representing calories in milk. This is a tool which can be used by the students to alter the number of calories until their total number is equal to 495.

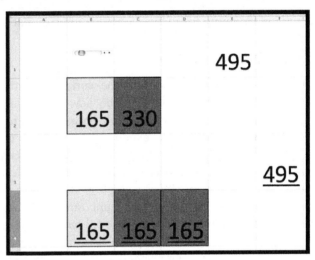

Figure 4.14 A spreadsheet for *Harry and the Hamburger* Spreadsheet.

Technology's Potential Contribution to Mathematics Classroom

Problems such as those shown in the *Harry and the Hamburger* scenario are all the more unfortunate since flexibility appears to be a characteristic valued in many domains. Researchers from many fields associate the flexible application of rules and strategies with expertise and higher levels of cognitive operations. Indeed, one key to evaluating successful learning in this newer approach to mathematics instruction would be student flexibility in choosing and using mental representations.

Technology in its myriad forms, which today includes object-oriented interfaces and tools geared specifically to enable students to perform specific actions upon specific objects (remember the verbs and nouns!), lends itself perfectly to action upon object models of learning and instruction underlying the examples from this introduction. Some of these include Step-by-Step Development of Mental Activities (Leontiev, 1979), Action Reification (Tall, Thomas, Davis, Gray, & Simpson, 2000; Sfard, 1991), and Action on Objects (Connell, 2001) to name a few. This linkage between suggestions from educational learning theory and the object classes created by technology is far too powerful to allow going to waste.

As these introductory examples show, computer generated visualizations and representations can be used to help the student create a new way of thinking, discussing, and building understanding in an inquiry-oriented environment. Finally, however, mathematical meaning is best made by students' performance with actual actions upon actual objects (real world ***nouns*** and ***verbs***, please!). In order for this to occur, the eventual objects created by the technology must become <u>real</u> in the minds of the students. It must become understandable and real to the students. It must possess well-defined attributes in the mind of the student such that the eventual symbol generated by the experience has well-defined properties.

Grade Level Examples

Bear in mind that these examples are not intended to be a cookbook or recipe. Instead, these examples should be considered as illustrations, showing how the principles described thus far might be used to guide technology. As you do so, you will see that there are some common instructional strategies present across all grade levels.

Remember an important lesson from *Harry and the Hamburger*! Technology should **never** be used to shortcut careful reasoning and planning. If students do not know what they are doing **without** technology, they will not know what they are doing **with** technology. The only difference being is that students will be able to hide their lack of knowledge behind the "correct answers" that they achieved by manipulations of numbers (without meaning) using tools whose computational accuracy is far beyond their own numerical literacy.

Pre-K to Grade 5

To encourage students to explore the world around them with mathematics, it is necessary to develop a classroom climate where problems can be viewed as having more than a single, correct, easily computable answer. In algebra, we learn that even simple problems can have one, none, or infinitely many solutions.

It is important that the experiences leading to these cases be developed early in children's mathematical experiences. In doing so it is sometimes necessary to simplify problems to allow the students' emerging understandings to be utilized in exploring the situation at hand. Students, in this example, will explore a situation where there is more than a single answer. Their work will be supported by initial hands-on activity which is then followed with appropriate supporting technology. This approach—hands on first, then technology for exploration second—is a very powerful model in developing this desirable classroom climate.

The children in this example, a classroom of second graders, were originally presented with a fairly open-ended problem requiring much more than the calculation of a single correct answer.

> *The average temperature for the week increased by 1°, and the temperature on Monday, Tuesday, and Wednesday did not change; then what temperature changes occurred on Thursday and Friday? Find and list all the possible combinations of temperature changes on Thursday and Friday.*

This problem has a "low floor and a high ceiling" in the words of Jo Boaler (2014).[2] As such, this means that the problem is relatively easy to get started on and allows for significant mathematics development. This "low floor, high ceiling" property will be seen in each of the chapter examples.

Originally, the students when asked this question (even in a spreadsheet environment that allowed for manually changing temperature through scroll bars and interactively observing the change in average temperature) were not able to handle the multiplicity of answers.[3] The maximum number of possible combinations of temperature changes found by one of the students was two:

> *"You have to change Friday 5 up. You move Thursday up 3 and you move Friday up 2."*

---

2. For a discussion of this phrase, together with a parent-friendly video on the importance of change in mathematics teaching see https://www.youtube.
3. A full discussion of this example may be found in Abramovich, Easton, and Hayes (2012).

Initially, children's concrete thinking proved to be a barrier for exploring the multiplicity of answers. It was found, however, that an initial concrete activity was effective in finding multiple answers. The second graders were given the following task: *How many ways can one put five rings on two fingers?* Experimentally, without using mathematics, the children found all six ways of putting five rings on two fingers and recorded their findings as shown in Figure 4.15.

After this experience, a second grader was able to answer the question about temperature as follows:

> *Fri increased by two and thurs increased by three. Fri increased by four and thurs increased by one. Fri increased by five and thurs increased by zero. Fri increased by three and thurs increased by two. Fri increased by one and thurs increased by four. Fri increased by zero and thurs increased by five. THAT WAS FUN!!!!!!!!!!!!!!!!!!!*

Figure 4.15   Concrete activity as a means of understanding multiple answers.

Seeing problem posing and problem solving as two sides of the same coin enables a child to attempt to answer self-posed questions either individually or with the help of a teacher. In this example the posing and solving of problems was supported by a spreadsheet. The students had been given a weather forecast for the next five days: Monday 6°, Tuesday 22°, Wednesday 24°, Thursday 18°, and Friday 20°. They were provided with a spreadsheet as shown earlier Figure 4.14, and with this support, a student was able to explore the following problem:

"What would happen to the average temperature if Friday's temperature dropped 20 dugrees?"

It should be noted that these, and the comments which follow, were her actual words and reflect the spelling that was used.

As you can see in Figure 4.16 the environment used by these students resembles a Nintendo DS. This is what Abramovich, Easton, and Hayes (2014) call an integrated spreadsheet. Such a spreadsheet is created by combining a traditional spreadsheet with images of technology—such as a Nintendo DS, a PlayStation Portable, or an iPhone—already familiar to young children. This is easily done by pasting a picture on the background of a spreadsheet. Such familiar images helped in reducing anxiety often felt by beginning. It also allows for a familiar interface for young children in presenting and processing information. In this example, the problems that children were exploring displayed on the colored "screen" of the Nintendo DS and the space for them to enter an answer is always in the transparent box.

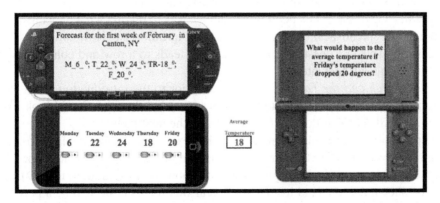

Figure 4.16   Posing a question (the top-right textbox).

Grade 6 to Grade 8

Aunt Sarah and the Farm. This activity illustrates how the appropriate use of technology can support extensive mathematical investigation, including making mathematical connections. As such, the "low floor, high ceiling" concept is directly utilized. The mathematics which underpins this activity is easily accessible and, with the support of technology, potentially quite rich. Indeed, this problem setting allows for multiple competencies (both on the part of the teacher and that of the student) to be addressed.

Without the use of supporting technology, it typically takes several days of tedious calculations for sufficient data to be generated to get to the richer underlying mathematics. Thanks to the modern spreadsheet, the explorations of Sarah's farm allow more time to be spent on building connections between deeper levels of mathematical content than was previously possible—including a powerful link forward from pre-algebra into limits and pre-calculus. As is recommended for all activities in this chapter, the initial problem setting and procedure choices are all done prior to the introduction of the spreadsheet technology.

Aunt Sarah and the Farm

Aunt Sarah wants to help her nephew Jack. However, she does not want to simply give him money. Instead she will provide him with a 10 dkm[4] × 10 dkm plot of land provided he keeps it fenced. At the end of the year she will reduce the width by 1 dkm and increase the length by 1 dkm so that in the second year he will have an 11dkm × 9 dkm plot. This will be done each year until there is nothing left but a fence (i.e., 20 dkm × 0 dkm). This way it will be up to Jack to work hard and make the most of this opportunity.

Help Jack explore what to expect over the next 10 years. As a start, for each year find:

1. How much land will Jack lose from the preceding year?
2. How much land will Jack lose from the first year?
3. How will the shape of his farm change over time?
4. How many feet of fencing will it take to fence it in?

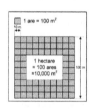

---

[4]A *decameter*—abbreviated as *dkm*, although rarely used, is part of the standard metric system and is equal to 10 meters. The benefit of the use in this problem is than an even more obscure metric unit—the *Are* —is equal to the area of a 10 meter × 10 meter square. Thus, the initial area of the farm is equal to 100 Ares, or 1 Hectare. So, each following calculation is easily expressed in terms of a percentage of the starting Hectare. So, Sarah can be used to reinforce the metric system together with its naming conventions as well as the immediate mathematics.

After reading through the problem situation, see if you can predict the various changes in area and perimeters after the first **three** years have been computed. By the time you have done you will generally be able to identify some of the connections in the problem. Typically, students by this time will recognize that they will be computing areas and perimeters and comparing one year to another.

A good teacher question to ask at this point is: "Is there a way to predict what happens in the 5th year? The 6th?" With the addition of spreadsheet, an excellent bridging question is, "How can we organize our work to make prediction easier?" This last question quite commonly leads to a row and column layout which can be directly translated into a spreadsheet later.

In exploring *Aunt Sarah and the Farm* problem, even prior to the introduction of the spreadsheet, some fascinating mathematics can be shown. If a student draws out what the farm would look like each year on a single figure, he or she will get the following (see figures on the next page):

From here, the possibilities for exploration open up. For example, to show the land lost for any given year relative to the beginning year (the fourth year is shown), take the rectangle of land gained for that year (A), rotate it (B and C), and place it inside the original figure to show the total amount lost (D).

It can quickly be shown that the land lost for each year that this is done will be a perfect square—which certainly hints at some interesting patterns to come!

Figure 4.17   The changing shape of the land.

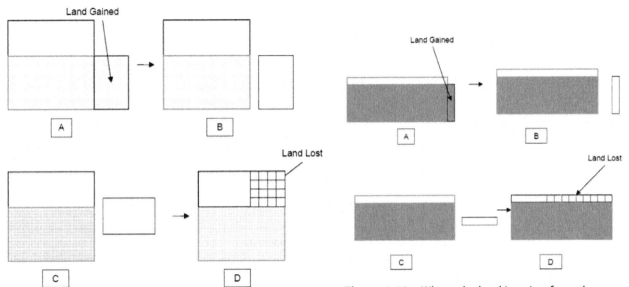

Figure 4.18   Where the land is going from Year One.

Figure 4.19   Where the land is going from the preceding year.

To show the land lost for any given year relative to the preceding year (the difference between the fourth and fifth year is shown), take the rectangle of land gained for that year (A), rotate it (B and C), and place it inside the preceding figure to show the total amount lost (D).

The sequence of odd-numbers this generates likewise hints at areas for investigation.

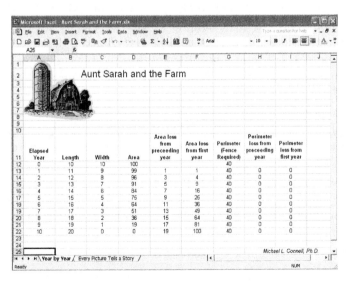

Figure 4.20   Data and calculations confirmed using a spreadsheet.

These examples draw heavily upon the dual process–concept nature of multiplication developed in the earlier chapter examples. As such, these sketches both represent specific processes **and** the solution to problems. This preliminary exploration provides a context for the following spreadsheet explorations as well as providing important clues for exploration. The following screenshot from **Aunt Sarah and the Farm.xls** shows one possible way of representing the problem situation.[5]

When relationships between cells are observed and can be generalized, the formula bar can be used to create many of the cells; for example, cell B12 was defined as being:

Figure 4.21 The Formula (Function) bar.

This makes it easy to copy cell B12, together with its attributes, and easily copy these – filling in the respective columns. This ability to copy relationships between cells, including functional relationships, helps in the students' understanding and exploration of the mathematical situation.

In a like fashion, each of the following cells can be defined using the formula bar as being:

Figure 4.22 Using the Formula (Function) bar.

The increment in year was then defined in cell A13 as being:

Figure 4.23 Last steps in creating the spreadsheet.

Once relationships are recognized and their underlying functions identified, it becomes easy to create meaningful function tables of values. In this example, we can see this by copying cell A13 into cells A14 through A22. In a like fashion, it is possible to copy cells B12, C12, and D12 into cells B13 through B22, C13 through C22, and D13 through D22. This is a bit different than the typical use of data tables serving as the basis for function identification. In this case, the function is created first and used to create a table of data for exploration.

An examination of the formula bar for Column B (fx = 10 + A12), Column C (fx = 10 − A12), and Column D (fx = B12*C12) provides a possible avenue to explore the concept of difference of squares (i.e., the length (10 + A12) and width (10 − A12)) being used in the area calculation. In this case, Column D's function is equivalent to B12*C12 which in turn is equivalent to (10 + A2)*(10 − A12).

Depending upon the classroom, this may not be followed up, but it does provide an important clue which could be utilized in further exploration into the mathematics underlying the *Aunt Sarah and the Farm* problem. By making explicit the relationships between cells, the formula bar can often be used in this fashion to gain hints as to potential mathematical underpinnings. The mathematics which may be found "beneath the rules" can then be made available for student explorations.

---

5. All screenshots were created using Microsoft Excel.

The remaining columns look at some of the other interesting interactions immediately springing from the problem situation. Each cell in Column E, E13 for example, was computed using the following convention:

$$E13 \quad \blacktriangledown \quad f_x \ =\!D12\text{-}D13$$

Figure 4.24   Differences from the preceding year.

When this is done, the sequence of odd numbers is generated, leading to questions concerning where this shows up in the graphical and functional representations generated in the group activity.

Column F was generated using the following:

$$F13 \quad \blacktriangledown \quad f_x \ =\!\$D\$12\text{-}D13$$

Figure 4.25   Differences from the first year.

The $ sign preceding the D and the 12 indicates that this location will be locked in and used as the reference for each of the cells generated by copying it. This ensures that each subsequent year's difference will be computed taking the first year as the comparison.

Now a sequence of squares is generated, once again leading to questions concerning where this shows up in the graphical and functional representations generated.

Using these columns the following graphs were generated:

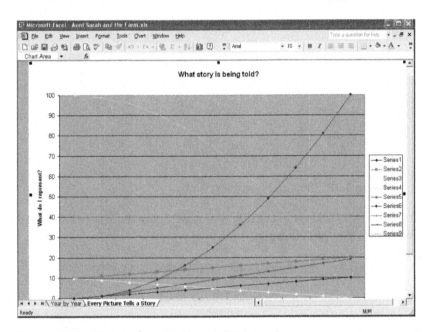

Figure 4.26   Data to function to graph to story!

It is now up to the students to describe which series gives rise to each graph and why. They should also be able to link their graphic representation created prior to the use of the spreadsheet (typically, done using graph paper) to these graphs.

An important conclusion that one can draw from this investigation is that given perimeter of rectangle, no smallest area exists, whereas square (i.e., rectangle with congruent adjacent sides) has the largest area. However, as noted by Kline (1985), "A farmer who seeks the rectangle of maximum area with given perimeter might, after finding the answer to his question, turn to gardening, but a mathematician who obtains such a neat result would not stop there" (p. 133). This note motivates extending *Aunt Sarah and the Farm* problem using the computational power of a spreadsheet.

Technology Enabled Sxtensions

Of course, technically, in order for a line graph to be properly used, a case must be made that there will not be any changes in the line as the difference between sampling times becomes infinitely small. This provides an easy link to the calculus which may be made via the spreadsheet.

This can be shown by first changing the spreadsheet so that the "change point" occurs every month instead of every year. This action effectively changes the difference between points on the line graphs by 1/12. This is easily done by changing cell A13 to be:

| A13 | ▼ | f_x =A12+1/12 |

Figure 4.27   Links to advanced math.

Now we can reconstruct the full table (all 120 rows of it!) with a simple set of copy instructions. The following shows the results of this action:

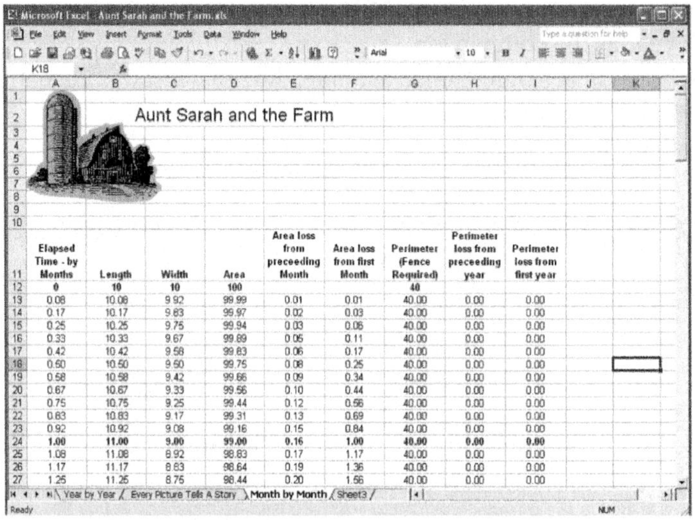

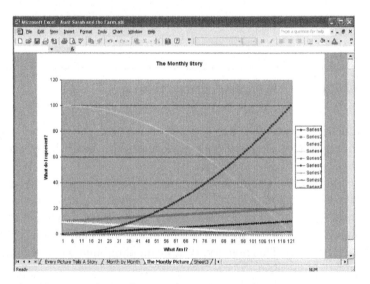

Figure 4.28   Ten times the data points.

We can now reconstruct the earlier graphs using this more finely tuned set of measurements. When this is done, the graphs created look like the following:

Figure 4.29   Identical curves from identical functions.

This is the identical shapes as shown in the earlier set of graphs. *The underlying equivalency can be better shown by changing the chart type to not plot the locations of the individual data points.* In a like fashion, we can narrow the limit to the day, the hour, the minute—to any degree we might choose . . . in each case since the underlying functions are the same, the graphs will maintain the same shape! Technology has enabled us to develop in a very intuitive fashion the notions of limit which underpin differential calculus. Without technology, this amazing development is not possible.

High School (Secondary)

One of the major tasks in the high school environment lies in developing the ability to work with abstract concepts. With its ability to provide an interface between functions and graphs technology can be an invaluable tool in this effort. The figures shown in this section were created with the *Graphing* Calculator (version 4.0) produced by Pacific Tech (Avitzur, 2011). However, any of a number of Web-based apps, programs, or handheld devices could have done just as well. It is a tribute to the power of technology that once the math is understood, there are a variety of tools which might be used. The opposite is also true, however. If the math is not understood, it does not matter how many tools you have access to.

Consider the question of constructing the graphs of the functions $y = x$ and $y = x^2$ in a single drawing. This construction is shown in Figure 4.26 and leads to the question of constructing just the parabolic segment as shown in Figure 4.30.

In order to construct the parabolic segment, one has to describe the points inside the parabolic segment in the form of inequalities. First, an x-coordinate of any point (x, y) that belongs to the parabolic segment satisfies the inequalities $0 < x < 1$, where $x = 0$ and $x = 1$ are the points of intersection of the graphs $y = x$ and $y = x^2$. Second, its y-coordinate satisfies the inequalities $f(x) < y < g(x)$ where $f(x) = x^2$ and $g(x) = x$.

These properties of the points that belong to the parabolic segment can be expressed in the form of simultaneous inequalities:

$$x - y > 0, \quad y - x^2 > 0, \quad x > 0, \, x < 1$$

In addition, the reflection of the parabolic segment in the line $x = 1$ can be expressed through another set of inequalities by substituting $2 - x$ for x:

$$(2-x) - y > 0, \quad y - (2-x)^2 > 0, \quad (2-x) > 0, \, (2-x) < 1$$

Likewise, the set of points that belong to the border of the parabolic segment can be described through inequalities. First, the graph of the upper border (a part of the line $y = x$) can be described as a set of points (x, y) for which the values of the coordinates x and y are ε—close to each other; that is, $|y - x| < \varepsilon$. Second, the graph

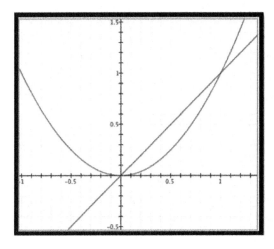

Figure 4.30   Y = X and Y = X².

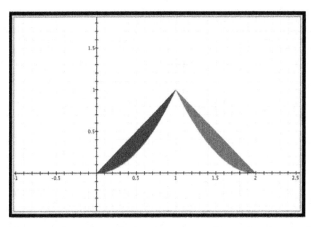

Figure 4.31   A parabolic segment and its reflection in the line $x = 1$.

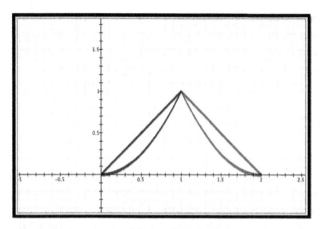

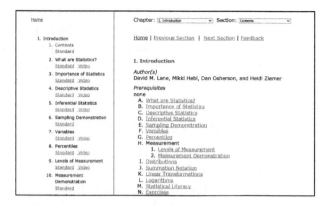

Figure 4.32   Digital fabrication of ε-thick borders of the parabolic segment and its reflection.

Figure 4.33   Online Statistic Education: An Interactive Multimedia Course of Study.

of the lower border (a part of the parabola $y = x^2$) can be described as a set of points (x, y) for which the values of y are ε—close to the values of x^2. Finally, once again, the inequalities $0 < x < 1$ characterize the points that belong to the border. In the context of the *Graphing Calculator,* these properties of the points that belong to the border of the parabolic segment can be expressed in the form of the union of simultaneous inequalities.

$$|y - x| < \varepsilon, \quad x > 0, \quad x < 1;$$
$$|y - x^2| < \varepsilon, \quad x > 0, \quad x < 1;$$

Adding another union of simultaneous inequalities

$$|y - (2 - x)| < \varepsilon, \quad 2 - x > 0, \quad 2 - x < 1;$$
$$|y - (2 - x)^2| < \varepsilon, \quad 2 - x > 0, \quad 2 - x < 1;$$

yields the right-hand side of the digital fabrication shown in Figure 4.32 . . . . Note that in Figure 4.32 $\varepsilon = 0.02$.

Using technology to enable students to construct graphs of areas in the plane and their borders by using two-variable inequalities illustrates "the way in which software can embody a mathematical definition" (Conference Board of the Mathematical Sciences, 2001, p. 132).

Finally, since students in the secondary environment are capable of a higher level of abstract reasoning and independent work they can directly benefit from many of the public domain "textbooks" that are available online. For example, the National Science Foundation supported the development of one such "text" for Statistics—*Online Statistics: An Interactive Multimedia Course of Study* (http://onlinestatbook.com).

This resource for teaching and learning introductory statistical analysis contains a complete textbook, a free PDF version, video vignettes, work templates, interactive demonstrations, specially formatted versions for mobile devices, and so on. For instructors wanting to use these materials, a free instructor's manual, PowerPoint Slides, and question sets are available.

Suggestions for Classroom Technology Use

From the examples presented in this chapter, we would like to offer the following suggestions for classroom technology use:

1. Begin by developing basic numeracy. Students cannot effectively act upon numbers, regardless of technology, without a rich understanding of number concepts. Be sure that students recognize that number can serve as both a **noun** and a **verb** and are able to provide examples of both situations.

2. Once numeracy, a deep understanding of the foundations of number and its uses, are in place, be certain that the basic operations are also thoroughly understood in both their **noun** and **verb** settings. It is far too easy for the correct answers provided by technology to hide student misconceptions and lack of foundational understandings. *Remember the hamburger!*

3. Whenever possible, use technology to confirm your thinking, not replace it. Perform a few sample calculations to test your ideas, use technology to check your calculations and confirm you are on the correct path, and then use the tools of technology to explore emerging ideas more efficiently.

4. Remember the examples of the embedded spreadsheets. Pick your technology to match the developmental needs and experiences of your students.

5. Take advantage of "beneath the rules" moments. Often technology can provide important clues as to connections which may be built in the emerging mathematics. In *Aunt Sarah and the Farm*, for example, there are multiple concepts which could serve as the basis of future explorations.

6. Remember to use technology to pose problems, not just as a means to increase speed of solutions. The ability to pose questions, even when their immediate methods of solution are not readily apparent, is a major goal in mathematics education.

7. If one truly understands the questions that one is asking, it becomes possible to select an appropriate technology to help explore possible answers. If the questions being asked are not understood, then **NO** technology will be able of assistance. Numerical answers can be generated, but these numbers might not even relate to the questions being asked.

8. Do use the massive amount of teacher resources the Internet has to offer with ideas for teaching with technology for all types of mathematics and various grade levels, for many types of technology usage, and many types of software and tools (i.e., Wii, blogs, tutorials, electronic whiteboard suggestions, YouTube videos, math memory songs, making electronic games, digital cameras use, WebQuests, apps, and many more).

9. Do take into account the time needed to teach the use of the technology tools so that students can use them quickly, easily, and without frustration.

10. Remember that classroom technology is a moving target. By focusing upon the mathematics that is to be taught, teachers should able to adapt when a newer program, instructional package, or textbook is to be adopted. Teachers should not allow themselves to become so centered on ***how*** to enter the correct keystrokes that they forget ***why*** they are doing so!

Summary

If we take the student-centered and meaning-driven approach to mathematics education advocated in this chapter, the question becomes what tools and abilities are necessary for success and how can educational technology be used as a tool in acquiring these?

This is a crucial question, as the nature of the "tools" which are provided to students to "think-with" come to significantly shape their performance and cognitive styles. For example, two-digit division may constitute a legitimate problem when paper and pencil are the only tools available for the student to use but are no longer a problem when calculators are available. When technology is available for the students' use, the situation shifts again. A legitimate problem with technology might involve the identification and selection of what data to include in the problem, identification of the problem goals, and selection of appropriate procedures and control statements to obtain and verify the desired results.

Let us be careful not to transfer a misplaced belief that mathematics education is solely about developing speed of process over to our thinking about technology uses. Modern technology is capable of blinding speeds of process—so this cannot be viewed as our end goal. If student are to internalize and construct meanings from experiences, there must be time to reflect upon the nature of the experiences and how they connect with the students' existing mathematical knowledge. Great care must be taken to allow students to construct their own knowledge and representations and then establish the linkages with other (also student-constructed) tools, representations, and concepts—many of which are technology dependent.

Listing of Recommended and Cited URLs and APPS/Programs

Council of State Science Supervisors. Data resources for classroom use. http://www.csss-science.org/classroom.shtml

Math2.org Math Tables: Multiplication Table. http://www.math2.org/math/general/multiplytable.htm

Multiplication: An adventure in number sense. http://naturalmath.com/mult/mult2.html

National Library of Virtual Manipulatives. Rectangle Multiplication. http://nlvm.usu.edu/en/nav/frames_asid_192_g_1_t_1.html?from = category_g_1_t_1.html

References

Abramovich, S. (2012). Counting and reasoning with manipulative materials: A North American perspective. In N. Petrovic (Ed.), *The interfaces of subjects taught in the primary schools and possible models of integrating them* (pp. 9–20). Sombor, Serbia: The University of Novi Sad Faculty of Education Press.

Abramovich, S., & Connell, M. (2014). Using technology in elementary teacher education: A sociocultural perspective. *ISRN (International Scholarly Research Network) Education*, Article ID 245146, 9 pages, doi: 10.1155/2014/345146.

Abramovich, S., Easton, J., & Hayes, V. O. (2012). Parallel structures of computer-assisted signature pedagogy: The case of integrated spreadsheets. *Computers in the Schools (special issue on Signature Pedagogy)*, 29(1-2), 174–190.

Abramovich, S., Easton, J., & Hayes, V. O. (2014). Integrated spreadsheets as learning environments for young children. *Spreadsheets in Education*, 7(2), Article 3.

Avitzur, R. (2011). *Graphing calculator* (Version 4.0). Berkeley, CA: Pacific Tech.

Campione, J. C., Brown, A. L., & Connell, M. L. (1988). Metacognition: On the importance of understanding what you are doing. In R. I. Charles & E. Silver (Eds.), *Teaching and assessing mathematical problem solving*. Volume 3 (pp. 93–114). Reston, VA: National Council of Teachers of Mathematics.

Conference Board of the Mathematical Sciences. (2001). *The mathematical education of teachers*. Washington, DC: The Mathematical Association of America.

Connell, M. L. (2001). Actions upon objects: A metaphor for technology enhanced mathematics instruction. In D. Tooke & N. Henderson (Eds.), *Using information technology in mathematics* (pp. 143–171). Binghamton, NY: Haworth Press.

Kline, M. (1985). *Mathematics for the non-mathematician*. New York: Dover.

Leontiev, A.N. (1979). The problem of activity in psychology. In J. V. Wertsch (Ed.), *The concept of activity in Soviet psychology* (pp. 37–72). Armonk, NY: Sharpe.

National Council of Teachers of Mathematics. (2000). *Principles and standards for school mathematics*. Reston, VA: Author.

Sfard, A. (1991). On the dual nature of mathematical conceptions: Reflections on processes and objects as different sides of the same coin. *Educational Studies in Mathematics*, 22(1), 1–36.

Tall, D., Thomas, M., Davis, G., Gray, E. M. & Simpson, A. (2000). *What is the object of the encapsulation of a process? Journal of Mathematical Behavior*, 18(2), 223–241. ISSN 0732-3123.

Chapter 5

Technology and Developmentally Appropriate Practice for Young Children

Amelia Hewitt, Carolyn Wade, *University of Houston-Downtown*

Hsin-Hui Grace Lin, *University of Houston-Victoria*

Meet Ben and Maya

Ben and Maya, two pre-kindergarteners, are chattering excitedly as they take turns playing with an iPad. "It's B, Ben. Choose B," squeals Maya.

Ben says, "I know, Maya, B **IS** the letter. It's **MY** letter for Ben." Ben chooses B, and the two children giggle when they see they chose correctly.

Maya says, "Okay, now me! My turn!" Several letters appear on the screen, and the two children watch for a moment. Both seem unsure, and Ben begins touching the letters.

"No, Ben! It's my turn! I'll do it," Maya yells. Maya begins frantically touching each letter to hear the sound the letter makes.

The excitement alerts the teacher, who is nearby. The teacher approaches the children, but she watches them before saying anything.

Ben says, "Maya, it's **THAT** one!" Ben points to the letter C. "C is for cat and cake. It's C, Maya! Pick C!"

Maya ignores Ben and continues touching each letter to hear the sounds. Maya laughs and says, "Look at that one! Look at the D. It's dancing." She presses D over and over and erupts into laughter.

Ben looks frustrated and looks up at the teacher for help. "She won't choose C! It's C! I told her!"

The teacher says, "I know, Ben. I heard you tell her that. I'm proud of you for knowing the correct answer, but right now, it's Maya's turn. Remember what we discussed about touching each letter first and repeating the sounds you hear before choosing a letter? Maya is trying all of the letters."

"But . . . she keeps doing it," Ben says.

"That's okay," says the teacher. "The D is silly!" The teacher then wiggles like the D, and the children laugh. The teacher stays near the children and watches for a few moments until she is sure the two have settled back into play. Maya eventually takes Ben's advice and chooses C. Both delight in the joy of the correct answer, and Maya hands the iPad to Ben. Ben begins the next round by touching each letter to hear the sound, and both children repeat the sounds the letters make.

The above scenario depicts play and interaction with technology in the pre-kindergarten classroom. This kind of play is optimal for centers when all children in the classroom are involved in content-related play (as guided by state and national standards). These two children chose the technology play center where the iPad is one of many options available to the children. What is clear from the scenario is that the teacher's rules for play with the iPad and the particular application the children were enjoying were made clear to the children before the two ever sat down to play. The teacher's role in this scenario is vital to the success of use of this technology in the classroom because she sets the rules and guidelines for play

Tania Kolinko/Shutterstock, Inc.

and interaction and must guide the children as they play with the technologies. Further, this teacher expanded the possibilities for the use of technology in her classroom to what is a more real world situation outside the classroom. Should she have one isolated child learning basic tablet skills silently with an application or two children interactively learning letters and letter sounds while negotiating the bumpy road of sharing and respectful socialization in the scenario? The teacher thoughtfully planned and created an environment for the children where they are learning how to navigate the iPad, how to identify letters and sounds, and how to take turns—all while following the classroom rules. This is an example of how, when implemented appropriately using planning and developmentally appropriate practice (DAP), technology can be an asset to the early childhood classroom.

Pedagogy by definition is the method and practice of teaching. Early childhood education naturally envelops the method of practice and teaching. Understanding pedagogy leads to early childhood teachers who interact and support children as they work—while also informing others of and advocating for the importance of developmentally appropriate teaching with peers, administrators, parents, and others. Understanding pedagogy assists early childhood teachers in recognizing the importance of appropriate teaching methods in helping children understand their environment and in learning new concepts and skills. Understanding pedagogy allows early childhood teachers to value the practice of teaching that encourages authentic, high impact experiences in order to make connections with the real world.

The most common pedagogical belief in early childhood is that play is at the center of learning. Play is a natural context whereby young children explore to grow, develop, and learn.

> *"When you asked me what I did in school today and I say, 'I just played.' Please don't misunderstand me. For you see, I am learning as I play. I am learning to enjoy and be successful in my work. Today I am a child and my work is play."* (Anita Wadley, 1974)

Through play, young children learn to make sense of the world around them while engaging in activities that promote higher-level thinking. Play is generally initiated by children and controlled by children. It allows children to collaborate with others while solving problems and practicing decision-making skills. Play offers children an opportunity to learn at their own pace and discover their own interests.

While "allowing children to play" sounds like a natural and simple directive, from a pedagogical perspective, there are many items to weigh and consider. An astute teacher knows that simply allowing children time to play is not enough to ensure appropriate and memorable learning opportunities for children. There are many pieces to the puzzle of the young child's classroom learning experience that include: (a) choosing the correct materials with which the children will engage, (b) planning the instruction about the materials and their use, and (c) assessing children's learning. Each of those items is an integral part of the learning process and environment of the early childhood classroom. Teachers who set up the correct environment will direct many of the outcomes that they desire subconsciously.

Monkey Business Images/Shutterstock, Inc.

There are also additional considerations when specific curricular standards are addressed. State and national standards may be mandated by schools, which further compound the teacher's role in the child's learning environment. Teachers must integrate the required standards (including technology standards), while carefully balancing the growth of the child's social-emotional, physical, and cognitive development. This extensive list of items with which teachers must grapple seems daunting. These issues can, however, be addressed knowing that such matters are interrelated and can be encapsulated under the umbrella of an early childhood teacher's most important pedagogical approach noted earlier as *developmentally appropriate practice*, commonly referred to as DAP, and as we clearly saw demonstrated in the scenario earlier.

When turning to the place of technology in the world today, we find that it has been improved significantly within the past few decades. New technology, including that for young children, has changed most people's lives in many different ways. Although benefits from the advances in new technologies have aided many facets of people's work and play, we should not ignore the pitfalls from using technology as well. When educators have a deep understanding of the impact of technology on young children's learning, they will be able to provide better learning environments in the classrooms.

Samuel Borges Photography/Shutterstock, Inc.

In this chapter, we discuss the importance of play, DAP, and planning for technology and learning in the early childhood classroom. We also discuss the advantages and pitfalls of technology and offer guidance for the many technological choices available for the early childhood classroom. Finally, we will look to the future possibilities of technology in classrooms for young children and the teacher's ongoing role as the facilitator to the young child's explorations and discoveries.

Developmentally Appropriate Practice (DAP)

Technology is an integral part of the world today and should be a part of the early childhood classroom; however, all teachers of young children, birth through age 8, must employ the tenets of DAP before any teaching activities, new curriculum, or instructional devices are deemed acceptable for use in the early childhood classroom. DAP is the lens through which early childhood education and best practices for children are viewed, as touted by the National Association for the Education of Young Children (NAEYC). Widely recognized as the prevailing authority on DAP guidelines and recommendations for young children, this association offers a set of DAP guidelines that teachers of young children follow, centering on a child's: (a) age, (b) individuality, (c) culture, and (d) developmental cognitive, social, emotional, and physical levels. DAP also supports a hands-on, active classroom where children use their existing knowledge to gain new knowledge through exploration and play (NAEYC, 2009). DAP classrooms are child-centered with the teacher taking the role of classroom facilitator. Therefore, a teacher must consider several factors according to DAP guidelines when planning for the early childhood classroom.

Dmitry Naumov/Shutterstock, Inc.

Age is the first determining factor of DAP, because it takes a child's chronological age as well as a child's developmental levels into account. A child's chronological age may indicate certain cognitive, physical, and social milestones that need to be addressed in the early childhood classroom. It is important that a teacher pays attention to these milestones, as they are developmental. This means that when a child has not yet reached a milestone, he or she may still be working toward it, or the child may be monitored and assessed for possible developmental delays. The teacher must take the child's development into account and understand that development (or lack thereof) in one area may affect a child's development in another area. For instance, a teacher who notices a child's language development is delayed may also notice that the child's social development has been affected by the language delay. A teacher who carefully considers the many facets of age indicators understands that, while a child may not have reached a milestone, he or she is developing and may need extra time, encouragement, and instruction to reach these developmental milestones. This is the start of differentiated instruction in today's classroom. This can be an important area for technology as young children fine-tune motor skills with mouse manipulation or appropriate touch screens that, in turn, aid in cognitive thinking (such as seriation or sorting) and social skills (such as problem solving in groups).

Because providing the extra time and attention children need to develop is part of the teacher's job, the teacher must create opportunities for the children to play and develop according to their individual needs. This second component of the definition of DAP, individual appropriateness, is also key to a child's progress in the classroom. Teachers have classrooms with many children, and each individual child comes to school with his or her own knowledge, development, likes, dislikes, learning preferences, and experiences. When planning for the classroom, teachers should evaluate the needs of the individual children and make decisions for the classroom based upon each child's needs.

The third part of the definition of DAP, cultural appropriateness, is also an integral piece of the DAP puzzle, and it works hand in hand with the child's age and individuality. Because children are unique and come from a variety of backgrounds and traditions, a teacher should make every effort to learn about each child's culture and create a classroom that nurtures respect, sensitivity, and understanding for all. This is especially important with technology, as children may come from a culture that values technology with parents who have the means to provide it from an early age, or, on the other hand, children may come from a culture and/or economic status that has not allowed them past (or current) technological access. Children can thrive and grow in classrooms that foster cultural awareness and appreciation for others, as those efforts can, in turn, nurture self-respect and self-acceptance within each child.

Along with considering a child's age, individuality, and culture, a teacher also needs to plan the method by which children will learn in the classroom. As noted, DAP supports the fact that children learn best through play. High-impact, real-to-life experiences where children can explore and have fun through play is a fundamental piece of the young child's learning process. Children's learning should be experiential and hands-on, as opposed to traditional classrooms that employ worksheets, silence, and teacher-directed activities as learning methods. When children's interest levels are high, as they are during play, learning and development are a natural outgrowth of the play process. With careful planning, a teacher can implement play as the primary method by which children are learning in the early childhood classroom. When considering technology with young children, this must be at the forefront of consideration in planning integration activities.

A remaining important element of an early childhood classroom is the idea of ongoing assessment. A teacher's job is to teach, but a teacher cannot know what to teach a child unless the child has been assessed. Assessment in the early childhood classroom is ongoing. It begins the very first day of school and is repeated each day until the very last day of school. Teachers of young children use observational assessment methods such as checklists, rubrics, rating scales, anecdotal records, and portfolios to record students' physical, cognitive, social, and emotional progress throughout the year. Assessments (that are highly aided by technology) provide valuable information about individual students as well as the general growth and development of all of the students in an early childhood classroom (NAEYC, 2009).

Technology Usage

When all of the elements of DAP, play, and assessment are considered, screening of possible technologies for the early childhood classroom can begin. The National Association for the Education of Young Children (NAEYC) and the Fred Rogers Center for Early Learning and Children's Media at Saint Vincent College, in 2012, released a joint research based position statement, *Technology and Interactive Media as Tools in Early Childhood Programs Serving Children Birth through Age 8 that* states that, "Technology should not be used for activities that are not educationally sound, not developmentally appropriate, or not effective (electronic worksheets for preschoolers, for example)" (p. 4). However, technology has grown dramatically during the past

half century and certainly has made a significant impact on people's lives. This can make choosing appropriate times for technologies and their applications difficult. For example, the list of popular technology products includes televisions, phones, computers, cell phones, cameras, electronic tablets, and video players, as well as software and applications. Software and applications are the programs run by technology products (Rideout, Foehr, & Roberts, 2010).

Also, technology usage may vary according to income levels. Wide ranges of technology products used among families with children and ownership of different types of technology products was found to be directly related to family income levels. Among all of the technology products, the television remains the most popular media for families (Gutnick, Robb, Takeuchi, & Kotler, 2011). TV is especially popular among younger children. In the United States, about 80% of families have cable or satellite TV; less than 50% of families with young children have television recording capabilities (DVR or Tivo). In addition, 75 % of families have cell phones, and two out of three families own computers. Almost all of these families have Internet services. Furthermore, these researchers tell us that more than half of the families in the United States own video game systems.

A national survey conducted in 2009 by the Kaiser Family Foundation showed that children between the ages 8 and 18 spend more than 7.5 hours each day (more than 53 hours weekly) using entertainment media (Rideout et al., 2010). These researchers also noted that the top four types of media that these children used in a typical day were TV (4.29 hours), music/audio (2.31 hours), computer (1.29 hours), and video games (1.13 hours).

Advantages of Using Technology

New technology has changed people's ways of thinking, entertaining, and connecting with the rest of the world. There are many ways that a person can find the information he needs by watching TV, listening to the radio, or searching information online. Smartphones, laptops, electronic tablets, and computers allow people to network and communicate with others through the Internet. Popular social media such as Facebook, Twitter, and e-mails provide venues for people to keep in touch with one another. We can expect that children will need and want to have skills to use these tools.

Some technology products are designed for learning in addition to fun. These products can be wonderful learning tools for enriching children's learning experiences and allowing them to learn at their own pace. For example, one study (Penuel et al., 2009) examined technology usage in a classroom and the students' learning outcome. This study included 398 preschool children whose teachers adopted a technology-enhanced curriculum by intentionally presenting curriculum content in videos, teacher-led activities, and computer games. Students watched the videos and participated in related large group activities. This meant that in the classrooms, their teachers co-viewed the videos and provided coherent activities. Students in this study showed improvement in their literacy skills, such as naming letters, knowing the sounds of letters, knowing concepts of story and print, and recognizing letters in a child's own name.

Maria Uspenskaya/Shutterstock, Inc.

Pitfalls of Using Technology

Although technology can bring many positive effects on people's lives, some negative outcomes with using technology have been found—particularly with young people. Children who spent many hours using technology products were predisposed to having multiple problems. First, this kind of activity had a negative impact on the children's health, resulting in lack of sleep time or development of irregular sleep patterns (Zimmerman, 2008). Second, some of these children were found to be incapable of paying attention and had difficulties following instructions (Hastings et al., 2009). Their attention spans were too short, which prevented them from learning effectively. Third, school-aged children were found to have lower grade performances and often had more learning problems as compared to their classmates. Furthermore, poor language development was also found to be associated with children who spent more time using technology (Hastings et al., 2009).

Additional research findings show that children who spent many hours using technology products tended to have poor social skills. These children often spent their time playing games and did not interact with others. Violent videos and technology games have become more accessible to young children. Due to their inability to distinguish between the virtual and real worlds, young children who spent more time watching violent videos or playing violent games were found to exhibit more behavior problems (Anderson, Gentile, & Buckley, 2007; Dubow, Huesmann, & Greenwood, 2007).

What is a better way for educators to provide positive learning opportunities for young children? Actually, technology devices can be used as appropriate tools for teaching young children, but the key is that technology needs to be used in a manner that can support children's development. Technology can be used to encourage children's curiosity and exploration. The solution, as mentioned, is to use DAP as guidance for implementing technology for teaching. First, teachers must always double check that the software and applications do not contain any sexual or violent content. Secondly, teachers should consider their students' ages, and the activities they select should match with the children's physical, cognitive, and social emotional developmental levels. Lastly, teachers should ask themselves, "What benefits can children obtain from incorporating technology into teaching?"

Technology in the Classroom

Most children come to school already equipped with a basic knowledge in technology. From the time they are born, children are now immersed in a world that is made up of technological advances. As teachers, we should make the most of the inherent knowledge shared by children and encourage technology in all areas of the classroom. Children need time to develop skills and learn to use technology in ways that benefit learning. Technology is a tool for young children to use that can assist in solving problems, locating information, and learning at their own pace. Teachers, however, must be cognizant of how young children grow, develop, and learn before introducing technology into the classroom. It is imperative for teachers to remember that children learn by doing, and, in a DAP environment, technology should be utilized as a way to engage children to explore, discuss, and document learning. As children become proficient with the use of technology as a tool in the classroom, teachers can and should take advantage of the great resources available. Teachers must also ensure that all children in the classroom are provided ample opportunities and time with technology (Copple & Bredekamp, 2009)

Approaches to Developmentally Appropriate Technology

Approaches to technology are abundant. With a plethora of information at one's fingertips, it is often daunting and sometimes difficult to choose those that are the most appropriate. Teachers must stay abreast of current technological trends and be knowledgeable about which trends offer the best opportunities for young students to learn. Teachers must also be cognizant of when and how to utilize technology for the best developmental experiences. They must make informed decisions about using technology based upon the activity(ies) occurring.

Information presented in the next section gives insight into technology approaches that offer developmentally appropriate practices to guide authentic learning. Teachers can build confidence about what technology to use, how to use it, and when to assess its effectiveness in the classroom. In essence, teachers become technology connectors using "*technivity*" to enhance and expand knowledge.

Developmentally Appropriate Devices Used in Technology

Kindle Fire or other ereaders. The Kindle Fire digital device is designed mainly for reading ebooks. The device allows the user to read newspapers, magazines, and other text. This particular device can also be used by children to highlight, copy, and save information to be downloaded at their convenience.

Technivity **with the Kindle**

1st Grade

Mrs. Clayborn's first-grade class reads the Kindle book *The Farm Yard* by Abby Sage. As they read, the children highlight high frequency words that they know. Once the story is complete, children list of all of the words they found in their personal Word Journal. Using words from their personal Word Journal, children write their own story about animals.

Andrey Shchekalev/Shutterstock, Inc.

iPad/iPhone/iPod/Windows Surface tablets. Smart devices are designed for the user to perform various tasks and encourage interaction with technology. Children in the classroom can play games, which is effective for practicing skills in various subject areas, as well as interacting with music and art. They can use smart devices to create videos of projects and/or take pictures to document the progress of assignments. Children can create virtual presentations, write stories, and illustrate stories with applications that allow them to draw and even "paint" their own art work virtually.

Vadim Ponomarenko/Shutterstock, Inc.

All of these devices make use of *apps* or software applications that are designed in the form of games and can be used for educational as well as entertainment purposes. Many of today's children grow up with knowledge about computer apps and are savvy about utilizing applications before entering the classroom. Teachers can facilitate that accumulated knowledge by preparing activities that take advantage of all that technology has to offer. In the classroom, applications offer hands-on experiences to children that connect skills to real life. For example, when children read about frogs on the iPad and then watch a video about the life cycle of the frog and the frog in its environment, they make connections about how the animal grows and lives as well as comparisons to themselves when they see how the animal moves, eats, and interacts. Following developmentally appropriate guidelines, teachers have the power to teach children how to use technology to its fullest potential and not just use it as a "time filler."

Technivity **with the iPad**

PK/K

Ms. Gomez reads the iPad book *Gossie* by Olivier Dunrea aloud in a small group, using a pointer to track the words read. Once the story is complete children create props and become characters or items from the book as they act out the story.

Digital cameras. Digital cameras use a lens to capture images and video that can be stored for later use. In the classroom, teachers can use digital cameras to record videos and take photographs that document and help to better assess learning. Teachers can assess children's progress by studying images that have been archived throughout the school year. Children can easily upload videos and photographs recorded during activities or projects to files on the classroom computer. They can use digital photographs to create stories, journals, and interest inventories to share ideas or document steps or progress on a project. Children can take their pictures one step further to create their own books out of the digital pictures taken. They can "read" their books in class and share with their peers. Although these examples of graphic literacy may not replace the picture on the refrigerator door, they will be precious to most parents when shared.

Technivity with the Digital Camera

2nd Grade

Mr. Wong groups children in the classroom into partner pairs. Children work with their partner to take photos of items and rooms around the school. Children create a collage of their photos and prepare a written paragraph description of *Our School in Pictures* using descriptive words.

MidoSemsem/Shutterstock, Inc.

Voice recorders. Voice recorders are small devices that are easily used to record verbal memos for later play back. These usually come with an output option (normally a *USB* port) so that recordings can be easily downloaded onto a computer. Children can use voice recorders in the classroom for all types of projects. For example, children can record narratives, interviews, sounds needed for particular projects, music, and performances. They can create their own unique rhymes and songs that assist with literacy and math skills, as well as, share their recordings with others.

Technivity with the Voice Recorder

Pk/K - 2nd Grade

Ms. Nguyen allows children to work individually or in partner pairs as a band. They plan a song, chant, or rhyme. Then, they create a tune for their song, chant, or rhyme. The children can create musical instruments or use ones from the classroom. They name their song, chant, or rhyme and record it using the voice recorder. Ms. Nguyen downloads the recordings to the computer and children type lyrics and create a music video to accompany the recording.

Interactive boards/electronic white boards. Interactive boards can now be found in many classrooms across the country. These boards project displays from the computer. They usually attach to a portable stand that can be moved around the classroom. However, they can also be attached directly to the wall.

Children can use interactive boards to participate in activities that the teacher has approved or created to practice skills they are learning in the classroom. They can also access Web sites and play games that the teacher has approved to assist in the transfer of information. Children can practice skills and interact with games while exploring concepts on the interactive board. They can work individually or in small groups as they interact with technology up close and personal.

Examples of such interactive Web sites are:

- Math Playground
  http://www.mathplayground.com
- FunBrain.com
  http://www.funbrain.com
- Cool Math 4 Kids
  http://www.coolmath4kids.com

- Kids Math Games
  http://www.kidsmathgamesonline.com
- Math Games—PBS Kids
  http://pbskids.org/games/math

Teachers who plan well will use interactive boards to watch live web lectures and have children participate in webinars. This device has the capability to engage and connect children from all over the world through live streams.

Technivity with the Interactive Board

K - 5th Grade

Mr. Garcia practices math skills by using the Web site *Mr. Wolfe's Math (https://sites.google.com/a/ norman.k12.ok.us/mr-wolfe-s-math-interactive-whiteboard/home)*. Children in the classroom practice various math skills while interacting with the program.

Developmentally Appropriate Tools and the Computer

Evgeniya Uvarova/Shutterstock, Inc.

Live video cams (Skype/Oovoo). Live video cams like Skype/Oovoo are basically video phone calls that allow the user to see with whom they are speaking through the camera on the computer. The basic services of these video cams are usually free to users. Basic Skype services allow for two users to communicate at one time. Basic Oovoo services allow for up to six users to communicate at one time. These live video cams assist teachers in bringing the outside world into the classroom. Teachers can partner with other teachers across the world and have live chats as well as teaching sessions that bring learning from around the world directly to the children they are teaching. Teachers can also bring in people from the community to help children understand concepts or gain information about topics being studied. For example, children would enjoy learning about the birth of a new giraffe at the local zoo.

Invite the zoo keeper to communicate with the class via Skype and open the children up to a whole new meaning of "trip to the zoo." By using these "video telephones," so to speak, teachers bring children from far way places or from the classroom next door closer and actually see other children in real time.

Technivity with the Computer

Any Grade Level

Mrs. Johnson sets up a video call to another grade level or partnering class in the same grade level. Children brainstorm, share ideas, and/or partner on projects by interacting and chatting live with the other students. Mrs. Johnson makes the first video call as a class. Children choose partners or small groups and then communication begins on an as needed basis. Mrs. Johnson collaborates with the teacher/s from the other class and shares lessons and/or reads stories during video calls as well.

Graphic organizers/PowerPoint/Draw. Graphic organizers and programs like PowerPoint/Draw are organizers to put information into visual formats. These programs help the user to record information in an organized manner. Children can create charts and graphs to record information for better understanding. They can then present information to others to show what they have learned. Teachers can utilize these programs for helping their lessons become more visual. They can organize facts and pictures into graphics to help connect information.

Technivity with a Graphic Organizer

2nd Grade

Mr. Lopez partners children during a themed study of the rainforest. Partner pairs create a graphic organizer to show what they are interested in researching about the rainforest. Graphics must include a topic, three questions children want to learn about the topic, and a project idea that will present the information learned upon completion of the research.

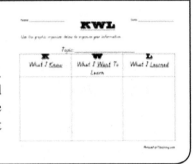

Windows Movie Maker. Windows Movie Maker is a program for the computer that allows the user to create movies and stories. Children can easily create movies and/or stories that represent content learned. Teachers can assist younger children by inserting illustrations into the program and having the students narrate their specific slides.

Technivity . . . Try It!

1st Grade

Ms. Dunn has her first-grade class work individually or in partner pairs to create a story. Children complete the story with illustrations using a draw tool or using paint or pencil paper methods. Ms. Dunn then inserts the illustrations into the Movie Maker program. Children narrate each slide of the story. They share with other classes or parents.

Approaches to using technology in the classroom encourage engagement and foster meaningful connections with information. They drive creative thinking and active participation. However, these approaches are only as good as the teacher who plans them. Teachers should think about technology as an intentional part of the classroom as they plan activities and information to present to children. "Technology does not drive purposeful learning; teachers' intentional instructional planning does" (Meaningful Technology Integration in Early Learning, 2008, p. 3).

Assessment Approaches to Technology

Teachers who utilize approaches to technology intentionally support developmentally appropriate real-world learning while facilitating purposeful activity. They encourage children to grow and learn to the fullest potential. As children interact and make advances technologically, it is essential for teachers to assess student outcomes. Technology can also help to create a very clear picture of the child and his/her abilities, which, in turn, drives instruction for the future. Because much of technology is most often used as a stage for other content knowledge, it is worth noting that assessment may sometimes need to be concerned with the physical ability of many young children to manipulate certain technology (rather than the actual knowledge he or she knows about the content area). This is much the same as a teacher who penalizes an assignment that is not neatly presented due to the lack of fine motor skills, even though the correct information may be there.

Authentic assessment aligns naturally with developmentally appropriate approaches to teaching with technology. Teachers must ensure that they are meeting standards and are teaching what is expected developmentally for the age, individuality, and culture of each child. According to Hewitt and Jenkins (2012), authentic assessment allows teachers to understand what is happening in the classroom while analyzing their own teaching style and approach to learning. Teachers become participants in the process of assessing and collecting important information that guides their teaching. The results obtained through authentic assessment can assist in "planning curriculum, making thematic unit decisions, selecting instructional strategies, partnering, or grouping students for projects or centers" (p. 13). One prime use of technology for teachers would be in creating individual portfolios. Digital portfolios for each child can be stored for quick accessibility and can include both student work and videos to help show growth or difficulties throughout the year.

Many states have standards and competencies set out for various levels of children. In the state of Texas, for example, the Texas Essential Knowledge and Skills (2013) require that teachers address children's technologically skills. It is suggested that children ages 5–8: understand basic knowledge and skills; communication and collaboration; research and information fluency; critical thinking, problem solving and decision making digital citizenship; and technology operations and concepts. Because the NAEYC (2012) set guidelines for technology that are rooted in developmentally appropriate practice, their position statement on technology reflects the importance of intentional teaching to benefit young children's development through the use of technology. A spiral curriculum ensures that teachers begin at the correct level and that these knowledge and skills increase appropriately in difficulty with age and/or development each year. Copple and Bredekamp (2009) state that for children who are in preschool through the primary grades, teachers should "make thoughtful use of computers and other technology in the classroom . . . (pp. 174, 242, 315). See Chapter 9 in this book for further information on integrating technology standards for teachers.

Observational, Authentic Assessments

Observational, authentic assessments are performance-based assessments that focus on what children know about the skills and activities being under consideration. They allow the teacher to assess student performance and measure student outcomes using developmentally appropriate methods. There are several observational, authentic assessments that are useful and support intentional outcomes when assessing the use of technology to enhance student performance.

There are a few apps available to assist teachers in assessing students. However, this area still has much room to grow. However, one such app is Confer. It is an app that can help the teacher create groups of students and take notes about them directly on an iPhone or iPad. Another app that has note taking capabilities is Teacher Pal. It facilitates taking roll, can take notes on behaviors, and can add notes about students. It is available for the iPhone or iPad in addition to the Android platform.

Anecdotal record. Anecdotal records are notes or anecdotes taken of actual activities and/or events that are taking place in the classroom. The content of anecdotal records can be about individual students or small group of students and tell a story about the students involved. Anecdotal records should reflect facts about the activity being observed. An anecdotal record may be taken on an event that lasts a short time or up to several minutes (see Figure 5.1 on the following page).

When writing an anecdotal record, a teacher should follow these simple steps:

- Describe the setting and time.
- Tell the names of the student's being observed.
- Write exactly what happened or is happening—use quotes when possible. Avoid judgments when writing the observation. Save these thoughts for the "comments" section.

Checklists. A checklist is a simple list of skills or items that the teacher creates to ensure children have accomplished particular skills. Teachers can observe children involved in technology use and simply check off the skills they have accomplished. A comment section can be added to the checklist for teachers to write particular information observed (see Figure 5.2 on the lower part of the following page).

Anecdotal Recording Form
Observer:
Child/ren Observed/Time:
Description of Observation:
Notes/Comments:

Figure 5.1   Anecdotal recording form.

When creating a checklist follow these simple steps:

- Determine the skill(s) to assess.
- Create a chart with child(ren)'s names.
- Create columns with dates/comment space for using checklist several times.
- Create a key for tracking assessment results.

The teacher can easily create cells for any skill that he or she wants to note with this type of technology.

	KEY		
	/ = skill visible needs more practice		
	* = skill accomplished skill first time		
	^ = skill not visible		
Child:			
Skill	**Date/Comment**	**Date/Comment**	**Date/Comment**
Child:			
Skill	**Date/Comment**	**Date/Comment**	**Date/Comment**
Child:			
Skill	**Date/Comment**	**Date/Comment**	**Date/Comment**

Figure 5.2   Checklist of technology skills.

Skill Assessed	3	2	1	Total:
Publish product using different media collaboratively	Uses at least 3 different media in product	Uses at least 2 different media in product	Uses at least 1 different media in product	
Select and use font attributes, color, white space, graphics for multiple communication media	Uses all of those listed for multiple communication media in product	Uses at least 2 of those listed for multiple communication media in product	Uses at least 1 of those listed for multiple communication media in product	
Collaborate with partner/s through personal learning communities	Collaborates with partner through personal learning community/ies 3 or more times.	Collaborates with partner through personal learning community/ies 2 times.	Collaborates with partner through personal learning community/ies at least 1 time.	
			Total Score:	

Figure 5.3   Rubric for Technology Application.

Scored Authentic Assessment

Analytic rubric. An analytic rubric is set of guidelines with specific criteria that allows the teacher to assign grades to projects or activities. It works well in grade levels where performance is rated through a grading system. It can be given to children prior to beginning an activity or project so that they will also know the expectation(s) for scoring and can better match their efforts to those as they are working. Analytic rubrics contain specific descriptors that define what to look for at each level of performance. Indicators are given to let the child and the assessor know what to look for in the work (see Figure 5.3 based upon third-grade Texas essential element objectives).

When creating an analytic rubric follow these simple steps:

- Determine the skill(s) to assess.
- Determine how much the assignment is worth in points. This varies by assignment. The figure above shows a rubric with points ranging from 1 to 3. The total score for this rubric is 9 points.
- Create criteria to meet each point value chosen. Let 3 be the greatest and 1 be the least.
- Create a grid/chart with the points and criteria that describe each point value.

When used appropriately, observational, authentic assessment takes into account all developmental levels and considers the needs of each individual child in the classroom. Assessing students should focus on information that allows teachers to make informed decisions about future curriculum while following developmentally appropriate guidelines. As children learn new technologies, they will progress at different paces; however, all children should make progress. Teachers must be well equipped with appropriate knowledge about how children grow and learn cognitively, physically, and socially. They must understand new technological advances and be cognizant of the fact that each child will assimilate new information at different rates. Most, importantly teachers must be well versed in state mandates and new advances in technology; they must be tech-savvy.

Be a Tech-Savvy Teacher

A "Tech-Savvy Teacher" always keeps 3 Ps in mind when teaching: Prepare, Practice, and Perform.

Prepare *in order to stay current and informed* as a tech-savvy teacher. It is imperative to be cognizant about new advances in technology and try out new things in the classroom. Children are often well informed when it comes to the latest and most exciting new technology. Teachers should encourage children to share with others and "teach the teacher." What better way to promote *"technivity"* than to have the child as the teacher! Other important information to keep in mind:

racorn/Shutterstock, Inc.

- Choose open-ended technology that offers children a chance to interact not only with the programs but with each other.
- Don't be afraid of technological advances.

Remember, the more teachers stay current in technological advances, the better prepared they are to assist children in their learning.

Practice *new technology often* to encourage children to interact and collaborate on building knowledge through interactions. Setting up activities and projects that promote collaboration among groups of children/partners or collaborative groups of four to six students will be of great benefit to children to keep working and to the teacher as children assist each other for "how to . . ." rather than calling on the teacher every time. Children working in these small collaborative partnerships groups often generate new ideas and work well above their developmental levels as they discuss and problem solve to inform their peers.

Teachers must practice new technology as much as possible. Even though it is sometimes intimidating to try new things, they must not let their own inhibitions limit what they can do in the classroom. By practicing what they don't know, it will help them to learn it and improve their skills. Practicing with children will help to perfect it, always keeping in mind that all technology choices should have the child at the forefront.

Perform *well with technology.* Once teachers are comfortable with new technology, they can bring about intended learning outcomes in the classroom by using various approaches to technology. Moreover, teachers can connect technology experiences with state-mandated guidelines to ensure well rounded exploration.

As mentioned, states establish guidelines for children to experience in technology. The NAEYC is working to ensure that those states involved in the new Common Core national standards adhere to the tenets of DAP, but they suggest that teachers may need additional training and appropriate tools (NAEYC, 2012). They also suggest that ongoing learning opportunities be made available to teachers in addition to appropriate curriculum materials. All of these will aid in teachers performing their best with technology to optimize the knowledge and skills of young learners. Each of these concepts is divided into specific skills that are appropriate for each grade level. Teachers are responsible for providing experiences that enhance children's growth and development with technology on a daily basis and can easily integrate these concepts into lessons that allow children to practice skills through hands-on applications. The NAEYC is working on ensuring that those states involved in the new Common Core national standards adhere to the tenets of DAP.

Teachers should make a point to perform with technology daily. Even simple tasks such as e-mail, note taking, or reading stories for fun can generate learning authentically. Whatever the technological task, teachers should perform it well and often.

Final Thoughts

Classroom teachers must meet the needs of all learners by making sure to utilize various teaching styles with technology. They must think about what's best for their children and plan accordingly. Grouping children encourages use of varied learning styles. For example, teachers pair visual learners with auditory and kinesthetic learners. When children in groups begin to discuss, clarify ideas, and evaluate others' ideas, they use higher-level thinking skills (Clifford, 2012). Gardner (1983) suggests that children have many diverse abilities that focus on multiple ways of learning. By focusing on relevant technological activities, teachers can ensure that children will make use of these diverse abilities and connect learning to the real world.

As an early childhood classroom teacher, assigning projects and activities for students to complete on their own should encourage challenges for children and develop their problem solving skills. Teachers must:

- be able and willing to facilitate new technology for children.
- be comfortable and well versed with the technology chosen.

Children who are provided technology that supports their individual styles of learning and levels of knowledge and skills will make progress in all areas of development (Gardner, 1999).

There is much thought that goes into technology learning for young children. Teachers who use high impact experiences while integrating technology facilitate appropriate activities and make intentional decisions about developmentally (and individually) appropriate approaches for children. They also consider the proper environment and equipment to support the growth and learning of new skills that foster higher-level thinking and a positive foundation for the years ahead of technology use that children will need in today's world.

Helpful Sites for Tech-Savvy Teachers

Early Childhood Teacher:
http://www.earlychildhoodteacher.org/blog/ece-technology-10-trending-tools-for-teachers

Using Technology in the Early Childhood Classroom:
http://teacher.scholastic.com/professional/bruceperry/using_technology.htm

Cool Culture:
www.coolculture.org

PBS Kids:
http://pbskids.org

Early Childhood:
http://www.earlychildhood.com

Gayles's Preschool Rainbow:
http://www.preschoolrainbow.org

The Activity Idea Place:
http://www.longman.com/young_learners/teachers/teaching_tips_pronunciation.htm

---

References

Anderson, C. A., Gentile, D. A., & Buckley, K. E. (2007). *Violent video game effects on children and adolescents: Theory, research, and public policy.* New York: Oxford Press.

Clifford, M. (2012). Facilitating collaborative learning: 20 things you need to know from the pros. Retrieved from www.opencolleges.edu.au/informed/features/facilitating-collaborative-learning-20-things-you-need-to-know-from-the-pros/

Copple, C., & Bredekamp, S. (Eds.). (2009). *Developmentally appropriate practice in early childhood programs serving children from birth through age 8* (3rd ed.). Washington, DC: NAEYC.

Dubow, E. F., Huesmann, L. R., & Greenwood, D. (2007). Media and youth socialization. In J. E. Grusec & P. D. Hastings (Eds.), *Handbook of socialization* (pp. 404–430). New York: Guilford Press.

Gardner, H. (1983). *Frames of mind: The theory of multiple intelligences.* New York: Basic Books.

Gardner, H. (1999). *The disciplined mind: Beyond facts and standardized tests, The K-12 education that every child deserves.* New York: Simon and Schuster.

Gutnick, A., Robb, M. B., Takeuchi, L., & Kotler, J. (2011). *Always connected: The new digital media habits of young children.* New York: The Joan Ganz Cooney Center at Sesame Workshop.

Hastings, E. C., Karas, T. L., Winsler, A. Way, E., Madigan, A., Tyler, S. (2009). Young children's video/computer game use: Relations with school performance and behavior. *Issues in Mental Health Nursing, 30*(10): 638–649.

Hewitt, A., & Jenkins, K. (2012). Assessment 101: Attitudes and approaches for effective and authentic assessment. *Early Years, 33*(2), 10–14.

Meaningful Technology Integration in Early Learning. (2008). Beyond the journal. Young children on the web. Retrieved from https://www.naeyc.org/files/yc/file/200809/OnOurMinds.pdf

National Association for the Education of Young Children (2009). *DAP Position Statement.* Retrieved from http://www.naeyc.org/files/naeyc/file/positions/PSDAP.pdf

National Association for the Education of Young Children. (2012). The Common Core State Standards: Caution and opportunity for early childhood education. Retrieved from www.naeyc.org/files/naeyc/11_CommonCore1_2A_rv2.pdf

National Association for the Education of Young Children and the Fred Rogers Center for Early Learning and Children's Media at Saint Vincent College. (2012). Technology and interactive media as tools in early childhood programs serving children from birth through age 8. Retrieved from http://www.naeyc.org/files/naeyc/file/positions/PS_technology_WEB2.pdf

Penuel, W. R., Pasnik, S., Bates, L., Townsend, E., Gallagher, L. P., Llorente, C., & Hupert, N. (2009). *Preschool teachers can use a media-rich curriculum to prepare low-income children for school success: Results of a randomized controlled trial.* New York and Menlo Park, CA: Education Development Center, Inc., and SRI International.

Rideout, V., Foehr, U. G., & Roberts, D. (2010). Generation M2 Media in the lives of 8-18-year-olds: A Kaiser Family Foundation Study. Retrieved from (http://kaiserfamilyfoundation.files.wordpress.com/2013/04/8010.pdf)

Rideout, V. (2011). *Zero to eight: Children's media use in America.* San Francisco, CA: Commonsense Media.

Texas Essential Knowledge and Skills (TEKS). (2013). Texas Education Agency. Retrieved from www.tea.state.tx.us

Wadley, A. (1974). *Just playing.* A narrative poem. First published in advertisement/enrollment brochure for Children's World Inc. Retrieved from http://www.cityofvista.com/departments/parks/documents/JustPlayingPoem.pdf

Zimmerman, F. J. (2008). *Children's media use and sleep problems: Issues and unanswered questions. Research brief.* Henry J. Kaiser Family Foundation. Retrieved from http://kff.org/other/issue-brief/childrens-media-use-and-sleep-problems-issues

Chapter 6

Technology and Special Education

Bernardo Pohl, John Kelly, and Katrina Borders
University of Houston-Downtown

Meet Stephen

Mrs. Wang is amazed at how much academic progress Stephen is achieving now in her class. He is not only making passing grades for her, but he is excelling and passing all of his classes with excellent marks. For the first time, he is being considered for honor classes for next year, and this year, he had even made the honor roll twice. This is a considerable difference from two years ago, when Stephen was failing every class and was considering dropping out of school for home-schooling and private tutoring—that is, until he arrived at Oak Park Senior High School.

Stephen, a tenth grader, was born with mild cerebral palsy affecting his motor skills. His disability affects his writing, as he writes very slowly, and this makes it difficult for him to keep up with the fast pace of the regular classroom. He has also been diagnosed with a learning disability in writing and reading comprehension. The introduction of technology as part of his accommodations helps him tremendously. He uses a laptop with word processing, text-to-speech software, and electronic textbooks, which help him to be at the same level with the rest of the class. The introduction of technology in Stephen's accommodations has made a huge difference in his life. Today, he uses the word processor to take notes in the class, allowing him to keep pace with the teacher's lecture and concentrate on the content rather than his handwriting. The text-to-speech software helps him tremendously in his reading and oral testing. The word processor also aids his writing skills, as he continues to struggle with spelling and grammar usage.

Lisa F. Young/Shutterstock, Inc.

Technology has made a world of difference in Stephen's life and in his education. Technology also has made a difference for his teachers. They no longer have to find the time for orally reading the materials to him or for testing him orally. They can more easily grade his work without having to decipher his writing or mark numerous grammar errors. Technology has made the educational process a "win/win" situation for all.

Objectives

After reading this chapter, you should be able to:

1. Understand what assistive technology (AT) is.
2. Explore the application of assistive and productive technology in the classroom available to disabled students.

Introduction

The education of students with special needs is wide, and it includes students with a variety of physical and mental disabilities *and* those with special gifts and talents (Valentine, 2007). This chapter addresses the primary technology tools used to enhance the education for this population of students.

In assisting those with special needs, teachers should understand the difference among *impairment, disability,* and *handicapped.* In the past, as stated by Roblyer and Doering (2010), these words have been used synonymously; however, a clear distinction needs to be made so that professionals who provide special services have a clear understanding when they are implementing and using technology with their students with special needs.

According to Roblyer and Doering (2010), **impairment** is an abnormality, which results in the absence of a physical or psychological function. This can occur at birth (congenital) or acquired later in life (accident or disease). A **disability** is a limitation caused by an impairment, which limits a human activity in a normal environment (moving, communicating, hearing, and manipulating) (Wise, 2012). A **handicap** is when there is an inability to perform a role due an impairment or disability (Elbro, 2014). It is important for those individuals and professionals who provide special need services to not make preliminary assumptions about individuals with impairments, disabilities, and handicaps. Individuals with special needs do not necessarily have limitations in performing a task and/or a lack of quality of life (Abberley, 1987; Baglieri & Knopf, 2004; Friend & Bursuck, 2015). Moreover, it is imperative to understand that a handicap is not what defines a human being (Pohl, 2013). Teachers must, however, see one of their roles as that of a "matchmaker" with the right technology to increase a student's chances of reaching his/her full potential in school.

In the United States, federal law ("PL 94-142: Education for All Handicapped Children Act," 1975) recognizes several types of disabilities. This law also entitles those who are affected by one or more of the listed disabilities to special services in a number of ways, including technology. Almost everyone is likely to know somebody whose life has been altered by one of these disabilities in some form: autism, visual/hearing impairment, emotionally disturbed, developmental delay, intellectually disability, orthopedic impairment, other health impairments (OHI), speech/language impairment, traumatically brain injury, and/or multiple disabilities. To begin to address these types of needs, the teacher first needs to understand the range of the most common categories of disabilities in the classroom: (1) physical [with use of mobility equipment or dealing with muscular dystrophy, Lou Gehrig's disease, sclerosis, or others]; (2) sensory [visual or hearing]; (3) cognitive [many levels of intelligence, memory, self-expression, information processing, and others]; (4) psychiatric [social phobias to bipolar or other personality disorders]; (5) health-related [chronic conditions such as diabetes, epilepsy, cancer, and others].

In recent years, the ongoing developments in technology have revolutionized the field of special education. The development of "touchscreen" computers and recent advancements in software and adaptive technology have provided the special education and regular classroom teacher with a plethora of options in assisting students who are differently. For example, software like MS PowerPoint, MS Word, and Prezi allows teachers and students (such as Stephen) to deal with the difficulty of taking notes and writing in class, thus allowing students to concentrate on the content of the class rather than the barriers to academics. The digitization of books and other written materials has made it considerably easier for students to tackle the difficulty of reading and understanding text. For example, a student with mild vision impairment who has a reading assignment in his/her textbook will find that all major publishing houses provide audio versions of textbooks with extra digital material. In the age of tablets, laptops, and smartphones, "text-to-speech" software is readily available and free of charge (or for minimal costs) for the student with special needs to use. Notably, advances in communication and technology allow teachers and students to move away from the impediments of the disability to learning. These are just a few of the modern-day tools for students in special needs situations. Every teacher and student should expect continuous developments to be on the horizon, so the commitment to stay "on the cutting edge" of adapting technology for students like Stephen must be made by teachers who are, in turn, assisted by their school's and/or district's special education team and technology specialists.

IDEA (The Individual with Disabilities Education Act), which was enacted in 1990 by Congress, defines assistive technology (AT) as any device that helps the individual access an environment independently (Roblyer & Doering, 2010), restores loss capacities (Turnbull, Turnbull, Whemeyer, & Shogren, 2013), and/or maintains or improves functional capabilities (Friend & Bursuck, 2015). The proper distribution and availability of AT is secured by the TECH ACT of 1988 (the Technology Related Assistance Amendment to IDEA) (Turnbull et al., 2013), which ensures the proper allocation of funds. This guarantees that the access of AT to special need students is free of charge. In this chapter, we discuss the hardware and software that is more commonly available to students with special needs to access the curriculum, examine applications, and see lesson samples and other curricular ideas.

The Least Restrictive Environment

Teachers in all grade levels will have students with special needs at some point in their careers. The Least Restrictive Environment (LRE) ruling requires that a student with special needs be placed in a regular classroom (rather than a separate/self-contained special education room) to the most extent possible. Placement is determined by an Admissions, Review, and Dismissal (ARD) (or IEP) Committee and the student's Individualized Educational Program (IEP) (Heward, 2013). This committee ensures the proper placement and services that the student with special needs will receive. This committee also determines what type of technology will best benefit each individual student, which must then be provided by the district at no cost to the parents. The regular classroom teacher will be a part of this committee, so it is his or her job and moral commitment to have knowledge of technology tools (as guided by the special education team) and, if selected for the student, to use them with the student in his/her classroom once available. It is essential that all teachers, general or special education, are very knowledgeable about the procedures of special education (Friend & Bursuck, 2015; Turnbull et al., 2013). It is also vital that they know the basic terminology used in special education.

Terminology

- **Individual with Disability Education Act (IDEA) (October 30, 1990):** A federal law which regulates how states and public agencies provide special education and related services to children with disabilities. It addresses the educational needs of children with disability from age 3 to 18 /21 in cases that involve any of the 14 identified disabilities.
- **Assistive technology (AT):** Any type of equipment or device, commercialized or freely acquired, which helps to improve access and functionality of individuals with disabilities.
- **Free and Appropriate Public Education (FAPE):** This part of Public Law 94-142 law guarantees those who are identified as disabled (from ages 3 to 22) access to a public education paid for by the district by requiring proper and accessible services, education that takes place with nondisabled students to the maximum extent possible, the right to nondiscriminatory evaluation, and the establishment of due process.
- **Less-Restrictive-Environment (LRE):** The right of a student with a disability to access the regular curriculum and attend classes with nondisabled students to the maximum extent possible.

- **Individualized Education Plan (IEP):** A document that describes the educational goals, objectives, and services for an identified student for the academic year determined by relevant professionals and parents (ARD or IEP Committee/Team).
- **No-Tech Solution:** Procedures and services that do not require the need for equipment.
- **Low-Tech equipment**: Inexpensive and non-sophisticated devices and equipment such as hard copies of notes, pencil grips, Velcro fasteners, and so forth.
- **Mid-tech equipment:** Sophisticated mechanical devices such as hydraulic lifts and wheelchairs.
- **High-tech equipment:** Devices or support that requires specialized and sophisticated equipment such as a computer, electronic equipment, and software. Often, it may require specialized training and support.
- **Response to Intervention (RTI):** A current approach to struggling students that emphasizes helping them early on prior to their identification as having a learning disability and supporting them with up to three tiers of quality, monitored interventions.
- **Differentiated Instruction:** Instructional approaches used to reach students with different learning styles, abilities to absorb information, and ways to express learned information.

Photographee.eu/Shutterstock, Inc.

Determining the Needs

It is highly unlikely that Mrs. Wang was able to assist Stephen with his academic success without any assistance and planning. Preparation by Stephen's ARD (or IEP) team and regular classroom teacher was required in order to determine what worked best for him inside the classroom. It is clear that Stephen's success required Mrs. Wang to develop a plan of action, which she could do by phases:

1. Phase 1: Assess the student's need(s).
2. Phase 2: Survey the environment and the students' physical mobility.
3. Phase 3: Assess AT available.
4. Phase 4: Determine learning outcome and objectives.
5. Phase 5: Prepare instructional setting.
6. Phase 6: Develop a response to intervention plan/instructional plan

Stephen's accommodations were not selected at random; the process required a team to assess his needs and the expectations for each change in his IEP that has finally led to success. Mrs. Wang started her assessment of Stephen's need by surveying his physical needs (see Table 6.1): vision, hearing, and motor. By doing this, not only did she know what was needed, but she also was able to discover what her classroom had and what the room was missing: Does she need a desk for wheelchairs? Does her classroom have motion sensitive switches? Is there a computer in the classroom with the proper software? These types of questions can be answered by completing this survey.

AT not only helps students with special needs to access the curriculum, it also helps the individual access the environment (Friend & Bursuck, 2015; Haq & Elhoweris, 2013). Stephen, for example, has mild cerebral palsy, and he does have some difficulty accessing the environment. Teachers do have an array of technology available that will help students move better within an environment. From motion sensors for lighting to magnetic keys, individual free access to the environment in schools could be (but, too often, has not been) updated to help students take advantage of all that is available to help them in their classroom and school. Table 6.2 shows some of the assistive and smart technology used for free access:

wavebreakmedia/Shutterstock, Inc.

Table 6.1 Technology checklist

Environmental survey related to physical needs identified in the student's IEP. **Directions:** Check proposed devices/tools that will enhance the student's learning outcomes.		Grading Cycle:_____ Student Name: _____ Student ID:_____ Subject:_____ HR Teacher:_____	
Vision	√	**Seating and Positioning**	√
Functions independently with standard classroom tools and layout		Functions independently with standard classroom tools and layout	
May benefit from the use of assistive technology in this area:		*May benefit from the use of assistive technology in this area:*	
Magnifier (Hand-held)/digital camera		Nonslip surface on chair	
Large print books		Bolster, cushion, foot blocks	
Antiglare filters		Adjustable tables, desks, equipment mounts, etc.	
CCTV (Closed Circuit Television)		Supports, restraints	
Screen magnifier		Adapted/alternate chair	
Screen magnification software		Custom fitted wheelchair	
Screen color contrast		Side layer	
Screen reader/text reader		Stander	
Braille materials/translation		Pressure monitors	
Enlarged or Braille/tactile labels for keyboard		Other:	
Alternate and assisted keyboard/enlarged keys			
Braille keyboard and/or note taker			
Monitor mounts (placement height for wheelchairs, etc.)			
Motion sensors			
Other:			
Hearing	√	**Mobility**	√
Functions independently with standard classroom tools and layout		Functions independently with standard classroom tools and layout	
May benefit from the use of assistive technology in this area:		*May benefit from the use of assistive technology in this area:*	
Pen and paper, email or Tweet reminders		Walker	
Computer/Portable word processor or tablet		Grab bars and rails	
Signaling device		Manual wheelchair, tray, parts	
Closed captioning		Powered wheelchair	
Real time captioning		Powered scooter	
Computer aided note-taking		Powered mobility toy	
Flash alert signal on computer		Moisture guards	
Personal amplification system/hearing aid		Adjustable wands, head pointers	
FM or Loop system*		Floor mounted grab bars in restroom with alert button	
Infrared system			
Other:		Other:	
*Frequency/system used in public settings to reduce background noise by delivering sound straight from the source to the participant's ear/head set.			

Table 6.2   Assistive and smart tools for operating within the environment

Assistive Customized Technology
• Loop induction amplifiers • Audible reminder devices • Keyless doors with magnetic cards • Video/voiced recognize entry system • Power assisted doors • Infrared sensors for sinks, soap dispensers, towels, and toilets in washrooms; roll under sinks; bars • Motion sensor light switches
Smart Technology
• Automatic switches (and those students can use by other means than touch [puffing, squeezing, etc.) • Automatic alerts systems for students who leave the classroom without permission • Turn off automatic switches • Open door alarms • Electronic pointers based on eye movement/brainwaves • Joysticks • Trackballs (movable ball on top)

It is important for students to be able to freely access an environment; however, it is equally important for students to have equal access to the curriculum. There is ample hardware and software that helps to ensure that students can properly perform in the classroom. From computers to scanners to spell-checkers to digital worksheets, this equipment can aid a student's productivity in the classroom. It is undeniable that Stephen's success was ensured by the proper access to the proper technology. However, careful planning and consideration went into the proper selection of the resources he needed to function in the classroom, and this will remain a continuous process of assessing and updating throughout his schooling to find the best matches. The availability of these products is extensive. Next, we will discuss the most commonly available technology (hardware and software) in the following sections.

Magnetic security lock for doors with two indicators and magnetic card key.

Hardware and Software

Today, the special education teacher and/or regular classroom teacher with mainstreamed students must consider the incredible availability of hardware for the classroom. The time has passed when students with special needs and their teachers fail to overcome many of the physical barriers imposed by a disability. Hugh Herr, an MIT professor who has designed and wears two "bionic legs" (due to a mountain climbing incident, yet remains a climber) and believes that there is no such thing such as a disability but feels, instead, that technology has just not caught up for everyone yet (Strickland, 2014). As teachers of students with special needs, keeping up with the latest technology can provide that "mountain climbing experience" academically when they provide students with better tools. Modern classrooms are equipped with electronic white boards, sound systems, digital projectors, headphones, laptops, and much more, allowing the student who is differently abled to eliminate many of the challenges created by a disability and focus on their content and lessons. From the simple acts of printing up hard-copies of notes to using headphones and speech-to-text software to read books, technology has revolutionized today's education classroom for students with special needs.

Of all tools available, the computer is the most fundamental and instrumental piece of technology in the classroom, perhaps making it the most valuable piece of hardware available to teachers of and students with special needs. Teachers benefit from this technology in many ways. The computer serves as a resource for lesson planning, research, and delivery of instruction for special needs. Lessons that have required extensive planning, materials, and team coordination can be completed with a click of a mouse because many options and ideas can be easily accessed from the Internet. The hardware works together with software such as MS PowerPoint to, for example, allow teachers to digitize notes, store them in a Web site, and then have students access them from virtually anywhere. Paired with specialized keyboards, there are touchscreen monitors, tablets, and other specialized equipment that give students many options. With some of the combinations above, the need for always providing a printed-out copy or having the student struggle with taking notes is eliminated. The teacher and the student can concentrate on the actual instruction. From delivering videos, connecting to the Internet, providing notes, drawing/painting, calculating, and creating music, the computer is often the key that opens new doors to students with special challenges. Today, for example, a high school student with special challenges can utilize CAD (computer-aided design) to create floor plans in a drafting class with the guidance of a laser pointer. Young students no longer need the help of an assistant to solve a 500 pieces puzzle. All of these and more can be done with a touchscreen monitor or with a mouse. Students with short-term memory can be reminded of assignments with a Tweet or a text message. Coupled with the right software and hardware, such as MS Office and microphones, the computer can help the teacher deliver instruction in a far more efficient manner.

It is hard to ignore what technology and hardware can do today for the student with reading comprehension, hearing/visual impairment, or communication problems. Microphones, headphones, speakers, and computers make an excellent team when paired with text-to-speech or speech-to-text software. Cassette tapes and analog recording have been replaced with digital recording, saving time and resources for teachers and students. As noted, districts and schools no longer have to spend countless hours recording a textbook. Teachers and students can use scanners and software to scan and digitally read a desired section of the book. A student with mild vision impairment can take a picture of the page in the book and have the page read to him or her through a smartphone, and a student needing oral testing administration can have a test be read at his or her own pace with the help of a tablet or laptop. Students with reading comprehension or visual impairment can use text-to-speech software such as JAWS®Screen Reader or optical character recognition (ORC) software to help them read and understand the text. Almost everyone is familiar with the famous scientist Stephen Hawking who cannot speak but still gives lectures. His computer generates his words orally via an infrared sensor, and a blink-switch on his glasses interfaces with his computer to use a voice synthesizer (text-to-speech/ TTS). This technology also allows him to access other computer tools such as emails and the Internet. These types of communication tools may become more applicable for students with aphasia or autism in the future. Table 6.3 shows some examples of helpful hardware available for teachers to use with different disabilities:

Table 6.3 Helpful AT hardware for accessing content and curriculum

Visual Disability	Auditory Disability
Screen magnifier Screen reader Speech recognition Speech synthesizer Large print Refreshable one-line Braille	Telecommunication Devices for the Deaf (TDD) Closed captioning Windows XP ShowSounds Computer sound light signalers
Cognitive Disability	**Motor Disability**
Reading tools Speaking text Word scanners Screen readers Grammar/spell checkers Automatic reminders	Pointing devices SIP devices Trackballs On-screen keyboards Keyboard enhancers/delayers Automatic key text

Software

The real value for teachers in AT lies in the endless availability of software, which, coupled with the power of the Internet, allows students and teachers to explore possibilities never imagined before. For example, MS Office, with its major components like Word, Excel, and PowerPoint, has become an indispensable tool for instruction and classroom work. MS PowerPoint gives teachers the seamless possibility of organizing instruction and delivering materials in ways that are particularly helpful to students with special needs. For instance, teachers using PowerPoint can "voice over" slides so that students can listen to presentations multiple times. Motivation for students is greater and attention is better during presentations with pictures, recordings, and embedded film clips. Research does show that students who have access to technology are more engaged in the classroom (Offen, 2013).

Technology is always changing and improving. Fortunately, for all of us, technology has also become more accessible than ever before, significantly enhancing the quality of life of the disabled. For example, the portability of tablets and laptops along with MS Word allows the student with handwriting difficulties to comfortably take notes and keep pace with the rest of the class so that the student can concentrate on the lesson instead of the actual and (often torturous) physical act of writing. Programs such as these allow considerable manipulation of content, freeing teachers and students from the worries of dealing the physical limitation(s) of a disability.

Software such as Microsoft's Windows Movie Maker or Paint, iPaint for Macs, or GarageBand, and other software are revolutionizing the classroom, and they should not go unnoticed by those who are educating students with special needs as alternative forms of assessment. Students can edit a movie or create a picture collage documentary or digital painting; these software programs can definitely help the student with challenges achieve his or her goals. Furthermore, as the principle dictum for IDEA is the least restrictive environment (LRE), teachers can use learning management systems (LMS) such as Edmodo and Blackboard to create chat rooms and blogs, allowing students to be fully integrated in the social aspect of the classroom. The major benefit of using a LMS is that teachers can maintain a controlled and safe environment (Scott, 2012). As social and independent skills are essential components of the IEP, social virtual spaces will become essential tools for the teacher.

It is undeniable that software has enhanced the learning experience of students because of its many classroom advantages. However, a teacher must weigh carefully the students' needs with what type of software he or she will use. Different software have different functions. Word processors are not simply tools used for writing. For example, a word processor's editing capabilities can help with organizational skills.

Word prediction programs in the market let users select a desired word from an on-screen window. These types of programs predict words from the first few typed letters. The word can then be selected from the list and inserted into the text by entering a number, clicking the mouse, or other means. Word prediction programs help support literacy, increase written productivity and accuracy, and increase vocabulary skills through word prompting. SoothSayer Word Prediction manufactured by Applied Human Factors is an example of a keyboard filter that helps with word prediction.

If a school budget does not permit expensive systems, the keyboard filters of MS Word also include several typing aids such as word prediction and add-on spelling checkers. These features can be used to reduce the number of keystrokes and make writing easier for special populations. As an example, imagine one must type the upper-case letter "V." Keyboard filters enable users to quickly access the letters they need and to avoid inadvertently selecting wrong key. Software that assists with word prediction and visual organization can assist with reading comprehension, and scanning software can help a student spell and edit his or her work. Table 6.4 shows how some software can assist the student with some basic skills.

A special type of software is operating systems (OS), which is an essential component of the system software in a computer system. Application programs such as MS Office usually require an operating system to function. OS manages computer hardware and software resources and provides common services for computer programs. In education, Microsoft Windows and Apple MAC OS are commonly known, followed by Google Chromium OS.

Table 6.4 Software that can be used as AT

Software	Spelling	Writing	Editing	Reading Comprehension	Organizational Skills
Word Processing	X	X	X		X
Talking text	X	X	X		X
Word prediction	X	X	X	X	X
Scanning software	X		X	X	X
ORC Software	X		X	X	
Visual Organizer		X	X		X
Spell Checker	X	X	X	X	
Electronic Highlighters		X	X	X	X

The Windows Control Panel is a part of the Windows OS graphical user interface which allows users to change accessibility options and control user accounts. Users can visit the "Ease of Access Center" to change and test keyboard settings, including the cursor blink rate and key repeat rate, change mouse settings, start on-screen keyboards, set up alternatives for sounds, and other functions. Once the setup is confirmed through the "Ease of Access Center" on the OS, all software applications take the instructions and function consistently. The Mac OS does have a control panel. However, most general system configuration can be done through the System Preferences within the Apple menu on the left corner of the screen.

Data inputs are usually accomplished through computer keyboards. The accessibility resources of most operating systems explain the ways to make keyboards quick and convenient methods for using keyboard shortcuts. Another way to customize users' experience is through keyboard settings. For students who frequently mistype due to paralysis or have difficulty releasing a key once it is depressed, Filter Keys can be turned on so that Windows ignores when students press the same key rapidly or when they press keys for several seconds unintentionally. For students who have difficulty to press complicated key combinations at the same time, such as the Ctrl+Alt+Del keys, Sticky Keys can be turned on so that students can press keys one at a time, and students who have a touch PC can type without an external keyboard.

Some software companies and Web sites are committed to building accessibility into products and to providing accessibility resources for educators and students alike (see Table 6.5). For instance, Microsoft Corporation's Accessibility in Education page provides resources for discussion blogs, a best practice video, a teacher training PowerPoint slideshow, and success stories for AT (Microsoft, 2014). Visitors can also download curriculum guides for educators written in both English and Spanish.

The Web

The information superhighway is one of the most powerful tools in a teacher's arsenal, and this should not be underestimated by teachers of students who are differently abled. The Internet offers a vast array of possibilities for teachers and their students. With the proper connection and a fair amount of access, teachers have a world of information about disabilities and ideas that may bring success to their students at their fingertips. One excellent example is the Web site LD Online (www.ldonline.org), which provides teachers with terms, expert advice, personal stories, and many more resources. Another site for teachers *and* students with learning disabilities is LD Pride Online (www.ldpride.net) with sections such as "Finding Your LD Pride" and

Table 6.5 Helpful Web sites AT

Web site	Disability	Description
Google Accessibility (www.google.com/accessibility)	Vision	Helps the visually impaired use Google's popular software such as Chrome, Android, Ebook, and Gmail
Blind Get Educated Blogspot (www.blindgeteducated.blogspot.com)	Vision	Provides an array of information for the visually impaired such as helping them to use the iPad or word processors.
National Center for Learning Disability (www.ncld.org)	Learning Disability	A rich Web site with a variety of information for the learning disabled; assists students with AT for dyslexia and dysgraphia
Beacon-Ridge (https://www.facebook.com/pages/Beacon-Ridge-School-Supplies/271882276159556)	Multiple	Assists in adapting low-tech AT

checklists for identifying various learning disabilities. Teachers can also explore virtual tours of museums, download songs to explore, analyze the latest pictures or other artifacts from the Smithsonian, and much more. With the Internet, the notion of LRE has a new meaning, as an entire classroom "can fly to Paris," tour the Louvre, and explore the countless treasures housed in this famed museum, as an example. This type of access to virtual fieldtrips can be of benefit to all children in a classroom, but, perhaps, even more so for students with special needs.

Despite the potential that the Internet offers, it does not come without certain drawbacks. A district's barriers to the Internet and determining the legitimacy of the information continue to be among the biggest concerns for teachers. For the most part, some districts have adopted an all-or-none policy, which has meant equal blocking of legitimate and illegitimate sites with Internet protection, or blocking barriers known as firewalls (depending on the district). This leaves teachers with very little choices as to what Web sites to use. Despite the great amount of irrelevant information on sites like YouTube or Wikipedia, teachers are often deprived from accessing legitimate information these Web sites have to offer. Teachers who do not have access to information at school should not ignore the possibilities of working at home to find out more information for their students, which could increase students' rates of academic success.

Technology in the Curriculum

As we have seen, the benefits of AT are vast, and teachers can effectively use technology to enhance the general learning of their students who are differently abled. Writing, reading, and mathematics are critical skills that all students must and should master as essential skills in their learning. In this section, we discuss different AT available to teachers in these three essential areas.

Writing

AT is designed to make hard, or seemingly impossible, tasks manageable. For students with disabilities, writing can often be the most difficult task of all. Since complications in writing are wide ranged and technology is evolving, finding the right AT device to incorporate into the student's accommodations can be time consuming. However, finding a fit can make a major difference to a student who is supported by special educational specialists. These specialists are more experienced with AT and other equipment, note taking, composition, productivity, and cognition. For example, special keyboards can enhance access for students with motor coordination problems, while text-to-speech programs assist those with visual impairments. Note-taking tools such as voice recording pens (electronic scribe pens) can help students record complete lectures and download them to a computer. Composition tools—such as word processors—can help the student with outlining, formatting, spell checking, and correct use of grammar and punctuation. Productivity tools such as proofreaders can assist the student in analyzing the text for style and appropriate sentence construction and can cross-check for plagiarism. A number of other tools are mentioned in Table 6.6.

Speech-recognition software allows users whose strengths lie in oral composition to dictate words and then capture them on the screen. In the end, technology is helping students acquire essential skills. The regular classroom teacher will, however, be expected to use it with the student—if it is identified as part of his or her IEP program. As a reminder, regular classroom teachers are supported by special education specialists who should know much more about AT and matching the correct AT to individual students.

Creative writing is an essential component that students should be encouraged to develop. In a language arts class, it is not uncommon for teachers to have students write stories by having a student in a small group start a story and, then, have others "Round Robin" to finish the story. This type of exercise motivates creativity and participation—if all are able. Several activities can assist the teacher in helping all his or her students develop their creative writing.

Ms. Morris is a creative writing teacher with upper-grade level students. One semester she begins a lesson on how to write a story. She begins by putting several desks into a circle (4–6 students works well). Students get a blank sheet of paper and a pencil on which they write their names on the back. All students start to write a story about any topic. Ms. Morris uses a timer and at the end of a short period (around a minute or less, but she uses her judgment, depending on the class), the students, then, must

pass their papers to the right. They continue the story started by the previous writer. The exercise continues until the paper ends up with the original author. This activity can bring excitement and liveliness into the classroom. However, the following year, Ms. Morris worries that her students with disabilities should not be deprived from participating in an exercise like this. When working with children with special needs, Ms. Morris modifies this lesson by incorporating technology (see Table 6.6). For example, she uses a computer lab set up to create stations within the room. Instead of passing papers, the students rotate from one station to the next. The computer keyboards are set with "typing helpers" and "modified mice" for two of her students.

This exercise finishes when the students are back at their original station. Then, she asks the students to read the story aloud. Her students with special needs are allowed to use speech software, when they have difficulty reading. This exercise has several variations, such as the beginning, middle, and end exercise, where a student starts a story, another writes the middle, and another finishes the story. AT can assist by involving all students in this activity.

Table 6.6 Writing solutions with AT

Low Tech	Mid-tech	High Tech
Modified pencils Templates Pre-written words Magnetic letters Big pen/pencils Printed graphic organizers Oversized ruled paper	Labeler Portable word processors	Text-to-speech software Oversized keyboard Word predicting software Accessible computers

Reading

Reading is one of the most essential skills that students must have. Research shows that children who fail to learn how to read by first grade will suffer academically later in life (Heward, 2013). For the most part, formal reading instruction tends to happen mostly in elementary schools during the most crucial developmental years. In the upper grades, instruction tends to focus on content, sometimes leaving an instructional gap for many students with disabilities who need more attention in developing crucial reading skills. AT for reading can help to greatly increase the quality of reading instruction for students in all grades and content areas. Text-to-speech technology helps students with difficulty pronouncing or decoding words to better understand a passage or text. For example, a student with good oral communication skills but who lacks the capacity for output (such as oral fluency or writing) can use presentation technology tools (e.g., Prezi or Voki) that can help him or her to share his or her ideas with the class. AT for reading can help students with reading speed, understanding, and comprehension.

Young children develop a better concept of the alphabet by knowing the sounds of the letter and how they are used. Phonetics becomes an important tool as children use familiar sounds to decode and learn new letters and words. Phonetics is only one aspect that new readers need to learn. Young children also must learn the semantic, syntactic, and pragmatic side of a language. The best time for learning the sound and proper use of letters and words is early in life. Students with problems decoding and analyzing the meaning of words will have a difficult time learning these skills (Heward, 2013). Furthermore, students with difficulty in handwriting will miss out on a very important component, which is to learn the printed aspect of word. The act of writing is crucial to learning the environmental component of word, which means the ability to use the word in the proper social setting. As children grow older, this helps them understand the order of words, when words are used, and where the proper placements of words occur (Friend & Bursuck, 2015). AT can help children with exceptionalities overcome these barriers with available technology (see Table 6.7). Word synthesizer software can help a student learn and understand the proper sounds of letters and words. Spellcheckers, the thesaurus, and other software can assist students with the proper writing and use of a word, and grammar checkers (*IF* students use it) can help students with or without special needs with proper construction of sentences and other grammar errors.

Research has proven that students learn best when they are active and engaged (McKenney & Voogt, 2012). For example, the teacher starts by introducing letters and words. The teacher asks the students what are letters and words that they may have seen before. Then, the teacher asks the student in which place the letters and words are more likely to appear: names, cereal boxes, games, cartoons, movies, or television shows. This is the perfect activity to spark children's curiosity and encourage them to ask questions. Using technology, the teacher can use the Internet with students who have reading comprehension and decoding challenges. For example, the teacher provides the student with a letter or word, and the student uses the Web to find where, when, and how these letters and words are used. Furthermore, the teacher can use a word synthesizer to help the student properly pronounce the word. In her class, Ms. Wang can use SpeechTRON or LingvoSoft to help Stephen understand the meaning and pronunciation of words. Software games can allow the student to rehearse the correct and incorrect use for letters and words. Electronic worksheets with word banks and fill-in-the-blank questions can replace the printed worksheet and can provide a manipulative (mouse or touchscreen) rather than constant writing.

Table 6.7   Reading solutions with AT

Low tech	Mid Tech	High Tech
Large prints Magnifying glasses Highlighted text Simple word texts Printed graphic organizers Printed word-to-pictures examples	Recorded text Hand-held word processors	Talking software Multimedia software Electronic graphic organizers Tactile-word processing software

We also suggest reading Chapter 1 for further ideas on teaching literacy. Many suggestions in that chapter may strengthen students with special needs as well.

Mathematics

Mathematics is another basic skill that all students need to master. From telling time to knowing the distance of a road trip to knowing how much the weekly grocery shopping trip costs, we all use mathematics for many essential daily tasks. AT has made significant progress in mathematics for those who have learning differences. Gone is the myth that only through paper and pencil can a student learn real mathematics (Haq & Elhoweris, 2013). Today, it is widely accepted that technology plays an important part in mathematics. Contrary to some myths, technology enhances problem-solving skills, helps develop better mathematical concepts, assists the student in drills, saves time, and improves the student's attitude of the subject (Haq & Elhoweris, 2013). Moreover, students who use technology in mathematics have shown better performance (Bottge et al., 2004; Roblyer & Doering, 2010).

With AT, students with exceptional challenges can compute, organize, align, and copy mathematical problems without the need of paper and pencil; furthermore, visual and/or audio support can assist the student in setting up and calculating mathematics problems. Today, calculators exist with speech synthesizers, allowing the student to verify the accuracy of the number pressed. Students with writing difficulties can use electronic worksheets, which allow students to organize and align math problems with more ease. Josue, in Mrs. Guadarrama's class third grade, for example, uses the Coin-U-Lator for money identification in addition to many free downloadable apps.

Identifying basic geometric shapes can be a good example of where AT can be of great use. In Mr. Green's class, for example, the teacher may ask students to identify basic geometric shapes. The array of exercises that he can employ for students is endless—from identifying the basic geometric shapes in a worksheet to constructing the shapes with glue and construction paper. Students with disabilities, however, may have difficulty with some of these exercises. For example, a student with difficulty grabbing a pencil can use a modified mouse and/or could identify basic geometric shapes with the help of software by simply clicking on the correct answer. Carla, who has difficulty with manual craft, can replace a glue and construction paper activity with three-dimensional software that can allow her to create the three-dimensional shapes. Furthermore, Mr. Green can allow her (and other classmates) to explore the complexity of creating more sophisticated shapes such as the construction of basic homes, cars, or airplanes. Carla can explore how basic shapes can make more complex shapes and can also help assist other children with difficulties in spatial skills.

Mathematics skills are vital, and AT is helping educators with the task of helping students learn these skills. No matter how many facts students know, it is imperative to apply this knowledge in meaningful ways. The students have an array of technology available at their disposal to achieve the following:

- **Virtual simulations** have become an integral part of the student's experience in the classroom. Teachers can use an array of software to help students explore scenarios where to use their mathematical knowledge. For example, students can use three-dimensional virtual models to calculate the stress of bridges.
- **Problem Solving** is vital in mathematics and having a sense of how to gather and use data is more important today than ever. Software and scientific calculators can help students gain a better sense and understanding of numbers. These data-gathering instruments allow the student to make mathematical representations more meaningful, so that the student can explore trial-and-error scenarios.
- **Mathematical representation** has become a norm in mathematics classes of today. Software allowing students to create three-dimensional representations are readily available. With the help of technology, students can see a graphical representation of many concepts.

The technology available to the mathematics teacher is abundant; therefore, careful consideration must be taken when assessing the use of technology in the class. Teachers must have a precise understanding of the learning objectives. Technology for mathematics classes is available in all arrays, from an abacus to spreadsheet software. Table 6.8 describes the most commonly used technology in the mathematic class.

Table 6.8 Math solutions with AT

Low Tech	Mid-tech	High Tech
Graph paper Manipulative Abacus	Non-scientific calculators	Scientific calculators Math lab Software Electronic worksheets Electronic whiteboards

Universal Design

We have discussed some specific areas and tools for students with special needs, but there is an overreaching set of principles that emphasizes a series of curricular practices that makes the curriculum more accessible to this population—the Universal Design for Learning (UDL). As one educational program (South Carolina Assistive Technology Program, n.d.) stated,

> "Universal Design for Learning" is a relatively new term, but it incorporates age-old, basic principles of good teaching through different modes. It involves using technology that allows students to access educational materials through their strongest learning mode. Universal design provides equal access to learning, not simply equal access to information. It does not remove academic challenges; it removes barriers to access. (para. 35)

UDL has become one of indispensable components in deciding what type of services and AT are required in the least restrictive environment (LRE) (see Table 6.10).

UDL has its foundation in the architectural concept of universal design. Universal design advocates for the increase accessibility of buildings and structures—entrance ramps, corners at street level, automatic doors, and hands-free fountains and restrooms are all examples of universal design. The concept of universal design is credited to the late architect Ronald Mace (1941–1998), who was bound to a wheelchair. Mace is also credited with founding the Center for Universal Design at North Carolina State University (http://www.ncsu.edu/www/ncsu/design/sod5/cud/). The Center for Universal Design specifies seven principles: equal use, flexible, perceptible, low or no physical effort, intuitive in use, low error tolerance, and appropriate size and space for use (Turnbull et al., 2013). These principles are the basic guides that help design and produce easy accessible buildings that meet the accessibility need for a large portion of a population. Over the years, the concept of universal design has been used to provide and implement a wide range of services and products. Education is not the exception.

These principles of universal design can be used in the classroom. Equal use can be used to design curriculum material that meets the expectation of a mixed pool of learners, including those with learning disabilities. Flexible material can be used to accommodate different learning preferences. Perceptible curriculum and equipment can address the need of those with visual disability. Cognitive impairment can be addressed with curriculum that promotes low error tolerance and low physical effort. Finally, issues of physical accommodation and factors as simple as font size can be addressed with size and space for use.

The Center for Applied Special Technology (CAST) is at the forefront and center of promoting universal design in the implementation of curriculum in schools, aligning educational initiatives with the use of technology. According to CAST, there are three main principles to the application of universal design in the school curriculum: multiple representations, multiple ways of action and expression, and multiple ways of engagement (Center for Applied Special Technology [CAST], 2011) (see Table 6.9).

The principle of Universal Design has emerged from our need to access the physical environment, which has benefited more individuals than originally intended. For example, ramps for buildings, initially designed for individuals with wheelchairs, have benefited elders with walkers, mothers with strollers, and so on. UD concepts have been applied specifically to help students with disabilities. An example is the access to software

Table 6.9 Guidelines for universal design

Multiple Means of Representations	Multiple Means of Expressions	Multiple Means of Engagement
Provide the learner with various opportunities to gain information and knowledge.	Provide the learner with different avenues to express knowledge.	Motivate and challenge the learner to participate in multiple engaging activities.

Table 6.10 Network for UDL

Networks of UDL
Recognition Network: The "what" of learning; how we gather facts and recognize what we read, hear, and see; how we identify what we learn.
Strategic Network: The 'how' of learning; how we organize and express what we learn; performing complex math problems, recreating an historical event through a play, or writing a report are examples of strategic network.
Affective Network: The "why" of learning; how learners are engaged and motivated; how they are challenged and excited about learning.

(CAST, 2011)

and computers. Accessibility software and hardware in computers, such as accessibility control panels, are standard features.

The current challenge for teachers working with disabled students, especially those in inclusion, is the need to constantly modify the curriculum, instruction, and assessment. Modifications are important, and will always be needed, as the majority of instructional materials continue to be designed without consideration for the classroom diversity (Roblyer & Doering, 2010). UDL attempts to erase this barrier by providing other ways to conceptualize accessibility. This can be achieved by exploring new ways of representing, expressing, and engaging. The following section explains the three main principles to the application of universal design in the school curriculum: multiple representations, multiple ways of action and expression, and multiple ways of engagement (Center for Applied Special Technology [CAST], 2011).

Multiple Representations

The traditional means of representing information and ideas has been the printed word. This includes work of fiction, nonfiction, and informational material such as textbooks. Over time, printed materials have proven to provide difficulties to those with visual impairment. It has also presented challenges to those with learning disabilities who have difficulties deciphering the meaning of words in textbooks and tests. Furthermore, different learners may prefer different means of obtaining the same information: pictures, audio, or video, for example.

The challenges that often cause the printed word to be problematic for the disabled have been addressed by advocating the use of digital text. In this format, textbooks or other printed material are scanned and digitized. Once in digital format, the learner can change the size of the font to his or her desire. Other learners can use text-to-speech software, creating an oral version of the text. Other software can render a visual representation of the text. Students with learning disabilities can use software that can modify and simplify the text with the additional help of electronic dictionaries and thesauruses.

Multiple Actions and Expressions

In the classroom, students are expected to display the knowledge they have learned. Traditionally, this has meant the production of printed reports, paper-and-pencil tests, and worksheets to demonstrate their understanding and acquisition of information. Multiple actions and expressions explore different and nontraditional ways to express the knowledge acquired: debates, plays, art, drawings, or oral reports. AT can be used with the disabled student to access software that can aid in the creation of multiple forms of expressions. For example, a student can use digital software or Web 2.0 tools such as Toondoo to draw or create a comic strip or political cartoon. These would be more engaging projects for many students.

Multiple Engagement

Traditional instruction relies heavily on teacher-directed instruction, textbooks, and worksheets. UDL encourages the teacher to explore and reassess the delivery and mode of instruction, considering learning modes such as cooperative learning, themed-based units, and student-centered activities that may provide greater learning motivation for students with special needs. Such methods of instruction can help the teacher recognize the true talents of his or her students with special needs, promoting learning that goes beyond the mere implementation of assignments for a grade.

For many decades, teachers have been perceived as the main source of knowledge in the classroom (Cowhey, 2006; Freire, 1970). Teachers utilizing technology can allow the student to become a knowledge producer rather than a knowledge recipient, and multiple forms of engagement can assist the teacher with that. For example, notes and worksheets can be replaced with WebQuests, having the student to investigate different angles of the same information. A student who is studying the battles from World War II (WW II) can read articles, visit museum Web sites, and access other sources such as film clips, helping him or her to gain a better perspective about an event at his or her own pace. Multiple engagements have many benefits. Students with disabilities often experience delay in processing information and often have difficulty in keeping pace with the rest of their peers (Friend & Bursuck, 2015; Turnbull et al., 2013). The "one-shot" classroom experience is no longer a limiting factor or students who need variety and "replay."

Activity: Applying UDL

The three main principles of UD (multiple representation, expression, and engagement) can be successfully applied to any lesson plan and with all students, but the disabled student can greatly benefit from this practice. We can illustrate this better by analyzing a WW II history lesson:

1. How would one incorporate multiple means of representation?
   Instead of using traditional textbooks, teachers can help disabled students by having them use Web sites, audio selections videos, and electronic textbooks. This will better help visual learners. Students who experience difficulties with reading comprehension can greatly benefit from multiple sources of information available on the Internet. The History Channel Web site, www.history.com, is an excellent source where students can gain information. A teacher should ask, "If I couldn't read well, how would I know?"

2. How could a teacher incorporate multiple actions and expression?
   In the past, students were often required to simply construct a written report. Today's students can express their knowledge in a variety of ways. For example, the disabled student, who may have difficulty with written expression, can benefit by creating a visual portrayal of WW II images using MS Movie Maker or IMovie. A simple Prezi presentation can become a collage of stories, and a simple written report can become a "newspaper article" with MS Word or Glogster.com. It is imperative for teachers to understand that the disabled student can also be creative and have imagination.

3. How would you use multiple engagements?
   Traditionally, teachers presented the lesson by assigning students to read a chapter, take notes, and complete worksheets and tests. In the past, this has created many disadvantages for the disabled student who finds it difficult to operate in the traditional instructional setting (O'Rourke & Houghton, 2006). The Internet can ease this burden for teachers, and WebQuests are excellent tools that teachers can use to engage the student. For example, during a WW II lesson, the teacher can engage his or her student with the help of WebQuests to explore the lives of those who were the children during WW II (http://www.uni.edu/schneidj/webquests/WWIIChildren/wb25/titlepg.html) to get a better background of the conflict (http://www.lhs.rcs.k12.tn.us/teachers/pughc/WWII%20Webquest.htm), and produce their own PowerPoint presentation (http://wwiiwebquest.wikispaces.com/World+War+II+WebQuest).

Instead of a traditional oral recitation of the paper in front of the class, these types of presentations can be rotated through a computer center where all students in the class view others' work. Students may also assume identities of historical notables, or, as mentioned above, a young person of the times and create a presentation from that perspective. Other types of presentations may include "moving maps" of how various invasions and battles changed during the war. Letting students become the teachers in an area of learning which is interesting to them (student choice) is more interesting *and* very empowering—especially to the student with special needs. A teacher who feels unable to support these types of products with his/her technical skills can easily go to the school or district technology specialist for assistance.

Although UDL is very well known in the field of architecture and special education, other areas can benefit from using it. Research has shown that English Language Learners (ELL) can greatly improve their language skills with the use of UDL (Lopes-Murphy, 2012), especially in the area of representation, engagement, and expression (King-Sears, 2014). As such, UDL is a useful tool for language acquisition for learners with special needs. The main goal for UDL is to bring lesson and instruction to the learner's academic level by providing access to the curriculum. With ELL students, exposure to the content is crucial, especially new vocabulary (Jang et al., 2013; Wallace, 2008), and this could apply to learners with special needs as well. Teachers can use technology and UDL to achieve this goal. An example of this is the use of digital texts. The use of digital texts with UDL as customary practice (Turnbull et al., 2013) is very common in subjects like science (Rappolt-Schlichtmann et al., 2013). Digital text is the electronic format of printed media that can be stored, changed, and manipulated. Digital texts not only provide access to the curriculum, they also provide information in a variety of representations and effective practice of new content (King-Sears, 2014). This can be crucial as students learn new vocabulary, practice the implementation of this new information, and express what they learn in different ways.

Teachers should have no trouble in accessing digital text these days. Because of New IDEA requirements, publishers must comply with the National Instructional Material Accessibility Standard (NIMAS). In this format, texts are created with a source file in XML format. This allows the publisher to produce the final texts in a variety of formats such as HTML for the Internet, Braille for the blind, or Daisy for digital voice. Project Gutenberg (www.gutenberg.org) and Bookshare (www.bookshare.org) are two online libraries where students and teachers can find an extensive collection of digital texts.

Your Turn

After viewing the Photosynthesis lesson that follows on the next page, incorporate the three UDL main concepts:

1. How would you incorporate multiple means of representation?
2. How would you incorporate multiple actions and expression?
3. How would you use multiple engagements?

We hope by now that you have some good ideas. Here are some suggestions:

1. How would you incorporate multiple means of representation?
   In this instance, the students have multiple opportunities to gain information and knowledge. Using technology, they can learn about photosynthesis using many different avenues such as Prezi presentations, Web sites, electronic encyclopedias, or online videos—as only a few of the resources available to use. The teacher can also use cooperative learning by dividing the classroom into four groups: Group (1) Sun and Light; Group (2) Chloroplast; Group (3) The Molecule; and Group (4) Light and Dark Reactions. In a Jigsaw configuration, each group will first research the Internet to find the information, which they will then present to the class using technology.
2. How would you incorporate multiple actions and expressions?
   In multiple expressions, students express their gained knowledge in different formats. In the case of a photosynthesis lesson, the teacher can have the students create a multimedia presentation. Platforms

Lesson Plan:

PHOTOSYNTHESIS

PART I: THE SUN AND LIGHT

Not all of the light from the **Sun** makes it to the surface of the Earth. Even the light that does make it here is reflected and spread out. The little light that does make it here is enough for the plants of the world to survive and go through the process of **photosynthesis**. Light is actually energy, electromagnetic energy to be exact. When that energy gets to a green plant, a number of reactions can take place to store energy in the form of sugar molecules.

Remember we said that not all the energy from the Sun makes it to plants? Even when light gets to a plant, the plant doesn't use all of it. It actually uses only certain colors to make photosynthesis happen. Plants mostly absorb **red** and **blue** wavelengths. When you see a color, it is actually a color that the object does NOT absorb. In the case of green plants, they do not absorb light from the green range.

PART II: THE CHLOROPLAST

We already spoke about the structure of **chloroplasts** in the cells tutorials. We want to reinforce that photosynthesis happens in the chloroplast. Within this **cell organelle** is the chlorophyll that captures the light from the Sun. We'll talk about it in a bit, but the chloroplasts are working night and day with different jobs. The molecules are moved and converted in the area called the **stroma**.

PART III: THE MOLECULES

Chlorophyll is the magic compound that can grab sunlight and start the whole process. Chlorophyll is actually quite a varied compound. There are four (4) types: a, b, c, and d. Chlorophyll can also be found in many microorganisms and even some prokaryotic cells. However, as far as plants are concerned, the chlorophyll is found in the chloroplasts. The other big molecules are water (H_2O), carbon dioxide (CO_2), oxygen (O_2), and glucose ($C_6H_{12}O_6$). Carbon dioxide and water combine with light to create oxygen and glucose. Glucose is used in various forms by every creature on the planet. Animal cells require oxygen to survive. Animal cells need an aerobic environment (one with oxygen).

PART IV: LIGHT AND DARK REACTIONS

The whole process doesn't happen all at one time. The process of photosynthesis is divided into two main parts. The first part is called the **light dependent reaction**. This reaction happens when the light energy is captured and pushed into a chemical called ATP. The second part of the process happens when the ATP is used to make glucose (the **Calvin Cycle**). That second part is called the **light independent reaction**.

Source: Biology4kids.com

---

such as Prezi can allow the students to create presentations that will incorporate multiple modes of learning. In their presentations, they must incorporate video, audio, and text. One group, for example, in Mr. Conde's class created a "TV New Flash" format video for their presentation.

3. How would you employ multiple engagements?

The idea of UDL is to have students involved in engaging activities. A lesson about photosynthesis is the perfect opportunity for students to do a meaningful project. The availability of light is vital for photosynthesis to occur. Students can put their knowledge to the test. Each group will be responsible for growing a plant. Each plant will have different amount of light. There are many ways to access or design tables using technology so that excellent data can be collected and displayed through various tables and figures. Digital cameras can record growth as well. At the end of a given number of days, each group will report their findings. The teacher can also have his or her students use virtual labs to simulate the process. With Glencoe Virtual Lab (http://www.glencoe.com/sites/common_assets/science/virtual_labs/LS12/LS12.html), students can decide which kind of light (e.g., orange, green, blue, or violet) they will use and which plants (e.g., radish, spinach, or lettuce). Student can see how much a plant will grow using different lights after 30 days. Using a light scale developed by the University of Reading (http://www.reading.ac.uk/virtualexperiments/ves/preloader-photosynthesis-full.html), students can regulate the growth rate of Elodea and watch the plant grow in real time. The same can be done with Johnston Photosynthesis (http://www.mhhe.com/biosci/genbio/biolink/j_explorations/ch09expl.htm).

AT in the Classroom

Remember Stephen from the case study at the beginning? In order to be successful in the classroom, Mrs. Wang must recognize Stephen's ability by examining the effectiveness of different tasks. She can do this by considering the AT and support discussed by parents and professionals (IEP/ARD Team) dealing with his challenges. Students with disabilities may have a number of challenges. For example, we noted that students with cerebral palsy or muscular dystrophy have difficulty producing legible handwriting, lacking the dexterity to write legibly or at a productive rate. Students with autism, Down syndrome, or a learning disability may have difficulty with fine motor coordination with dysgraphia and/or illegible handwriting. Students with difficulty producing legible handwriting often have difficulty producing final products, expressing ideas, and editing their own work.

It is clear that Stephen will need intensive means of instruction at different level of academic intervention to improve his fine motor skills, especially in the area of writing. This goal can be accomplished by the use of response to intervention instruction (RTI), which is a multilayered approach to implement academic instruction and assessment (Byrd, 2011; Hoover & Love, 2011). Even before an IEP committee makes proper recommendations, Stephen's teachers can implement some strategies that can help him improve and deal with his learning skills. Since it might be difficult for Stephen to draw diagrams, Mrs. Wang can have him use Inspiration or FreeMind to create digital graphic organizers. This can help Stephen organize his ideas. Writing for Stephen can be a challenge. Besides using MS Word, he can benefit from utilizing Dragon or Write:Outloud, which offer vocabulary prediction. In the end, teachers can be proactive about helping the student with his or her struggle.

How does a student get the technology he or she needs? Let us revisit how AT arrives in the classroom for children. To have a better understanding of the student's need and the proper implementation of AT, usually a nondiscriminatory assessment and evaluation process take place. This process includes an initial screening of the student's learning ability, an exhaustive assessment of the student's performance, the proper consideration of the LRE, related services needed, and the present level of academic performance. An IEP is developed with measurable goals and objectives, supplementary aids, modifications and accommodations, and a proper standardized assessment format.

The use of AT should be considered by the ARD (or IEP) team in the implementation and discussion of services for students with disabilities. The screening process should include the consideration of possible technologies to be used. For the teacher, an AT checklist such as the one listed can help the teacher and the IEP team evaluate the student's need. Such a checklist can help better identify the areas of strength and weaknesses. Usually, the AT checklist is also part of the overall process in determining the proper annual goals and objectives for the student IEP (see Table 6.1). In some cases, an AT checklist is also part of the original screening process.

Usually, the IEP teams make one of four decisions in determining the implementation of AT for a student with disability:

1. No AT is required.
2. AT is considered, but additional screening is needed.
3. AT is recommended, and a proper list is provided.
4. AT is recommended, but a full assessment evaluation is required. (In some cases, the IEP/ARD team might need further assistance in determining the proper assistive technology for the student.)

Activity: Implementing AT and the IEP

Let's look again at Stephen from the vignette at the start of this chapter. As noted, Stephen has cerebral palsy, and his condition affects his writing skills. (For the purpose of this exercise, we can also determine that Stephen is also confined to a wheelchair and has difficulty with his fine motor skills.) Also, remember that Stephen has also a learning disability in the areas of writing and reading comprehension.

Using the AT checklist and Stephen's IEP goals and objectives, consider Stephen's proper needs for AT.

Stephen's IEP Goals

Goal 1: Demonstrate the proper independent reading skills:
Objective: When given a reading assignment, Stephen will accomplish with 70% accuracy:

1. identifying the implied main idea,
2. drawing conclusion and inferences, and
3. summarizing a reading selection.

Goal 2: Demonstrate the proper independent writing skills
Objective: When given a writing assignment, Stephen will with 70% accuracy:

1. write complex and compound sentences,
2. write five words paragraph with no more than two spelling errors, and
3. use proper writing rule and mechanics,

Goal 3: Demonstrate proper use of fine motor skills:
Objective: When in the classroom, Stephen will with 70% accuracy:

1. write clear and legible letters, and
2. demonstrate the ability to draw, construct models, and produce crafts model.

The above IEP goals and objectives suggest that Stephen will need assistance in the areas of reading, writing, and mobility. By referring to the AT checklist (see Table 6.1), Mrs. Wang can immediately deduce that Stephen will greatly benefit from a word processor with a spell checker; she can use voice-to-text software that can help Stephen read and assist him with his reading comprehension, and software can be used that will assist Stephen with his writing and model production. However, as we noted earlier, Mrs. Wang was not waiting for the ARD or IEP committee to make recommendations; she was knowledgeable enough to start implementing some RTI interventions with the proper use of technology.

AT can offer a better learning environment for the student. In doing so, the teacher must constantly evaluate and reassess the student's need for AT in accordance with the student's IEP goals and objectives. To accomplish this, the teacher can follow these steps:

1. Review existing information regarding the student's ability
2. Schedule meetings with members of the ARD (or IEP) team.
3. Identify the problem
4. Prioritize potential solutions to be considered
5. Generate solutions
6. Implement a plan of action

An ARD (or IEP) committee must meet at least once a year, but can be called at any time by a member (including the regular classroom teacher). If the classroom teacher believes that certain technology is needed or is not working, he/she should meet with the team to request it.

Such exercise can help the teacher best assist the teacher in understanding the learning environment for the student. Teachers can best make decision about the proper implementation of AT when they have a full and complete knowledge of the resources available, the needs of the student, and a proper plan of action in assisting students with disability.

Differentiated Instruction

Differentiated Instruction (DI) refers to a series of classroom practices that tailors instruction to a learner's styles, interests, and needs, taking into consideration the individual's prior knowledge, social exposure, and educational experience. If national, state, or district standards tell us what knowledge a learner must acquire, DI is the blueprint that allows teachers to create a more dynamic and exciting learning environment where the student can learn in a more purposeful way.

The premise behind DI is to introduce meaning and dynamics into the learning process. Guided by a constructivist approach, the belief behind DI is that learning occurs best when learners make meaning out of the information. DI is much more than distinguishing the heterogeneous component of the learning environment. It means taking into consideration the readiness, learning needs, and interests of *each* student. When implementing DI, teachers must consider careful planning and the dimension of the learning environment. They can do this by considering the instructional dimension of DI. Teachers must take into account the content to be learned, process of instruction, and desired product. Furthermore, teachers must include the student's interest, readiness, and profile.

The goal of DI is to engage each learner by offering multiple ways for individuals to demonstrate the learning and understanding—particularly those with special needs (Heward, 2013). Over the years, technology has assisted the teacher with effective tools to achieve this. Furthermore, technology lets the teacher embrace the student's different learning styles. It provides an engaging and motivating learning environment with the opportunity for grouping so that the students can use various products to demonstrate their learning. Technology facilitates the gathering of data, which helps teachers and students to monitor the progress of learning and guiding future instruction. DI attempts to captivate the student's interests, thus encouraging interaction, participation, and creativity.

When using technology, the first step for teachers is to gather and use data. By using data driven decision, teachers can better understand the student's progress. Web sites, such as Student Progress Monitoring, give the teacher a better understanding of how the student is performing in his or her class. With data, communication between parents, teachers, and students has become indispensable for success. As such, in recent years, online grading has opened a crucial line of communication. Web sites, such as Engrade (www.engrade.com), help the teacher to create online grading, attendance records, assignments calendars, and progress reports, which can be shared with parents and students. With DI, giving students ownership of their own learning is also crucial. For example, creating a Graph (http://nces.ed.gov/nceskids/createagraph/) helps students to visualize and understand their own learning.

Table 6.11 Guidelines for DI

Content	Different levels of reading or resource materials, reading buddies, small group instruction, curriculum compacting, multilevel computer programs and Web Quests, tape-recorded materials, etc.
Process	Activity choice boards, tiered activities, multilevel learning center tasks, similar readiness groups, choice in group work, varied journal prompts, mixed readiness groups with targeted roles for students, etc.
Product	Tiered products, students choose mode of presentation to demonstrate learning, independent study, varied rubrics, mentorships, interest-based investigations
Interest	Options in content, topic, or theme, options in the tools needed for production, options in methods for engagement
Profile	Consideration of gender, culture, learning styles, strengths, and weaknesses
Readiness	Identification of background knowledge/gaps in learning, options in amount of direct instruction, options in amount of practice, options in pace of instruction, options in complexity activities, options in level of analysis/exploration of a topic

Having the student to explore new ideas is very motivating with DI. Different Web sites allow students to download podcasts, use virtual cameras, and access thousands of videos. It is important that students explore their interests. This allows the student to take ownership of the learning process, motivating the student to be engaged.

Table 6.12 Useful Web sites for DI

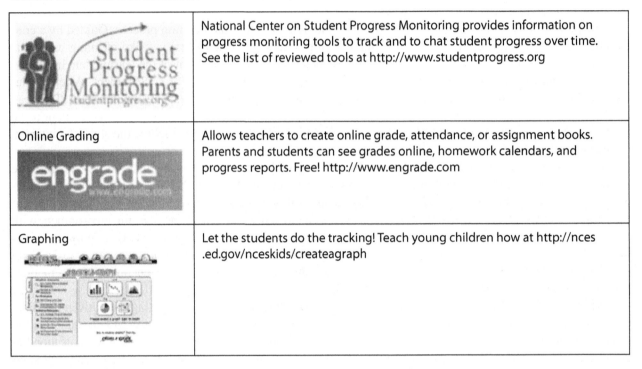

	National Center on Student Progress Monitoring provides information on progress monitoring tools to track and to chat student progress over time. See the list of reviewed tools at http://www.studentprogress.org
Online Grading	Allows teachers to create online grade, attendance, or assignment books. Parents and students can see grades online, homework calendars, and progress reports. Free! http://www.engrade.com
Graphing	Let the students do the tracking! Teach young children how at http://nces.ed.gov/nceskids/createagraph

Table 6.13 Useful tools for DI

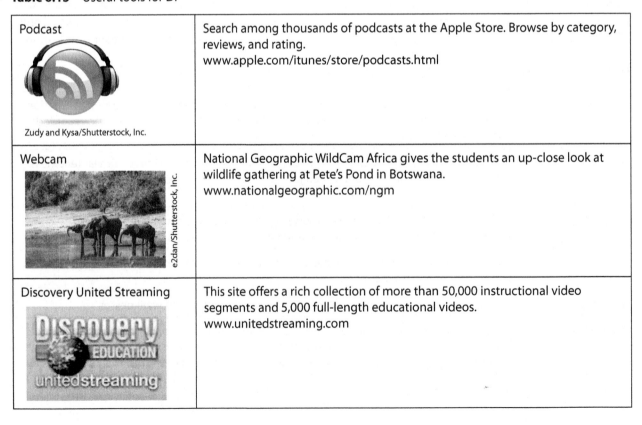

Podcast	Search among thousands of podcasts at the Apple Store. Browse by category, reviews, and rating. www.apple.com/itunes/store/podcasts.html
Zudy and Kysa/Shutterstock, Inc.	
Webcam	National Geographic WildCam Africa gives the students an up-close look at wildlife gathering at Pete's Pond in Botswana. www.nationalgeographic.com/ngm
e2dan/Shutterstock, Inc.	
Discovery United Streaming	This site offers a rich collection of more than 50,000 instructional video segments and 5,000 full-length educational videos. www.unitedstreaming.com

Table 6.14 Useful WebQuest tools

WebQuests were designed to help students learn to navigate the Web and locate information in a meaningful way.
http://www.thirteen.org/wnetschool/concept2class/month8/index.html   Concept to Classroom is a collaboration between Thirteen Ed Online and Disney Learning Partnership. This URL features Concept to Classroom's take on WebQuests.
http://webquest.org/index.php   This site is designed to serve as a resource to those who are using the WebQuest model to teach with the Web. By pointing to excellent examples and collecting materials developed to communicate the ideas, teachers experimenting with WebQuests will be able to learn from each other. A WebQuest is an inquiry-oriented activity in which most or all of the information used by learners is drawn from the Web. WebQuests are designed to use learners' time well, to focus on using information rather than looking for it, and to support learners' thinking at the levels of analysis, synthesis, and evaluation. The model was developed in early 1995 at San Diego State University by Bernie Dodge with Tom March.
www.iptv.org/exploremore/ge/teacher_resources/webquests.cfm#   This "Explore More" site offers a number of WebQuests in various subject areas for middle and high school teachers along with other projects and lesson plans.

Collaboration and production is at the core of DI. Technology can definitely facilitate this. In the twenty-first century, technology provides endless possibilities for students with special needs to excel. A WebQuest is a perfect tool for collaboration and production. There are many advantages to WebQuests. First, they allow the student to learn about a topic by exploring information sources that build on his or her interests. Second, they make the student an expert in the topic. Third, they promote higher-level thinking. Students are not just learning information but using it to create a product.

In the twenty-first century, teacher-centered instruction is only one of the many choices in instruction. Student-centered instruction has proven to be much more effective because the student becomes active and engaged rather than a passive listener. To comply well with DI, student-centered instruction is promoted. As

Table 6.15 Useful Web sites for social media

Blogs & wikis	Blogger Learn what a blog is and how to create your own in three easy step at www.blogger.com. pbwiki Get an ad-free wiki started with pre-made templates, free videos, and lots of help. http://pbwiki.com/
Presentation software voicethread	Add voice to presentations, pictures, or text with VoiceThread. www.voicethread.com
CENTER for DIGITAL STORY TELLING	Use digital stories to motivate students to share their stories in a unique and creative way. Digital stories can be used as alternatives for projects, summaries, and presentations. http://www.storycenter.org/

such, blogging, presentation software, and digital story-telling are indispensable tools for the teacher. Blogging allows student and teachers to take the classroom to a different level. The classroom is no longer four physically defined walls, but virtual spaces where new ideas and horizons can be explored. Blogging can increase a student's participation, motivation, and collaboration. In the case of special education students, this is a very important skill that they must master. Blogging gives the student with exceptionalities the opportunity for active participation. For example, students with speech difficulties will not have the fear of interaction. Liam, for example, experiences speech aphasia from a head injury during a biking accident. He is no less intelligent than his peers, but he has trouble with word finding at times, especially during stressful situations. Blogging provides him with a tool to participate as an equal and for others to see him as a valuable resource.

Another aspect of the twenty-first-century classroom is the creativity of student products, which is at the core of DI objectives. New software and Web 2.0 tools, such as word processors and drawing software, allow students to enhance the production of their work. The days of only paper-and-pencil reports are past. Today, teachers are encouraged to tap into students' imagination and ingenuity. New technology, such as VoiceThread (www.voicethread.com), allows the student to incorporate voice and sound into their final product. Furthermore, such creativity can be enhanced by creating digital stories, which students can use to display final presentations.

Technology Strategies for Gifted and Talented

Gifted and Talented (GT) is often defined as the category of individuals identified as possessing extraordinary qualities that provide the potential for high quality performance in intellectual activities, leadership roles, creative endeavors, and artistic performances with a high degree of commitment (Heward, 2000; Renzulli, 2011). Many teachers are surprised that these students are labeled as those with special needs, but the definition of "needing special attention to obtain their maximum potential" fits GT students handily. According to Roblyer and Doering (2010), the primary concern for teachers should be to identify the students who merit these services not ordinarily available in the general curriculum. Comprehensive discussions of how best to service these students are provided by Heward (2000) and Renzulli (2011).

Roblyer and Doering (2010) observe that technology has increased the potential abilities of students, providing the student with greater freedom and independence to create. They find that technology integration for the gifted and talented should evolve around three major areas:

- **Virtual Communication**—the ability to electronically communicate with other cultures and people from other regions of the world should exponentially enhance students' potential for expression.
- **Research**—the ability of resources (e.g., the Internet and electronic databases) allows gifted and talented students to explore new ideas and events in greater depth, so that students truly investigate a particular subject.
- **Independence**—the availability of various tools for interactivity and representation provides gifted and talented students with opportunities to explore new discoveries and display their creativity freely.

Finally, we all agree that gifted and talented students are highly creative and motivated students (Renzulli, 2011). Teachers must not only provide the tools and opportunities for these students to excel, but they must also provide for the opportunity for cooperation and group work. When educating the gifted and talented, teachers tend to focus on the academic outcome of the student, often overlooking vital social skills components (Coleman, 2014), but socialization of the gifted and talented continues to be an area of concern (Coleman & Cross, 2014). According to Roblyer and Doering (2010), working in the creation of Web sites or multimedia project provides the opportunity for gifted and talented students to participate in the motivational tasks that they need, while providing them with the chance to develop important social skills needed in the work place.

Final Strategies for Teachers

Teachers in the special and non-special education classroom face the ever-increasing challenge of meeting the needs of exceptional children (Roblyer & Doering, 2010), and the demand to provide these services is mounting (Pohl, 2013). Here are some suggestions that teachers can apply to meet these needs:

- Become familiar with the student's need as soon as possible. If the student qualifies for special education services, it is important for the teacher to review the IEP to ensure understanding and determine how to support the student most effectively. Contact the school special education administrator to learn about the student before he or she arrives in your classroom.
- Continually survey the classroom with a checklist to see if the environment meets the needs of the student in term of accessibility and AT.
- Check to see if AT is required or enhanced by the student's modification and accommodation.
- Always use resources such as *Wave, Closing the Gap Solution,* and professional development training to check for Web accessibility. Be on the guard for the latest technology, and stay on the alert for new information (Roblyer & Doering, 2010).

Conclusion

In this chapter, we provide an introduction to the basic concepts and implementation of AT for students with disabilities. An underlying principle of AT is to provide independence and full participation of the student in the learning environment while minimizing any stigma that might occur as a result of being a differently abled learner to provide a way for the child to reach his/her full potential. AT can help to level the playing field in creating learning situations for equalizing the environment so that may happen. AT is not cheap, and it adds substantially to the cost of educating a student. However, it may make a lifelong difference in the life of a child (and society) in untold ways. The teacher who realizes the potential of students with special needs to become independent learners and contributing members of their communities may, at times, need to become an advocate for a student in obtaining the technology. When implementing AT, the district, school administrators, teachers, and other professionals must be knowledgeable of the correctly applicable equipment, costs, usage, tech support, and various other services that go hand in hand with the technology. Communication and cooperation among members of the IEP/ARD team are crucial. Finally, a teacher must be knowledgeable on how to translate the IEP goals and objectives into the use of AT and be wholehearted in following through with its use in the classroom.

References

Abberley, P. (1987). The concept of oppression and the development of a social theory of disability. *Disability, Handicap & Society, 2,* 5–19.

Baglieri, S., & Knopf, J. (2004). Normalizing differences in inclusive teaching. *Journal of Learning Disabilities, 37,* 525–529.

Bottge, B. A., Heinrichs, M., Mehta, Z. D., Rueda, E., Hung, Y.-H., & Danneker, J. (2004). Teaching mathematical problem solving to middle school students in math, technology education, and special education classrooms. *Research in Middle Level Education Online, 27*(1), 43–68.

Byrd, E. S. (2011). Educating and involving parents in the response to intervention process: The school's important role. *Part of a Special Issue: Collaboration, 43*(3), 32–39.

Center for Applied Special Technology (CAST). (2011). *Universal design for learning guidelines version.* Wakefield, MA: CAST. Retrieved from http://www.udlcenter.org/sites/udlcenter.org/files/updateguidelines.pdf

Coleman, L. J. (2014). The Power of specialized educational environments in the development of giftedness: The need for research on social context. *Journal for the Education of the Gifted, 37*(1), 70–80.

Coleman, L. J., & Cross, T. L. (2014). Is being gifted a social handicap? *Journal for the Education of the Gifted, 37*(1), 5–17.

Cowhey, M. (2006). *Black ants and Buddhists: Thinking critically and teaching differently in the primary grades.* Portland, ME: Stenhouse.

Elbro, C. (2014). Dyslexia as disability or handicap? When does vocabulary matter? *Journal of Learning Disabilities, 43*(5), 469–478.

Freire, P. (1970). *Pedagogy of the oppressed.* New York: Herder and Herder.

Friend, M. P., & Bursuck, W. D. (2015). *Including students with special needs: A practical guide for classroom teachers* (7th ed.). New York: Pearson.

Haq, F., & Elhoweris, H. (2013). Using assistive technology to enhance the learning of basic literacy skills for students with learning disabilities. *International Journal of Social Sciences & Education, 3*(4), 880–885.

Heward, W. (2000). *Exceptional children: An introduction to special education* (6th ed.). Upper Saddle River, NJ: Prentice Hall.

Heward, W. (2013). *Exceptional children: An introduction to special education* (10th ed.). New York: Pearson.

Hoover, J. J., & Love, E. (2011). Supporting school-based response to intervention: A practitioner's model. (Sage Publications Inc. February 1, 2011). Retrieved from https://ezproxy.uhd.edu/login?url=http://search.ebscohost.com/login.aspx?direct=true&db=tfh&AN=57405584&site=eds-live&scope=site

Jang, E. E., Dunlop, M., Wagner, M., Kim, Y.-H., & Gu, Z. (2013). Elementary school ELLs' reading skill profiles using cognitive diagnosis modeling: Roles of length of residence and home language environment. *Language Learning, 63*(3), 400–436.

King-Sears, P. (2014). Introduction to learning disability quarterly special series on universal design for learning: Part one of two. *Learning Disability Quarterly, 37*(2), 68–70.

Lopes-Murphy, S. (2012). Universal design for learning: Preparing secondary education teachers in training to increase academic accessibility of high school English learners. *Clearing House, 85*(6), 226.

McKenney, S., & Voogt, J. (2012). Teacher design of technology for emergent literacy: An explorative feasibility study. *Australasian Journal of Early Childhood, 37*(1), 4–12.

Microsoft (2014). Accessibility in education. Retrieved from http://www.microsoft.com/enable/education

Offen, K. (2013). Historical geography II: Digital imaginations. *Progress in Human Geography, 37*(4), 564–577.

O'Rourke, J., & Houghton, S. (2006). Students with mild disabilities in regular classrooms: The development and utility of the Student Perceptions of Classroom Support scale. *Journal of Intellectual & Developmental Disability, 31*(4), 232–242.

PL 94-142: Education for All Handicapped Children Act. (1975).

Pohl, B. (2013). *The moral debate on special education.* New York: Peter Lang.

Rappolt-Schlichtmann, G., Daley, S. G., Lim, S., Lapinski, S., Robinson, K. H., & Johnson, M. (2013). Universal design for learning and elementary school science: Exploring the efficacy, use, and perceptions of a web-based science notebook. *Journal of Educational Psychology, 105*(4), 1210–1225.

Renzulli, J. S. (2011). What makes giftedness? Reexamining a definition. *Phi Delta Kappan, 92*(8), 81–88.

Roblyer, M. D., & Doering, A. H. (2010). *Integrating educational technology into teaching* (5th ed.). Boston: Allyn and Bacon.

Scott, S. M., shanscot@nova.edu. (2012). Go ahead . . . be social. *Distance Learning, 9*(2), 54–59.

South Carolina Assistive Technology Program. (n.d.). SC Curriculum Access through AT. Retrieved from www.sc.edu/scatp/cdrom/atused.html.

Strickland, E. (2014). The end of disability. *IEEE Spectrum, 51*(6), 30–35.

Turnbull, A. P., Turnbull, R., Whemeyer, M., & Shogren, K. (2013). *Exceptional lives: Special education in today's classroom* (7th ed.). New York: Pearson.

Valentine, J. (2007). How can we transgress in the field of disabilities in urban education? In S. R. Steinberg & J. L. Kincheloe (Eds.), *19 urban questions: Teaching in the city* (pp. 127–142). New York: Peter Lang.

Wallace, C. (2008). VOCABULARY: The key to teaching English language learners to read. *Education Digest, 73*(9), 36.

Wise, P. H. (2012). Emerging technologies and their impact on disability. *Future of Children, 22*(1), 169–191.

Chapter 7

Technology to the Rescue: Helping English Language Learners Advance in English Proficiency and in Content Knowledge

Myrna Cohen, Colin Dalton, Laura A. Mitchell, Stephen White
University of Houston-Downtown

Meet Mrs. Davidson

Mrs. Davidson worked with her five ELL (English language learner) students in different ways in order to have them practice speaking more. She noticed, however, that Binh, a student from Vietnam, was going through a silent period—a well-known time to second language educators when children will not speak the new language at all in front of others. Mrs. Davidson, therefore, had Binh work on technology projects such as screencasts (see example at tube.sandi.net/video/videos/2564/beginning-esl-autobiography and at tube.sandi.net/video/videos/2565/beginning-esl-autobiography). In this way, Binh was able to use headphones and a microphone to speak her new language in private instead of speaking in front of others, which is embarrassing and scary for students in the silent period.

Second Language Acquisition Principles and Technology

The ways in which technology can be effectively used to facilitate learning for all students are vast. However, using technology to teach English language learners (ELLs) can make the ELL teacher's job much easier than in the past. This is because technology offers many ways to implement best practices in second language teaching. These best practices, often seen in the most popular ESL (English as a Second Language) teaching strategies, have been developed and adapted over the past decades and are based on the fundamental principles of second language acquisition that have been well researched and are widely accepted in the field. It is important for teachers to understand these principles in order to use technology wisely for ELLs.

Several of these principles are discussed in the following paragraphs. These principles guide teachers of ELLs as they consider: the level of English to use with their ELLs; the sequencing of instruction that is most effective; distinguishing among the different language domains to enhance proficiency the role of emotion in second language learning; and why it is crucial to differentiate between conversational and academic language. An understanding of these principles will help teachers make decisions about the technology tools that are best for their ELLs and about using the technology tools to their students' best advantage. Note that ELL teachers need not speak two languages. Many effective teachers of ELLs are monolingual but have a good grasp of second language acquisition principles and the appropriate technology to support them.

One of the most important considerations for learning a second language is to have access to *comprehensible input* (Krashen, 1985) or *accommodated language*. This means that the learners have *"clues"* to help them understand *the message* being communicated, rather than having *"just the words"* of a new language. There are many ways to help make the new language *comprehensible*. For instance, adding pictures, objects, gestures, intonation, and cognates (words that are similar in both languages) to spoken or written language can help comprehension. Consider an ELL hearing the sentence "The Arctic Circle is in the Northern Hemisphere, and the temperature there is ice-cold." Just hearing or reading this sentence may be hard to understand for a beginning ELL. However, the teacher could make this sentence much more *comprehensible* by pulling a globe off of the shelf, pointing to the Northern Hemisphere, tracing the Arctic Circle with her finger, using the cognate *zero* (for temperatures below zero) and by shivering to indicate the ice-cold temperature. In addition, seeing the globe would probably activate the student's prior knowledge about the Northern and Southern Hemispheres and the North and South Poles. In the former *incomprehensible* sentence, the student might be so clueless about the meaning that he might not even know that he has the prior knowledge for it! Making the new language comprehensible to the learner is a key component of ESL strategies. Technology is an attractive way to accomplish this goal with its ready access to pictures, sound, video, illustrations, games, maps, and so forth.

In order to advance in a second language, the *level* of the second language needs to be appropriate for the learner. Krashen (1985) suggests that the learner is best served by experiencing language that is slightly more difficult than his or her proficiency level. Krashen uses the term "i" to indicate the current proficiency level of the learner. This is the level where language is produced and comprehended without effort. He uses the term "i+1" to indicate the next higher level where the learner has to struggle slightly to use the language but where comprehension and production are possible with the appropriate accommodations. The "i+1" level is a "slight stretch." Therefore, according to Krashen, the "i+1" level of language is the most fruitful for the second language learner. If learners stay at their comfort level, they will be able to function easily in the new language at that level, but no further language progress is likely to take place. If the learner jumps to a level that is too far above the current level, he or she will not be able to comprehend the language, frustration will set in, and no language progress will occur. However, with the "i+1" level, the learner will be able to stretch just enough to advance. For example, let's say a learner knows the words "gift," "birthday," and "yesterday" and is familiar with the irregular past tense "gave." He will understand the sentence "Yesterday, he gave me a gift for my birthday" without difficulty and will not advance in his language proficiency because, for him, it is at the "i" level. If a learner does not know the words "gift," "birthday," "gave," or "yesterday" and hears that sentence, he probably will not understand it at all because it is too difficult, and he will not advance. However, if a learner knows the words "gift," "birthday," and "yesterday" but is not familiar with the irregular past form "gave," he probably can figure out the meaning of the sentence by inferring the meaning of "gave" from the words "yesterday," and "birthday," and "gift." For this learner, the sentence is on the "i+1" level. This is the English language level for which teachers should aim as they work with their ELLs and as they choose technology tools to enhance instruction.

It follows that in order to teach at the "i+1" level, teachers need to know the current proficiency level of each of their ELL students so that teachers can stretch each student beyond his or her level. In Texas, for example, a great deal of effort has been invested in identifying and describing second language proficiency levels through the Texas English Language Proficiency Assessment System (TELPAS). These TELPAS levels are incorporated into the state's English Language Proficiency Standards (ELPS). The TELPAS has developed a rubric of Proficiency Level Descriptors (PLDs) that is an effective tool for Texas teachers. Four levels of language proficiency are described (1) beginning, (2) intermediate, (3) advanced, and (4) advanced high in each of the four language domains (listening, speaking, reading, and writing). Many excellent resources regarding the TELPAS and the ELPS can be accessed from the Texas Education Agency (TEA) Web site (http://www.tea.state.tx.us).

Teachers can learn a great deal about their students' English language abilities in each language domain by referring to the descriptions of each of the four proficiency levels in that domain. For example, it should be clear that *listening* in English is quite different at each of the four proficiency levels. It is evident from the PLDs that a student at the beginning level of proficiency (1) in *listening* will struggle to understand simple English, even when the topics are familiar and even when extra linguistic clues are available. The beginner most likely will not ask questions about what they are hearing but will rather remain silent. For instance, if Rosa, a third grader from Puerto Rico who just arrived in the United States without knowing any English, hears the teacher talk about the supplies the children need to bring to class each day, she will not understand, even if she is familiar with school

supplies in Spanish and even if she may see examples of scissors, markers, and pencils. She probably will not ask questions of the teacher or of her classmates. This is typical of the beginner stage (1) in *listening*.

Once Rosa progresses to the intermediate stage (2) in *listening* she will understand the main ideas (the gist) of her teacher as he talks about the daily schedule and the class rules because these topics are now familiar to her in English. However, when he explains and discusses with the class the traditions and history of Thanksgiving, she will most likely not understand unless the teacher uses a number of pictures, cognates, short sentences, and other accommodated language. At this point, Rosa may ask her teacher or classmates to speak more slowly or to explain some words. This is typical of the intermediate stage (2) in *listening*.

Once Rosa reaches the advanced stage (3) in *listening* she will understand her teacher and a class discussion about the solar system in English because she is somewhat familiar with the information, but she still may need to see some diagrams or three-dimensional models to aid her understanding. Even if the teacher speaks in long, complex sentences, she has a good chance of understanding him. This is typical of the advanced stage (3) in *listening*.

When Rosa reaches the advanced high stage (4) in *listening*, she is almost at the level of her native English speaking classmates, although she may not understand idioms, subtle nuances, and very low frequency vocabulary. For example, when the teacher says, "If you follow the study guide as you prepare for the test, it will be a piece of cake," Rosa may be confused as to why her teacher is suddenly talking about cake. Because she has not yet mastered the many idioms and figurative expressions in English, she may think that there will be a party tomorrow after the test. This is typical of the advanced high stage (4) in *listening*.

In the PDLs, the four proficiency levels are described in detail for the language domains of *speaking, reading*, and *writing* as well as for *listening*. The PDLs can be accessed from the TEA Web site (http://www.tea.state.tx.us/student.assessment/ell/telpas). Teachers of ELLs who want to use technology effectively should understand what each of the four levels entail for each language skill so that the technology used for instruction is applied most effectively.

Another important consideration for learning a second language is related to the emotions (or affect) of the learner. Krashen (1985) proposes that if the learner feels comfortable, safe, and at ease, second language acquisition will be facilitated. On the other hand, if the learner feels tense, at risk, or anxious, acquisition will be hampered. He refers to this as the "affective filter." Technology, in particular, can contribute to a low affective filter because the learner can often be anonymous when he or she wishes; whereas, in a classroom, using a new language publically can be anxiety-evoking for a learner. In addition, the game-like nature of so many of the technology tools adds enjoyable, pleasant connotations to learning.

Second language theory also recommends a preferable *sequence* of instruction. It is suggested that the ELL should experience the second language along two continuums. The first moves from *context embedded* to *context reduced*. This means that the language, at first, should have many context clues or that it should be very accommodated. As the learner advances, the language should become less and less *context embedded*, having fewer and fewer context clues and should become less accommodated. The other continuum addresses how cognitively demanding the language is. The learner should first experience language that is less cognitively demanding and should gradually move to language that is more cognitively demanding (Cummins, 2000) (refer to Figure 7.1). Teachers using technology need to be aware that their ELLs should experience gradually less *context embedded* language if they are to advance in English. This is a challenge for teachers of ELLs because context-embedded language is common when using technology. Teachers and students may have to make a conscious effort to gradually reduce the context clues in order for the learner to become more proficient.

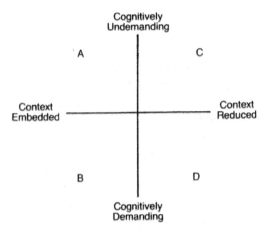

Figure 7.1   Range of contextual support and degree of cognitive involvement in language tasks and activities. Reprinted from *Language, power, and pedagogy: Bilingual children in the Crossfire* (p. 68), by Jim Cummins, 2000, Great Britain: Cromwell Press Ltd.

One of the major goals of ESL strategies is to help the ELLs acquire *academic language* in English. Academic language refers to language that is context reduced and abstract. This is the kind of language mostly used in school. It is referred to as "Cognitive Academic Language Proficiency," or CALP. Language that is conversational and less school-like is referred to as "Basic Interpersonal Communication Skills," or BICS (Cummins, 2000). It is important for teachers to help their ELLs to use technology that develops their CALP, or academic language.

Lastly, second language learning is most effective when the language experienced is holistic in nature so that the learner is exposed to all four language skills: *reading*, *writing*, *speaking*, and *listening*. Technology is adept at allowing for this integration, as visual and auditory language is so accessible. Moreover, ESL strategies encourage the learning of the second language through the learning of content—whether it is social studies, mathematics, science, literature, or other subjects. The emphasis should be on the *meaning* of the ideas, not simply a focus on the language itself (and its rules). In this way, while concentrating on the *content*, the learning of language "comes in through the back door." In other words, the language is the "means" to an end (understanding the idea) but is not the "end" itself.

As an example of this principle, Ms. Halloway is working on a unit about civil rights in her tenth-grade history class. The students are engaged in a heated discussion about the pros and cons of using violence when fighting for social justice. The students are captivated by this question. Marko, an ELL, is so drawn in by the discussion that his thoughts are all focused on the question of using violence. He has an opinion, and he expresses it without even realizing that he is talking in English. His motivation to express his ideas is so forceful that he does not have the time to be self-conscious about his new language. Technology can be a wonderful way to advance this because the range of content is abundant, and its presentation can be so motivating that the learners may become less conscious of the language, making their second language acquisition a by-product.

In this chapter, we explore several possibilities of how to use technology for English language learners. It is important to understand *why* each technology tool is effective for ELLs so that teachers can make wise decisions about how or even *if* they should use the new tools for their ELL students. It is crucial to have an understanding of how to use comprehensible input, the affective filter, the suggested sequence of language learning, BICS and CALP, academic language, and holistic language. When reading about and evaluating the use of video games, electronic publishing, e-readers, computer assisted language learning (CALL), apps, social media, and personal communication tools for ELLs, one should keep in mind how all of these technology tools are supported by the second language principles described above.

Teaching English as Second Language with Video Games

Today's video games feature sophisticated plots, complex characters, vibrant settings, and realistic sound tracks. These modern video games allow players to control many aspects of the game, including the characters' appearances, actions, and even personalities. When students engage with the language of the game through the personas of the game's characters, their language learning anxieties are reduced. Krashen (1985), as may be remembered, refers to this aspect of successful second language education as lowering the "affective filter." The complex plots of the games require players to listen to and read detailed instructions in order to play. Additional reading and listening must be accomplished to comprehend the plot of the game and the characters' background information.

Sergey Novikov/Shutterstock, Inc.

Academic Language Instruction: Language Arts

Just as every K-12 content area teacher is a language teacher, every K-12 language teacher is a content area teacher. Video games provide a platform for ESL teachers to teach subject-specific academic language pertaining to language arts. Knowledge of subject specific academic language (or Cognitive Academic Language Proficiency [CALP]), as opposed to BICS, should feature prominently in the language goals of every lesson in a K-12 ESL classroom.

Language Arts in the ESL Classroom: Elements of Fiction. Video games provide the perfect platform for teaching students the structure of a dramatic work (similarly found in novels, plays, and films), including exposition, inciting incident, rising action, climax, falling action, resolution, and denouement (or conclusion) of the plot. These commonly taught elements of a dramatic work stem from the nineteenth-century German novelist and playwright Gustav Fretag's (1863) analysis of the common patterns in the plot of stories and novels. Video games contain the *common elements* of fiction: plot, setting, characters, conflict, symbolism, flashbacks, foreshadowing, personification, style, and point of view. Conflict, a major literary element of the genre of fiction, clearly exists in video games. Themes of "Person vs. Self," "Person vs. Person," "Person vs. Society," "Person vs. Nature," "Person vs. Supernatural," "Person vs. God," "Person vs. Fate," and "Person vs. Machine" play out in novels, plays, *and* many video games alike. Similarly, character types exist in video-game plots as they do in fiction on the page. Protagonists, antagonists, static characters, dynamic characters, foil characters, supporting characters, and minor characters have their entrances and exits on the virtual stage of video games. ESL teachers should provide students with a lesson on the elements of literature prior to playing the video game. After playing the game, students can use this language arts specific academic language in their reading journals, just as they would after reading traditional literature.

Video Role-Playing Games in the ESL Classroom. Perhaps the most unique genre of video games for use in the ESL classroom is the role-playing game. Role-playing games require players to assume the role of characters in a fictional setting tasked with accomplishing a predetermined goal. Some of these are: creating or nurturing a society from mud huts to space travel in *Civilization Revolution,* designing bacteria and guiding them through a millennium of evolution in *Spore,* or managing an amusement park in *Thrillville: Off the Rails.* To accomplish these goals, players must read manageable amounts of material, including directions for playing the game, descriptions of the game's setting and characters, and information pertaining to the goal and plot of the game. Additionally, students must listen and respond to vast amounts of in-game dialogue, both directional and character based, in order to accomplish the task of the game.

Dikiiy/Shutterstock, Inc.

Table 7.1 Template for Video game character sketch

Character	Appearance	Personality	Motivations	Actions	Allies	Enemies

Post-Game Reading Journal Entries. A reading journal provides students with a place to react to their experience playing the game, utilizing the academic language taught prior to playing the game in conjunction with the language utilized in the game. Students can practice summarization skills, outline written character sketches (appearance, personality, behavior, motivations, and actions), reflect on the events of the game, or respond to specific teacher generated writing prompts pertaining to the cultures, politics, metaphors, life lessons, and so forth expressed in the game (see Table 7.1).

Oral Language Activity: Readers Theater. ELLs require opportunities to reread texts in order to develop sight word vocabulary, reading fluency, and comprehension skills. Additionally, they require *scaffolded* (or supported) experiences to practice pronouncing new vocabulary and grammatical structures with character-specific inflection, expression, and varied volume. Readers Theater, which requires students to read character dialogues in the form of a play, allows for the development of these interrelated language skills. Students can read teacher-generated or student-generated Readers Theater scripts based on the setting, characters, and plot of a recently played video game. Mrs. McAffee assigns her students their Readers Theater roles well before the actual in-class performance, allowing her students to rehearse their parts before performing in front of the class and thus lowering the affective filter. Readers Theater allows students to further immerse themselves in the plot of a video game and reread its vocabulary and grammatical structures, thereby acquiring the language utilized in the game in a natural, fun way.

Clearly, video games should not replace traditional methods of ESL instruction but rather should provide students with a supplement to relevant content area curriculum. It must be noted that not all video games are suitable for classroom use. Obviously, violent games that award points for killing, maiming, or other violent/antisocial acts should be avoided. Also, games devoid of language content should be avoided. Just as with literature offered in class, games should be age and school appropriate. Since video games mostly require students to read and listen, students should be encouraged to talk about their experiences after playing the game to practice pronouncing their newly acquired vocabulary and grammatical structures. Similar after-game-playing language practice should occur in writing in students' reading journals in order to link language learning across the *listening, speaking, reading,* and *writing* spectrum.

Utilizing Electronic Publishing Platforms to Teach English as a Second Language

The purpose of language is to communicate with others. In the twenty-first-century world, many aspects of communication via publications have moved online. Therefore, ESL teachers should include aspects of electronic publication into their teaching. Electronic publishing platforms, both online and software formats, allow ELLs to acquire language in a natural environment with a low affective filter. Additionally, utilizing electronic platforms in the ESL classroom allows teachers to connect with students on their level and better obtain student buy-in, motivation, and participation (Wright, 2010).

Digital Stories

ESL teachers can utilize digital storytelling platforms like Microsoft Movie Maker and Microsoft Photo Story to publish any manner of language acquisition projects. Teachers can develop activities where students create personal narratives—for example, students documenting their family's sociocultural histories and traditions by incorporating images, narratives, text, video clips, and music. Also, students can create traditional research projects utilizing a digital story platform. Moreover, research projects utilizing a digital story format require students to interpret, analyze, and evaluate visual images—important visual literacy skills. Posting digital stories on social media Web sites, podcasts, video blogs, and video posting Web sites provides an incentive for students to produce their best work, knowing the far-reaching distribution of these online publishing platforms.

Omer N Raja/Shutterstock, Inc.

In one adult ESL class, several students have created digital narratives that they have used to describe events that were very important to them. Sadie created a digital narrative that combined her wedding ceremony with the important traditions in a small village in Oaxaca, Mexico. She described the events through pictures and videos that they had taken during their wedding while she narrated the story through her own emotions and experiences. Sadie described how her husband, who grew up in this village, asked her if she would be willing to travel to Oaxaca to share their wedding with the community where he grew up. When she agreed, she did not realize that she would be inviting over 1,000 people to her wedding because everyone in the village attends weddings in the community. Sadie had the opportunity to learn about the local customs and traditions. It was good luck for their marriage to have a rooster wake them up on their wedding day. As they celebrated the wedding mass, a baby was baptized as a sign of prosperity. The women in the village made a beautiful bag for the couple to contain grain so they would not go hungry. As they left the church, bells were ringing to celebrate the mass and people were shouting, "*Beso, Beso, Beso*" or "Kisses, Kisses, Kisses" just like in the movies. As Sadie told her story, she not only shared about an important event in her life, she gave her audience a glimpse into the cultural lives in a different country and a different place. She shared how much she valued the culture and life of her husband's family and community. Younger students find empowerment as well in sharing their life events with others.

Facebook

Facebook, the most pervasive online social networking service, boasts a membership over one billion active members. Users create and manage a personal profile—including photos, personal information, contact information, interests, and life events—in order to remain in contact with friends, family, classmates, and acquaintances. The platform also allows users to send messages, email, voice call, and video call to other users. When ELLs utilize this collaborative technology to interact with their peers in English, it becomes both an independent and collaborative natural English acquisition environment. The Facebook platform provides students with an effective publishing platform for audio and visual recordings of them

Bloomua/Shutterstock, Inc.

performing speeches/presentations, original poems, Readers Theater performances, and even songs. Additionally, students can publish their thoughts, feelings, and opinions on a variety of topics, including restaurants, films, music, politics, world events, and sports. Students can even publish, using appropriate privacy settings, a class Facebook page where they post photos and descriptions of class events, fieldtrips, and school activities.

Business-Oriented Social Networking Services

Online business-networking platforms, for example LinkedIn, allows users to communicate with professional colleagues, customers, distributors, clients, classmates, and employees. Users build a contact network in order to find jobs, build a customer base, obtain information about a company, and congratulate colleagues' successes. In 2013, LinkedIn reported 259 million members in more than 200 countries utilizing the Web site, which is available in 20 languages. Despite these diverse language offerings, ELLs should set up an account in English. This activity can work with high school students with part-time jobs, designated career ambitions, and career specific classes. Setting up an account, which includes developing a professional profile, provides students with a perfect publishing platform to learn business English in a natural setting.

Wikis for Collaborative Writing

A wiki, unlike a blog, allows an online community of people to contribute to the content of an informational webpage on a specified topic. Since the web-page structure is present, a Web-based wiki allows students to easily create a webpage by concentrating on content rather than format. For example, the structure of the most commonly used *wiki,* Wikipedia, is already in place, and contributors can easily add or edit an existing article, thus making it a perfect platform for collaborative writing projects. Students can write individual or group contributions to a wiki site and peer edit each other's writing at the same time. Also, students can add images, videos, audios, and links to other Web sites to enhance the content of a wiki. Since contributions to a wiki appear instantly on the wiki Web site and are accessible by anyone with an Internet connection, contributors are highly motivated to put forth valuable content using their best writing. Students keenly allow their peers and teachers to provide content input and editing advice. Wiki sites allow contributors and readers to track individual contributions to the sites, providing teachers with

Tyler Olson/Shutterstock, Inc.

a valuable assessment tool. The history tool also allows teachers to track students' work continuously as they revise their writing, a valuable tool that permits teachers to monitor students as they continue to work through the writing process. Commonly used wikis in classrooms include: PBworks (www.pbworks.com), Wikispaces (www.wikispaces.com), and Wetpaint (www.wetpaint.com).

Teaching English as Second Language with E-Readers

Advances in technology have been changing the ways in which we use language along all dimensions, including the ways in which we read. The popularity of electronic reading has been growing at a remarkable pace (Yoon, 2013). Electronic reading includes reading online documents from Web sites or reading online versions of newspapers or magazines that once could only be accessed in printed form. It also includes reading books (ebooks) on screens that include not only personal computers, laptops, and tablets but also on e-readers such as the Kindle and the Nook. Debates are ongoing as to whether paper books will one day be

Tom Wang/Shutterstock, Inc.

obsolete, giving way entirely to electronic media or whether it is unreasonable to think that a complete take-over by online reading will ever occur. The answer to this debate is interesting, but the essential question for educators of second language students is how to maximize electronic reading options to enhance the ELLs' language development as well as their content knowledge through English.

For teachers of ELLs who engage their students in independent reading, the International Digital Children's Library (IDCL) (http://en.childrenslibrary.org) is an excellent resource. The library contains over 4,500 books in 59 languages. One important feature for teachers of ELLs is that it is easy to find books that are of interest to older students even though they are written in simple English. On the IDCL Web site there is a category of books that have received the distinguished White Raven label because of their universal themes and innovative style and design. Within the White Raven Catalogue on the IDCL site, there is a subcategory of "easily understandable" books that are of interest to mature readers but that are written in relatively simple language. These books allow ELLs to explore sophisticated ideas and themes in understandable English.

Consider the use of e-readers as you imagine Mr. Horace's ninth-grade history class is comprised of 24 students, 8 of whom are ELLs. Of the 8 ELLs, 5 students are on the intermediate level, and 3 students are on the advanced level. Mr. Horace is responsible for integrating all of his students into this class so that the same learning objectives apply to all students. However, he needs to accommodate language for his ELLs and make it comprehensible for them, while not sacrificing the level or rigor of the content curriculum. The class is studying the Great Depression years and how that period affected different regions in the United States. The students are reading *To Kill a Mockingbird* by Harper Lee (1960) in order to understand the Deep South during that time. The book will also provide background for his upcoming unit on civil rights. Because all students have tablets with e-reader apps, everyone in the class is reading the electronic version of the book, the features of which allow Mr. Horace to implement effective differentiated reading instruction for students.

Dimitri, an intermediate level ELL student in Mr. Horace's class, can listen to sections of the text in English while reading along silently. Moreover, he can look up unfamiliar key vocabulary words by clicking on them and by accessing the simplified versions of the words, pictorial illustrations of the words, or translations of the words into his first language. For very difficult passages, he can employ Google Translate which will present the entire selected passage in his first language. Fatima, an advanced level student from the Middle East, is lacking knowledge of the Deep South during this period in general, so she accesses the Internet to view short documentary film clips and explanations about this era. These clips also expand her vocabulary as she both hears and sees illustrations of key words such as "rural," "mansion," "segregated," "civil rights," "discrimination," and so forth.

Tuyen, a Vietnamese student on the high-advanced level is interested in the legal aspects of the novel. She wants to concentrate on the parts of the book that relate to the law. Mr. Horace helps her to identify the "legal" vocabulary words in the book such as "jury," "defend," "accuse," and "prosecute." She uses the Web search tool on her tablet to locate the sections of the novel where these words appear in order to help her highlight and compare these passages so that she can better understand the court system described in the book.

These students highlight sections of the book that they think are significant for either language or content so that they can easily return to them at a later time. They also enter comments and make notations using the note-taking tool on the tablets. Some students may enter questions that they would like to ask in class about different parts of the book. As Mr. Horace guides his ELL students through their reading of the text, he helps them use the technology tools wisely. For example, he emphasizes that they should not look up every unknown word; they should only look up the words that are essential for comprehending the important ideas. He encourages them to guess at what unfamiliar words mean before clicking on them and to see whether or not they guessed correctly. He is conscious that they still need to develop inferencing skills in their second language and that these tools should not be overused. He also helps them choose appropriate short videos to develop the prior knowledge necessary for comprehension of the text and of this period in American history. Mr. Horace remembers that years ago he invested a great deal of time figuring out ways to make English comprehensible for his ELL students. The e-readers offer multiple and individualized ways to do so and free him to invest his time helping his students in other ways.

Ms. Gino appreciates e-readers for her younger students. She teaches second grade and has several ELL students in her class. She provides them with the opportunity to hear professional readings of the electronic books that she will read with her students in class by referring them to the Actors Guild Web site (http://www.sagfoundation.org/childrens-literacy). She knows that many of her students whose first language is English most likely have family members at home who can read English books aloud to them, but this is probably not the case with her second language students. A few days before she is to read *The Rainbow Fish* by Marcus Pfister (1995) in class, she has her ELL students listen to the electronic book read by Ernest Borgnine, who was a famous American film and television star, while reading along with him silently. This allows her ELL students to have heard the text read with skillful expression and correct pronunciation of vocabulary prior to their encounter with the text in class. This activity will make the whole-class instruction effective for the ELL children because they have had the opportunity to build schema for the ideas and language of the book.

Rodolfo Arpia/Shutterstock, Inc.

The descriptions of Mr. Horace's and of Ms. Gino's activities using e-readers need not be restricted to ELL students. Certainly, students whose first language is English can also benefit and enjoy these strategies. However, using ebooks for ELLs in this fashion is essential for the language development and content knowledge of ELL students.

Reading proficiency in a second language should best follow the *sequence of context-embedded* text to *context-reduced text*. Electronic texts can be *context embedded* simply by the reader accessing related pictures, diagrams, graphics, and sound that provide him or her with clues to the meanings that go beyond the mere words of the language. In any effective ELL lesson, the teacher provides these extra-linguistic clues to make the language comprehensible. With e-readers, the ELL student is empowered to self-provide these clues on demand and to regulate the amount of context embedded clues needed. It is the responsibility of the teacher to help the ELL student find the optimal level of context needed to supplement the text so that the text remains challenging but not frustrating. Being able to do this enables ELL students to be self-regulated learners as they continue to pursue all forms of ereading, which, undoubtedly, will become more and more sophisticated in time.

CALL (Computer Assisted Language Learning) and Tools

Computer Assisted Language Learning (CALL) programs provide an effective learning environment so that students can practice language in an interactive way using multimedia content. Learning can take place either with the supervision of teachers or individually at one's own pace. As CALL becomes more engrained in the ELL classroom, many educators are interested in figuring out how to use CALL programs in meaningful ways for their students.

As we know, the ELL classroom is made up of many different levels of proficiencies within the skills of *listening, speaking, reading,* and *writing*. For example, consider Mr. Boone's classroom. Xochilt has just arrived in the United States. When she was given the language proficiency test she scored a 1 in English and a 1 in Spanish based on a scale of 5. She has never attended a school. Clara is also a recent immigrant. Clara's oral proficiency test scores were a 5 in Spanish and a 4 in English based on a scale of 5. From these descriptions, one can see that Xochilt is a beginner with only listening and speaking skills in her native language, and Clara, who is an advanced high, is totally proficient in her native language. As an ELL instructor, how does one meet all of the needs of teaching English when students come with such a wide range of language skills?

Web-based commercial programs can help the school and district with generating score reports and can help the classroom teacher with individualizing instruction. For example, the tests that are administered to ELLs in Texas provide important results for teachers. These English Language Proficiency (ELP) scores align to language standards so that teachers can easily understand their ELLs strengths and weaknesses and make sure that ELL students receive the right support. ELP scores help teachers analyze their students' proficiency gains and serve as a guide for differentiated instruction. The scores also help in the documenting and tracking of ELL students' progress after they exit ESL programs. The reports can help classroom teachers set specific goals for each student by language domain, based on proficiency level and standards. The software options noted in the following paragraphs show how Web-based commercial programs can help students who are at beginning levels as well as those at advanced-high levels by allowing the teacher to provide differentiated instruction while using authentic language for *listening, speaking, reading,* and *writing.*

Teachers of ELL children must become knowledgeable about the wide variety of educational software available to help enhance all skills of learning a language. For example, numerous software programs can help ELL learners with survival and real-life reading skills. Students learn to read labels, menus, advertisements, job ads, job applications, banking forms, travel schedules, and maps on many of the software programs available. Core Reading and Vocabulary Development are designed for low-level literacy learners and ELL students who require a basic foundation in vocabulary, spelling, and comprehension. *Internet Pictionary Dictionary* (www.pdictionary.com) is an excellent Internet site that offers materials in five languages including English. Learners build vocabulary through motivating activities that include flashcards, fill-in-the-blank games, word scrambles, spelling challenges, and so forth. Each activity can be chosen at a variety of levels, and all activities offer self-checks. This kind of site is excellent for individual practice and differentiated instruction. Easy Writer Interactive Software lets the learner read, choose, and edit compositions that ELL students from all over the world have written. Longman English Interactive is a four-level, video-based integrated skills software program that has engaging video, audio, animations, and extensive practice activities to develop essential skills for beginners to intermediate high. Exercise Generator Plus CD-ROM is for busy teachers who want to produce really professional looking paper-based reading and vocabulary activities, exams, and homework materials. Story Word CD-ROM brings to life well-known children's stories and songs to help them to build on their knowledge and use of English language. Road to Citizenship was designed to help qualified people become U.S. citizens. As one can see, there are numerous software programs that can help the ELL teacher. Depending upon the student's needs, most likely there is a technology program that will help ELLs develop academic language and become more proficient in English.

Video conferencing options that can enhance the educational experience for ELLs are numerous. These video conferencing options offer the same opportunities for students no matter where they live—in small towns, rural communities, or big cities. Students, no matter where they are located, can connect with other students across the United States and the world. One can even connect with experts to begin to develop not only essential communication skills but also an awareness of global issues. It is a truly valuable educational experience to talk with experts and peers face to face through Skype. Students in a classroom in Houston, Texas, can work with students in a classroom in Madrid, Spain. If the ELLs are

Spanish speakers, *they* are able to become the experts in the conversation. While in the past, collaborative activities might have been limited to one classroom or one school, video conferencing allows students from multiple schools around the world to work together on relevant issues. One benefit of such an exchange is that learners can receive different views and fresh ideas from students who are miles away. Students in schools with ELLs can benefit from communicating with ELLs in other schools to broaden their perspectives and, of course, the ELLs benefit from "teaching" their online peers about their cultures and experiences. Teachers can explore the Web site of the international organization Teachers of English to Speakers of Other Languages (TESOL) (http://www.tesol.org). In doing so, they can network with other teachers of English as a second language around the world in order to initiate such partnerships.

The interactive electronic whiteboard is another tool that can help in demonstrations and that can accommodate different learning styles and language proficiency levels. Since the board can be used with any software, it is extremely adaptable for numerous uses and does not require acquisition of additional software. Its creative use is limited only by the imagination of teachers and students. It can interface well

with a document camera and video camera. With the document camera the presenter can show an object such as a story, and then the skills being taught can be highlighted. The board is excellent for lessons where the participants need printed copies of a brainstorming activity. Copies of the resulting document can be printed and distributed and/or can be saved for future work. With proper planning, preparation, and training, it is a powerful instructional tool that can be adapted for use with a wide range of subjects and ages. Many ELL learners may have limited vocabulary in the new language, but having them contribute visual examples will help increase their understanding. For example, Mrs. Keen is teaching the rectangle shape in her first-grade class. She gives out digital cameras to pairs of students in the classroom, and they take pictures of books, the whiteboard, and other real-life rectangular shapes in the school and post them on the interactive whiteboard showing their knowledge and offering many visuals for other students to see.

Whenever possible, teachers should provide learners with the opportunity to practice with technology. Computer skills should be a regular part of the learning process. In one of the classroom described above, there were two students with very different language proficiencies. By using CALL programs, teachers can individualize instruction for each student, especially when they have a classroom with multiple levels of proficiencies. Using computers and other technology devices help deliver material in class (video, clips, images, etc.) and help learners improve their language skills and sources of information. The more that learners are exposed to technology, the more comfortable they feel using it. The benefits and features of technology will help the teacher in preparing lessons, tracking students, and in using authentic language to help them become more proficient.

Tablets and Smart Apps

Apps and online resources can make learning English fun. Instead of repeating common English phrases in a classroom setting, ELL students play games and complete exercises while learning the ins and outs of the language, even if they are far away from a teacher or school. For instance, the Internet *TESOL Journal* (www.tesol .org) created a site comprised solely of quizzes, tests, exercises, and puzzles for ELL students. With thousands of contributions from teachers, students can take advantage of exercises that suit their needs. Users are allowed to choose their level of difficulty in grammar, vocabulary quizzes, and even crossword puzzles. In addition, the site offers a range of podcasts and YouTube videos, including those that allow students to listen and read along.

Mr. Gomez had a variety of students in the same ESL classroom. Bianca who is in her second year in the ESL program moved here from Mexico but knew no English when she arrived. She was retained once in her old school. Henri is a student who moved here two years ago from Haiti. He speaks Haitian-Creole and French and can read and write French, although he was several years below grade level in these skills. Based on these two scenarios, the ESL instructor needs to have a variety of tools to meet the needs of these students as well as to differentiate for each student based on their level of proficiency.

Although ESL lessons can be extremely beneficial, they often focus solely on the basics. Online resources and apps can supplement basic skills to allow students to learn slang and idioms. This creates more natural sounding dialogue and allows the student to better understand phrases and terms that are not available in a dictionary. Sites like manythings.org not only feature games, quizzes, exercises, and vocabulary words but also a collection of slang terms, English songs, proverbs, jokes, and American stories. Podcasts such as the Learn a Song Podcast, Jokes in English, and Listen and Repeat Podcast can also be enjoyable ways to not only learn the language but to "soak up" the culture as well. Since culture and language are strongly connected, this is an important part of learning English.

Convenience is another major benefit of utilizing apps and on-line resources. ESL students can learn on their own time and tailor a program to fit their needs. YouTube and podcasts allow the student to hear English language being spoken. The well-respected VOA Special English program offers streaming podcasts, Facebook lessons, YouTube tutorials, mobile phone applications, and webcasts—free of charge. There are some YouTube sites that even show clearly where to place the tongue in pronunciation of sounds. Apps are ideal for ESL students on the go.

SGM/Shutterstock, Inc.

Relying solely on a classroom approach to learning English can be unsatisfactory for certain types of learners. To maximize a student's ability to absorb new information, it is important to expose them to a variety of learning styles. Internet resources and apps are the perfect way to teach all students, regardless of their learning needs. By choosing the type of resources or apps that work for them, the student can create a personalized program. Active learners can use chat rooms, games, or competitive tools. Reflective learners can use informative lessons, concentration games, and vocabulary tools. As for visual and verbal learners, charts, diagrams, video lessons, listen and speak apps, pictures, and reading exercises, satisfy both types of learning styles. In addition, many online resources and apps such as Parlo use diagnostic tests to determine the ESL student's skill level before providing appropriate exercises.

The following apps are extremely useful tools to implement in ESL: (a) FaceTime is a video phone app built into the iPad, and it is an excellent way to have students practice speaking and listening. This app can be used to arrange various types of conversations with different speakers and can be used to arrange conversations between ESL students and English language native students; (b) Camera app, with the built in camera lets a user record audio and video so that ESL students can use this feature to record themselves and then send the recording to others to seek feedback; (c) Conversation English app is dedicated to helping the user practice and improve conversational English skills; (d) Sentence Builder is aimed towards elementary ages and helps children learning to build grammatically correct sentences in English; (e) Intro To Letters app is an application that runs through all the letters of the English alphabet, introducing users to the structure and pronunciation through tracing, audio, digital flashcards, and phonogram puzzles; (f) IDaily PRO HD, is an innovative app that turns English language news into valuable lessons in listening, grammar, and sentence structure with its custom dictionary, allowing users to save words and phrases that need clarifying; (g) Hello-Hello is an amazing app which helps users with their conversational English, providing lessons chosen and selected from real-life scenarios, flash cards, note-taking exercises and more; (h) Phonetics Focus app, one of the iPad's most popular ESL applications, offers a phonetic typewriter, games, flash cards, audio recording and playback; (i) Puppet Pals HD is an app suitable for ESL K-10 students to practice their fluency and language skills; (j) The Cat in the Hat - Dr. Seuss app is wonderful for ESL students K-2 and helps students practice reading fluency through echo reading. This app offers students three different ways to read: Read to Me – Read It Myself – Auto Play. As is evident, there are numerous apps for the ESL classroom, and, no doubt there will be more in the future.

ELL students who immerse themselves in the new culture often have an easier time picking up on the cultural nuances that exist in all languages. For example when a student lives the new culture, he or she goes to the school cafeteria to get his/her lunch. The student will have the real-life experience of getting into line, picking up a tray, making food decisions, deciding on a drink, and hearing questions such as, "What side (order) do you want?" From this experience the student will learn new vocabulary words in context. Online resources are not as powerful as real-life experiences, but they do offer opportunities that go beyond what can be traditionally learned in a book. Students can chat with native speakers and learn about holidays, sports, and pop culture. Apps and Internet sites offer stories, news, videos and pictures about many practical topics that can add to understanding.

Perhaps the greatest advantage of using online resources and apps for ELL students with limited resources is cost-effectiveness. There are thousands of Web sites that offer free lessons, activities, and resources for ELL students. Even those students who do not own a computer can take advantage of the resources by using the

Internet at a library or community center or from cell phones. While apps are sometimes available for a charge, the fee is usually never more than a few dollars. There are a fairly large number of apps that are free. Athabasca University recently released a free app called Mobile ESL with 86 sections of lessons and activities.

When the right educational iPad application is integrated into a content-rich lesson, it provides multi-sensory access to that content, facilitating comprehension and allowing ELLs to participate more effectively in academic subjects. Apps can be used to scaffold activities that may otherwise be difficult for ELLs to understand. In addition, using multimedia apps to deliver content enhances traditional methods of delivery that are largely text based. This opens up the door to critical thinking by lowering the language barrier and channeling the instructional focus to academic content. Some of the advantages of recommending language learning apps to students are: (a) convenience—the mobility of these devices provide students with the chance to study/review any day, any time, without the need to bring their books or class material; (b) efficiency—most apps are tremendously user friendly and well organized into topics, meaning that students do not waste any time looking for what they want to practice; and (c) engagement—language learning apps are the ideal tool to engage learners who are very tech-minded and naturally enjoy using gadgets and to engage learners who may not be tech-minded but who use applied technology in their daily lives. There are many useful apps that incorporate images, videos, audios, writing, and drawing to create interactive multimedia presentations and videos.

For ESL students with limited resources, apps and online resources provide a fun way to learn and a way to supplement basic knowledge with an understanding of cultural factors, idioms, and slang. In addition, the use of apps and online resources is cost effective, convenient, and customizable to fit the ESL student's individual learning needs. The vast quantity of apps and online resources ensures that there is something for every ESL student. The iPad, smart phones, and tablets provide the multimedia support for content that ELLs need and also allow ELLs to demonstrate mastery of a topic—regardless of their English proficiency.

AntonioDiaz/Shutterstock, Inc.

Teaching English as Second Language with Social Media

Social media technologies offer wonderful opportunities for teachers of ELLs to find motivating tools to engage the students in the process of learning English. Social media is the organization and creation of new ideas that are shared with others through tools such as blogs, podcasts, and video sharing. Social media refers to the many ways that people communicate with each other to share information and can be as simple as writing a letter, drawing pictures, and/or sharing ideas in groups that use media tools to create interactive and global communication. These tools include Skype, Whatsapp, and Google Hangouts, to name just a few. Students of the twenty-first century, more than ever, use and follow social media to gain information, share ideas, maintain relationships with others, and keep up with relatives and friends. These social media tools are ones that ELL students may already know how to use in their first language, and they can find new uses for them to learn a second language. In fact, even when students use social media to enrich their first language, they are strengthening their second language. The reasoning behind this is that the richer the knowledge of one's first language, the better able he or she is to learn a second language (Cummins, 2000). Moreover, the skills that students have in social media communication in their first language will transfer over to their second language. For example, if there is a meaningful abbreviation like "LOL" in their first language that is prevalent in social media communication, they will recognize that there are such abbreviations in their second language as well.

The task for teachers in this technology age is to find ways to transfer the technology skills that students have for personal use into classroom learning environments. In the traditional classroom, communication may have consisted of teacher lectures, students taking notes, pen pals, letter writing, journal writing, and passing notes in class. With today's social media, the classroom communication may now consist of blogging, Facebooking, Instagramming, and social videos such as YouTube, Tumblr, and MySpace. The plethora of tools to choose from can create a conundrum for teachers as they decide how to use them in the classroom. Teachers should recognize that these tools can lead to stronger communication skills for ELL students and should embrace them. For example, social media tools can bring ELL students who may be isolated from their peers because of language or cultural differences to a social learning environment that increases their communication and relationship skills.

In Mr. Robinson's middle school classroom, one sees literature circles (Daniels, 1994) with ELL students added into the groups. The students choose a novel that focuses on a social studies concept and their reading levels. They use social media tools to interact with the novel, individually through reading responses, while dialoguing about the novel, questioning each other about different parts of the book, and completing a project (such as a video) together. As the students work together, the ELL students receive excellent language support through social media tools to develop academic language by interacting with peers. For example, students in a social studies class are reading the book, *Roll of Thunder, Hear My Cry* by Mildred D. Taylor (1976). As they are completing their reading assignments at home, they post their reading responses to the group in their assigned blog. While writing their reading responses, they ask each other questions about parts of the book. As the ELL students participate in this process, they read the blog to see how the more advanced language students are using the concepts and the vocabulary words in the context of the book.

In setting up an online environment for a class, Ms. Nieto expected the students to communicate with each other through the messaging tool and to create presentation groups based on the topics they were choosing. A student asked, "How are we supposed to form a group when we are working online?" Following that comment, Ms. Nieto discovered that the students who used Facebook and Instagram on a daily basis had not thought about how to transfer those skills into a classroom environment. When she suggested to the students that they contact each other using the tools in the online environment (much like they would do in Facebook), they were able to connect with each other and form their groups. As teachers implement social media tools in their classrooms, they need to realize that the tools need to be explicitly taught so that the students can transfer their everyday knowledge of the tools into an online class environment.

Blogs

Blogs are electronic journals where people share unique perspectives, news, and world events that are happening in their own lives. Blogs are connected electronically and linked to Internet news so others can read the entries and follow the links or connections that the authors make. Blogs reflect the personal journal writing and opinions of authors. Sometimes blogs can be used as a place to maintain personal information, events, and photographs or space to express personal opinions of current or world events. Information links and entries are added on a regular basis. Followers of blogs can be family and friends. Journalists will follow blogs by looking for key words to identify trending topics or ideas. The owner of the blog controls who can read the blog. It can be maintained by a set of people or be open to the public. Those who have access can add comments to the blogs. Bloggers create communities of blogs by connecting links and blogs together. This allows groups to work together and to maintain connections when working at a distance. Some interesting blogs for ELLs may be family, travel, or food blogs. Students can create the blogs for real events or as information for class assignments. Often, teachers assign reflective journals as a part of the course assignments. Students can use a blog as an interactive journal between the teacher and the reflective journal entries.

In Ms. Jackson's high school English class, students create their own blogs to add their individual reading responses about what they are reading. The teacher may give prompts or questions for the students to respond to based on the reading selection. The teacher sets up the blog so that only the teacher and the student and/or the literature circle group can read the blog. The teacher also interacts in the blog by writing comments to students about the blog entries.

Wikis for Collaboration

Wikis create collaborative spaces for groups of people to work together from a distance so they can add information to a text and view, contribute, and edit content. Wikis can also build collaborative language groups for ELLs. This collective space gives groups the opportunity to maintain their creativity within the project without having to save, edit, or email new documents. They can add or change information in real time and work from a distance on the same text. The wikis tool allows teams to work on projects in real time. In a mixed class, even beginning ELLs can benefit by the collaborative process as they can learn a great deal by observing how the English-proficient students use language and can apply their own knowledge to the process.

Ms. Jackson found that when students start a project at school, they can add to the project at home and come back to school to continue working on the project. By collaborating on a project both at home and school, they are able to build files so they can capture and share each other's work in real time. For example, in Ms. Jackson's class students are working online in groups. They are putting together a brochure for traveling abroad to a new country. The group starts the work at school, and then each student continues to work on it at home. In her class the literature circle groups have a group wiki as well. Group members write to each other and describe what they are learning from reading their novel. They ask each other questions to clarify specific points or to check their own understanding of the novel. The literature circle group may also determine a project that they can complete in response to the end of the novel. They are able to work in their wikis to create the project, working at school and home.

Facebook, Instagram, and Pinterest.

Facebook, Instagram, and Pinterest are social media tools that allow for exciting and innovative ways to share life events with friends through photos, videos, and comments. Each tool has a unique approach to connecting people together. While Facebook focuses on groups of friends and sharing life events, people share their life events through a series of pictures in Instagram and Pinterest, which is a pin board-style photo sharing Web site. Each of these tools allows for individuals to create groups of family, friends, and/or colleagues to share life events, interests, and hobbies. These tools focus on the relationship building of groups so that families can be connected from distances, friends can keep in contact with each other, and colleagues can keep up with the latest trends in their fields. The social messages that are shared throughout these social media tools connect people to each other and give them understandings and perspectives through shared comments, pictures, and other media. Students can also use their smart phones or tablets to participate in these social media experiences.

Pinterest works much like fashion magazines. Once readers create boards in Pinterest, they create their own interests and a following among other Pinterest readers. Pinterest followers will see what others have pinned, will add their pins, and will begin following various readers. The Pinterest boards then are created based on those interests. The reader flips through the Pinterest boards much like they would flip through a magazine. When they find a recipe or a hair style that they like, they can pin it to their own personal boards. In this way, they save the recipe or hair style for later use while also connecting with others who may be interested in those same items. The Pinterest boards continue generating links and pins based on those interests. As this tool becomes more popular, teachers will find ways to use Pinterest to develop the students' interests and to motivate them to find more information about their topics. They can share their pins with others and continue to find more pins that may interest them. The special advantage of Pinterest for ELLs is that the topics are expressed with visual information in addition to written text, providing them with accommodated language.

Mr. Robinson uses social media in his middle school class in a way that helps his ELLs develop their literature knowledge and their English language proficiency. Students are placed in literature circle groups, and, as they continue to read their novels, they may respond through social media tools from the perspectives of the characters in their books. For example, the students may want to take on the character's perspective of Cassie Logan in the book, *Roll of Thunder, Hear My Cry* (Taylor, 1976). Cassie is upset because the students in her school received used and unwanted books from the school for White children. An ELL student could take on the perspective of Cassie. The student may consider sending out a post about the injustice of receiving the used textbooks. The students in the literature circle groups could interact with each other through the social media tool in the way that they believe their characters would interact with other characters from the novel or from that time period. The students create authentic dialogue based on their character's voice and post this in social media tools. Writing in direct speech in dialogue form can be easier for many second language learners than writing in third person. This format would thus be advantageous to ELLs. Moreover, students can find different photos or videos to illustrate what they want to say, thus making their language more *context embedded*. Students in this activity focus on how to understand the perspectives of their characters and find ways to give them a voice using these new tools. This creates a shift in thinking about the possibilities that "could be," while developing the voice and perspectives of characters in language that is comprehensible to ELLs.

Social Videos

Social video tools such as YouTube, Tumblr, and Myspace have become strong teaching tools in the classroom. Students like the social video tools because they can learn at their own pace. They can watch a video, pausing or repeating it to get the information, or they can move through it quickly when they already understand the information. Students can also create their own videos and post them in YouTube, Facebook, or Instagram for others to see. When students have access to these tools in the classroom, the instruction can be tailored to their specific learning needs. Teachers can find materials for students based on their achievement levels, interest, or academic needs. When students view a video on a particular topic, they can often understand the content more easily than when teachers give a "one-shot" lecture on the topic, or the content can be reinforced for better understanding. Note that there are some videos that are not useful or are inappropriate, so part of a teacher's job is to create an index to direct students to videos that are appropriately connected to their topics.

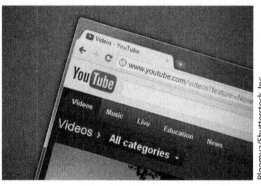
Bloomua/Shutterstock, Inc.

Creating videos has become easier with the digital video editing tools that are available to students. They can create videos to demonstrate their understanding of concepts, topics, or as a reflective process in an autobiography. The videos can be used in different social media tools to share with others. This process has opened up the teaching process for students and teachers. It has literally *flipped* the classroom so that a student-centered classroom is created rather than a traditional, heavily lecture-based classroom. In flipped classrooms, students learn the content before they come to class. During their class time, the teacher and students respond to the content through classroom activities. This is particularly advantageous to ELLs as they can preview the class materials before going to class with the help of simplified language, translations, added context, voice recordings, and so forth. They then can have a better understanding of what is happening in the lesson as they participate in the applied classroom activities. For instance, two teachers created a collaborative social studies project between two grade levels using social video tools. Ms. Rodriguez in a fourth-grade ESL content class planned with Mr. Smith in a fifth-grade sheltered class. The students were reading different books about communities in the early 1600s. Both groups needed to create a project to demonstrate their understanding. The teachers decided to put the students into groups made up of two fourth graders and one fifth grader. The fifth graders knew how to use the digital story-telling tools very well and taught the fourth graders how to use the nuances of the technology. The fourth graders wrote the storyboards or scripts for the digital narratives and shared their work with their fifth-grade partners. The students worked in collaborative teams to create a digital narrative about communities.

In Mrs. Goldman's sixth-grade classroom, social videos are used to develop a deeper understanding of the science content that students are exploring. They search for videos that are based on their concept. They create a digital narrative that explains the science concept and how it is applied. The ELLs have opportunities to develop a concept map or a story dialogue of the scientist(s) who is famous for the concept while matching it with video or photos that show how the concept is used in the real world. Students show not only their understanding of the science concept, but they also demonstrate their understanding of its application in real life. The videos and visuals provide them with the context clues that enrich their understanding of the academic language.

Personal Communication Tools for Sociocultural Enhancement

As noted, ELLs can connect with their family and home with different communication tools. Literacy includes cultural and linguistic diversity because of global literacies, connections, and migration. Many students may be connected globally because of their family's displacement from their home countries or because of travel or work (Giroux, 1993). They can find ways to connect with their friends and/or family through video conferencing and continue personal communication through emails and instant messaging. The ELLs will also find that they can develop their home language through this family communication. Often, students will tend to develop their English language skills, especially reading and writing, but ignore those skills in their home language. For example, many times ELLs come to the United States with their parents and siblings, but their grandparents stay behind. By communicating with their grandparents in their home countries the ELLs not only maintain personal relationships with their grandparents, they also develop the necessary reading and writing skills in their first language. Students find that through video conferencing, they can talk with their family members who live far away from them. The students can interview grandparents about when they were little children and perhaps develop a digital narrative about their grandparents' lives as a story to share with the class. The students can add pictures and video to the story as they also incorporate grandparents' voices from the interview, or the students can, for the same purpose, develop digital narratives with cousins or friends to get a peer perspective on "what's happening" in their former home.

Digital tools call for a new understanding of literacy and literacy development. The emergence of hybrid digital forms such as wikis, blogs, online databases, and online news calls for a new understanding of teaching in the classroom. Textual features require students and teachers to learn new technology proficiencies. In the classroom, students may be motivated to inform their technology and literacy groups based on friendship and interest groups. They may find opportunities to use video conferencing, social media, and electronic communication to enhance personal communication skills. In their class, students create multimodal texts to communicate messages with family and friends. They may use a combination of text with visual, audio, spatial, and gestural modes to communicate.

Global Communication and Maintaining Culture

Many ELLs live in a society that maintains home and global connections. The ELLs find that they must maintain both their home language *and* English to communicate with all of their family and friends. Young people may use their home language to communicate with parents, grandparents, and possibly aunts and uncles or friends back home. They may use English to communicate with their brothers, sisters, nieces, nephews, and friends in their new home. Often, they find that the personal communication with their family from their home country will be through video conferencing such as Skype, Viber, or Whatsapp. They may also use electronic communication such as email and instant messaging. At the same time, they feel enormous pressure to fit in with their school friends using English communication skills. Their context for communication often requires distance communication with family and direct communication with immediate family and friends.

With the transition of the global society, many traditions have changed drastically. An important tradition in the Latino American home, for example, is to visit the grandparents or *abuelos* on Sunday. Many families will spend all day together eating traditional foods, playing games such as *Lotería*, and visiting with each other. Now that Camila lives in the United States, she cannot visit with her grandmother on Sundays. Now Camila conference calls her *abuela* every Sunday through Skype, and her *abuela* can still share favorite recipes for traditional foods with Camila and give her advice on how to cook her favorite tamales or enchiladas. Camila maintains her home language with her *abuela,* while learning new things about her family background and heritage. Many of these traditions can be continued with digital conferencing tools. Parents and grandparents can conference call with their children or grandchildren miles away while still maintaining the tradition of sharing Sunday with the family. ESL teachers can encourage the technology skills needed for this type of communication, and students can later share these experiences with others in the class in English.

Class Communication

Teachers can generate purpose and meaning within these contexts for personal communication for BICS and CALP. In a primary language arts classroom, students create their purposes and audiences for writing and developing multimedia products. The students work in small groups to decide which form of communication they will use to communicate with family members. They develop questions to interview various family members about a particular event in their life (getting married, having their children, going to school, etc.) or about particular events that occurred in history. The group then interviews the family member through Skype, Viber, or Whatsapp. This creates a purpose for communicating with family in various settings while also developing the communication skills in their home language.

To develop this further, ELLs can use a virtual tour to tell classmates and friends about their former home. Through the use of Google Earth, they can collect pictures of their communities from a distance. As they create a virtual tour of their home, they can describe their home, school, and local community. The ELLs will be able to share a part of them with their new classmates and friends while also describing their identity. The ELLs utilize technology tools such as photos, video clips, and recordings from their homes. Dialogues can be recorded with digital software programs that explain their homes and communities. The virtual tours can also give the ELLs an opportunity to proudly share their former homes with friends and classmates whom they now have in their new country. As a note, teachers should be sensitive to some situations in which an ELL may not want to share—or even remember—his or her home country. Some families may not be documented; others may have lived in extreme poverty or may even be refugees from fighting or political violence. If that is the case, the teacher must certainly find alternative assignments.

ELLs can develop their BICS language skills by writing emails about general information type of writing. They can have pen pals within the class or school or students from other cities, states, or countries. They also text or write emails to their family and friends. Instant messaging is a tool that creates immediate responses. Students find information quickly by using this tool. They also develop good questioning strategies and learn how to write questions to find information.

Academic language is developed through the multimedia products that the groups of students complete. They may choose to create multimedia presentations of informational texts. They also choose to write an informational text such as a nonfiction book, a brochure, or a class newsletter. Students can import lyrics of a favorite poem or song and then analyze the lyrics to find ways to incorporate them into a multimedia project. Music is an excellent teaching tool for language, and the availability of songs in many languages on the Internet is a dramatic addition to ESL instruction. Pairing ELLs with various partners can help the students share in the writing/reading strategies. By incorporating both partners into the writing process, both groups of students will contribute their ideas into the multimedia process.

Conclusion

Clearly, there are many technology tools currently available to enhance learning for students for whom English is their second language, and many more will become available in time to come. It is important for teachers of ELLs to understand how to evaluate the usefulness of current tools and of tools of the future (see Table 7.2).

Table 7.2   Criteria to choose the most effective technology tools

Criteria	Questions to ask
Engaging in Learning	Does this tool engage my students? Are the topics and the tasks interesting to them? Do they have the prior knowledge necessary to comprehend the ideas?
Using Language I+1	Is the English language in this tool just a little bit above their current level in English so that they can make educated guesses for vocabulary or grammatical structures that are unfamiliar to them?
Integrating Language and Content	Does this tool add to the content knowledge of my students as well as to their English language development?
Integrating Language Skills Listening, Speaking, Reading, Writing	Does this tool use several language skills?
Providing collaborative experiences	Can my students use this tool to work with other learners either face to face or electronically?
Lowering Affective Filters	Will this tool be enjoyable to my students and will they feel comfortable and relaxed when using it?
Possible sequencing from context-embedded to context-reduced	Does this tool allow me to gradually expose my students to less context-embedded language?
Providing comprehensible input (accommodated language)	Will my students be able to access clues to the meaning of the content in addition to the language itself?

The rubric summarizes the ways in which teachers can evaluate the effectiveness of technology tools for their students and reviews the principles of second language learning presented in this chapter.

Understanding how to best use technology for ELLs is imperative for all teachers in school districts whose populations include students for whom English is a second language. It is safe to say that most teachers will have second language learners in their classrooms at some time during their teaching careers. For examples, in the Houston Independent School District, the largest school district in Texas, 29.8 % of the student population was determined to be limited English proficient in years 2012-2013 (http://www.houstonisd.org/domain/7908). In a nearby district, Alief ISD, the home Web page of the district can be translated into 80 home languages. The potential for using technology to help advance ELLs in both content knowledge and in English language has never been more exciting. Teachers should embrace all that our growing technology has to offer and should use good judgment by choosing the tools that best support the principles of second language acquisition.

References

Cummins, J. (2000). *Language, power, and pedagogy: Bilingual children in the crossfire.* Clevedon, Great Britain: Cromwell Press Ltd.

Daniels, H. (2002). *Literature circles: Voice and choice in book clubs and reading groups.* Ontario: Markham Publishers.

Freytag, G. (1863). *Die technik des dramas.* Germany: S. Hirzel.

Giroux, H. (1993). *Border crossings: Cultural workers and the politics of education.* New York: Routledge.

Krashen, S. (1985). *The input hypothesis: Issues and implications.* New York: Longman.

Lee, H. (1960). *To kill a mockingbird.* New York: Grand Central Publishing.

Pfister, M. (1995). *The rainbow fish.* New York: North-South Books

Taylor, M. (1976). *Roll of thunder, hear my cry.* New York: Puffin.

Wright, W. E. (2010). *Foundations for teaching English language learners: Research, theory, policy, and practice.* Philadelphia, PA: Caslon.

Yoon, T. (2013). Beyond the traditional reading class: The application of an E-Book in the EFL English classroom. *International Journal of Research Studies in Language Learning, 2*(1), 17–26.

Part II
Using Educational Technology for Best Practices in Schools and for Teacher Education

Chapter 8

Using Technology with Models of Teaching

Janice L. Nath
University of Houston-Downtown

Meet Miss Givings

Sarah Givings, a first-year, fifth-grade teacher, had felt prepared to go into teaching. However, after her first six months, it seemed as if *she* was doing the majority of the "thinking work" in the classroom; that is, she was presenting all the information, while her students waited for her to assign their lower-level independent work. She had had good methods classes in her teacher education program for the content areas that she currently taught, but something just wasn't working as well as she had envisioned for a learner-centered classroom. Was she falling back into the ways that some of her own teachers had used most often when she had been in school; that is, simply giving the students the information and then having them apply it in some way (most always through a worksheet or writing assignment)? The "kicker" had come this very afternoon, when Jorge in sixth period had noted on his way out of the room in a "stage whisper" (which she was surely meant to hear) that her class today had been particularly boring and "lame." What was missing? What could she do?

Models of teaching are exciting ways of having students learn because these instructional methods of teaching encourage *active* rather than *passive* student learning; that is, the learner is more active than the teacher in constructing knowledge. A model of teaching is a format in which almost any content area can be "inserted"—and, in addition, model formats can be modified to work for all school-age learners. One popular and well-known model of teaching, for example, is cooperative learning, which can be used in mathematics, science, language arts, social studies, music, and so forth. However, there are many more models of teaching that offer student-centered (rather than teacher-centered) learning, and many of these develop students' higher-level thinking abilities as well. Coupled with technology, these models offer teachers novel ways of teaching that actively engage students in stimulating instruction. This chapter will discuss the following models of teaching and their integration with technology: Concept Attainment, Cooperative Learning, Memory Models, and Concept Development.

Models of teaching have been examined at length by researchers such as Joyce, Weil, and Calhoun (2008). These and other educators (Kilbane & Milman, 2014) have noted that each type of model has a distinct purpose (i.e., creativity, social skills, forming or developing concepts, mastery, review, and so forth). A teacher who has knowledge of these models can use them wisely to create variety in his or her instruction and specifically target the academic and social needs of a class.

These models of teaching can stand alone without technology, but coupled with technology, they can have a powerful effect on instruction. When computers first began to be viewed as a future educational tool, Bruner (1960) noted that "what one does and how one teaches [with technology] depends upon the skill and wisdom that goes into the construction of a program of problems" (p. 83). The teacher who considers models of teaching along with technology in his/her repertoire of "solving student learning issues" will be rewarded with actively engaged students who gain in multiple areas of learning.

Concept Attainment

The Concept Attainment model has as its main purpose helping learners to form and remember concepts. It is based mainly on the work of Jerome Bruner, Goodnow, and Austin (1965), who purported that without the ability to *categorize*, human beings would not be able to identify objects/concepts in order to make sense of the world. Defining and learning concepts is part of categorization or organizing one's world.

Perhaps one of the first questions asked in beginning to create a lesson with this model might be, "What do we mean by a concept?" The answer can be simple—"a thing or idea"—but it is, at times, much more complex in instruction. Gunter, Estes, and Schwab (2003) state that "Concepts are defined by the attributes we give them" (p. 82). A concept that a teacher may want children to learn, for example, might be as simple as "general transportation," or he or she may want to narrow it down to "transportation without wheels" (hot air balloons, sleds, helicopters, skates, etc.). Instruction may focus yet on another concept such as "walls", and, based upon the content area, grade level, or purpose, the organization of the concept may be very different. In one lesson, instructors may wish students to touch on *all* types of walls—or he or she may want to narrow the concept to simply walls that are vertical structures made of concrete types of materials (wire, wood, stone, chain-link, etc.) or famous walls from an historical context (the Berlin Wall, the Great Wall of China, Hadrian's Wall, the wall at the Warsaw Ghetto, etc.). He or she may even consider the more abstract concept of walls which "one puts up to others" (protectionism, fear, isolationism, separation, etc.). Therefore, in planning, a teacher must consider that a concept has particular attributes and boundaries that make it unique, and he or she must decide ahead what those boundaries/attributes will be in order to have students obtain that exact concept through many offered examples and nonexamples. To give a very simple example of this process, let us consider the following simple examples and nonexamples and ask ourselves, "Of what could the teacher be thinking here, or/what could this concept be?"

Examples	Nonexamples
Sprite	water
Mountain Dew	milk
Dr. Pepper	juice
7-Up	tea

By looking at the examples and the nonexamples, one can almost immediately see that the concept is "soda" or carbonated beverages. By the teacher offering examples and nonexamples *a bit at a time* (rather than just giving students a definition with a few examples), the learner engages with this idea and mentally builds a place in his/her mind for this category of drinks. The learner is likely to form a more permanent storage area for the concept because the information was not simply "served up" by the teacher. As the learner sees each example and nonexample, the brain engages in hypothesis testing to try to "make a category" and/or to fit in other known examples/nonexamples. Therefore, the learner could ask, "Is Coke an example?" or "Are Kool-Aid and lemonade nonexamples?" When the teacher confirms a student's input, the learner (and the class) firms up the category or concept even more clearly—or, conversely, realizes that his/her train of thought is going in the wrong direction, so a new pathway must be found. This is the beginning of forming a concept in this model.

Let's try another simple concept as Mrs. Clayborn might actually teach it as a "practice game" for students to understand the format and the rules of the game. After she sets the stage with a statement such as, "I have something that I am thinking of, and I want to see if you can guess what it is." She then adds, "I am going to give you some examples of 'it' and some nonexamples, or things that are 'not it'" (note that she could easily use technology to generate pictures of these examples and nonexamples as well [e.g., soda cans as in the earlier "game" or pictures of real fruit and vegetables if using those concepts]). For further directions, she gives the rules of "the game," which include not calling out without raising one's hand and not guessing the concept itself until cleared by the teacher to do so. She tells students that only examples or nonexamples may be given until she feels that most of them have a good idea of what the concept is. Mrs. Clayborn then puts the first two examples below on the board along with one nonexample. Learners may then participate by adding examples or nonexamples to "test their hypothesis" about the concept Mrs. Clayborn is "thinking of." She adds the learners' responses to the correct side. This practice game is presented below.

Mrs. Clayborn begins by putting up two examples and one nonexample:

	Examples	**Nonexamples**
	apple	beans
	orange	
A learner asks, "Is *lettuce* a nonexample?" The teacher confirms by placing it in the correct column.		lettuce
Next, Mrs. Clayborn adds:		book
Callie asks about:	banana	
Jack also says:		pencil
Then the teacher asks where peas, cherries, & dog would go and writes them in the correct columns:	pears cherries	peas dog
(Notice that a nonexample does not have to be "an opposite," but for a simple practice game, it can help the learner see the process more easily. Also, using "opposites" works well for very young children.		

Mrs. Clayborn adds other examples as students brainstorm. By now, learners have certainly understood that the category was fruit, and they can test their hypothesis further by suggesting strawberries as an example or corn as a nonexample and so forth. Once Mrs. Clayborn has the sense that the class, fairly much as a whole, has the concept, she calls on one student to say it or ask the whole class to say it together—fruit!

One benefit of this game is that by the end of the process, the teacher will have an excellent idea of the overall knowledge of the class about this concept because students, once they have the concept, will list all examples they know. When prompted to add, "What other fruits do you know?" they may say, "Lemons, grapefruit," and so forth. This is valuable information for the teacher because it lets him/her know where to *start* teaching in terms of the concept. For example, if students did not respond well, she may want to delve into the concept from the beginning, or, if the game was too easy, move to fill in the blanks on obvious areas the students did not list or move to the more difficult areas of the concept.

Once a teacher has taught this model a time or two, the flow will become very easy, but it is important for the learner's thinking processes to prepare and teach the model in this discussed format for the model to work well. Again, the teacher first gives the general goal of the game (e.g., "Today we are going to play a game where I am thinking of something, and you are going to try to guess what 'it' is. I am going to give you some hints [examples] and some things that are 'not it' or that don't include an idea of the concept."[nonexamples]). Next, the teacher then gives the class some strict rules that should always include:

1. always raising one's hand if he or she has an example or a nonexample to try,
2. not shouting out what he/she thinks what the concept is (only offering examples or nonexamples), and
3. waiting for the teacher to "clear" an individual or the class to guess the concept.

These rules are very important for the teacher to follow, and Mrs. Clayborn makes sure that she redirects students during the practice game so that during the real game, students don't give the concept away early. Of course, students are often very excited to guess what the concept is when they think they know, so there will be some slips in the rules—especially in calling out the concept—but the teacher must be firm to say, "I need to hear you give me an example or nonexample to test your hypothesis" (even if the learner should happen to guess the concept correctly). Reminding the class or individual of these rules often will prevent the game from being over before it starts. The teacher may say, "Remember you are not allowed to guess the concept until I ask for it, so try an example or a nonexample to see if you are still on the right track in your mind."

There are other important considerations in teaching this model's format. This is one of the main reasons for beginning with a simple practice game like the ones above. Children learn the format quickly, and, when learners break the rules during a practice game, the teacher can remind them before the "real game." Again, when the teacher thinks that a good many students have gained the concept, she or he can ask for an educated guess of the concept. A teacher can also control how long the game goes by: (a) giving more examples quickly, (b) having student caucus in groups to see if they can generate more examples/nonexamples/ideas, or (c) simply telling learners the concept if time or examples are running out and students are "stuck." Students are next asked to give examples and what they know about the concept ("milking it")—when the concept is confirmed. Another important part of having students really think hard is to be sure *not* to give them the objective(s) of the lesson until *after* playing the game. If, for example, the teacher wrote on the board, "Today, you are going to identify shapes with corners" and then began putting shapes upon the board for the game, students would not have to think hard at all about what the concept might be. They would it guess quickly—and the object of the model, of course, is to have students engaged in active thinking.

The teacher should also know that there are other phases in the thinking aspect of this game. The order of the game is listed below.

1. Give the goal and rules;
2. Play a simple practice game for students to see the game format (this should be very short and obvious concept for all grade levels so that the instruction can move on to the "real concept" of the day);
3. Give the examples and nonexamples, starting with two examples and one nonexample (so that the students can begin comparing and contrasting right away);
4. When the teacher "reads the audience" that a number of students probably have an idea of the concept, he/she changes "modes" to give students words/pictures/real items to have students classify each as an example or nonexample (e.g., in the game above, the teacher might say, "On which side would I put grapefruit (as an example or a nonexample), cabbage, kiwis, onions?";
5. When the teacher sees that, indeed, most students have gained the concept itself, he or she has a student or the class tell what the concept is. If incorrect, the teacher would continue on, but, if correct;

6. Have students give *all* the examples that they know and can generate ("milk it"); and
7. Have students construct a list of the attributes that make up the concept;
8. If students question some of the examples/nonexamples and their placement in a category, the class "talks it through" after the concept is revealed. For instance, if tomato was given as a nonexample in the game above, the teacher might have "put it in the middle" and come back later to discuss it as a fruit;
9. Have students reflect on and discuss the strategy(ies) that allowed them to "get it."

The advantages of integrating technology into this game are that for almost all concepts, there are instant images, videos, and/or animations available, and images are sometimes much more vivid and can convey more than words in print. The old saying that "a picture is worth a thousand words" is not misplaced here. If Mr. Kumar in science class, for example, wanted to teach the concept of "force" with relationship to movement, he might have to draw or comb through many magazines for pictures of images that fit the definition if it were not for technology. If he had to write or tell about the examples, he might also give the concept's attributes away by having to write descriptions (for instance, "a man kicking a ball" and "a statue just sitting on a stand" rather than letting students see the movement [or lack thereof] in the image that contributes to the definition). With technology, however, he might be able to offer pictures (as seen below) of force in nature, force in work, force in play, force in weapons, and so forth, and its many nonexamples rather than just give the formula and "talk about it." Mr. Kumar constructed the game below. He gradually offers the pictures and time for thought, and, as above, has students construct the concept as they try to guess what it could be.

Examples	Nonexamples

Images © Shutterstock, Inc.

(continued)

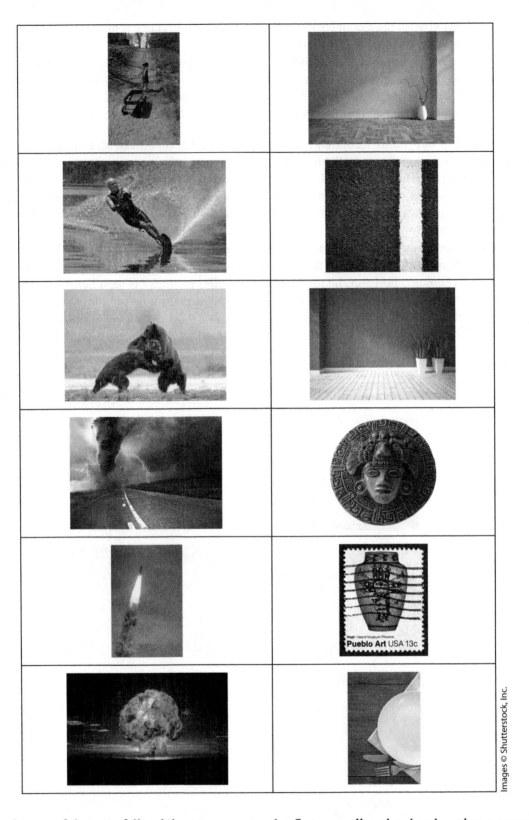

He offers pictures of the waterfall and the wave as examples first, as well as the chessboard as a nonexample. He then flips up examples and nonexamples one at a time. He may also create a presentation as the one shown below in the next example. Here, the teacher has added the example and nonexample pictures as she goes along to keep them firmly in the students' minds.

Not only are the images more vivid but these types of pictures can be easily put on a PowerPoint as a slideshow or on a Web-based presentation such as Prezi and shown to Mrs. Bostic's young learners as follows in her reading lesson. She did so as the class sit in a circle around the screen. See if you can guess the concept.

Slide 1

It (Examples)	Not It (Nonexamples)
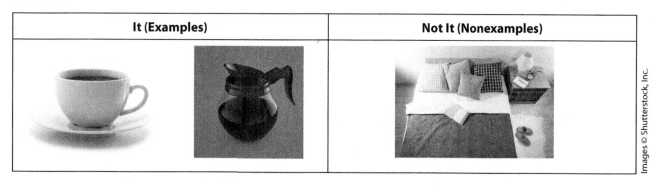	

Images © Shutterstock, Inc.

Slide 2

It or not it?

Images © Shutterstock, Inc.

Slide 3

It	Not It
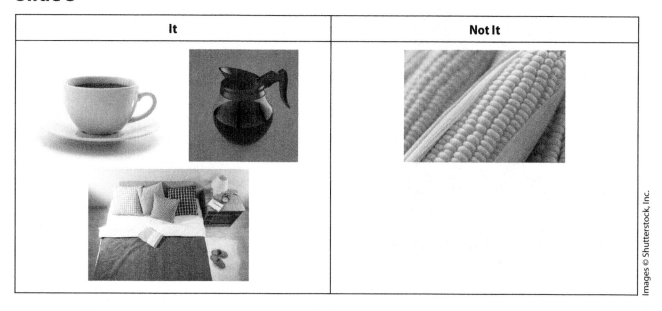	

Images © Shutterstock, Inc.

Slide 4

It or not it?

Images © Shutterstock, Inc.

Slide 5

It	Not It
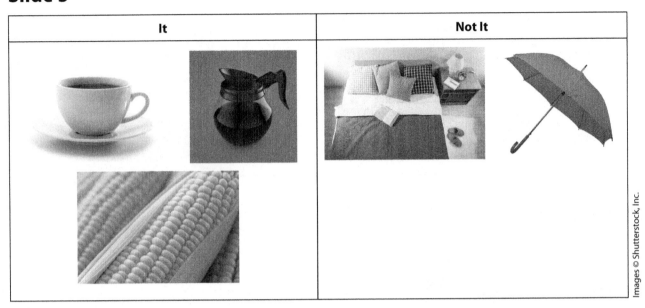	

Images © Shutterstock, Inc.

Slide 6

It or not it?

Images © Shutterstock, Inc.

Slide 7

It or not it?

Images © Shutterstock, Inc.

Slide 8

It	Not It
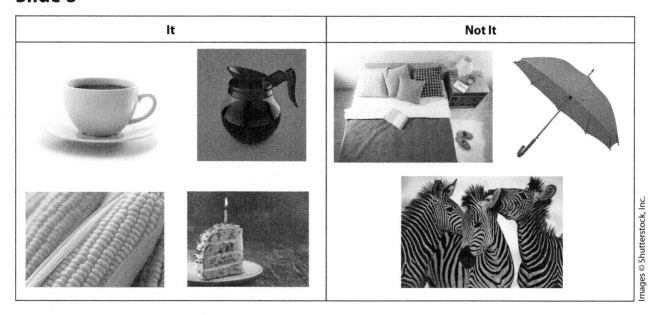	

Slide 9

Slide 10

Slide 11

It	Not It

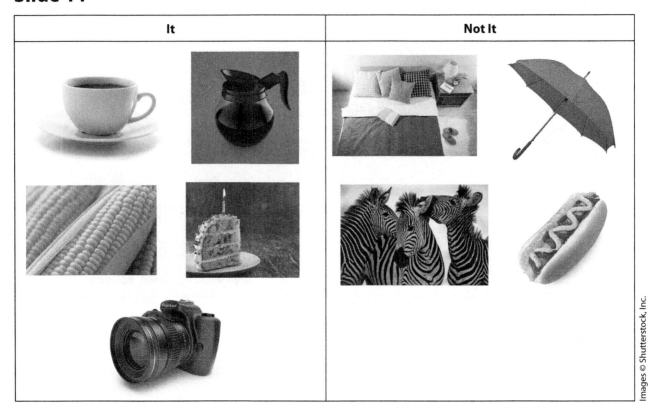

Slide 12

It or not it?

Slide 13

It or not it?

Slide 14

It	Not It

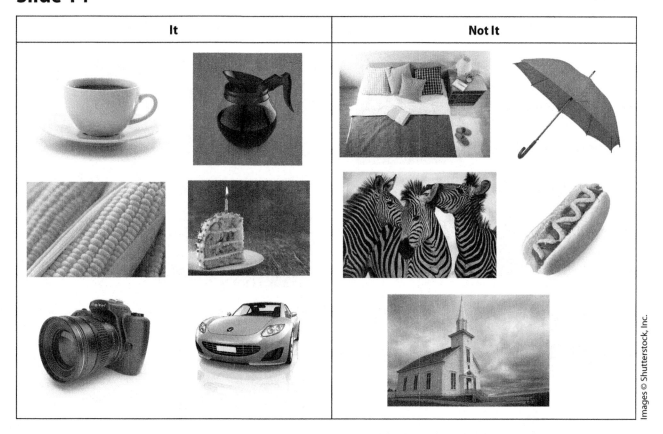

Images © Shutterstock, Inc.

Slide 15

It or not it?

Images © Shutterstock, Inc.

Slide 16

It or not it?

Images © Shutterstock, Inc.

Slide 17

It	Not It

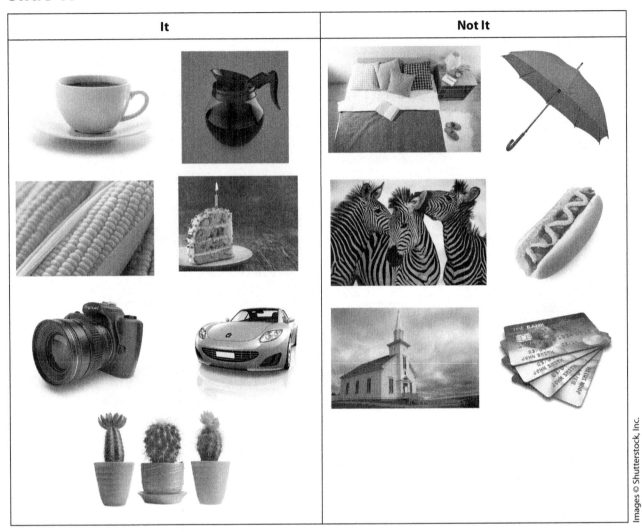

Images © Shutterstock, Inc.

Slide 18

It or not it?

Images © Shutterstock, Inc.

Slide 19

It or not it?

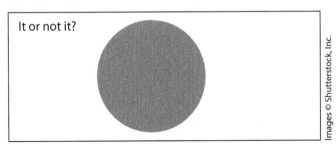

Images © Shutterstock, Inc.

Slide 20

It	Not It

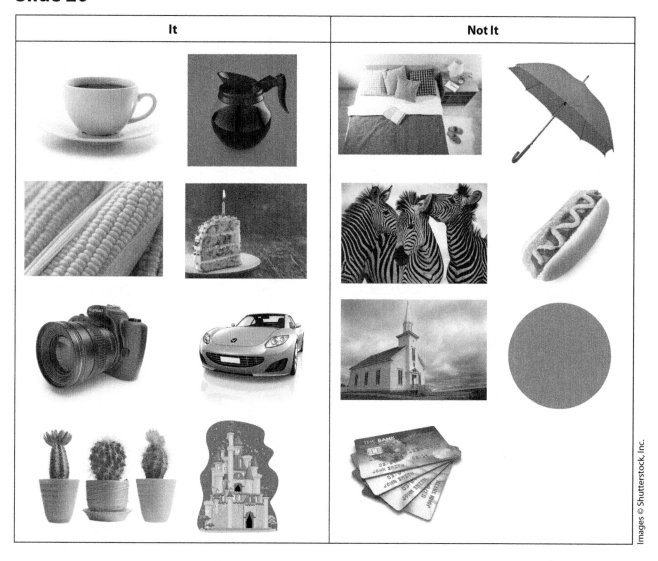

Slide 21 - A Final Look

It	Not It

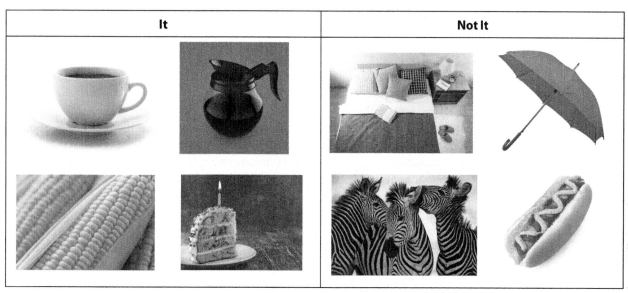

Slide 21 - continued

It	Not It

Slide 22

What else could we add to the list?

Mrs. Bostic is teaching the concept of words that have the /k/ sound but begin with the letter "c." She has chosen a number of images above that illustrate the /k/ sound for examples, and other nonexample images that do not have this sound. When examining how children might think through this model, we can imagine that in the beginning of the game they might believe when presented with the first few images, the concept might be "things we eat or drink." They test their hypothesis by asking the teacher if pizza would be an example. She says that it is not. When Mrs. Bostic continues with the example of cake, learners may still believe it is food or drink, When the picture of the camera goes up as an example, however, they realize that it is something else entirely, and they begin to have to rethink their ideas. A teacher may design this game to show all nonexamples without a "c", but Mrs. Bostic knows students have already had some experience with this sound, so she puts in items as nonexamples that begin with a "c" but have blends or the /s/ sound (circle). When she puts the game into her computer center for children to review, she adds even more nonexamples like a chick, a check, and so forth.

Throughout this narrative on Concept Attainment, one sees the words "the teacher will," but groups of learners and individual learners also love to create Concept Attainment games for their peers, so it is beneficial to remember that "the teacher" could be a student, or, even better, groups of students who generate a Concept Attainment game (after they understand the format and have played several times). For instance, Mr. Aldana assigned his seventh-grade groups to design a PowerPoint game for each of the geographic regions of Texas. They were to include examples of both words/phrases and pictures or even film clips. The group assigned the Coastal Plains area included pictures of oil wells in the Gulf, wind farms, rice fields, pine forests, big ships in the channel, fishing boats, the skylines of Houston and Corpus Christie, and so forth. Mr. Aldana made sure that each group kept their region a secret as they were working so that the other students would have to guess when groups made their presentations. This is truly higher-level thinking at its best, and the computer or the Web is able to store these for further retrieval for interest, addition, review, and/or remediation.

How and When to Use the Model

This model can be used in a number of ways during a lesson. Most often, perhaps, we see it used as a focus activity, for if the teacher uses direct instruction, he or she will have given away the concept; learners, as mentioned earlier, will not have to think as much. As a focus, the model puts the learner into a motivating game immediately. However, this model can be used during a lesson as students come to a concept in the middle of a lesson. For instance, Mrs. Kiley, a high school geography teacher, had been talking about various ways that natural disasters influence the growth of cities and nations. She decided to insert a Concept Attainment game into the middle of her lesson on current "Ring of Fire" cities. She selected pictures of areas that had experienced disasters from long ago and the more recent past and included a map picture of the country or state with the city marked to illustrate the concept of major earthquakes and volcanic eruptions as the focus of natural disasters. She included pictures of cities that have recovered and some that have not in her concept game. At the end of the game, she involved students in predicting where this type of disaster may occur again and had them discuss why some cities recovered from these types of disasters and some remained in ruins.

Finally, this model can also be used as an evaluation tool (closure). After a fourth-grade class has read *The Secret Garden* (Burnett, 1911), Mrs. McNamera used this game to see how well students remembered the parts of the book, characters, plot, and so forth. She began with two of the more difficult examples and one nonexample, and students then offer examples and nonexamples to "fill in" the rest (following the format of "playing the game" discussed earlier). Using technology, she added a number of images downloaded from "Images for The Secret Garden" (following technology usage requirements/laws).

One suggestion for using this model is that students continue to develop a concept using a shared electronic folder to which students can add images from their own or school digital devices or from the Internet. Students can review these concept folders as often as desired or be directed to review them as the teacher sees that it could be needed.

Teachers constructing a Concept Attainment model can use the following steps to be sure that they isolate the concept well and have clear examples and nonexamples ready:

1. Select a concept and write a definition as to how the teacher wants it to be used. Make the definition of the concept very specific and clear so that examples and nonexamples can be generated (e.g., if the concept was vegetables, the game cannot change in the middle to be only "green vegetables").
   • Select attributes and boundaries that are then checked for clarity as an example or nonexample.
2. Develop examples and non-examples:

words	phrases	sentences	film clips
pictures	tangible items	computer images	animations

   • The teacher/leader should generate at least 10 of each (and place these into lesson plans to avoid having him or her scrambling to remember these "on his/her feet." After completing the list, one should go back yet again to ensure each clearly fits the attributes and definition of the concept.

3. Order the examples and non-examples.
    • The examples and nonexamples should be arranged with the "most difficult" first to "easiest" so that students must think harder.
4. It is not necessary to "match" nonexamples, but this can be easier for younger children. Using opposites usually means students "get it" more quickly.

A Review of the Real Game

1. The teacher/leader of the game should present examples and nonexamples one at a time, but should always begin with at least two examples and one nonexample.
2. The leader should ask students to "test their hypothesis" by offering their own examples or nonexamples. A leader should also ask players if they would like to be given another example or nonexample at times when they may be slower to play. To make sure of participation, the leader should call on individuals to contribute an idea, even if they are not raising their hands.
3. When it seems as if students may have an idea of the concept, the leader switches modes to present an example (or nonexample) and then ask players to classify it into the proper column.
4. If students become "stuck," the leader can have them use groups to generate ideas.
5. When it seems that most students have gained the concept, the leader asks for an answer.
6. The leader then asks for all examples that the entire class knows ("milks it" for all the examples known by the entire group and everything known about the concept).
7. The leader asks for a good definition and checks for understanding.
8. The leader has players reflect on strategies that helped them "get there" or attain the concept.

There are many, many concepts that a teacher can use in this model for all areas of learning and all grade levels—early childhood to high school. The teacher can easily use this model in almost any content area to help students think in an active way. The example below shows a variation on the game in an early elementary science lesson on animals that live in the sea. For high school, it might be modified to show examples of microscope slides, figurative language, specialized vocabulary, and so forth.

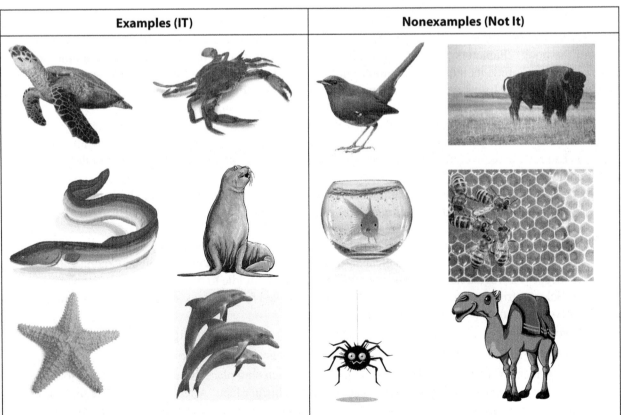

Examples (IT)	Nonexamples (Not It)

The following is another way to look at using this model for mathematics, remembering that the numbers would be introduced by starting with two examples and one nonexample. After some thinking time, the teacher would ask students to test their ideas about the concept. Then, as in the games above, the teacher would introduce more examples and nonexamples one at a time. The teacher may also want to add a "hypothesis" column when playing so that students can keep up with their ideas as they go. There are many variations on how teachers can use this model to fit their learners' needs. Teachers should use these variations to "make them their own" for their learners and for their content area, remembering to keep the general teaching format discussed in order to better engage the brain in higher-level thinking.

Examples	Nonexamples	Hypothesis
1 ½	55	Fractions; small numbers
22 ½	4/5	Numbers with 1 and 2
131 1/3	4/3	Whole numbers with a fraction, eliminate small numbers
28 3/5	1	Yes, that stands! Let's test more to be sure!
5 7/8	34	Mixed numbers!!!

The following is a "writing starter" for language arts. Look carefully at each picture to see what it might have in common with the ones below it, remembering that a teacher/leader would begin with two examples and one nonexample and add the ones below one at a time.

You Can See An Example Here	You Can't See It Here

You Can See An Example Here	You Can't See It Here
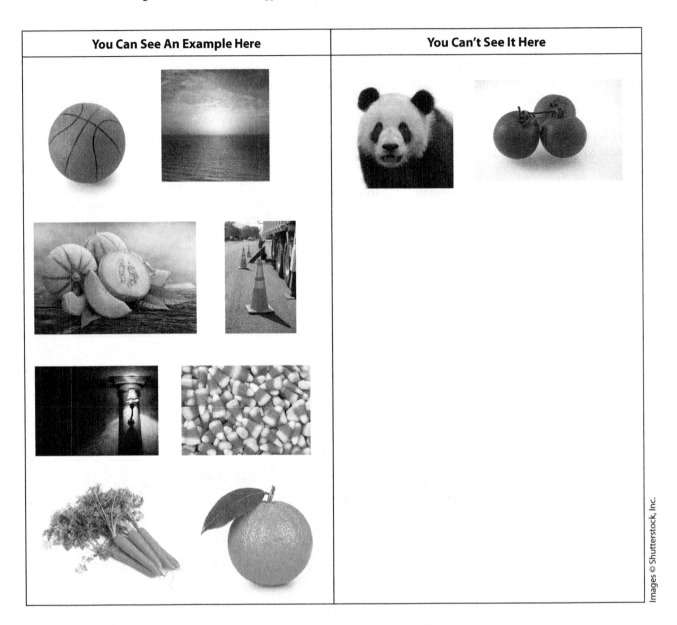	

Students in this language arts class are using images to learn about similes, metaphors, and adjectives for the "color orange." Now when they write, they have these more vivid varieties in their heads (such as "orange as a cantaloupe," or "candy corn orange," or "the sun hung like an orange lifebuoy in the sky").

Students can also use text using their word/picture answers and write them onto the electronic white board. Clip art images, photos, and so on, can also be used from software packages such as Kidspiration and Inspiration, both of which offer images, text boxes, graphic organizers, and much more. Students and teachers may also use videos (from YouTube or other sources) to enhance learning concepts in this model. Mrs. Long, for instance, teaches a World War II Concept Attainment on the Allies and Axis powers using short film clips. On the example side, she chooses short film clips such as the President Roosevelt declaring war after the attack on Pearl Harbor, Winston Churchill's "finest hour" speech, and clips of the Battle of Britain, D-Day, the flag raising at the Battle of Iwo Jima, the French Resistance, the bombing of Hiroshima, and so forth. On the non-example side, she selects clips of Hitler's speeches, Hirohito's reviewing the troop, the attack on Pearl Harbor, the Bataan Death March, Mussolini's speeches, and more that identify the Axis forces.

This model gives teachers a great deal of important information and provides many other benefits for instruction. The most beneficial is active thinking on the part of the learners. Strategies that students use can be observed and strengthened, group work becomes enhanced as members see each other as resources, and the teacher is provided, in the end, with all the knowledge a class knows about the concept. This allows him or her to build on that or teach to fill in the blanks. Technology allows these concepts to come to life in vibrant and motivating ways by bringing in colors, images, lights, sound effects, transitions, time effects, animations, and many more.

Cooperative Learning/Grouping

There are many, many cooperative grouping "submodels," and each one offers a teacher a different goal or goals for his or her class. For example, Mrs. Avalos may know that, in addition to academics, she can also target students' social or emotional needs by selecting the right fit with a particular type of cooperative grouping structure. With technology, teachers can also include technology goals by using various peer groupings—pairs or small numbers of students—who work together on a specific effort using computers, phones, digital cameras, clickers, and so forth. Working together not only strengthens social skills but meets the needs of technology instruction at times when there is not enough equipment for each student to have his or her own for an activity (Dockterman, n.d.). Various submodels of cooperative learning can also work well with technology when students have outside of class assignments and members work asynchronously (on their own time). The discussion in this section goes over some of the important planning issues of using technology with groups along with some of the submodels of cooperative learning that are particularly suited to technology integration.

When teachers begin to incorporate cooperative groups, they have several decisions to make. The first, of course, is "What are my goals academically?" and then, "What are my students' needs outside of academics?" Academic goals are excellent for cooperative grouping because the literature shows that most students learn well academically from being placed in groups due to the *active* (versus passive) nature of peers working with peers (Joyce, Weil, & Calhoun, 2009). Mrs. Krowley, for example, knows that when she teaches a topic, *she* learns it better—and her students are the same. She often sets up cooperate groups requiring that the students who are placed in small groups "teach each other" so that they become more actively involved with the materials. She also knows that this works because students can often explain something more easily to their peers on their own' level, and/or they can help to create more meaningful connections that may sometimes make more sense of materials than can an adult's explanation. Lessons involving technology are typically excellent for using pairs or small groups because one person in the group may be "an expert" who can help others to problem solve with the use of the technology. All group members can all move past the technology issues and on to the academic goals.

Let us examine some thinking processes for a group lesson with technology. Because Mrs. Krowley knows that some students do not always do their independent work well alone, she sometimes creates a "group goal," so that the peers in the group will work together towards that shared goal. Teachers already understand that goals are "broad but guiding learning ideas" such as "Students will learn about conservation," or "Students will learn to use figurative language in their writing." Now, Mrs. Krowley must also decide on a social/emotional skill that his/her class(es) may need. For example, Mrs. Krowley notices that her middle school students need lots of reinforcement. She also knows that her own "teacher's public reinforcement" at this age level can be more embarrassing than effective; however, peer praise is avidly sought and *is* effective. Therefore, her social goal (alongside her academic goals) for students becomes, "The students will appreciate giving and receiving praise." She plans a "sub lesson" that goes into many of her cooperative group lessons.

Mr. Bradley also teaches this type of sub lesson to his fourth graders. He begins his lesson by asking students what praise looks like, and students answer him by giving examples such as "That was cool," "Good job," "Great," "Awesome," and so forth. He has one student come up and Google "praise words" on the electronic white board (where they find a site with 150 words of praise that could be used with classmates). He also asks them to try some more meaningful praise and uses as a reference a project that the class had completed not long ago. "Try to think of some examples of what your partners did on the last project that you really liked," he encourages. "For example, you might say, 'That image or picture you picked really made your poster stand out.'" The class follows with some good examples that coworkers could use. Then Mr. Bradley tells them that they were half done, because when someone gives praise, the receiver has to acknowledge it in some way. He goes on to say, "If someone says to you, 'Wow! I like that shirt,' and the first person does not acknowledge that compliment, it makes them doubt their judgment or feel uncomfortable . . . so what are some ways we verbally acknowledge someone's compliment or praise?" Students think for a moment and say, "Thanks," "I appreciate that," or "That was nice," and so forth. Mr. Bradley asks that the student at the electronic whiteboard now go to a site on "how to take a compliment," and some ideas pop up on the site he had designated. Now Mr. Bradley asks the class to turn to their partners and practice using some of the words/phrases that they have generated (or some new ones). The first partners would give three praise words or phrases, and the second partners would acknowledge them. Then they would reverse roles. Mr. Bradley gives students four minutes to practice this skill.

In the next phase of the mini-lesson, Mr. Bradley asks students how we give praise nonverbally. After thinking about that for a moment, students reply that thumbs up, high 5s, silent cheers, a pat on the shoulder, fist in the air, and others that show praise. The class is asked again to practice this with their partners. Now students have some concrete ideas to use during the group lesson. However, Mr. Bradley knows that "just knowing it and using it" are two very different things, so he tells the class that during the lesson, he will be looking for the "Social Skill of the Day (praise)," and when he sees it, he will give that group a point. At the end of the class period, the group with the most points would receive a prize.

Mr. Bradley is now ready to begin his academic lesson. Kilbane and Milman (2014) also suggest that teachers may even want to have students write and film a short "documentary" of their groups as they are role-playing how to be supportive when working in small groups. "They could ask students to model positive and negative examples of supportive feedback," these researchers continue, "and then later use these videos to reflect on and compare how they actually practiced these skills in reality" (p. 337).

Using groups with technology can be very successful, but the process must be highly structured. This format of using groups can provide good management just through motivation, because technology provides interest and active learning when students are talking and learning for the sake of learning—simply because it is more fun. However, it can all fall apart if the teacher is not careful to structure each part of the lesson so that students feel that they have fair usage of technology and that time issues are carefully regulated. That is not to say that each member of a group will have a turn with the technology during every activity, but students must feel that they get their "fair share" (perhaps even later during the week). The younger the child, the more keenly this will be an issue. That is one reason Ms. Simms makes sure to have roles in her class for each group activity that she uses. A key role is the time keeper of the group so that in "take turns activities," everyone has the same amount of time with technology, or it is understood that in the next activity, they will change roles and have equal time then.

Ms. Simms uses a group learning project with her 20 third graders (and 5 computers) where each group of students must come up with a poster for a mammal of their choice. On the poster, children must download a picture of the mammal and, also, they must have a summary paragraph that includes the mammal's habitat, what it eats, what preys on it, and if it appearance changes seasonally. By assigning the role of timekeeper to each group, Mrs. Simms makes sure that all students get equal time on the computer to download the information and a picture which they will eventually print out and paste onto a poster. She also assigns to each group of students the role of a "checker," who is the person who will make sure that in each summary, each group member has the required information. The "quality engineer" will make sure that the poster and its summaries/pictures are all finished in a way that is attractive and that each student's name is on his/her contribution. Finally, there is a "materials manager/presenter" whose role includes getting anything else the group needs for the poster as they work towards their joint project together, and, in the end, present it to the class. For this grade level, the information and picture is glued onto poster boards, but Mr. Johnson may have his older students present their similarly structured slideshow on the electronic white board. This encourages each student to do his/her best using peer pressure to move in a structured way to both an individual academic task and an interdependent task. Assigning roles provide a great deal of structure when using groups and technology.

As Ms. Simms gets ready for this lesson, she also plans carefully as to what her directions will be for groups. How will she get children into five groups around the technology if they are not already in long-term groups? Who will she put together this time? How will she make sure she creates diverse groups academically (and with computer skills), so there are no "win/win and lose/lose" groups? One of the best reasons for using groups is to make sure that students work with those who are different from themselves ethnically, academically, gender-wise, and so forth, so she carefully designs her groups. At times, she also may use as a reward having pairs choose their partners, but normally she structures her groups carefully. In doing this, she does not want confrontation as she directs children to work together. To prevent this, she beings by placing a color-coded card face down on each student's desk as she begins the technology part of the lesson. When all the cards have been passed out, she asks students to move into groups one by one with their matching colors ("If you have a red card, please move together in the right corner of the room now."). It seems that each card is the "luck of the draw," but Ms. Simms has carefully "stacked the deck" so that when a student complains that he/she does not want to work with someone in the group, Ms. Simms can say, "Well, next time the cards will probably come out a different way" (and she does make sure they do). This usually does much to deescalate the situation of "I don't want to work with him/her!" rather than pointing to students and saying, "You ARE working with him/her today, and that is that" (which often sets up a power struggle and starts the project off with a negative environment as one child gets farther into the confrontation and the other cringes because he/she is an unwanted group member).

Ms. Simms also thinks carefully through how much time each student will need on the computer, if applicable, during this lesson and how groups will decide who goes first (she has them number off before they do anything so she establishes the order and the roles using these numbers). It is sometimes difficult to plan for exactly the right amount of time for each group member's activities on and off technology, but thinking about this ahead of time will assure better classroom management and help members see that all "jobs" are valuable in a group effort. She also reminds them of the "first three, and then me rule," which means that if someone in the group doesn't know how to do something on the computer (or the answer to other questions), he or she must ask everyone in the group prior to all group members raising their hands. This ensures that each group uses its members as resources first and gives Mrs. Simms more time to facilitate issues where no one in the group knows the answer. She also thinks about the seating situation with technology and, in addition, she decides what work students will be doing when it is not their turn on the computer (or with other digital devices) so that engagement and management are maintained throughout the experience.

Several chapters in this book, particularly about social studies, may mention projects where classrooms may work together from different locales—even from different countries on a particular project. This is one aspect of group work that can be easily managed by today's technology. Again, to do this, careful planning must be a top priority. First, the teacher must decide if this should be synchronous (in real-time) or asynchronous (at one's own convenience, such as with email). One issue when working with groups outside the school is timing. Times when groups may be available online to chat at the same time (in chat rooms, Google Hangouts, or Skype connections) must be considered carefully, especially if time zones are an issue (for example, in middle and high schools where a teacher may want different periods during the day to participate, but school may be over in different parts of the world by the time that some classes are in session). The types of technology available (and various firewalls which a school may have) must also be considered when connecting to other classrooms. Clear contributions for each participant need to be carefully thought out and set up prior to beginning. Equipment that all can use may also be of concern. Many students in U.S. classrooms may have availability to digital cameras, for example, where students in other countries (or other parts of the United States) may not have those same options. It also becomes a management problem when teachers have made plans for groups to be online, and, for a variety of reasons, the connection is not made. Teachers must have a backup plan for groups to connect at a later time and an assignment or instruction ready for now. A calendar is also a must in planning these types of group adventures with mini- and final project goals clearly laid out and interim deadlines established. During communication times, time slots should be set forth clearly so students understand that they must complete their messages within a certain limit (especially if it is synchronous/real-time). Depending on one's district, there may be course management tools such as Blackboard, or Zoho.com that offer chats, connections, documents, discussions, email, meetings, projects, and wikis, as well as business and productivity applications. Moodle.org offers its learning platform free as a "build for free."

Miss Verma, a high school social studies teacher, makes arrangements for her students to conduct a project with a counterpart class in India. First, she gives her students a brief time zone lesson of the two locations by asking students to try out Web 2.0 time zone tools such as Time Zone Converter or World Time Buddy. To manage the scheduling issue across two continents, she uses Web-based scheduling tools such as Doodle and Meeting Wizard to decide meeting times of the two classes. Then to remind teachers and students of alike of events and activity dates, the Web-based Google Calendar is set up to share with all participants. Miss Verma also incorporates the project's Google Calendar into her homepages created on Weebly. Miss Verma thinks that in addition to the social studies content that students will learn in their projects, knowing how to interact with people from a different culture, understanding how international time zones work, knowing how to manage big projects that involve many parties, and being able to conduct effective business scheduling are important work force skills for her students.

Another area to consider for those using groups is self-evaluation. Some of the controversial issues of being in a group are: that not everyone participates equally (riding on coattails); some members may try to manage the team too forcefully; some may not share digital time well; all members may not adhere well to deadlines; and so forth. These should be carefully considered in group reflections. In the real world, without skills that make a group work well together, the productivity is not high and negative feelings of working on a team are generated. Because preparing students to do well in the real world is of paramount importance, students need to reflect on their productivity skills so they can become better for the next time—and for the future. Luckily, there are some quick technology assessment tools that can help students look at this in a quick and metacognitive way. For instance, SurveyMonkey, Socrative, or Google Forms allows students to sign on quickly and record their answers so that the teacher can see if students are feeling positive or negative about their group and what areas they see as strong or, conversely, problematic. They can also rate their own participation.

Jigsaw

Mr. Stanton teaches world history, and he wants to use a submodel of cooperative learning called Jigsaw. He begins by explaining that today, each member of the well-established long-term group is "going away" to another group to become an expert in *one* area of the Mayas—the topic for today's lesson. In their new expert group, they will be reading a short summary, and each expert group will also be seated at one of the four computer stations in the classroom, so that they will be able to get further information (for which URLs have been bookmarked) about "their piece of the puzzle" on the computer. The aim of the expert groups is to come up with the "most important information about their assigned area (Group 1: Short history; Group 2: Religion/war; Group 3: Agriculture/economy; and Group 4: Famous landmarks/artifacts). He continues to give all directions before asking students to move—since he knows they will be distracted once they begin moving. He then has students number off in their long-term groups. "I will have all the roles on the board for your expert groups," he tells them. "When you get to your new expert group, renumber in your new group, and then I will show you the roles for the day." Your mission in your expert groups is to design a way to teach your long-term group about the details of the readings and the information you found out from your computer. Everyone in your group should have the same exact memory model that you all design together (and/or other graphic organizers) to take back to your long-term group by the end of the time so that no member of the expert groups forgets to teach all the information that you found out. That will be your individual responsibility when you get back to your original group at the end of this activity—to teach them your piece of the puzzle so that we can pass a test on all the information. For example, if a group felt like it was important to remember that most of the cities had pyramids, the group might download pictures of some of the major ones that are still available to see . . . or they may draw a group of pyramids on a map of Mexico and other Central American countries about where the pyramids are located to show their group. . .or they might even draw a funny picture of many pyramids along with other information they find in their chapter to make a memory model. It is a group's decision as to how they design materials that will best be remembered. "Alright," he directs, "let's pack up our belongings, and all those who are 'ones,' come to Computer Station 1." He waits until that move is settled before calling the next stations.

The flowchart on the following page demonstrates how students might move from original groups to expert groups and back.

Numbered Heads

Mr. Abboud plays Numbered Heads, another submodel of cooperative learning with his young students in mathematics using images flashed up on the computer screen. This cooperative structure requires that students number off in their groups. After showing a picture on polygons, for example, he has "think time" (in which there is a pause for students to come up with an individual answer), "talk time" (in which groups all agree on one answer), and then he calls a group's name and a number. If that student knows the answer, he or she gains

---

6 Long-Term Groups of 4 Number off 1-2-3-4S

Move Into Expert Groups

All ones move to one area (where one laptop is positioned)
All twos to another area (where one laptop is positioned)
All threes to another area (where one laptop is positioned)
All fours to another area (where one laptop is positioned)
Academic assignment

1. Read short information packet/chapter that is bookmarked (group members can use "Round Robin" read-aloud if needed)
2. Retrieve addition information on the Internet
3. Design a memory model or graphic organizer to "take back" to long-term group (use clip art/graphics, etc.)

Roles:

1. Timekeeper
2. Artist/graphic artist (can be done with technology)
3. Checker (to make sure everyone has a copy of the information from which they will teach (when they move back into their original group)
4. Praiser
5. Gatekeeper (to be sure that everyone in the group contributes equally)
6. Reflector (to determine "how we did/what could we do better next time")

Move Back to Original Groups

1. Renumber and reassign roles: timekeeper, gatekeeper, roundup (revisits big picture/main points), and reflector/celebrator
2. Each member teaches the rest of their group (Round Robin style) about what was discovered by their expert group and demonstrates the memory model they created. Afterwards, the reflector of the group has the entire group give one suggestion about what they did well together and what they could work on the next time. He or she leads the group in a celebration of having completed all this material with everyone's help.
3. The quiz on this material is assigned for tomorrow. This gives all members the chance to go back over the other chapters on their own once more, but the teacher knows that all students have already had an active experience with the material today. The "puzzle" of reading long sections alone was broken up into "doable" pieces in expert groups and put back together in long-term groups.

---

a point for the whole group. If not, Mr. Abboud goes to a different group. For a practice question, Mr. Abboud flashes the following picture up:

He then calls out "think time" and, after a short pause, "talk time," and, finally, he calls on the T-Rex group, Number 2. Steve, who is Number 2 in that group, answers, "A rectangle," and Mr. Abboud confirms that Steve's answer is correct. He then proceeds to the real game in which he mingles real-life pictures with the shapes as seen below. He shows examples like these one at a time.

Images © Shutterstock, Inc.

After flashing up each picture, he calls the name of a new group and a new number within the group.

This submodel provides an excellent and supportive structure because students have their group members to consult if they don't know the answer. Interdependence is enhanced, and students are actively talking about the question. The competition between groups provides motivation to get the answer right within each group.

A long history of research shows the positive results of using cooperative learning groups during instruction—both academically, motivationally, and socially/emotionally (Slavin, 1987; Stahl, 1994, Stevens & Slavin, 1995). This type of instruction can be joined with technology, but a teacher must structure these experiences to have the potential of the group experience and the technology work well together.

Ms. Tran recently learned of the interactive Web site, Socrative (www.socrative.com), from a teacher conference and eagerly tried it out with Numbered Heads. She had been inspired by a conference presentation where a high school AP (Advance Placement) teacher, Mr. Hart, incorporated it into his physics lessons. The Web tool has the ability to quickly and interactively gather feedback from students by offering many possibilities for gauging opinions, testing understanding, and engaging all participants. Ms. Tran had used Quizlet, Cram, and Flashcard Machines to host online flashcards and quizzes for students before but thought the Socrative interface would be more appealing to adolescent learners. Ms. Tran modified Mr. Hart's teaching strategies in order to fit her seventh-grade math class. She likes to be able to display the break down analysis of student responses in percentage as well as diagram formats. After implementing this interactive Web site, one student found out that she could respond to Socrative by using her own smart phone rather than computers or proprietary hardware in real time such as a physical voting handset (e.g., clickers). This makes implementing this type of interactive Web site even more convenient. One feature of this site that groups can use with Numbered Heads is the Space Race that allows teams to compete. As they answer electronically, the teams can see immediately on a display who is winning.

There are good examples of this submodel on YouTube that can be found by typing in "Numbered Heads Together YouTube" on a search engine. One elementary example with Mrs. Hines (Numbered Heads Together 0001) is at www.youtube.com/watch?v=v8uYS488BIUw (or search for Mrs. Hines and Numbered Heads) and a high school example is at www.youtube.com/watch?v=ADmXhDuHpD4, although there are many more.

Group Role Play

Dockterman (n.d.) describes a cooperative learning submodel requiring both cooperation *and* conflict that generates good discussion through dissonant points of view. A situation which requires a decision about a particular compelling issue is required. If background material is needed, it is taught or reviewed, and then each student is given a well-supported opinion (of which there are many), with the end objective being a whole group decision. Teams of about four students are given advisory roles or "put on a committee." For instance, for an environmental decision in a town or city through a mayor's office with a reelection on the horizon, there may be teams of environmentalists, scientists, economists, reelection specialists, public advocacy, or others. Each group will have targeted information bookmarked that is coming from their perspective roles. Dockterman gives the following as one such scenario:

> *Dead fish! The headline glares at you from your desk. The danger forced you, the mayor of Alpine to close Snyder Pond. Could the nearby dump be polluting the pond and killing the fish? Or is it some other cause . . . .? Many people suspect the town dump! Who knows what the mining company is dumping there? Are Malaco and its jobs really good for alpine? What if the company seeks to mine beautiful Gab's Gully? You are the mayor, and it's an election year.* (p. 41)

Part of the instructions for each advisory committee would be to summarize the materials on what their position should be and then rank their goals for a decision. In the case above, goals would be to win reelection, protect the environment, hold down costs, preserve the economy, and so forth. Based upon their rating, groups then individually begin to form their case (based on the bookmarked or other information they find online) to the mayor. Cases are presented, and the class must then come to a consensus after much high-level, persuasive discussion. As one can see, these types of role play can cover mathematics skills, language arts, science, social studies, and so forth. Students become invested in their positions, so involvement is more intense. There are a few software applications for these types of role play, but the teacher is able to create cases easily in his/her content area that support a particular class.

Memory Model

The memory model is one that is most useful in helping learners remember the vast amount of information that teachers ask of students throughout their schooling. Although there are some memory submodels that do not require technology, many of these submodels can be enhanced through its use.

One of the submodels that is very effective with technology, for example, is using ridiculous images. Teachers often use this submodel to help students remember vocabulary words. The word "litany" for instance might be depicted as the "mind jolter" below:

Images © Shutterstock, Inc.

The vocabulary word "litany" means a form of prayer. The common elements that help the mind "click in" when the definition cannot be remembered is that someone turned over a candle during prayer and set his knee on fire . . . or "lit-an-knee" (litany) = prayer. The ridiculous association picture pops readily to mind when the word is heard. Often the memory model will use a "play on words" such as this one to associate the real meaning with the ridiculous. For another example, one may want to teach the word "discommoded." A picture of a frustrated person standing over a toilet will surely bring up the funny phrase, " 'Dis' commode is broken, and so I am very annoyed." The definition of discommoded is annoyed.

Images © Shutterstock, Inc.

One element that makes technology a boon to creating memory models is that these "ridiculous association" pictures may sometimes require art work, and many students do not feel confident in their drawing. Using clip art, they can quickly search for art images that might help make up their ridiculous image. In doing so, they are seeing a number of images, which makes the word more likely to "stick in the brain." For example, there are more than 100 clip art images to choose from in the prayer category above for litany on bing.com/images. The artist creating the memory model has to examine each to see if the image is suitable for making into his/her or a group's imagine, so already the focus on the word *litany* as associated with a form of prayer is making pathways into the brain through activity. If using small learning groups, there can be quite a bit of discussion

Bear Cubs (A Litter)

as to the choices and arrangement of the items used. This also helps the image and vocabulary word to "stick" in the brain. If students are drawing, there may be quite a bit of erasing or starting over, but using technology is quick and easy. This can be used for many different concepts. For example, if Mr. Farr wanted students in science to remember the terms for some "animal babies" so he might help students design the following:

The ridiculous image is the three bear cubs with trash/litter all around.

Another science class was studying "animal groups" and came up with a memory model for a group of caterpillars. One may be able to guess by looking at the picture below that a group of caterpillars is an army.

Similarly, a group of coyotes is. . ..?

. . . a band. When asked to remember that dogs, however, in a group were a pack, one group came up with a picture of dogs going into a suitcase (packing), while another came up with an image of a six-*pack* of soda with dogs coming out of it.

If Mrs. Bures was having her students remember the years of World War II in her social studies class, she might ask students to create "an image" for some major events using a rhyming scheme for numbers. This rhyming list stays the same for all numbers and is created by the class.

1 = sun
2 = shoe
3 = tree
4 = door
5 = hive
6 = sticks
7 = heaven
8 = gate
9 = dine
10 = hen

Therefore, we might see 1939 as the following picture/ridiculous image:

One = sun, 9 = dine, 3 = tree, 9 = dine, and we have added to the "dine" a Polish sausage and a Polish group starts the picture to remind students one of the beginning events of WWII was the invasion of Poland by Germany in 1939. This could also be enhanced by an image of Hitler's moustache superimposed over "the diners at the table."

Mr. Wood, a science teacher, has his students use ridiculous images to help remember Newton's three Laws of Motion.

1st Law of Motion: An
object at rest wants to stay
at rest.

2nd Law of Motion (two elephants for the 2nd law): When two forces are acting on each other, the greater dominates.

3rd Law of Motion (three pairs of pears to help remember this is the 3rd law): Force exists in pairs.

Tips for Using Memory Models

As with all models of teaching, this model can be used with most content areas. It can also be used with and without technology. Teachers may want to investigate more usage of the model in other ways such as visualization, mnemonics, and silly songs (of which there are an amazing number as resources on the Internet). Most preservice teachers remember various Schoolhouse Rock songs, and many can probably still remember the lyrics to this day. Teachers can search for songs in content areas such as science or more specific areas within the content area (e.g., the rainforest). Many Web sites have animations to go along with the songs (David Williams' Rainforest Song – YouTube). Groups may create and film their own songs and/or animations to help remember content information.

Indeed, there are many other ways to help students remember various things that we need to teach. With the ideas that have been introduced here, there are some factors to remember. The teacher must clearly understand that to work, a memory connection must be meaningful for the learner. If the association doesn't "ring a bell" with the student, he or she cannot make the connection to put it into memory easily. Teachers are often much older than their students, so students may have no idea of a connection that a teacher makes in terms of a concept. Therefore, the teacher should always give students an idea(s), but he/she should also give students time to generate their own so that there is a meaningful connection. Groups are supportive for creativity in generating these ideas.

Part of the reason that this model works is that learners pay more attention to the material, so *activity* must also be in place during the lesson for this. Students must have some time to work on memory connections of their own. "Anything that captures students' attention and engages their mind has the potential to produce learning," notes Banikowski (1999). She continues with, "of course, the opposite is also true: No attention, no engagement, no learning."

This model works in a number of other ways as well. Banikowski (1999) also reminds us that "a picture is worth a thousand words," and the numbers and variety of pictures available through technology are vast. Humor is also an element that causes ridiculous associations to be caught in memory because these images are often funny and unusual.

The more students use this technique and are directed to where it might be used, the more they may be able to see its application in other content areas and in life (for instance, even remembering homework assignments or a list for shopping). A social studies teacher, Mr. Barton, tells his class, "I know you are studying *Hamlet* with Mrs. Cole this term in English. We are going to use the same memory model format that you worked with in her class that helped you remember the story line and characters of *Hamlet* to remember the main events of the American Revolution in my class." The more that teachers can use these elements in memory models, the better chance students may have to access their memories of the vast amount of information that they learn throughout their time in school and onward.

Concept Development

Mrs. Brandenburg was planning to begin a unit with her high school English students on *Romeo and Juliet*. She knew that they already had some experience with the story, but she wanted to find out how much they knew. On the electronic whiteboard, she asked students to brainstorm what they thought of when they heard the title *Romeo and Juliet*. Students begin to "toss out" the following ideas, and Mrs. Brandenburg wrote them in as they did:

Romeo and Juliet

a play	Shakespeare	old English	sad	movie
stabbed	feuding families	died	young	

With this, the students began to taper off. Mrs. Brandenburg was surprised! She thought they would know more. She saved the brainstorm on her computer as 1st Period— *Romeo and Juliet* Concept Development and moved on with her next lesson on the play.

At the conclusion of the unit, she brought the brainstorm back up on the computer screen and asked the same question, showing them what they had known before. "What can you add now?" she asked. They contributed the following:

Romeo and Juliet

a play	Shakespeare	old English	sad	movie
stabbed	feuding families	died	young	Paris
Capulet	the nurse	Friar Laurence	Verona	Mercutio
Montague	street fight	the party	balcony	secret marriage
sleeping drug	banishment	"O Romeo, Romeo, . . .	poison	crypt/tomb
"star-crossed"	tragedy	wherefore art thou	16th century	love at first sight
lovers	"sun hides its face	Romeo?"	men actors	comedy to tragedy
women's roles	in sorrow"	hatred	feud	Juliet's room
forced marriage	Capulet's house	orchard	Mantua	church
forbidden love	*West Side Story*	ballet	movies	*High School Musical*
Shakespeare	*Romeo & Juliet* (the	"Parting is such	love is as	swordplay
In Love	movie, 2013)	such sweet sorrow"	"boundless	. . . "what light through
masks	themes	light/dark	as the sea"	yonder window
time	fate/fortune	Prologue	Justin Bieber	breaks. . ."
"Bye Bye"	"You Had Me at	timeless	songs	plaza/public square
party crashers	At Hello"	Capulet's tomb	Tybalt	revenge
the prince				

After listing, Mrs. Brandenberg looked at the list and asked if anyone else had anything else they could think of to add and made sure that students knew they could do so if they thought of anything as they went along through the model. She told them that she was going to read the list, and if anyone had another idea that she would add it. Also someone didn't know why a term was added or what it was, he or she should raise his or her hand, and they would revisit the reason the term had been added. She began to read the list and came to the word Mantua, when Brad held up this hand. "I don't know what that is," he said. "Who put Mantua up?" Mrs. Brandenberg asked, and Kaylynn said that it was her. "Can you tell Brad why you added that?" the teacher asked. "It was the place where Romeo got banished to by the Prince," Kaylynn told him, "you know, after Romeo killed Tybalt who had killed Mercutio." "Oh, okay," answered Brad, "I didn't remember that." The teacher moved on down the list, and there were a few more terms that were discussed and some that students wanted to add.

For the next step, Mrs. Brandenburg told students that they would be finding words /phrases/concepts that belonged together and give them a category name. They were to use all the words on the list. Mrs. Brandenberg asked them what might go with Verona, for example, and Angie said, "The balcony, the public square, Capulet's orchard, Capulet's house, and the tomb." "What could we call this category?" Mrs. Brandenberg continued. "It could be the settings for the scenes," another student chimed in, "so then we would add Mantua." "That's a very good idea," said Mrs. Brandenberg.

Settings

    Verona
    the balcony
    the public square
    Capulet's orchard
    Capulet's house
    the tomb/crypt
    Mantua

She continued telling students to find their computer groups, because they would be working on the computer to use all these terms listed in this way. She emailed the list to the accessible class email so that students could put it up at their stations and work on it. She also had cards at each station with roles and time limits so that all students would have some time on the computer. As they used each term, they used the cross out feature of Word. One group began classifying the terms in the following way (although other groups make other categories):

Romeo and Juliet

~~a play~~	~~Shakespeare~~	~~older English~~	sad	movie
stabbed	family didn't want	died	young	~~Paris~~
~~Capulet~~	~~the nurse~~	~~Friar Laurence~~	<u>Verona</u>	~~Mercutio~~
~~Montague~~	~~street fight~~		~~balcony~~	~~secret marriage~~
sleeping drug	~~banishment~~	"O Romeo, Romeo, . . .	poison	~~crypt/tomb~~
"star-crossed"	tragedy	wherefore art thou	16th century	love at first sight
lovers	"sun hides its face	Romeo?"	men actors	comedy to tragedy
~~women's roles~~	in sorrow"	hatred	feud	~~Juliet's room~~
forced marriage	~~Capulet's house~~	~~orchard~~	Mantua	~~church~~
~~forbidden love~~	*West Side Story*	ballet	England	*High School Musical*

Shakespeare	*Romeo & Juliet* (the	~~"Parting is such~~	~~love is as~~	swordplay
In Love	movie, 2013)	~~such sweet sorrow"~~	~~"boundless~~	~~..."what light through~~
~~masked ball~~	~~themes~~	~~light/dark~~	~~as the sea"~~	~~yonder window~~
time	~~fate/fortune~~	Prologue	~~Justin Bieber~~	~~breaks..."~~
~~Elizabethan~~	~~"You Had Me at~~	~~timeless~~	~~songs~~	~~plaza/public square~~
party crashers	~~At Hello"~~	~~Capulet's tomb~~	~~Tybalt~~	~~revenge~~
~~the Prince~~	~~wedding~~	*~~New Moon~~*		
~~"How Do I~~				
~~Live Without You~~				

The following categories emerged from one group.

Settings	Characters	Themes
Verona	Romeo	revenge
the balcony	Juliet	fate/fortune
the public square/plaza	parents	light/dark
Capulet's orchard	Tybalt	roles of women
Juliet's room	the Prince	forbidden love
Capulet's house	Capulet	love at first sight
Capulet's tomb/crypt	Montague	
Mantua	the nurse	
Church	Mercutio	
	Paris	
	Friar Laurence	

Events	Author	Movies/Plays/Books/Songs
wedding	Shakespeare	*New Moon*
street fight	timeless	Justin Bieber songs
masked ball	sonnets	"You Had Me at Hello"
banishment	Older English	"How Do I Live without You"
secret marriage	Elizabeth	
Juliet is buried	England	
Romeo takes poison		
Juliet stabs herself		

Famous quotes

"... what light through yonder window breaks..."

love is "boundless as the sea"

"Parting is such sweet sorrow..."

For students to interact more with the important vocabulary words within *Romeo and Juliet*, Mrs. Brandenberg asked students to copy and paste a number of key word lists to word cloud sites such as WordItOut (http://worditout.com/word-cloud/make-a-new-one) or Tagxedo (www.tagxedo.com/). To extend even more, one student found the entire *Romeo and Juliet* play from the Shakespeare homepage at MIT (http://shakespeare.mit.edu/romeo_juliet/full.html) and created a word cloud of the entire play through a word cloud generator such as http://www.jasondavies.com/wordcloud/#. Some students liked the word clouds so much that they ordered customized t-shirts with the word clouds online from sites such as www.spreadshirt.com/word+cloud+t-shirt. Several students express that these word clouds made learning English literature more artistic and educated fun.

Images © Shutterstock, Inc.

Mrs. Brandenberg's class is having so much fun with the words, phrases, and quotes in *Romeo and Juliet* that one student created a meme on the quote " "Parting is such sweet sorrow . . .".

Parting is such sweet sorrow. . .

Images © Shutterstock, Inc.

The bell was about to ring, so Mrs. Brandenberg had students save their work for tomorrow so they could come back to it and finish up using all the terms on the brainstorm list. One group's categories are listed above, but other groups came up with some differences. The teacher let them make the list in the form above, or they could download or create a graphic organizer that suited their purpose. One group used a web for theirs, adding some other things as they worked (see next page).

The next day, Mrs. Brandenberg had them go straight to their group computer station and pull up their saved documents. Each group was to continue to work on using all the terms in the brainstorm. At the close of the time limit on this activity, the teacher asked each group to select two categories each to share with the class orally and to read all the terms underneath the category. If a group had already shared a particular category, the next group should try to pick a different one if they had one (if not, they could repeat). After completing this activity, each group was to take one of the categories they had chosen and summarize it by using all of the terms they had used underneath it. Mrs. Brandenberg gave them a time limit and set them to work. One group constructed the following summary from the category they created on main events:

The main **turning points** of this play were key in having the fate of these two star-crossed lovers come out the way it did. First, they met and fell in love at first sight at a <u>masked ball</u>. They pledged their love and <u>were married secretly</u> by their friar. Romeo went to the plaza where he got into a <u>street fight</u> with some Capulets over sneaking into the party, and his friend is killed. Romeo, in retaliation, kills Tybalt (a Capulet). Because of this, he is <u>banished</u>, but, meanwhile, Juliet's <u>parents push her to marry Paris</u>. The friar <u>gives her a drug</u> that will make it look like she died, and <u>she is buried</u> in the family crypt. Romeo <u>doesn't get the message</u>, so he finds Juliet in her crypt and <u>takes poison</u> to join her in death. <u>Juliet wakes up and sees Romeo dead</u> and <u>stabs herself</u> with this dagger to join him. The Prince points out what they have done though their hate and feuding to cause all these tragedies.

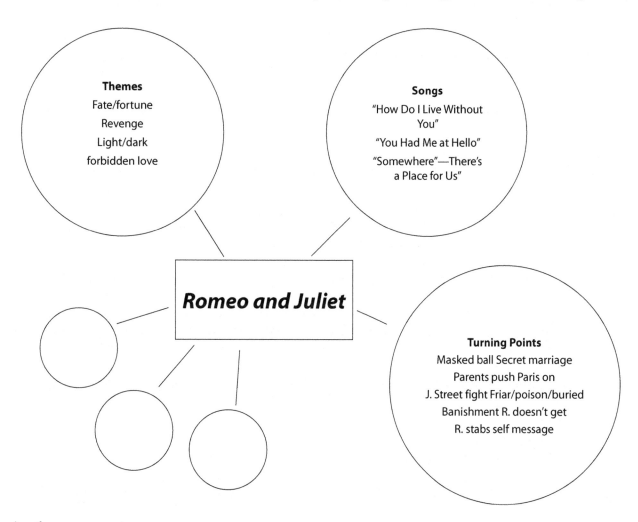

Another group wrote:

> Shakespeare is the author of the play, *Romeo and Juliet*. He lived in England during Elizabethan times in the later 1500s and early 1600s. He wrote many plays in sonnet form in older English, so it is difficult to understand some of what he is saying without studying it, but when we do, many of his ideas are timeless.

Each of the groups covered the main categories with each other. Mrs. Brandenberg asked them to remember how much they hadn't known about the play at the beginning and how much they knew now. She went back and reinforced a few ideas that had seemed a bit weaker for students during the model. A few days later, she tested them on the play, and her assessment showed that they had all learned *much* more than her classes from the past year before when she had not used the Concept Development model as a closure or used as much exciting technology.

Tips for Using Concept Development

Students must know something about the concept/subject before they can generate the number of terms needed to complete this model well. This is an excellent model to use as a focus activity—but only if students have some prior knowledge about it. If they do not, it is a very effective closure activity to sum up everything they have learned. The broader the topic, the more terms they will be able to add. One must also remember that younger children will not need to contribute as many examples as older children, and the teacher may need to help young children over time to do each phase according to their skills. Mrs. Knight, for example, has children pick out pictures of birds from her animal cards or from a technology folder in the class shared drive on the school network and then asks them to make their categories in stacks or by moving the pictures into another folder. Children usually do this based on colors or sizes. She does not require them to do very many, but she does ask them to orally give her a summary sentence about the categories.

Students can use technology to seek more information about contributions. For example, several students in Mrs. Brandenburg's class had not heard of the musical *West Side Story* or the song "Somewhere." They looked it up on the Internet to listen and view the lyrics. Others wanted to know how far it was from Verona to Mantua (where Romeo was banished), so they brought up an interactive map of Italy online with that information.

This method of forming and developing concepts can be used with all subjects and concepts within subject areas (including technology). "What comes to mind when we think of the *Internet*?" might be used to generate all the terms associated with that area of technology or "What do we know about *Word*?" Questions like this can remind students of broad associated terms, very specific terms, ethical areas, or historical information—among others.

This model can also be continued to increase higher-level thinking. This is based upon Taba's (1962, 1967) belief that thinking can be taught. Asking students to predict consequences, explain unfamiliar phenomena, hypothesize, analyze, and so forth might be a next phase. For instance, an English teacher using this with *Romeo and Juliet* as above might ask if there are still arranged marriages in some cultures and, if so, what are the consequences for going outside family's wishes. Questions that could be asked of groups to delve into this area would be, "What would happen if . . .," why do you think this would happen (supporting the predictions and hypotheses and determining links), and verifying predictions ("What would it take for this to be generally true or probability true?"). Are there modern day interactions to support Shakespeare's story? Why does this story have such universal appeal even today? Other questions and verifications can be brought into play with consideration to the content area.

Teachers should also allow students to contribute terms that seem unlikely—*if* the student can make the connection to the concept. The only time a term should not be included in listing is when it is inappropriate or intended to create disruption. As with all the models, establishing time limits for each phase and providing roles for structure increases participation and success. Allowing for and/or providing for technology use during the activity (once initial listing has occurred) helps students to follow up on their interests generated during this inductive model.

Concluding Thoughts

There are a number of other models of teaching (along with their submodels) that can be used to engage students in active learning. Many of those, as we have seen with the models discussed here, can be combined with technology to enhance the learning experience in various ways. The use of models of teaching creates variety, promotes "minds on" thinking, increases students' curiosity to search deeper, and finds a way into many of areas of teachers' concerns (management, motivation, etc.). A teacher who is creative with this excellent combination of models of teaching and technology will motivate students and enrich his or her own practice in exciting ways for learners. The ideas for combining these two areas are part of what establishes teaching as a creative process and a satisfying endeavor.

References

Bruner, J. (1960). *The process of education*. Cambridge, MA: Harvard University Press.

Bruner, J., Goodnow, J., & Austin, G. (1965). *A study of thinking (6th printing, 2009)*. New Brunswick, NJ: Transaction Publishers.

Banikowski, A. (1999). Strategies to enhance memory based on brain research. *Focus on Exceptional Children*, 0015511X, *39*(2). Retrieved from scboces.org/english/IMC/Focus/Memory_strategies2.pdf

Burnett, F. H. (1911, 1962). *The secret garden*. Philadelphia, PA: Lippincott.

Dockterman, D. (n.d.). Cooperative learning and technology. Retrieved from www-tc.pbs.org/teacherline/courses/math230/docs/clt.pdf

Gunter, M., Estes, T., & Schwab, J. (2003). *Instruction: A models approach*. Boston, MA: Allyn and Bacon.

Joyce, B., Weil, M., & Calhoun, E. (2008). *Models of teaching* (8th ed.). Boston, MA: Pearson.

Kilbane, C., & Milman, K. (2014). *Teaching models: Designing instruction for 21st century learners*. Boston, MA: Pearson.

Slavin, R. (1987). Developmental and motivational perspectives on cooperative learning: A reconciliation. *Child Development*, *58*(5), 1161–1167.

Stahl, R. (1994). The essential elements of cooperative learning in the classroom. ERIC Digest (ED370881).

Stevens, R., & Slavin, R. (1995). The cooperative elementary school: Effects on students' achievement, attitudes, and social relations. *American Education Research*, *32*(2), 321–351.

Taba, H. (1962). *Curriculum development: Theory and practice*. New York, NY: Harcourt College Publishers.

Taba, H. (1967). *Teacher's handbook for elementary social studies*. Palo Alto, CA: Addison-Wesley.

Chapter 9

Integrating Technology Standards for Teachers

Irene Chen, Libi Shen
University of Houston-Downtown, Education Consultant

Meet Miss Brown

Miss Brown was considering a lesson on the life cycle of the plants with her third graders. She wanted students to be able to complete the following objectives in her science lesson:

- Students will follow an inquiry process to answer questions.
- Students will use an existing WebQuest to find information about the life cycle of the plants.

While preparing the lesson plan, she decided to use the National Science Education Standards (NSES) available online for the science content. However, she also remembered that the district encouraged all teachers to integrate the state technology standards in lessons.

As Miss Brown sat down to the computer, she pulled up a split screen of the science education standards, the state technology standards, and even the national technology standards in order to integrate into her curriculum. She also considered the Common Core standards. This made her wonder if she had to refer to all of these standards in order to be a *twenty-first century digital teacher*.

Standards are set by a number of groups—national content area specialists' organizations (such as in mathematics and science), states, districts, and so forth. By setting guidelines in various content areas (including technology), they hope to ensure that students are taught "the essentials" for the specific subject. These standards are normally set up to progress in age appropriate steps so that students will have the skills they need from year to year in order to easily move up to the next level.

As a new teacher, one is likely to make the connections of how objectives for learning are linked to standards through: (1) certification exams, (2) job interviews, and (3) lesson plans. Teacher certification examinations often include questions directly related to the knowledge and skills of the standards, including technology. Interviewers for teaching positions can also ask questions about what children should know and be able to do at certain grade levels or in particular content areas where positions may be open. Because of the emphasis on students' state test scores (which connect back to standards), a teacher candidate can be sure that a school wants its new teachers to clearly understand how important these standards are for students to learn.

Teachers are routinely asked to display objectives *and* specific standards for their lesson plans. They are also often required to turn in these objectives and standards on lesson plans to their administrator(s). This procedure is in place to help schools, districts, states, the nation, and, ultimately, children to be assured that their knowledge is on level with what is expected by the experts who created these standards. On top of taking attendance, learning students' names, and maintaining classroom management, teachers may wonder how they can accomplish all that! The process becomes very automatic once teachers have worked with this requirement, and there are even programs and apps that list and "plug in" standards at the touch of a fingertip (e.g., http://www.shop.professorsoft.com).

The best way to ensure that the required standards are covered in the curriculum is to include them right from the start of any planning phase by determining specific learning objectives. Hill (1995) stated that,

> Good teachers have standards in mind when they set their lessons up, where the idea of a "standard" represents a specific idea of what the teacher expects a student to recall, replicate, manipulate, understand, or demonstrate at some point down the road—and of how the teacher will know how close a student has come to meeting that standard. Standards, in other words, are conceptually nothing new—but they did receive a new emphasis over the last decade, through state initiatives and through the passage of the Goals 2000: Educate America Act. (para. 1)

It is important to match learning objectives with the standards that are to be covered. For example, if a state standard asks that students evaluate their products before final submission, then towards the conclusion of a lesson or a project, the teacher would need to have students go through a final checklist, peer check the project, or complete another activity designed to include self-evaluation as a part of the project or assignment. The best projects and lessons focus on one or two specific standards instead of trying to cover too many. Most standards are designed to be covered during a year's time. By looking at the objectives and standards, teachers develop instructional procedures, assignments, projects, and other components in their lesson plans. With the last two steps, learning outcomes are then easily measured in assessment. Connecting broader expectations with standards and objectives makes it easier to ensure that curricular goals are met and so that students gain essential knowledge and skills.

What Are Curriculum Standards, Benchmarks, and Technology Standards?

Some major educational developments during the past few decades are the pervasive impact of computers and the Internet in schools and the implementations of academic standards. Many researchers consider the publication of *A Nation at Risk* (National Commission on Excellence in Education, 1983) that was published in 1983 as the initiating event of the modern standards movement. Later, with the passage of the *Goals 2000: Educate America Act* in 1994, U.S. lawmakers acknowledged the importance of high standards in improving education (North Central Regional Educational Laboratory, 2000). Curriculum standards, for example, have recently emerged at the national level for those participating in the Common Core in order to convey the educational requirements in each subject area at each grade level that students are expected to learn and teachers are expected to teach. Again, these standards are broad statements that identify the knowledge and skills that students should acquire. The domains (or main fields) normally remain constant, but the difficulty of the content and the complexity of student work increase as the child progresses through the grade levels. This is called a spiral curriculum in which learning is revisited but in a "wider and deeper" manner.

Each standard then provides specific information in a hierarchical view. The lowest levels of the hierarchy are offered as "benchmarks" (refer to Figure 9.1). A particular curriculum standard will contain many educational benchmarks which consist of keywords and directions that educators will use to further build their lesson plans. Benchmarks may be specific to a grade level or provide a learning target for a span of grades, such as grades K-2. Each standard is an essential piece to ensure rigor and to challenge current student performance. Implementing curriculum standards requires a system of supports, which include benchmarks, grade-level expectations, curriculum, teacher professional development, and assessments. Most schools and school districts test students against these benchmarks so that teachers are held accountable for children to have learned the knowledge and skills set forth prior to official state testing. An example standard with benchmarks from first-grade math reads:

Mathematical process standards. The student uses mathematical processes to acquire and demonstrate mathematical understanding. The student is expected to:

A. apply mathematics to problems arising in everyday life, society, and the workplace:
B. use a problem-solving model that incorporates analyzing given information, formulating a plan or strategy, determining a solution, justifying the solution, and evaluating the problem-solving process and reasonableness of the solution;

C. select tools, including real objects, manipulatives, paper and pencil, and technology as appropriate, and techniques, including mental math, estimation, and number sense as appropriate, to solve problems (See http://ritter.tea .state.tx.us/rules/tac/chapter111/ch111a.pdf)

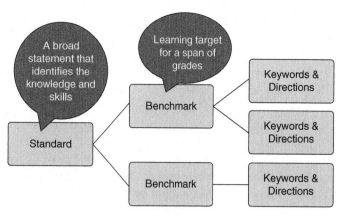

Figure 9.1 Standards and benchmarks.

As one can see, the standard is supported by the benchmarks listed in detailed language below it. For quick access to a collection of national and international standards, visit: http://correlation .edgate.com/standards/index.html.

Texas, along with Delaware, New York, and Massachusetts, were early adopters of standards. The Texas Essential Knowledge and Skills (TEKS), for example, are the state standards for what students should know and be able to do (Texas Education Agency, 2014). The TEKS include divisions for subject areas such as English language arts, reading, mathematics, science, social studies, and, for our particular interest here, Technology Applications (TA TEKS) from kindergarten through high school levels.

National standards are created by a variety of national organizations, such as the National Association for the Education of Young Children (or NAEYC), the National Council for the Social Studies (NCSS), the National Research Council (NRC), and the National Council of Teachers of Mathematics (NCTM). Unlike state standards, which all public schools in a particular state are required to use, national standards set by organizations are voluntary and K-12 students are not officially held accountable to them (The Great Schools Partnership, 2014). However, some states use national standards as guidelines for creating their own state standards or simply adopt them as state standards.

In addition to state curriculum standards and national curriculum standards of some subjects, the Common Core State Standards were launched in 2009 with support from 43 states, two territories, and the District of Columbia (National Governors Association Center for Best Practices & Council of Chief State School Officers, 2010a). "State school chiefs and governors recognized the value of consistent, real-world learning goals and launched this effort to ensure all students, regardless of where they live, are graduating high school prepared for college, career, and life" (National Governors Association Center for Best Practices & Council of Chief State School Officers, 2010b, para 1). At this time, Texas, Indiana, Virginia, Hawaii, Minnesota, and a few other states, have not adopted the Common Core Standards for various reasons, including the belief that they may have more stringent standards and may better understand their localized needs.

With the passing of No Child Left Behind (NCLB) (2001), stricter certification, higher expectations, and more stringent hiring policies for new teachers have been implemented by school districts across the nation. NCLB requires teachers to meet the criteria of "Highly Qualified Status" in subjects that they will be teaching. Standards are increasingly imperative in the practice of all teaching fields. In addition, NCLB, Title II Part D, or the Enhancing Education through Technology Act of 2001, requires that all teachers be technology literate and be able to integrate technology into content areas across the curriculum. More emphasis was placed on the technology literacy and integration requirements for students, teachers, and school staff in NCLB so that national education could be enhanced through technology.

Why Is It Important for Beginning Teachers to Know Technology Standards?

The TA TEKS are intended as a planning aid and a vehicle to support technology integration across the curriculum to help students develop twenty-first-century skills. In general, state curriculum standards impact teachers by:

- providing teachers with consistent goals and benchmarks to ensure students are progressing;
- providing teachers with consistent expectations for students who relocate to their districts from other states;

- providing teachers the opportunity to collaborate with other teachers as they develop curricula, materials, and assessments linked to high-quality standards;
- helping colleges of education and professional development programs to better prepare beginning teachers;
- promoting equity to ensure that all students are well prepared to collaborate and compete with their peers; and
- matching what is taught in the classroom to the standards, so that students and parents will know what students should be learning and on what they will be tested.

Although improved student achievement is the most important goal, other unexpected outcomes of curriculum standards, such as teacher morale, are also important because, ultimately, they affect student achievement. Teachers know what they should expect of students so that they can more clearly plan for and address instruction with confidence.

As in the case of the International Society for Technology in Education (ISTE), many professional organizations have taken on the challenge of creating educational standards to be used on a national or, sometimes, an international level. Most states, like the state of Texas, adopt and modify these national or even international standards by soliciting the experience of teachers, subject matter experts, and leading thinkers in the field. They then incorporate evidence-based research, literature, and theories with feedback from the public (National Academy of Education, 2009, p. 8). With such close alignment as this, a beginning teacher can be assured that he or she is meeting separate state technology standards as well as national technology standards— as they are comparable (refer to Figure 9.1). A beginning teacher can normally follow one set of standards, knowing that the experts have examined all of them and merged many of them together.

Generally, technology application standards describe **what** needs to be taught but not **how** to teach the content. This is important for beginning teachers to understand because each child is unique with his or her own pattern and timing of development. Teachers will need to plan curriculum to respond not only to their class as a whole but also to individual differences. Teachers are also expected to use information about typical development within a specific age span that is provided through standards and benchmarks to plan an effective learning environment and applicable experiences.

One way for states to ensure that teachers know about standards is through state certification exams. As noted, a number of questions on the state examination for teacher certification in Texas, for example, are closely related to technology (more specifically, Competency 9 of the Pedagogy and Professional Responsibilities/PPR TExES [TEA, 2012, p. 14]). Prospective teachers are also expected to be capable of integrating technology skills when they walk into their first classrooms, so those who demonstrate excellent technology knowledge and skills (see Chapter 12 on e-portfolios) are in great demand in the hiring market.

Hopefully, beginning teachers will use the international, national, state, districts, and/or school technology standards as a foundation to implement their curricula. Many districts and organizations have lesson plans that provide excellent ideas for these types of activities, but they do not necessarily make sure that each teacher implements them (other than through the lesson plans they have turned in to administrators). It is every teacher's responsibility to do so. By using the required standards and many ideas already generated as resources, teachers can create solid objectives for their lessons; thus, students will learn the way they should learn for their individual needs and to prepare for the world ahead.

National Educational Technology Standards

Computer technology has germinated, evolved, and advanced for more than three decades, but classrooms are often left behind because of initial cost and professional development for teachers. Teaching and learning need to be changed as society changes to match the needs of the workforce and social uses that are so much a part of the world today. These necessities address the demands of a wide base of affected adopters for using classroom information, and communications technology has emerged accordingly.

To examine more of the "big picture" of how these standards work, we can see that one way of ensuring that schools stay up to date is to have the national and/or state governments or influential organizations establish specific goals and directives as pertains to their focus (mathematics, science, etc.). Most of these types of standards ask teachers to meld technology with a specific content area, but there are standards that center on technology alone as well. With this in mind, schools understand what skills and knowledge their students should have from the frameworks recommended by experts in the industry, education, and other fields (see Figure 9.3). The National Educational Technology Standards (NETS) (refer to Table 9.1), for example, come from the International Society for Technology in Education (ISTE). The American Association of School Librarians (ALA) also provides Information Literacy Standards for Student Learning (ILSSL) to help students become skillful producers and consumers of information. The International Technology Education Association (ITEA) provides Standards for Technological Literacy, which is intended to help educators define and recognize quality technology instruction. Among the three entities (ISTE, ALA, and ITEA), ISTE has the most commonly referred to set of standards (NETS) in schools and colleges of education across the United States and even worldwide for technology.

Table 9.1 ISTE Standards for Students (2007)

The ISTE Standards for Students
(1) creativity and innovation (2) communication and collaboration (3) research and information fluency (4) critical thinking, problem solving, and decision making (5) digital citizenship (6) technology operations and concepts

The standards for using computer technology in schools were first developed in the 1980s (Roblyer, 2000). Based on Bitter (as cited in Roblyer, 2000, p. 134), "some states set their own computer literacy standards, and various national groups recommended that students should learn some computer skills at each grade level." Later, ISTE has "worked in conjunction with the National Council for the Accreditation of Teacher Education (NCATE) to generate standards and a vision statement for how teacher education programs should address technology" (Roblyer, 2000, p. 135) (refer to Table 9.2). The NETS project was sponsored by NASA in consultation with the U.S. Department of Education, the Apple Computer, and the Milken Exchange on Education Technology (Roblyer, 2000). ISTE provides a list of standards that are applied to learning, teaching, and leading in a technological society (see Tables 9.1 and 9.2). These offer teachers a framework for integrating technology in teaching and learning.

Table 9.2 ISTE Standards for Teacher (2008)

The ISTE Standards for Teachers
(1) facilitate and inspire student learning and creativity (2) design and develop digital-age learning experiences and assessment (3) model digital-age work and learning, (4) promote and model digital citizenship and responsibility (5) engage in professional growth and leadership

In addition to standards and performance indicators, ISTE also published "Essential Conditions" (2009) to explain the necessary conditions to effectively leverage technology for learning. The "Essential Conditions" require teachers' full cooperation in implementing the following aspects to enable students to learn effectively and live productively in an increasingly digital society (ISTE, 2009):

- Shared Vision
- Empowered Leaders
- Implementation Planning
- Consistent and Adequate Funding
- Equitable Access
- Skilled Personnel
- Ongoing Professional Learning
- Technical Support
- Curriculum Framework

- Student-Centered Learning
- Assessment and Evaluation
- Engaged Communities
- Support Policies
- Supportive External Context

By reviewing the ISTE Standards for students (Standards•S) and teachers (Standards•T), it is noticeable that simply being able to use technology is no longer sufficient. Today's students should be able to use technology to analyze, learn, and explore. Digital skills are vital for preparing students to work, live, and contribute to today's society.

While knowing how to use the technology is still important, it is no longer the primary focus of the standards. The standards provide teachers with more guidance on assigning tasks that are authentic and relevant to learners, where tools and skills are a means to a purposeful end. They emphasize the process of student learning over a continuum with rich and authentic assessment tools, resources, and standards-aligned content and curriculum to measure multiple levels and styles of learning. They seem to place emphasis on creativity and globalization, communication, collaboration, problem solving, and decision making. Teachers are expected to encourage students to look at real-world problems and use technology tools to solve them. Students are expected to be given more opportunities and take responsibility for their own learning that is meaningful to their lives.

Overall, the standards reflect twenty-first century learning skills and appear to be very specific and measurable. There is a great focus on application and communication using technology within the global society. ISTE standards have an impact on teacher education. As stated by Cohen and Tally (2004),

> They call for new teachers to demonstrate mastery in general computer operations, in content-specific applications, in evaluating software and Web material, in gathering and managing information, in creating and publishing multimedia products, in communicating and working with others electronically, in thinking critically, and in acting ethically with technology. (p. 5)

The ISTE's NETS have put technology integration on the map for educators and provide a useful reference point for new teachers towards appropriate technology to help ensure that U.S. students will stay in step with an increasingly global society (Cohen & Tally, 2004).

State Technology Application Standards for Students and Teachers

States and school districts can also determine goals and standards that teachers and students must reach. For instance, in Texas, it is important for teachers to be familiar with these resources: (a) Texas Long-Range Plan for Technology (LRPT), 2006–2020 (TEA, 2006a), (b) School Technology and Readiness Chart (STaR Chart) (TEA, 2006b), and (c) TA TEKS (TEA, 2014).

The passing of the federal No Child Left Behind (NCLB) Act in 2001 led to the 2002 update to the Long-Range Plan for Technology, 1996–2010 (TEA, 2006a) to make sure Texas goals and objectives were aligned with the federal plan. In view of the quick advances of information technology, Texas once again updated the Long-range Plan for Technology, 2006–2020 in 2006 to set new strategies for all school districts in response. An electronic resource allows districts and charter schools to prepare and submit a technology plan to the state for review and approval in a completely online process. Through the ePlan system, districts address the following areas in the LRPT: teaching and learning, educator preparation and development, leadership, administration and instructional support, and infrastructure for technology.

vasabii/Shutterstock, Inc.

An online resource tool called the Texas STaR Chart is used to assist Texas teachers in self-assessing efforts to effectively

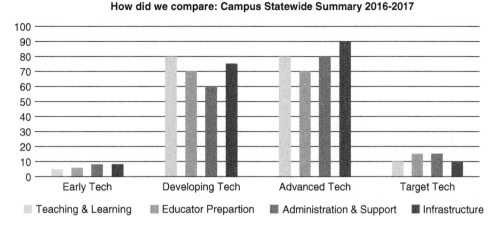

Figure 9.2   A sample STaR Chart to compare campus and statewide reports.

integrate technology across the curriculum (Texas Education Agency, 2006b). The STaR Chart focuses on the following four areas of Long-Range Plan for Technology, 2006–2020: (a) teaching and learning; (b) educator preparation and development; (c) leadership, administration, and instructional support; and (d) infrastructure for technology. One can access the charts at: https://www.txstarchart.org/.

The Performance Descriptions of the STaR Chart categorize teachers' technology skills into (a) early technology level, (b) developing technology level, (c) advanced technology level, and (d) target technology level (see Figure 9.2). The system assists the state and districts in the measurement of the impact of state

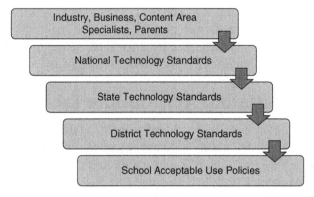

Figure 9.3   A flow chart on how the standards are developed.

and local efforts to improve student learning through the use of technology as specified in NCLB. It helps schools to identify needs for ongoing professional development and raise awareness of research-based instructional goals. It also assists teachers in assessing needs and setting goals for the use of technology in the classroom to support student achievement. The STaR Chart also lists the Technology Applications Standards for All Teachers as described by State Board for Educator Certification (SBEC) (see Table 9.3). More details can be found at: https://www.txstarchart.org/standards.html

Table 9.3   Technology Applications Standards for All Teachers (in Texas)

Technology Applications Standards for All Teachers

Standard I. All teachers use technology-related terms, concepts, data input strategies, and ethical practices to make informed decisions about current technologies and their applications.

Standard II. All teachers identify task requirements, apply search strategies, and use current technology to efficiently acquire, analyze, and evaluate a variety of electronic information.

Standard III. All teachers use task-appropriate tools to synthesize knowledge, create and modify solutions, and evaluate results in a way that supports the work of individuals and groups in problem-solving situations.

Standard IV. All teachers communicate information in different formats and for diverse audiences.

Standard V. All teachers know how to plan, organize, deliver, and evaluate instruction for all students that incorporates the effective use of current technology for teaching and integrating the Technology Applications Texas Essential Knowledge and Skills (TEKS) into the curriculum.

TA TEKS for Students from the Kindergarten to the 12th Grade

As noted, many states have developed their own set of technology standards for students based on ISTE Standards performance indicators. The technology applications curriculum developed in Texas, for example, has the following six strands:

- Creativity and innovation;
- Communication and collaboration;
- Research and information fluency;
- Critical thinking, problem solving, and decision making;
- Digital citizenship; and
- Technology operations and concepts.

The latest Chapter 126 TEKS (available at http://ritter.tea.state.tx.us/rules/tac/chapter126/ch126b.html) was adopted for the school year 2012-2013 and contains subchapters for the elementary level, the middle school level, the high school level, and other Technology Applications courses. The details of Subchapter A. Elementary and Subchapter B. Middle School attempt to align the skills addressed in each of those projects with the approximate grade level where they will be utilized in the curriculum, while Subchapter C High School and Subchapter D Other Technology Applications Courses describe technology application courses such as Digital Video and Audio Design, Web Design, and other courses.

Integrating Appropriate Technology Applications

In addition to national and state standards, future teachers become familiar with what "developmentally appropriate" means in terms of technology through professional organizations such as National Association for the Education of Young Children (or NAEYC), National Council for the Social Studies (NCSS), National Research Council (NRC), and National Council of Teachers of Mathematics (NCTM). The national council of these organizations each makes recommendations regarding technology use for their content area. Central to their recommendations is the concept that development and learning are influenced by multiple social and cultural contexts. Knowing what is typical at each age and stage of human development is crucial. This knowledge helps teachers decide which experiences are best practices for children's learning and development, so it is essential for teachers to note the following three important terminologies (see Figure 9.4):

Developmentally appropriate practice (or DAP). Teachers use knowledge about child development to create a program that is suitable for the age and stage of development, as well as the individual needs of children. (See Chapter 5 in this book for further information on the use of technology with young children.)

Age-appropriate practice. Teachers use information about typical development within a specific age span to plan a learning environment and experience.

Individually appropriate practice. Teachers understand each child is unique with his or her own pattern and timing of development.

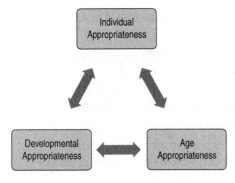

Figure 9.4 The three anchors of appropriate technology applications.

Technology also offers options for students with special needs. Some students may benefit from the more constrained and engaging task situations possible with computers and other assistive technologies. Students with physical challenges can become much more engaged in learning using special technologies. Teachers plan their curriculum to respond to individual differences. When planning technology-based activities for students with high-incidence disabilities, it is important to consider how the learning will be structured and how much direction and guidance should be given to a student (Gardner & Wissick, 2002). (See Chapter 6 for further information on the use of technology with children who have special needs.)

As noted, the Texas legislation requires that all students should be technology literate by the time they leave the eighth grade. In the years preceding the eighth grade, students may need instruction and support to use these skills, although many students will be able to perform the skills much before the target years. Teachers must, however, remember that children come from many backgrounds that may not have provided them with early access to technology.

Joe Salinas was a preservice teacher who was excited to begin his semester with fourth graders. He was currently involved in his fieldwork as a university senior and was asked to teach several lessons by his teacher education program. As he opened a conversation about planning the science lesson, his mentor teacher reminded him to include technology. He began to ask himself, "How do I know what fourth graders ought to be taught in technology?" When he asked his mentor this question, she told him that, luckily, the experts had researched it well and provided them with standards. In addition, the district provided them with benchmarks. She gave him the Web sites, and he began to put together the science content with the technology. When he taught the lesson, he felt like the match had been a good one. Students were challenged but successful in both areas.

Best Practices of Integrating Technology Standards

While national technology standards set goals, they do not define how the standards should be taught or which materials should be used to support students because local needs and support for technology vary. It is up to the states to define the full range of support appropriate for these students. States and localities often take different approaches to implementing the standards and providing their teachers with the support they need to help students successfully reach the standards. However, decisions on how to implement the standards are most often made by classroom teachers. Teachers usually know about what works well in the classroom for their particular students (Dean, Hubbell, & Pitler, 2012). This is a rationale of why the standards establish what students need to learn but do not dictate how teachers should teach. Instead, schools and teachers decide how best to help students reach the standards. As noted, technology application standards describe **what** needs to be taught but not **how** to teach the content. Teachers are expected to use information about typical development within a specific age span provided through standards and benchmarks to plan a suitable learning environment and applicable experiences for their classrooms, although there are many resources (especially online) to support them.

Very Young Children

When used intentionally and appropriately, technology and interactive media are effective tools to support learning and development. NAEYC is the organization that offers key messages for teachers of young children (see Table 9.4). NAEYC (2012a) has suggestions for effective classroom practice for preschoolers and kindergarteners in terms of using technology tools and interactive media. NAEYC's Key Messages (2012b) for technology and interactive media serve as tools in early childhood programs for children from birth through age 8.

Table 9.4 NAEYC's Key Messages for technology and early childhood programs

NAEYC's Key Messages for technology and early childhood programs
• When used intentionally and appropriately, technology and interactive media are effective tools to support learning and development.
• Intentional use requires early childhood teachers and administrators to have information and resources regarding the nature of these tools and the implications of their use with children.
• Limitations on the use of technology and media are important.
• Special considerations must be given to the use of technology with infants and toddlers.
• Attention to digital citizenship and equitable access is essential.
• Ongoing research and professional development are needed.

Figure 9.5 An example of "lapware."

Figure 9.6 The finger of a toddler selecting the correct letter on a touchscreen tablet with learning software.

For very young children, play is an important vehicle to develop self-regulation and promote language, cognition, and social competence. Children's experiences shape their motivation and approaches to learning. When children are appropriately challenged, development and learning advance. Baby software, designed for children ages 6 months to 2 years old, is nicknamed "lapware" because the parent holds the child while he or she plays (see Figure 9.5). Baby software lets tiny fingers "whack away" at the keyboard without destroying data (see Figure 9.6). Most lapware programs rewards babies or toddlers for doing what comes naturally by responding with a variety of sounds and dancing shapes whenever they touch the keys (Figure 9.8). It teaches them cause and effect, which is important for babies and young children to grasp.

For the many benefits of technology, there are also some concerns for its use with young children. Excessive screen time is linked to a host of childhood problems, including poor school performance, attention issues, sleep disturbance, obesity, and more (Page, Cooper, Griew, & Jago, 2010) (see Figure 9.7). Mobile touch devices and screen devices are so omnipresent that it is getting harder for parents and teachers alike to figure out how and when to set limits. Because the explosion of smart phones and tablets is relatively new, most of the research on the harmful effects of technology on young children is associated with television, but emerging studies are beginning to raise concerns about the time and appropriate use of smart phones, iPads, tablets, and other types of digital media (Page et al., 2010) (see Figure 9.9).

Although the American Academy of Pediatrics recommends that children under age 2 avoid TV and computer screens, the goal can be unrealistic in practice because TVs, DVD, telephones, PCs, and telephones fill

Figure 9.7 Toddler and children focusing on the computer.

Figure 9.8 A cartoon robot asks children to write text on the board.

Figure 9.9 *Little Red Riding Hood* in digital format.

Miss Clay, a day-care teacher, understands that during the earliest years, infants and toddlers interact primarily with people. Whenever technology tools are used, she makes sure to allow children to explore digital materials with an adult as mediator and/or a co-player. Her young children are drawn to push-button switches and controls. The classroom is surrounded by toys and technology tools that infants and toddlers might use that are safe, sturdy, and not easily damaged.

As with shared book reading, Mrs. Clay uses shared technology time as an opportunity to talk with children, use new vocabulary, and model appropriate use. Since children need to freely explore and try out everything in the environment in the early years in today's world, this includes the exploration of technology tools and interactive media.

In the daily classroom and at school events such as parents' nights, Miss Clay is always there, holding her cameras to make digital audio or video files to document her students' progress. She is often able to share examples of children's growth with parents.

She uses technology as an active and engaging tool to provide toddlers with access to images of their families, friends, animals, objects in their environment, and a wide range of different images of people and things they might not otherwise encounter. Among her favorite activities is sharing her collection of photos of children from other countries.

Miss Clay tries to avoid passive screen time for toddlers in her class. Miss Clay does not think that infants and toddlers learn from docilely watching videos. She also believes that if infants are distressed, they need the comfort of a caring adult, not an electronic toy.

She noticed that some of her students watched videos for hours at home. She probably should persuade parents not to use TVs or videos for hours as a baby-sitting tool. Instead, parents should mediate or play digital materials with very young children to provide human interactions.

How does she persuade busy parents not to allow children watch TVs or videos for hours as a baby-sitting tool?

our lives as well as those of children (Alterio, 2006). Alterio also noted that some educators tend to be cautious of using technology for babies and toddlers because the child is, too often, a passive observer of the action (refer to Figure 9.11). Manufacturers of digital media for young children distance their products from video and television by marketing educational apps and games as "educational," but Goodwin and Highfield (2012) found that only 4% of the apps marketed as education for young children promote open-ended and constructive learning.

Teachers must use information to carefully evaluate equipment or software that they already have available or they request. There are rating systems for movies (Motion Picture Association of America) and video games (Entertainment Software Rating Board), which are tools for parents and educators when deciding if the content is appropriate for their children, but there is still not a universal rating system for software applications and tools. Some companies such as "Your Sphere for Parents" offer Certified App Review Programs where they review apps for Apple and Android platforms and put them under more stringent standards than either Apple or Google. Teachers can have parents view lists of approved applications from these institutes when picking media resources.

Figure 9.10   Teacher as a co-player.

Figure 9.11   An example of passive screen time.

Table 9.5   Category Comparison between Computer Literacy and Technology Applications

Categories of Computer Literacy	Categories of Technology Applications
• Email and Internet • Network and computing skills • Word processing • Graphics & presentation • Spreadsheets & databases	• Creativity and innovation • Communication and collaboration • Research and information fluency • Critical thinking, problem solving, and decision making • Digital citizenship • Technology operations and concepts

The NAEYC (2012a) also recommends that young children explore digital materials in the context of human interactions with an adult as mediator and co-player (Figure 9.10). As with shared book reading, teachers use shared technology time as an opportunity to talk with children, use new vocabulary, and model appropriate use. Most educators agree that unlike software for preschoolers that aims to teach reading, numbers, or other complex skills, software for young children is meant to be simply fun, and it is not designed to be a substitute for play between parent and child.

Kindergarten Through Eighth-Grade Students

Most states start their curriculum framework and technology standards from the kindergarten year and, again, require that all students should be technology literate by the time they leave the eighth grade. Most states publish specific guidelines which are intended as a planning aid and a vehicle to support technology integration across the curriculum to help students develop twenty-first century digital knowledge and skills.

As might be expected, different entities may view concepts in different ways. Some states define the "21st Century digital knowledge and skills" as a set of basic computer literacy, while others describe the skills as technology application skills (see Figure 9.12). Both act as a key for the students of today and tomorrow. Fluency with technology applications may require more intellectual abilities than the rote learning of software and hardware associated with computer literacy, but the focus is still on the technology itself (ALA, 2014). This section will first discuss the skills from the computer literacy perspective and continue the discussion from the technology application perspective.

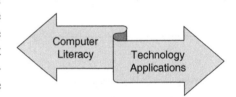

Figure 9.12   Two views of "21st Century Digital Knowledge and Skills."

A number of states view twenty-first century digital knowledge and skills as **basic computer literacy**, and they publish computer skills scopes and sequences that represent reasonable expectations of student skills that they expect all educators to make a part of how their classroom functions to improve student learning. The states and districts that view twenty-first century digital knowledge and skills as **basic computer literacy** provide specific information in the following five computer literacy areas:

- Email and Internet
- Network and computing skills
- Word processing
- Graphics and presentation
- Spreadsheets and databases

In the area of **email and Internet**, from the kindergarten year through the eighth grade, students grow from: following a Web link; using the browser; using Internet bookmarks; creating book marks; sending and replying to email; sending and reading attachments; and managing address books. They move on to evaluating search tools, finding information and using appropriate search strategies, and, finally, to assessing the quality of Internet resources.

In the area of **network and computing skills**, from the kindergarten year through the eighth grade, students develop skills from starting up and shutting down a computer and handling CDs and other media to logging on to the network. They continue with launching programs, copying and pasting between windows, switching among open windows, and managing directories to navigating file systems and local area network. They complete basic trouble shooting skills by the eighth grade.

In the area of **word processing**, from the kindergarten year through the eighth grade, students improve skills from keying in letters and sentences, editing by inserting and deleting letters, and formatting text (e.g., changing sizes, fonts, colors, cutting, formatting page layout with margins and tabs, adding headers and footers). They progress to using outline tools for prewriting purpose and using a combination of tools to create publication quality documents.

In the area of **graphics and presentations**, from the kindergarten year to the eighth grade, students grow from drawing using computer programs, taking pictures using digital cameras, inserting clip art, creating multimedia presentations, and importing pictures to using appropriate animations or transition to enhance presentations. They move to being able to create self-timing presentations, save graphics in a variety of format, and capture and utilize digitized videos.

In the area of **spreadsheets and databases**, from the kindergarten year through the eighth grade, students begin early by locating data in a spreadsheet or a chart, being able to enter data, and locating a spreadsheet cell by its column and row. Students move forward to being able to insert simple calculations, create formulas, format data, print spreadsheets, use absolute and relative addressing, and differentiate between records and fields in a database.

It is hoped that future teachers will begin to grasp the general scope and sequence of teaching technology to children. Again, these scopes and sequences are aligned with state technology standards, which are then aligned with ISTE national and international standards. Teachers need to integrate directly or indirectly each of the stated skills into lessons in ways that are appropriate.

Figure 9.13   When using a mouse, the small muscle movements of a child's fingers coordinate with eyes.

Catalin Petolea/Shutterstock, Inc.

Mrs. Rodriquez's preschool students are curious about the world around them and about learning. They are finding out their ability to create and communicate using crayons, markers, and their bodies to represent ideas and experiences. In addition to crayons, markers, paints (and other art materials), blocks, dramatic play materials, and miniature life figures, Mrs. Rodriquez uses digital technologies to provide her preschool students one more outlet for them to demonstrate their creativity and learning. Most of her students are eager to use the two tablets and one desktop she has in the classroom to explore touch screens loaded with a developmentally appropriate interactive media.

Han, a student who comes from a lower SES family with a number of siblings, is not eager to get to the tablets. Mrs. Rodriquez notices that Han has not developed the fine motor-skills of coordinating the small muscle movements of his fingers in coordination with his eyes when using the computer mouse and keyboard.

Mrs. Rodriquez allows Han a little more computer time to provide opportunities for him to explore and feel comfortable using a traditional mouse and keyboard.

Keyboarding is a foundational skill largely related to motor skills. The standards Mrs. Rodriquez looked up indicate that based on the child's developmental readiness, it may be appropriate to begin keyboarding training in grades 2–4.

Is it too early to "correct" Han's mouse and keyboarding problems? What else can Mrs. Rodriquez do to bridge the digital gap for preschool students like Han?

In addition to the five computer literacy areas discussed above, keyboarding and the teaching of the ethical, human, and social issues are two areas that need special attention. Keyboarding is considered a foundational skill largely related to motor skills (see Figure 9.13). Most states recommend that it is appropriate to begin keyboarding training in grades 2–4, based on the child's developmental readiness. Therefore, Mrs. Rodriquez may want to wait until later to enhance Han's keyboarding skills, as he may not be developmentally ready as a preschool student. Most states also suggested that the ethical, human, and social issues related to uses of technology should be addressed as appropriate each time they arise in the classroom. More about this area will be addressed in Chapter 10. Educators are to model and practice Internet safety at all times.

As mentioned earlier, Table 9.5 illustrates how "21st century digital knowledge and skills" can be viewed by some states as basic computer literacy skills, while other states describe the skills as technology application knowledge. An analysis of the more recently required technology competencies of Texas and a number of states reveals an emphasis by some on **technology applications** over **computer literacy**. Fluency with applications requires more intellectual abilities than the rote learning of software and hardware associated with computer literacy. According to the American Library Association (2014),

> "Fluency" with information technology may require more intellectual abilities than the rote learning of software and hardware associated with "computer literacy," but the focus is still on the technology itself. Information literacy, on the other hand, is an intellectual framework for understanding, finding, evaluating, and using information—activities which may be accomplished in part by fluency with information technology, in part by sound investigative methods, but most important, through critical discernment and reasoning. Information literacy initiates, sustains, and extends lifelong learning through abilities which may use technologies but are ultimately independent of them. (para. 11)

Individuals are faced with abundant information choices in their academic studies, in the workplace, and in their personal lives.

> The uncertain quality and expanding quantity of information pose large challenges for society. The sheer abundance of information will not in and of itself create a more informed citizen without a complementary cluster of abilities necessary to use information effectively. (ALA, 2014, para. 6)

In view of the complexity of information applications, Texas and other states design its curriculum framework and standards from the perspective of **technology applications**. The technology application curriculum (Technology Application TEKS, or TA TEKS) starts with the kindergarten year and requires, as many of these do, that all students should be technology literate by the time they leave the eighth grade. Texas, like most states, publishes specific guidelines which are intended as a planning aid and a vehicle to support technology integration across the curriculum to help students develop tomorrow's digital knowledge and skills.

Table 9.6 illustrates the growing expectations of the TA TEKS in terms of **creativity and innovation** through various age ranges. Note that in the creativity and innovation strand of the TA TEKS, students in K-5,

Table 9.6   Expectations of creativity and innovation competencies for K-8 students

	Kindergarten-Grade 2	Grades 3–5	6th Grade	7th Grade	8th Grade
(1) Creativity and innovation.	(B) create original products using a variety of resources;	(A) create original products using a variety of resources;	(B) create original works as a means of personal or group expression;	(B) create and present original works as a means of personal or group expression;	(B) create, present, and publish original works as a means of personal or group expression;

Note: Adapted from "Chapter 126. Texas Essential Knowledge and Skills for Technology Applications" by L. Chen in 2014. Copyright 2014 by Texas Education Agency.

Table 9.7 Communication and collaboration expectations within technology standards for K-8 students

	Kindergarten-Grade 2	Grades 3–5	6th Grade	7th Grade	8th Grade
(2) Communication and collaboration.	(C) Format digital information, including font attributes, color, white space, graphics, and animation, for a defined audience and communication medium.	(C) Collaborate effectively through personal learning communities and social environments.	(C) Read and discuss examples of technical writing.	(C) Create products using technical writing strategies.	(C) Create and publish products using technical writing strategies.

Note: Adapted from "Chapter 126. Texas Essential Knowledge and Skills for Technology Applications" by L. Chen in 2014. Copyright 2014 by Texas Education Agency.

according to the spiral curriculum, are expected to create original products using a variety of resources, while students in the sixth grade are expected to **add personal and group expressions** to the work. Students in the seventh grade add **presentation of their work**, in addition to the expectations for the sixth-grade students. Furthermore, eighth-grade students are expected to also **publish their work** as a supplement to the expectations of the sixth- and seventh-grade students.

Table 9.7 shows the growing expectations of TA TEKS in terms of **communication and collaboration** through various age ranges. Note that in the communication and collaboration strand of the TA TEKS, students in K-2 are expected to **format digital information** for a defined audience, and students in grade 3 through 5 are expected to **collaborate** effectively through personal learning communities and social environments. Later, in the sixth grade, students are expected to read and **discuss technical writing**. Technical writing is a written form of professional communication used in a variety of technical and occupational fields, such as engineering, health science, chemistry, finance, and biotechnology. On that foundation, students in the seventh grade should begin to **create products** using technical writing strategies. Furthermore, eighth-grade students are expected to also **publish** their work as a supplement to the expectations of the sixth- and seventh-grade students.

Table 9.8 highlights the growing expectations of the TA TEKS in terms of **research and information fluency** through various age ranges. Note that in this strand, K-2 students are expected to **manage information** to build a knowledge base regarding a task, and students in grades 3 through 5 are expected to **collect and**

Table 9.8 Research and information fluency expectations within technology standards for K-8 students

	Kindergarten-Grade 2	Grades 3–5	6th Grade	7th Grade	8th Grade
(3) Research and information fluency.	(B) use research skills to build a knowledge base regarding a topic, task, or assignment;	(B) collect and organize information from a variety of formats, including text, audio, video, and graphics;	(B) discuss and use various search strategies, including keyword(s) and Boolean operators;	(B) use and evaluate various search strategies, including keyword(s) and Boolean operators;	(B) plan, use, and evaluate various search strategies, including keyword(s) and Boolean operators;

Note: Adapted from "Chapter 126. Texas Essential Knowledge and Skills for Technology Applications" by L. Chen in 2014. Copyright 2014 by Texas Education Agency.

organize information from a variety of formats, including text, audio, video, and graphics. Students in the sixth grade should be able to **discuss and use search strategies**, including keyword(s) and Boolean operators in addition to the expectations for the grades 3 to 5 students. On that foundation, students in the seventh grade should be able to **evaluate** various search strategies in addition to using search strategies.

As for communication and collaboration, seventh-grade students **create personal learning networks** to collaborate and publish with peers, experts, or others by using digital tools such as blogs, wikis, audio/video (rather than simply participating in those activities). They are able to form technical writing strategies when creating products instead of simply creating and discussing the products. They **use and evaluate** various search strategies, including keyword(s) and Boolean operators, rather than simply discussing and using various search strategies as most sixth-grade students do. Eighth-grade students are expected to also **plan** their search strategies in addition to using and evaluating search strategies. In the tables below, one can see how the standards advance in difficulty through the grade levels.

Nathan, a third grader, watched how his brother, who goes to a community college, uses digital technologies at home. Nathan emulates the usage, first through imitation, and then later he does not even have to count on his brother's help, for example, when creating PowerPoint presentations or doing things on the Internet.

Nathan loves to go to school. Among all things, he likes how his teacher, Mr. Washington, provides digital microscopes and other digital tools for science investigation and how he installs geometry software that allows the class to explore the concept of shape by stretching, bending, shrinking, or combining images. Like most third graders, Nathan does not like drill and practice.

Nathan has found that on the days they have technology, he is more excited than ever to be at school. What do the standards mean to Nathan?

Table 9.9 summarizes the expectations of TA TEKS in terms of **critical thinking, problem solving, and decision making** through various age ranges. Note that in this strand, K-2 students are expected to identify **what is known and unknown and what needs to be known** regarding a problem and **explain the steps to solve the problem**; **evaluate** the appropriateness of a digital tool to achieve the desired product; and **evaluate** products prior to final submission.

Students in grade 3 through 5 are expected to identify information regarding a problem and explain the steps towards the solution like K-2 students. They should also be able to **collect, analyze,** and **represent** data to solve problems using tools and **evaluate technology tools** applicable for solving problems.

Table 9.9 Critical thinking, problem solving, and decision making expectations within technology standards for K-8 students

	Kindergarten–Grade 2	Grades 3–5	6th Grade	7th Grade	8th Grade
(4) Critical thinking, problem solving, and decision making.	(A) identify what is known and unknown and what needs to be known regarding a problem and explain the steps to solve the problem;	(A) identify information regarding a problem and explain the steps towards the solution;	(A) identify and define relevant problems and significant questions for investigation;	(A) identify and define relevant problems and significant questions for investigation;	(A) identify and define relevant problems and significant questions for investigation;

Note: Adapted from "Chapter 126. Texas Essential Knowledge and Skills for Technology Applications" by L. Chen in 2014. Copyright 2014 by Texas Education Agency.

Figure 9.14   Laptop, microscope, telescope are tools for science investigation.

Mr. Washington provides digital microscopes and other digital tools for science investigation (see Figure 9.14). As noted, he installs geometry software that allows Nathan's third-grade class to explore the concept of shape by stretching, bending, shrinking, or combining images. These science and math investigation tools are used by students to collect, analyze, and represent data to solve problems, and these practices are aligned with TA TEKS. By complying with standards such as the TA TEKS, Mr. Washington offers lessons that are motivating and developmentally appropriate in Nathan's class.

Students' critical thinking, problem solving, and decision making skills in the sixth grade are to plan and manage activities to develop a solution, design a computer program, or complete a project; collect and analyze data to identify solutions and make informed decisions; use multiple processes and diverse perspectives to explore alternative solutions; make informed decisions and support reasoning; and transfer current knowledge to the learning of newly encountered technologies. Students' critical thinking, problem solving, and decision making skills mature in the sixth grade and are refined in the seventh and throughout the eighth grades. In other words, students should all be literate with problem solving and critical thinking skills by the time they leave the sixth grade.

As Table 9.10 illustrates, children's **digital citizenship responsibilities** grow along with ages as well. Note that in the digital citizenship strand of the TA TEKS, students in kindergarten through the second grade are expected to **adhere to acceptable use policies,** reflecting appropriate behavior in a digital environment. As they grow older, from the third grade through the fifth grade, students are to adhere to acceptable use

Table 9.10   Digital citizenship within technology standards for K-8 students

	Kindergarten-Grade 2	Grades 3–5	6th Grade	7th Grade	8th Grade
(5) Digital citizenship.	(A) adhere to acceptable use policies reflecting appropriate behavior in a digital environment;	(A) adhere to acceptable use policies reflecting positive social behavior in the digital environment;	(A) understand copyright principles, including current laws, fair use guidelines, creative commons, open source, and public domain;	(A) understand and _practice_ copyright principles, including current fair use guidelines, creative commons, open source, and public domain;	(A) understand, explain, and _practice_ copyright principles, including current laws, fair use guidelines, creative commons, open source, and public domain;

Note. Adapted from "Chapter 126. Texas Essential Knowledge and Skills for Technology Applications" by L. Chen in 2014. Copyright 2014 by Texas Education Agency.

Table 9.11   Technology operations and concepts within technology standards for K-8 students

	Kindergarten-Grade 2	Grades 3–5	6th Grade	7th Grade	8th Grade
(6) Technology operations and concepts.	(A) use appropriate terminology regarding basic hardware, software applications, programs, networking, virtual environments, and emerging technologies;	(A) demonstrate an understanding of technology concepts, including terminology for the use of operating systems, network systems, virtual systems, and learning systems appropriate for Grades 3–5 learning;	(A) define and use current technology terminology appropriately;	(A) define and use current technology terminology appropriately;	(A) define and use current technology terminology appropriately;

Note: Adapted from "Chapter 126. Texas Essential Knowledge and Skills for Technology Applications" by L. Chen in 2014. Copyright 2014 by Texas Education Agency.

policies (AUP), reflecting **positive social behavior** in the digital environment. In addition to being expected to adhere to AUP, students starting in the sixth grade are asked to also **understand** copyright principles, including current laws, fair use guidelines, creative commons, open source, and public domain. Students starting in the seventh grade are asked to understand and **practice** copyright principles, including current fair use guidelines, creative commons, open source, and public domain, while students starting in the eighth grade are expected to also understand, **explain**, and practice copyright principles, including current laws, fair use guidelines, creative commons, open source, and public domain.

As Table 9.11 illustrates, children's **technology operations and concepts** grow along with ages as well. Knowing and using basic technology terms is also expected. From kindergarten through the second grades, students should be able to **use appropriate technology terms** such as hardware and software and use appropriate tools for input, output, and storage. They know how to **open** an application and **create, modify, print, and save** files (refer to Figure 9.15). They also know how to use the online "help" function and demonstrate basic keyboarding skills (Figure 9.16). School-aged children are able to **evaluate** the usefulness of acquired digital content. They can use simple **search strategies** to access information regarding a topic and develop habits to adhere to **acceptable use policies** reflecting appropriate behavior in a digital environment.

According to the TA TEKS, older children, from the third through the sixth grades, should be able to follow the rules of digital etiquette; respect the intellectual property of others; use search strategies such as keywords and the Boolean identifiers *and*, *or*, and *not* and other strategies appropriate to specific search engines; validate and evaluate the relevance and appropriateness of information; draft, edit, manipulate files using appropriate file management system; and publish

RedKoala/Shutterstock, Inc.

Figure 9.15   Common multimedia file type icons.

dslaven/Shutterstock, Inc.

Figure 9.16   School-aged children need to know how to seek online help.

products in different media individually and collaboratively. They also manage to troubleshoot minor technical problems with hardware and software using online "help."

The sixth-grade students should be able to **identify, create, and use files in various formats** such as text, raster and vector graphics, video, and audio files. They create original works as a means of individuals or groups. Students understand and use operating systems; perform more advanced troubleshooting techniques such as resolving software compatibility, verifying network connectivity; and demonstrate effective file management strategies such as conversion. Sixth graders use technology to discuss trends and possible outcomes and create a research plan to guide inquiry as well. They use productivity tools including word processors, spreadsheet workbooks, databases, and digital publication tools. More importantly, this level creates nonlinear media projects using graphic design principles and that integrate two or more technology tools to create a new digital product. They can also discuss how technology has changed throughout history and the relevance of technology to daily living. They **understand** the negative impacts of inappropriate technology use, including online bullying and harassment, hacking, intentional virus setting, invasion of privacy, and piracy of software, music, video, and/or other media. Rather than simply protecting and honoring individual privacy, just as with their younger counterparts, they venture into the direct implications of these issues. The expectations for seventh-grade students are very similar to that of the sixth-grade students. The differences are in the expectation for the seventh graders to **discuss trends** and **make predictions** instead of just discussing possible outcomes.

Students from the 9th through the 12th Grades

Adolescence is viewed as a transitional period between childhood and adulthood. The age at which particular changes take place varies between individuals, but adolescence is also generally regarded as a time for rapid cognitive development (Arnett, 2009; Steinberg, 2008) (refer to Figure 9.17). Piaget (1969) describes adolescence as the stage of life in which the individual's thoughts start taking more of an abstract form, and their ability to think more deductively and logically emerges. This allows the individual to think and reason in a wider perspective.

By the time the individuals have reached about age 15, their basic thinking abilities are comparable to those of adults.

Figure 9.17 New family communication concept by technologies.

These improvements occur in five areas during adolescence: (a) attention, (b) memory, (c) processing speed, (d) organization, and (e) higher-level cognition (Daddis, 2011; Graca, Calheiros, & Barata, 2013; Sylwester, 2007). They gain more in the areas of behavior autonomy, cognitive autonomy, and emotional autonomy.

In gaining **behavioral autonomy**, adolescents are developing the ability to regulate their own behavior, to act on personal decisions, and to self-govern (Sylwester, 2007). With **cognitive autonomy,** they partake in processes of independent reasoning and decision making without excessive reliance on social validation. With **emotional autonomy**, they develop more mature emotional connections with adults and peers. During adolescence, there is a high emphasis on approval of peers due to adolescents' increased self-consciousness. In general, adolescents think more quickly than children. Their thinking is also less bound to concrete events than that of children because they also have developed the skills of hypothetical and abstract thinking (Sylwester, 2007). The thoughts, ideas, and concepts developed at this period of life greatly influence one's future life. Where does technology come into play in these changes? Simply being able to use technology is no longer enough. Today's teenagers need to be able to use technology to analyze, learn, create, and explore.

The TA TEKS cover computer literacy in grades K-8, but there are many other areas in which students should grow throughout their K-12 experience in order to enhance the use of technology in learning. There are technology-related courses designed for high school students to prepare for successful transitions to postsecondary education and employment beyond the eighth grade.

The percentage of U.S. students enrolling in college in the fall immediately following high school completion was well over 60 percent in 2012 (National Center for Education Statistics, 2012). No matter whether students choose to enroll in college or look for employment after high schools, they need to

Figure 9.18   Scientists using microscopes and digital tablets in a laboratory.

acquire additional technology skills beyond basic computer literacy. The world's best companies are redesigning themselves to increase productivity, quality, variety, and speed, which can only be accomplished by "tech savvy" employees (National Center on Education and the Economy, 2008). Digital age skills are vital for preparing students to work (refer to Figure 9.18), live, and contribute to society. The following courses are often offered as electives on the high school level (ninth grade and above) for students who have built a computer literacy foundation in grades K-8. These are the areas in which students should grow throughout high schools in order to bridge the gap from high school to work or high school to colleges:

Computer Science I, II, & III	3-D Modeling and Animation
Digital Forensics	Digital Communications in the 21st Century
Game Programming and Design	Digital Video and Audio Design
Mobile Application Development	Web Communications
Robotics Programming and Design	Web Design
Digital Design and Media Production	Web Game Development
Digital Art and Animation	Independent Study in Technology Applications

In the two-semester Computer Science II Honors/AP course, for instance, students usually learn Java programs and object oriented programming, array lists, Boolean logics nested control structures, and other concepts. The course description typically indicates that "The course will develop the skills using Java as a means for learning programming. The types of problems solved by means of programing will vary (i.e., mathematics, science, finance, and graphics)."

High school students who are enrolled in career and technical education programs also have opportunities to take additional technology-related courses, including animations, audio/video production, graphic design and illustration, touch system data entry, business information management, virtual business, computer maintenance, telecommunications and networking, computer programming, and Web technologies. Industry has considerable influence in the standards in courses such as these. These courses offer school-to-work opportunities for students to earn portable job skills; prepare students for jobs in high-skill, high-wage careers; and increase students' opportunities for further education, including education in colleges or universities.

Conclusion

The Texas legislation requirement that all students should be technology literate by the time they leave the eighth grade is important one for emphasis in this chapter. High schools also offer technology-related electives courses in which students can grow from the ninth grade through the twelfth grade in order to bridge the gap from schools to work or K-12 to colleges. Future teachers should know the national ISTE Standards•S (for students) and state TA TEKS; both describe what K-12 students should know about and be able to do with technology. Prospective teachers should also understand the ISTE Standards•T (for teachers), the state level Technology Applications Standards for All Beginning Teachers, and Technology Applications Standards for All Teachers, which are the standards for evaluating the skills and knowledge that educators need to teach, use for work, and learn in an increasingly connected global and digital society. In addition, when teaching content areas, teachers also have recommendations from teachers' councils and associations such as the NAEYC for early childhood and the NCTM for mathematics education.

Technology standards were developed to provide benchmarks and guidelines for helping beginning and current teachers develop strategies for using technology in effective and meaningful ways with their students.

The standards, indicators, and student profiles encourage K-12 students to have ownership and responsibility for their learning. They also reflect the importance and the infusion of twenty-first century technology skills to assist and guide students to be productive, responsible citizens and to emphasize the importance of life-long learning with changing technology.

Teacher education programs introduce the basics of standards to beginning teachers, but ongoing exposure and familiarity with relevant details in various fields of specialization is a part of continuing professional development for educators. New teachers must become familiar with standards at all phases—from field testing in the work setting to professional development in their best use and application so that technology becomes the norm in their classroom.

There are clear implications for adopting various technology standards. The teacher needs to learn cutting edge ways of teaching. Helping teachers change their teaching styles to meet the vision described in the standards is not an easy task. This may involve a fundamental shift in the way some teachers work. Technology can serve as a catalyst to move teachers towards an instructional style that is more student-centered, active, and relevant to the world in which we live. Technology also provides learners with the opportunity to visualize and make more concrete the abstract world of some subjects.

Beginning teachers must know their technology for today, but they must also know that they are the agents of change in this process for the future and are at the active center of the life-long learning process. Technology cannot replace the teacher nor can it be used as a replacement for basic understandings and intuitions. Teachers have to make prudent decisions about when and how to use technology and should ensure that the technology is enhancing students' learning and thinking. Technology should become a tool to enhance all other learning and skills.

References

Alterio, J. M. (2006). Lapware introduces babies to computers. *The Journal News*. Retrieved from http://www.giggles .net/pressArticles/JournalNews/

American Library Association (ALA). (2014). Information literacy competency standards for higher education. Retrieved from http://www.ala.org/acrl/standards/informationliteracycompetency

Arnett, J. J. (2009). *Adolescents and emerging adulthood: A cultural approach* (4th ed.). New Jersey: Prentice Hall.

Cohen, M., & Tally, B. (2004). New maps for technology in teacher education: After standards, then what? *Journal of Computing in Teacher Education, 21*(1), 5–9.

Daddis, C. (2011). Desire for increased autonomy and adolescents' perceptions of peer autonomy: "Everyone else can; Why can't I?" *Child Development, 82*(4), 1310–1326.

Dean, C. B., Hubbell, E. R., & Pitler, H. (2012*). Classroom instruction that works: Research-based strategies for increasing student achievement* (2nd ed.). Alexandria, VA: Association for Supervision & Curriculum Development (ASCD).

Delaware Center for Educational Technology. (2005). Computer skills growth chart. Retrieved from http://www.dcet.k12 .de.us/instructional/skills/CSGCltr.pdf

Gardner, J. E., & Wissick, C. A. (2002). Enhancing thematic units using the World Wide Web: Tools and strategies that integrate technology for students with mild disabilities. *Journal of Special Education Technology, 17*, 27–38.

Goodwin, K., & Highfield, K. (2012). iTouch and iLearn: An examination of "educational" apps. Paper presented at the Early Education and Technology for Children Conference, March 14-16, 2012, Salt Lake City, Utah. Retrieved from http://www.academia.edu/1464841/iTouch_and_iLearn_An_examination_of_educational_apps

Great Schools Partnership. (2014). The glossary of education reform. Retrieved from http://edglossary.org/ learning-standards/

Graca, J., Calheiros, M., & Barata, M. (2013). Authority in the classroom: Adolescent autonomy, autonomy support, and teachers' legitimacy. *European Journal of Psychology of Education, 3*, 1065.

Guth, G. J. A., Holtzman, D., Schneider, S., Carlos, L, Smith, J., Hayward, G, & Calvo N. (1999). *Evaluation of California's Standards-Based Accountability System. Final Report.* (ED439137).

Hill, C. (1995, September 6). Re: Education: Developing educational standard page. [Electronic mailing list message]. Retrieved from http://cartman.mofet.macam98.ac.il/~dovw/aa/0066.html

International Society for Technology in Education. (2007). National education technology standards and performance indicators for students. Retrieved from http://www.iste.org/docs/pdfs/20-14_ISTE_Standards-S_PDF.pdf

International Society for Technology in Education. (2008). National education technology standards and performance indicators for teachers. Retrieved from http://www.iste.org/docs/pdfs/20-14_ISTE_Standards-T_PDF.pdf

International Society for Technology in Education. (2009). Essential conditions necessary to effectively leverage technology for learning. Retrieved from https://www.iste.org/docs/pdfs/netsessentialconditions.pdf

Mid-Continent Research for Education and Learning. (2014). Content knowledge: A compendium of standards and benchmarks for K-12 education. Retrieved from http://www2.mcrel.org/compendium/docs/purpose.asp

National Association for the Education of Young Children. (2012a). Technology and interactive media as tools in early childhood programs serving children from birth through age 8. Retrieved from http://www.naeyc.org/files/naeyc/PS_technology_WEB.pdf

National Association for the Education of Young Children. (2012b). Key messages of the NAEYC/Fred Rogers Center Position Statement on Technology and Interactive Media in Early Childhood Programs. Retrieved from http://www.naeyc.org/files/naeyc/file/positions/KeyMessages_Technology.pdf

National Academy of Education. (2009). Standards, assessment, and accountability: Education policy white paper. Retrieved from http://www.naeducation.org/cs/groups/naedsite/documents/webpage/naed_080866.pdf

National Center for Education Statistics. (2012). Fast facts. Retrieved from http://nces.ed.gov/fastfacts/display.asp?id=372

National Center on Education and the Economy (U.S.). (2008). *Tough choices or tough times: The report of the new commission on the skills of the American workforce.* San Francisco: Jossey-Bass.

National Commission on Excellence in Education. (1983). *A nation at risk: The imperative for educational reform. A report to the nation and the Secretary of Education, United States Department of Education.* Washington, D.C: National Commission on Excellence in Education.

National Governors Association Center for Best Practices & Council of Chief State School Officers. (2010a). Common Core State Standards Initiative: Standards in your state. Retrieved from http://www.corestandards.org/standards-in-your-state/

National Governors Association Center for Best Practices & Council of Chief State School Officers (2010b). Common Core State Standards Initiative: Development process. Retrieved from http://www.corestandards.org/about-the-standards/development-process/

No Child Left Behind (NCLB) Act of 2001, Pub. L. No. 107-110, § 115, Stat. 1425 (2002).

North Central Regional Educational Laboratory. (2000). Critical issue: Integrating standards into the curriculum. Retrieved from http://www.ncrel.org/sdrs/areas/issues/content/currclum/cu300.htm

Page, A. S., Cooper, A. R., Griew, P., & Jago, R. (2010). Children's screen viewing is related to psychological difficulties irrespective of physical activity. *Pediatrics, 126*(5), 1011–1017.

Piaget, J., (1969). In D. Elkind & J. H. Flavell, J. H. (Eds.). *Studies in cognitive development: Essays in honor of Jean Piaget.* New York: Oxford University Press.

Roblyer, M. D. (2000). The national educational technology standards (NETS): A review of definitions, implications, and strategies for integrating NETS into K-12 curriculum. *International Journal of Instructional Media, 27*(2), 133–146.

Steinberg, L. (2008). *Adolescence* (8th ed.). New York: McGraw-Hill.

Sylwester, R. (2007). *The adolescent brain: Reaching for autonomy.* Thousand Oaks, CA: Corwin Press.

Texas Education Agency. (2006a). School Technology and Readiness Chart. Retrieved from http://www.tea.state.tx.us/WorkArea/linkit.aspx?LinkIdentifier=id&ItemID=2147501875&libID=2147501869

Texas Education Agency. (2006b). Texas Long-Range Plan for Technology, 2006-2020. Retrieved from https://www.txstarchart.org/docs/TxCSC.pdf

Texas Education Agency. (2012). TExES™ Pedagogy and Professional Responsibilities (PPR) EC–12 (160): Test at a glance. Retrieved from http://cms.texes-ets.org/files/9113/4193/1936/ppr_EC_12_160_TAAG.pdf

Texas Education Agency. (n.d.). Texas Essential Knowledge and Skills for Technology Applications. Retrieved from http://ritter.tea.state.tx.us/rules/tac/chapter126/

Texas Education Agency. (2014). Texas Essential Knowledge and Skills. Retrieved from http://www.tea.state.tx.us/index2.aspx?id=6148

Chapter 10

Technology Legal and Information Literacy Essentials

Sue Mahoney, Irene Chen, & Janice L. Nath
University of Houston-Downtown

Meet Mrs. Keith

Mrs. Keith was working on a PowerPoint slideshow for her presentation to her class on frogs. She really wanted to catch the attention of her young students by using a picture of Kermit, the Frog (see Figure 10.1). She downloaded a picture from the web and was ready to insert it into her presentation when she remembered that she should think about the copyright rules governing the use of the image. Can she use the image in her slideshow?

Technology Responsibilities

Technology encompasses numerous powerful and exciting tools, but with these tools comes the responsibility of using them legally, ethically, and appropriately. It is important that all parties—parents, teachers, and students—comply with the acceptable use policies (AUPs) developed by their school district and based on laws and accepted ethics. Teachers should introduce the school's acceptable use policy to their students (and to their parents) because it provides them with appropriate guidelines for technology use. Classroom teachers should also be mindful that they are role models for students and that they should always model the legal, ethical, and appropriate use of technology.

Classroom teachers have multiple responsibilities to their students when integrating technology into the curriculum. These responsibilities include knowing:

Figure 10.1 Kermit the Frog is a popular Sesame Street puppet character.

Harmony Gerber/Shutterstock, Inc.

- the content and how best to present it to ensure student mastery;
- the tools available and how best to include them in the content presentation;
- relevant ethical responsibilities associated with using technology tools in a manner that conforms to the teachers' ethics code and for being in compliance with international, federal, state, and school district rules and guidelines;
- the legal responsibilities with regard to copyright laws and plagiarism; and
- how to communicate effectively and appropriately with students and parents. Not all families have computers and/or Internet access, and teachers must be cognizant of this fact. These students and their families are experiencing the digital divide or technology gap.

Content Knowledge

Content knowledge is key when preparing lessons and using resources properly. The district and state curriculum requirements (e.g., the Texas Essential Knowledge and Skills, or TEKS, in Texas and Core requirements in many other states) provide guidelines for what content information is to be taught in the classroom. The curriculum and the lesson content guide what type of technology should be used with lessons, but technology "for technology's sake" should not guide the lesson content. Many states also have separate technology knowledge and skills requirements. Required state assessments and other formative and summative assessments determine if teachers have taught and students have learned.

Figure 10.2   Available resources in the Web 2.0 environment.

New teaching tools—software, Web 2.0 applications (refer to Figure 10.2), phone apps, and many others—arrive in the marketplace on a continuous basis for use with content areas and for technology knowledge and skills. It is the responsibility of each teacher: to examine and evaluate any new resources that may be of benefit to instruction, individual students, or to the school in other ways; to seek professional development opportunities and resources when appropriate; and to comprehend and follow the legal and ethical issues associated with using these tools.

Social and Ethical Issues of Integrating Technology for Learning

Ethics refers to a moral duty and obligation to try to do what is principled (Merriam-Webster, 2007). There are many issues in the use of technology which not only concern laws but also "doing what is right" for all users, particularly students.

The Digital Divide is an economic and social inequality according to categories of persons in a given population in their access to, use of, or knowledge of information and communication technologies. The Digital Divide is normally the result of inequalities between individuals, households, businesses, or geographic areas and is most often due to different socioeconomic levels.

The Digital Divide exists for many students, as many of them are also first generation immigrants from developing countries and/or live in lower SES situations. According to recent research, one of the major barriers to raising student literacy levels and computer skills is a lack of parental assistance at home (Daugherty, Dossani, Johnson, & Oguz, 2014). Research also shows that computer-based information, communication, services, and instruction are less available to those who are poor, live in rural areas, are members of minority racial/ethnic groups, and/or have disabilities (National Telecommunications and Information Administration, 1999). To tackle this challenge, educators have to work collaboratively and creatively with school districts and grant funding sources for solutions.

To help bridge the Digital Divide gap, teachers can serve as the advocates for their technology disadvantaged students. Trainings for teachers in integrating technology and the particular impact of the Digital Divide can be emphasized. Future teachers can brainstorm solutions on how they can assist in bridging the gap, but they must always consider if their assignments (especially homework) they are giving will be equitable in students being able to complete them (and complete them in equitable ways quality-wise). There are other places where students can use technology (such as public libraries), but parents may not be able to always get their children there, and older students may often need to work during public library hours. Teachers must also consider if parents are able to receive technology communications, and, if not, the teacher must ensure phone or paper alternatives.

Educators can extend their linkage with other appropriate agencies and organizations to offer computer literacy training courses to parents and community members. For community adult computer courses, acquiring basic computer skills, such as surfing the Internet, setting up and using e-mail, learning basic keyboarding, word-processing skills and data entry are taught. Participants experience the value of technology utilization as a tool for life. Schools can encourage faculty and staff involvement in community service.

There are a number of ways that a teacher may try to help gain more technology for his or her students—from business donations of old equipment to writing large and small funding grants. This type of advocacy for the preparation of students may need to occur if one's district cannot support large budgets for technology. However, a teacher must always be sure to follow district guidelines in seeking equipment or funding from the outside. The more that can be obtained, the more students will be able to develop their technological knowledge and skills. A district may provide funding and help obtain grants, but it may, at times, also be up to the teacher to initiate the process.

New Literacies

The meaning of literacy commonly signifies interpretation of a written text. *Visual literacy, graph literacy,* and *media literacy* are relatively new phrases amid the rising wave of multimedia technology. Visually pleasing, accurate charts enable users to easily find critical information or recognize important relations between data. *Visual literacy* is the ability to make meaning from information presented in the form of an image. *Graph literacy* is the ability to read and understand messages presented graphically. The skill of reading and understanding tables, diagrams, flow charts, timelines, maps and pie charts is becoming essential in the contemporary workplace. The third term, *media literacy* refers to the ability to read, analyze, evaluate, and produce communication in a variety of media forms including audio and video. Media literacy is critical in everyday life: information that is viewed on TV and on the Internet is used for decisions, including transportation, medical, grocery shopping, financial, and others.

Information literacy is "the set of skills needed to find, retrieve, analyze, and use information" (American Library Association, 2014, para. 1). This term encompasses all three kinds of literacies—visual literacy, graph literacy, and media literacy:

> It allows us to cope by giving us the skills to know when we need information and where to locate it effectively and efficiently. It includes the technological skills needed to use the modern library as a gateway to information. It enables us to analyze and evaluate the information we find, thus giving us confidence in using that information to make a decision or create a product. (para. 6)

It is important to note that information literacy skills are relevant to all content areas in K-12 schools. With these new concepts, laws and regulations have and will continue to be developed.

Teachers must be aware of the laws and guidelines at the international, national, state, and local levels that govern, for example, the usage of copyrighted materials including materials used under fair use and plagiarism.

Technology Standards

The International Society for Technology in Education (ISTE) is a nonprofit organization whose purpose is to assist educators and education leaders in advancing technology use for learners (www.iste.org). To this end, ISTE has developed standards for teachers and students. These standards identify the skills and expertise both groups need to function in today's digital environments. Teacher standards focus on facilitating, inspiring, modeling, and promoting digital citizenship, technology skills, and learning experiences, as well as continued professional development and leadership (ISTE Standards for Teachers, 2008). Student Standards correlate with the Teacher Standards while placing emphasis not only on the technology skills needed but students' ability to think critically, communicate, and function ethically and appropriately in the digital world (ISTE Standards for Students, 2007).

States and school districts may have their own set of technology skills and standards that teachers and future teachers must meet. Teachers must equip children with various technology skills (along with content) in specific terms, and this technology knowledge is often measured through certification testing for teachers and state and district testing for children. For example, the Texas technology components of the TExES™ Pedagogy and Professional Responsibilities (PPR) EC-12 (Texas Education Agency, 2012) exam are found in Competency 9 (Nath & Cohen, 2011) and in the Technology Application (TA) Standards I-V. Both documents identify the knowledge and skills required for beginning teachers.

Teacher and Student Behaviors/Practices

Professional and appropriate behavior is a requirement for all teachers in many areas of their lives, including their technological actions. Likewise, students should also practice appropriate behavior in the face-to-face classroom and in the digital environment. This section discusses some critical topics and resources relating to these topics. It is important that teachers and students be aware of the issues involved in these areas and engage in "best practices" for all parties involved. Many states, including Texas, may have certification sanctions and even civil lawsuits regarding misbehavior with technology (see Figure 10.3).

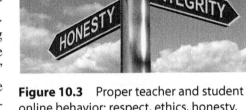

Figure 10.3 Proper teacher and student online behavior: respect, ethics, honesty, and integrity.

Acceptable Use Policy (or AUP)—This is a written agreement among involved parties that provides guidelines for behavior on the Internet or intranet, which is a network that uses technology to share information or computing services within an organization. Most school districts have developed an AUP (see Figure 10.4). This policy includes what the school district will do to protect students from inappropriate online materials, student practices with regard to Internet usage, and parental understanding that the school district will do its best to provide a secure, safe environment for its students but that sometimes students venture to inappropriate Web sites. Very often, parents must sign ahead of time for their children to be able to use the computer at schools.

Netiquette/Online Manners—Because electronic communication does not include the body language so necessary to the full understanding of some messages and because the writer is often in a hurry in today's busy world, messages sent via email, text message, or discussion board can be easily misunderstood. Knowing the proper etiquette for communicating in the online environment can make a difference in how a message is perceived. This is particularly true of teachers who are writing to parents, colleagues, administrators, and, sometimes, students, but school age learners also need to be taught how to avoid conflicts and misunderstandings. Proper online communication includes the following conventions:

Figure 10.4 Acceptable Use Policy equals Terms of Use Guidelines for Internet or intranet use in a school.

- Always identify oneself (include title and/or place where one teaches, especially if writing to parents or other administrators) (e.g., Sincerely, Jane Smith, Katie's Teacher at Sandy Creek Elementary).
- Use appropriate language.
  - Refrain from using sarcasm.
  - Avoid obscenity.
  - Do not be offensive online with language or pictures. Keep a high standard of behavior for the online environment.
  - Do not use all caps because this means that the sender is "SCREAMING" at the person receiving the message.
- Use spelling, punctuation, and grammar checks in messages.
- Be alert to copyright and plagiarism issues.
- Be respectful and sensitive to others in both copying and sharing messages and with regard to diversity issues.
- Use emoticons appropriately and be cautious with using humor—sometimes humor does not translate to text properly.

- Avoid forwarding spam and/or suspicious messages with possible viruses.
- Avoid forwarding "chain letters" (from the teacher's message box in particular).

Emily, a student teacher, was asked by her mentor teacher, Ms. Jefferson, to send out reminders to students' parents and invite them to the school open house next Tuesday. Ms. Jefferson said it was fine for Emily to send the invitation from her school's email account with the sender's name as "Ms. Jefferson". Should Emily follow Ms. Jefferson's advice since she is her mentor?

Emily noticed that most teachers remind students to follow Netiquette guidelines at the beginning rather than in the middle of the semester. What is the rationale behind this instructional decision?

According to proper online communication (Netiquette), Emily has to "always identify oneself." Even though Ms. Jefferson, her mentor teacher, said it was fine for Emily to send the invitation from her own email account with the sender's name as "Ms. Jefferson," she still had to send the message to students' parents and invite them to the school open house from her own email account with her own identity or *clearly* indicate this was not Ms. Jefferson's letter.

Most teachers around Emily remind students to follow Netiquette guidelines at the beginning rather than in the middle of the semester. Netiquette refers to the etiquette for students to follow when going online for e-mail, chat, and discussion forums. Again, these Netiquette guidelines are usually introduced to students early on in the school years to clarify expectations, set up class norms, to explain to students what technology behaviors are acceptable and what are not, and to put into effect online behavior guidelines. Some teachers even invite students' input to create an honor code so they become invested in it. A savvy teacher will know that particular assignments or situations are times when students may need reminders, so he or she does so again prior to those times.

Computer and Cyber Ethics—The Computer Ethics Institute provides a forum and resources for the identification, assessment, and responses to ethical issues associated with the advancement of information technologies in society. The institute has also published the Ten Commandments of Computer Ethics (http://computerethicsinstitute.org/images/TheTenCommandmentsOfComputerEthics.pdf) which provides guidelines for ethical behavior in the computer world (Computer Ethics Institute, n.d.):

1. Thou shalt not use a computer to harm other people.
2. Thou shalt not interfere with other people's computer work.
3. Thou shalt not snoop around in other people's computer files.
4. Thou shalt not use a computer to steal.
5. Thou shalt not use a computer to bear false witness.
6. Thou shalt not copy or use proprietary software for which you have not paid.
7. Thou shalt not use other people's computer resources without authorization or proper compensation.
8. Thou shalt not appropriate other people's intellectual output.
9. Thou shalt think about the social consequences of the program you are writing or the system you are designing.
10. Thou shalt always use a computer in ways that ensure consideration and respect for your fellow humans.

These rules of etiquette for the computer have expanded over time to include concepts relevant to the expanded use of computers, the Internet, and the ongoing innovations that appear daily in the technology world.

Teachers and students need to be constantly alert to their actions and the actions of others with regard to ethics in today's world. Teachers and students need to be appropriate in all their communications—they must think before they send any communication, and, when in doubt about the appropriateness of the message, not send it. School districts have policies about responsible computer use, communication with parents and students, and social media use. Teachers and future teachers must familiarize themselves with these policies! They must not post inappropriate comments or pictures on their Facebook or Twitter pages, even though it is "outside school." To keep one's job, they must act responsibly and use good judgment.

Bullying and cyberbullying are unacceptable practices for students and teachers, whether it is perpetuated face-to-face or through electronic technology. Either type of bullying is an unsolicited aggressive behavior towards another person (see Figure 10.5).

Student- and school-related abuses of computer and communication tools are widely reported in the media. In 2012, the word *sexting* was listed for the first time in Merriam-Webster's Collegiate Dictionary. Sexting is the act of sending sexually explicit messages, primarily between mobile phones. "Staff must not use social networks to communicate with students" is the guidance given in some schools' e-safety policy, nor should staff "have students classed as 'friends' or the equivalent." In recent years, Facebook, MySpace, and other social networking sites have sometimes been involved with cyberbullying issues which, in turn, have been blamed for incidents of teenage students' fear, embarrassment, and other problems in some states. A number of recent lawsuits have looked at the role a school or teachers could have played in preventing students from being cyberbullied and causing them anguish (even to the point of committing suicide). This is a serious issue that includes the teacher being aware of inappropriate pictures and/or messages sent to and about students. Two resources available are:

- Stopbullying.gov (http://www.stopbullying.gov/index.html) provides information about the types of bullying, who is at risk, how to prevent it, how to respond to it, and how to get help immediately. This Web site contains information that is relevant to students, teachers, parents, and the community.
- Cyberbullying Research Center (http://cyberbullying.us/) is an organization that is committed to providing the public with information about cyberbullying among adolescents. The Web site has resources for educators, parents, and teens. The center also has several publications available about cyberbullying and the center's research about cyberbullying.

It is important for teachers and guardians to closely monitor children's use of electronic devices, computers, and cell phones alike and to note any behavior that seems out of the ordinary.

The Cyberbullying Research Center (2009) lists the following as red flags that a child maybe a victim of cyberbullying if he or she,

- unexpectedly stops using the computer
- appears nervous or jumpy when an Instant Message text message, or email is received
- appears uneasy about going to school or outside in general
- appears to be angry, depressed, or frustrated after using the computer
- avoids discussions about what they are doing on the computer
- becomes abnormally withdrawn from usual friends and family members. (para. 2)

The Cyberbullying Research Center (2009) lists the following as red flags that a child maybe cyberbullying others if he or she,

- quickly switches screens or closes programs when you walk by
- uses the computer at all hours of the night
- gets unusually upset if he/she cannot use the computer
- laughs excessively while using the computer
- avoids discussions about what they are doing on the computer
- uses multiple online accounts or uses an account that is not his/her own.

It is also a good practice to remind older students to keep a clean online presence of themselves if they have social network profiles on sites such as Facebook or Twitter. Recruiters often use the Web as a place to search for talent and conduct employment background searches for job applicants. Any hint

Figure 10.5 The "Stop Bullying Now" sign.

of inappropriate posting can cause one to not be hired in the first place or an employee to be sanctioned. One must also remember what he or she may not consider offensive could be to others. If in doubt, a teacher or prospective teacher should not send or post. Also, teachers must always remember that their technology belongs to the school district, and the district has a right to monitor emails and school computers (including search histories). Downloading or searching inappropriate sites can be cause for a teacher to be fired and/or, in worst case scenarios, prosecuted. This is particularly true of anything that may be associated with pornography.

Academic Dishonesty and Plagiarism

Academic dishonesty is present in any classroom, in any school, in any university—but now it goes beyond cheating on a test. Due to technological advances, there are different types of dishonesty, such as claiming someone's work as your own, paying for someone else to do an essay, and not citing the sources used to create your own work. Statistics have shown in high school that more than 70% of students inside a classroom admitted to cheating (Rodrigues, 2011).

The question that needs to be addressed is why are these students cheating? Are students aware that it is against school rules and that plagiarism outside of school is considered a crime? If so, do they still find it acceptable?

It is now commonplace for students to bring PDA's and smart phones into the classroom, which gives them swift access to the Internet. While this technology is a benefit for students conducting research for a project, it can also be detrimental for educators who need to assess students' content mastery. Some students say they cheat because "this is my safety net" and/or "it is no big deal" (McMahon, 2007). However, we also know that later on it can not only cost grades but also the loss of a student's professional program (such as becoming a teacher), embarrassment, loss of a job, or many other detrimental actions.

Plagiarism is defined as the act of using another person's words or ideas without giving credit to that person (Merriam-webster.com). To plagiarize is to:

- steal and pass off (the ideas or words of another) as one's own
- use (another's production) without crediting the source
- commit literary theft: present as new and original an idea or product derived from an existing source (Merriam-webster.com).

When using someone else's materials, ideas, and so on to create documents, credit must be given to the sources used. Many teachers and instructors have spent an abundance of time explaining plagiarism with regard to assigned papers. The Online Writing Lab (OWL) at Purdue University (https://owl.english.purdue.edu/owl/) is a useful resource—for both students and teachers. The scope of information provided on multiple writing and writing related topics, including plagiarism, is outstanding. The OWL lists some common examples of plagiarism:

- If you buy, steal, or borrow a paper and turn it in as your own.
- If you hire someone to write a paper for you, then turn it in as your own.
- If you use a source too closely when you are paraphrasing information.
- If you build on someone's ideas without citing or giving proper credit.
- If you copy from another source without giving proper credit.

More and more school districts and universities subscribe to plagiarism checking services such as TurnItIn (www.turnitin.com) to check students' papers against its huge database of previous work, dissertations, theses, newspapers, and other paper and online sources over the Internet for similarities. The Originality Check feature provides a summary of matching or similar areas of text found in a submitted paper. The higher the similarity percentage, the greater the amount of text in the submission that appears as matching (to have been copied) against information in the database repositories.

For those schools who have not subscribed to TurnItIn or other plagiarism checking services, teachers can try out other free plagiarism detection Web sites such as Grammerly, PaperRater, and Dupli Checker, for occasional searches.

Some teachers make it a requirement that students submit "originality reports" generated from TurnItIn to accompany all major class papers. Instructors can also set up a view to see all class papers with similarity indices in class assignment inboxes. Some schools are more general about the "similarity indices" in order to call a paper "clean" or "original," while others give specific percentage numbers. Teachers not only have to become familiar with technology-based plagiarism checkers, but they can educate students about how to avoid plagiarism by using free cartoons, games, and other interactive Internet resources (see Additional Resources at the end of the chapter for recommended sites). After these activities, students should have less of an excuse to say that they do not know they have committed plagiarism. Part of the technology knowledge that can be taught from a very early grade level and onward is having students give credit when it is someone else's work.

Multimedia must conform to the same guidelines as a research paper which means citations and references are required. Quotation marks with a citation on the slide/screen and a full reference in the Credits/References at the end of the document are required if text is quoted verbatim. Using information from a source requires that the source have a citation in the document with a full reference at the end of the document. In summary, when creating any kind of document, credit must be given to the author, photographer, artist, musician, Web site, or others in the document.

Teachers should incorporate anti-plagiarism mindfulness in their classrooms by doing the following: include the school's academic honestly policy and penalties associated with plagiarism in the course syllabi as well as explain plagiarism at the beginning of a semester and refresh students' memory multiple times throughout the year as they venture into projects where students might be most apt to plagiarize. The school librarian would also be a relevant resource for reinforcing the anti-plagiarism mindset. Teachers and students should also be aware of the school district's policy and the guidelines for handling any plagiarism incidents that occur.

Authors, software creators, artists, composers, and others are paid and/or recognized for their efforts, and they have the right to agree to let others use their work (see Figure 10.9). Most will agree to use for teachers in schools, but they *must* be asked. Many make their living selling excellent products to schools, so they can ask for compensation for usage. Taking that from them is really a form of stealing. When others claim that something is their own work, the value of the creator's work is diminished. If there is financial or other type of recognition lost, it is doubtful that their creative efforts will continue. This includes copying others' textbooks or chapters in textbooks without permission by the publisher. At the college or university level, the librarian is also an excellent resource for plagiarism rules, copyright issues, fair use guidelines, and other guidelines.

Software Issues

When **purchasing software**, one is **purchasing a license** and with the license comes **terms of use**. The options can include purchasing a single license and a license for a network. Both of these state the number and guidelines of installations that can be made. Simply because a license has been purchased does not mean that one can install the software on as many machines as desired. This unauthorized copying is termed piracy. The limitations of the contract must be followed on installations, even for school use.

There are also several other types of software available:

- **Freeware** is copyrighted software that the author allows for free use. Examples of freeware include ClassRoom GradeBook (http://www.classroomgradebook.com), which is designed for teachers for record keeping and grading. EaseUS Todo Backup Free (www.todo-backup.com) lets teachers and students create backups of important files or entire computers. In both cases, the authors retain the copyright, which means that a user must conform to the author's copyright guidelines (Webopedia, 2014d).
- **Shareware** is also copyrighted software that is distributed free of charge, but the author of the software requests a small fee if a user likes the software and uses it regularly. Dino Numbers is a shareware

math computer game designed for children that allows them to practice arithmetic skills. Magic Photo Editor is a shareware digital image editor for creating collages, frames, and portraits. It's free to try with a 30-use limit. Shareware is inexpensive, often produced by a single programmer, and is offered directly to users (Webopedia, 2014e).

- **Public-domain** software (refer to Figure 10.6) is software that is not copyrighted. It is free and can be used without restrictions (Webopedia, 2014f). For instance, the public-domain software, BLAST (Basic Local Alignment Search Tool, http://blast.ncbi .nlm.nih.gov/) allows high school biology teachers to perform similarity searches against constantly updated databases of proteins and DNA.

Figure 10.6   Creative Commons Public Domain Logo.

- **Open source software** is software in which the source code is available to the general public for use and/or modification from its original design free of charge (refer to Figure 10.7). It is usually developed in collaboration with other programmers and is under a license defined by the Open Source Initiative (OSI) (see Figure 10.7). Not all open source software is distributed under the same licensing agreement (Webopedia, 2014g). More information about OSI can be found at http:// opensource.org. Mozilla Firefox, the Web browser used by many educators and students alike, is a free and open-source Web browser developed by the Mozilla Foundation. Another open source software example is Moodle. Used by many school districts, Moodle can be customized as a learning management system (LMS) for students without any licensing fees.

Figure 10.7   The Open Source Initiative helps users identify open source software.

- **Creative Commons** is a nonprofit organization that provides free copyright license tools that allow authors to customize the copyright terms for their creations (http://creativecommons.org) (refer to Figure 10.8).

Using the Internet, educators can more easily find quality shareware or freeware products while still preserving the ability to find obscure niche software. Major download sites, such as CNet's Download.com, rank titles based on user reviews, editors' reviews, and a few other ways. There are also user blogs and forums that assist individuals to spread news about titles they like.

However, educators also have to note that a limitation of open source resources, freeware, and shareware programs is potential instability and/or poor quality. When looking for open source resources, freeware, and shareware programs, educators should be cautious of the credibility of the hosting servers from where they plan to download the program so that a computer virus, such as Trojan Horse, will not become a threat to one's computer.

Figure 10.8   Creative Common's CC button.

Figure 10.9   The many aspects of copyright.

Which Is It? Trademark? Patent? Copyright?

Mashups are combinations that bring together different content into one place. They can combine pictures, audio, text, maps, and videos from various sources. **Remix**, a related term, refers to combing multimedia elements that were not originally intended by the creators. Yahoo's Pipes and Google Mashup Editor are more specialized tools to create online mashups. Mashups can be music pieces, videos, audios, games, word clouds, Web contents, and even books.

Some mashups that teachers often use are blogs on Blogger, Edublogs, or WordPress on which teachers can post materials, such as video helps or instructions on assignments necessary for students to complete work while at home. The electronic presentation on Prezi or PowerPoint in class that teachers use typically pulls information and materials from several sources.

Mashups can be included in reports and assignments to provide a visual representation. Students can create mashups as class projects for assessment to replace the traditional written reports or PowerPoint presentations. Mashups rely on open and discoverable resources, open and transparent licensing, and open and remixable formats. However, most publicly available data used in mashups today (such as graphics from Flickr or videos from YouTube) are not designed for educational purposes. Educators must be wary of issues of plagiarism and copyright infringement in those mashups they present to their students and the mashups created by students. For the future generation of the Americans to become more aware of intellectual property at an even younger age, schools need to start educating children as early as possible on the nuances of intellectual property, innovation, and patents.

Teachers need to inform students that trademark, service mark, patent, and copyright are not synonyms (refer to Figure 10.11). The following definitions come from The United States Patent and Trademark Office (http://www.uspto.gov/trademarks/basics/definitions.jsp).

- A **trademark** is a word, phrase, symbol, and/or design that identifies and distinguishes the source of the goods of one party from those of others.
- A **service mark** is a word, phrase, symbol, and/or design that identifies and distinguishes the source of a service rather than goods (see Figure 10.10).
- A **patent** is a limited duration property right relating to an invention, granted by the United States Patent and Trademark Office in exchange for public disclosure of the invention.
- A **copyright** protects works of authorship such as writings, music, and works of art that have been tangibly expressed (see Figure 10.9).

Each of these terms has a set of criteria which must be followed in order to be in compliance with the governing agency: the United States Patent and Trademark Office (an agency of the Department of Commerce) (2013) and the U.S. Copyright Office (a division of the Library of Congress) (2012). More often than not, students and teachers are concerned about copyright issues. Therefore, it is expected that students and teachers be aware of the legal issues surrounding the use of copyrighted materials.

Teachers play a key role in students' lives and should model the appropriate behavior with regard to the literacies, ethics, and laws that revolve around schools, classrooms, the community, and society as a whole. Let us return to Mrs. Keith at the beginning of the chapter. She is practicing a good teaching strategy of engaging students' attention by inserting the picture

Figure 10.11   Common infringement symbols: copyright, registered, trademark, and patent.

Figure 10.10   A fictional logo using the service mark symbol.

of Kermit the Frog in a presentation, but she has to model proper online behavior to her young students by downloading a picture from a source to which she has legitimate access and citing the source properly (or not use it otherwise).

The **1976 Copyright Act** (copyright.gov/title17) provides guidelines for use of copyrighted materials. The following information comes from the document, *Copyright Basics*, provided by the U.S. Copyright Office in Circular 1 (2012) (http://www.copyright.gov/circs/circ1.pdf). Copyright is a form of protection provided by U.S. laws to authors of "original works of authorship," including literary, dramatic, musical, artistic, and certain other intellectual works. Section 106 of the 1976 Copyright Act generally gives the owner of the copyright the exclusive right to do and to authorize others to do the following:

- Reproduce the work in copies or phonorecords
- Prepare derivative works based upon the work
- Distribute copies or phonorecords of the work to the public by sale or other transfer of ownership, or by rental, lease, or lending
- Perform the work publicly, in the case of literary, musical, dramatic, and choreographic works, pantomimes, and motion pictures and other audiovisual works
- Display the work publicly, in the case of the literary, musical, dramatic, and choreographic works, pantomimes, and pictorial, graphic, or sculptural works, including the individual images of a motion picture or other audiovisual work
- Perform the work publicly (in the case of sound recordings) by means of a digital audio transmission

Circular 40 (http://www.copyright.gov/circs/circ40.pdf) provides information about Copyright Registration for Pictorial, Graphic, and Sculptural Works. Copyright protection comes into existence at the time the work is created in a fixed, tangible form. Prior to March 1, 1989 the use of a copyright notice was mandatory on all published works, but after March 1, 1989 the use of a copyright notice is optional. A copyright notice includes the copyright symbol ©, the owner of the copyright, and a date—for example: © John Smith 2014.

What is protected by copyright? Original works of authorship that are fixed in a tangible form of expression. Works created in one of the following categories are considered to be copyrightable:

- Literary works
- Musical works, including the accompanying words
- Dramatic works, including any accompanying music
- Pantomimes and choreographic works
- Pictorial, graphic, and sculptural works
- Motion pictures and other audiovisual works
- Sound recordings
- Architectural works

Copyright law also allows educators the use of copyrighted materials under the doctrine of fair use (2012) (http://copyright.gov/fls/fl102.html). The doctrine of fair use has evolved through multiple court decisions and is found in section 107 of the copyright law. This doctrine allows for the reproduction of materials for the purpose of criticism, comment, news reporting, teaching, scholarship, and research. Four factors are to be considered in determining whether or not a particular use is fair.

1. The purpose and character of use, including whether such use is of commercial nature or is for nonprofit educational purposes
2. The nature of the copyrighted work
3. The amount and substantiality of the portion used in relation to the copyrighted work as a whole (see Table 10.1)
4. The effect of the use upon the potential market for, or value of, the copyrighted work.

Table 10.1 Amount Desired to Be Copied. *Modified table used under a Creative Commons BY license from the Copyright Advisory Office of Columbia University, Kenneth D. Crews, director*

Amount Desired to Be Copied	
Favoring Fair Use	**Opposing Fair Use**
• Small quantity is to be copied. • Portion used is not central or significant to entire work. • Amount is appropriate for favored educational purpose.	• Large portion or whole work is to be used. • Portion used is central to or "heart of the work."

To copy or not to copy? These elements must be carefully weighed. A chart such as the one below may help to tip the educator's decision one way or the other (refer to Table 10.2):

An Attribution (BY) licensee can be obtained, if the work is correctly referenced to the author, to copy, distribute, display and perform it.

Educators can refer to the Fair Use Checklist put out by the Copyright Advisory Office at Columbia University Libraries (http://copyright.columbia.edu/copyright/files/2009/10/fairusechecklist.pdf) for complete rulings on copying. Another very handy series of charts to help judge whether copying is Fair Use or not is shown at http://home.moravian.edu/public/reeves/library/Fair%20Use%20Flow%20Chart.pdf. The distinction between what is fair use and what is infringement in a particular case is not always be clear or easily defined. The law calls for a balanced application of these four factors: purpose, nature, amount, and effect. The Copyright Advisory Office of Columbia University (n.d.) calls this a "balancing test" and states,

> To determine whether a use is or is not a fair use, always keep in mind that you need to apply all four factors. For example, do not jump to a conclusion based simply on whether your use is educational or commercial. You still need to evaluate, apply, and weigh in the balance the nature of the copyrighted work, the amount or substantiality of the portion used, and the potential impact of the use on the market or value of the work. This flexible approach to fair use is critical in order for the law to adapt to changing technologies and to meet innovative needs of higher education. (para. 10)

Table 10.2 *Effect in copying works.* Used under a Creative Commons BY license from the Copyright Advisory Office of Columbia University, Kenneth D. Crews, director.

Effect in Copying	
Favoring Fair Use	**Opposing Fair Use**
• User lawfully purchased or acquired it for consumable purposes (many teacher workbooks can be bought for the purpose of copying). • Only one or few copies will be made. • No significant effect is made on the market or potential market for copyrighted work. • No similar product is marketed by the copyright holder. • There is no licensing mechanism.	• Could replace sale of copyrighted work • Significantly impairs the market or potential market for copyrighted work or derivative. • Reasonably available licensing mechanism for use of the copyrighted work. • Affordable permission is available for using work. • Numerous will be copies made. • The copier will make it accessible on the Web or in other public forum. • Repeated or long-term use.

Let's apply the "balancing tests" on the scenarios of Miss Brown and Jason.

Miss Brown, a mathematics teacher, thinks a shareware tutorial software program that she uses in class can be helpful for a group of disadvantaged children that she volunteers to mentor after school in a community center. Should she request to purchase as many individual copies of the software as needed in the community center as required by the software company? Can she use the school software CD to install a copy for the community center?

Miss Brown's school purchases one copy of a typing tutorial program, which is housed in the library. It is checked out to individual students to take home for two-week periods. This is permissible under what conditions?

At one time or another, most teachers and students have found that "perfect piece" of video, music, or art for a presentation and hoped that the use of it fell into the category of "fair use." Miss Brown should check the software company homepage and the documents that come with the shareware tutorial software program and the school AUP to see if she can install the software program in the community center where she volunteers. The typing tutorial program should be checked out to individual students to take home for two-week periods only if the software is removed from school and home computers after use.

Jason, a student in the high school Web design class, finds a photo online dramatizing a pre-Columbian Viking landing in America. Since the school symbol is the Viking, he uses this photo as a graphic element on the school's Web page—giving credit to the site from which it was copied. Is this Fair Use? Why or why not?

Jason also takes a video class alongside his Web design class. His class produces a student video yearbook to add to the school homepage that they sell at community events to raise money for equipment for the school. They use well-known popular music clips. The money all goes to the school and the songs are fully listed in the credits. Jason wonders if this is covered under Fair Use? Why or why not?

School districts are liable for any copyright violations committed by their staff and students, and the area with the greatest potential for liability is the district's public Web site. Even though Jason plans to give credit to the site from which the Viking photo is found, it is still not a good practice to add the graphic element on the school's Web page without written consent from the original graphic owner. Again, using well-known popular music clips on a video yearbook to add to the school homepage without written consent is not permitted, even if it is for a good cause. There is not always a clear line between fair use and infringement. The best rule of thumb is that when in doubt, get permission from the copyright holder in writing. Many authors, composers, photographers, and others allow this through their Web sites.

The key concept that should be taken away from this government publication is that copyright is important! Copyright violation can result in civil and/or criminal sanctions as well as substantial fines depending on the nature of the violation.

When teachers are looking for high resolution stock photos for illustration or other visual need, they can first try out loyalty free sources such as Morguefile. There are also stock photo services such as Shutterstock or iStockphotos that charge by annual subscription fees or download fees per

Figure 10.12   Educators can purchase stock pictures online.

Figure 10.13   If using an image from a Web site under Fair Use, it is imperative that the source information be included.

picture (see Figure 10.12). Stock photos are copyrighted images. For instance, with Shutterstock, users must purchase permission to use an image or subscribe to a photo service much like subscribing to a magazine in order to use these images. If a user has a license for a software package that includes clip art/photos, the user can use the clip art/photo images that are associated with the software usually without any additional charges, depending on how they are being used. The user should always review the software licensing agreement for the "terms of usage" to insure that images are used within the limits of the licensing agreement.

If using an image from a Web site under Fair Use, it is imperative that the source information be included under the image in a small font size (e.g.,—Source: http://complete. url.information.com) (see Figure 10.13).

If one uses personal photos in a document and he or she is the owner of these photos, a notice of copyright should be included in the information with the photos. This information should be in a small font size underneath or to the side such as in Figure 10.14 (Tyler Olson/Shutterstock, Inc.) and include a notice of copyright.

Figure 10.14   Notice of copyright for the photograph.

Two pieces of federal legislation, the Digital Millennium Copyright Act of 1998 (DMCA) and the Technology, Education, and Copyright Harmonization (TEACH) (Copyright Clearance Center, 2005) were created to govern issues related to digital distance education. If one is participating as a teacher in digital/online delivery of materials, he or she should check with school district resources to be sure to comply with the institution's requirements.

Best practice dictates that teachers and students be acquainted with copyright laws, fair use doctrine, and any future laws pertaining to copyright. It is also best practice to ask for permission in writing to use copyrighted materials when creating multimedia documents. Again, the school librarian is a useful resource for what is allowed.

Students and teachers must be mindful of copyright laws. Copyright law changes, and teachers serve as models for proper copyright protocols.

Citations and Reference Guidelines

The American Psychological Association (APA) Style Guide (2012) is used as the formatting guide for documents created in the field of education. Among many, the APA Web site (http://www.apastyle.org) provides resources and guidance for users. Typing in "APA electronic citations" or "APA electronic references" will bring up a number of sites and examples in a search engine (also see Table 10.3).

According to current APA guidelines (2014), if citing an entire Web site and not a specific document found on that site, it is sufficient to include the web address (URL) in parentheses in the text. However, the guidelines change when citing a particular document or information from a Web site, and this requires a listing in the reference list as well as an in-text citation.

Table 10.3 The Online Writing Lab (OWL) at Purdue University. More can be found at https://owl.english.purdue. edu/owl/resource/589/2/

> Citations and References are required when you . . .
> - use words or ideas presented in a magazine, book, newspaper, song, TV program, movie, Web page, computer program, letter, advertisement, or any other medium
> - use information gained through interviewing or conversing with another person, face to face, over the phone, or in writing
> - copy the exact words or a unique phrase from a source
> - reprint any diagrams, illustrations, charts, pictures, or other visual materials
> - use or repost any electronically available media, including images, audio, video, or other media

Music and video must also be properly cited and referenced. The following examples are from the *APA Style Guide to Electronic References, Sixth Edition* (2012).

Music recording, full album
Writer, A. A. (copyright year). *Title of album* [Recorded by B. B. Artist if different from writer; Medium of recording: CD, mp3, record, cassette, etc.]. Retrieved from http://xxxx (Date of recording if different from album copyright date)

Music recording, single track on an album
Writer, A. A. (copyright year). Title of song [Recorded by B. B. Artist if different from writer]. On *Title of album* [Medium of recording: CD, mp3, record, cassette, etc.]. Retrieved from http://xxxx (Date of recording if different from album copyright date)

Music recording, single track, republished
Lennon, J., & McCartney, P. (2000). I want to hold your hand [Recorded by The Beatles; mp3 file]. On *The Beatles 1*. Retrieved from http://www.amazon.com (Original work recorded 1963)

Streaming video (e.g., YouTube video)
Author, A. A. [User name]. (year, month day). Title of video [Video file]. Retrieved from http://xxxx
User name. (year, month day). Title of video [Video file]. Retrieved from http://xxxx

The person who posts a video is credited as the author. If the person's real name and user name are both available, the real name must be provided in the format: Author, A. A., followed by the user name inside brackets. If the real name is not available, one must include only the user name without brackets.

Citations and/or references are critical in any document created. If there is a resource that needs citing and it is impossible to figure out how to do it, the school librarian can be asked for assistance (refer to Table 10.3). Sometimes Web sites offer citation assistance. For example:

- Van Gogh Gallery—http://www.vangoghgallery.com/: Scroll to the bottom of the webpage . . . "How to Cite this Page"
- Wikipedia—http://www.wikipedia.org/: Although Wikipedia should not be used as a primary and the only reference for researching a subject, if used, it should be included in the references. Wikipedia provides citation help in its menu: Toolbox > Cite this page.

Driven by the rapid expansion of published and online literature, a new generation of online citation generators, or citation management software, is available for authors to record bibliographic references (Table 10.4). These online tools facilitate the creation of bibliographies or reference sections. Citation generators work by asking users to fill out Web forms to take input and format the output according to guidelines such as MLA from Modern Language Association, APA from American Psychological Association, and the Chicago Manual of Style. The excuses used by students who plagiarize are sometimes that they do not know how to cite properly. These sites prevent problems.

Table 10.4   A list of citation generators for students

Citation Generators	Web Address
Citation Machine	http://www.citationmachine.net
EasyBib	http://www.easybib.com
Citation Builder	http://www.lib.ncsu.edu/citationbuilder
KnightCite	http://www.calvin.edu/library/knightcite

When the citation process is made easy by introducing the citation generators, hopefully, instances of plagiarism should decrease. Nevertheless, teachers have to beware that not all citation generators are created equally. For instance, some citation generators target APA style formats, while other may be more accurate with MLA or other styles. Teachers are recommended to find the citation generators that best fit the practices of their subject areas and produce the most accurate bibliographies.

It is imperative to remind teachers and students alike that citations and references are provided in any type of document created. If the information required for a specific citation/reference is not readily available, it is a definite responsibility to locate the information and properly cite/reference any source used.

Confidentiality

Part of an ethical conversation about technology revolves around the plethora of data that teachers collect on students, including grading. There is student and parent information on teachers' technology tools that cannot be shared with others. Much care must be taken to ensure that none of this type of information be seen and/or taken. This could occur, for example, when a teacher leaves his/her screen on where others (including other parents) may view it. A student and his/her parents (according to FERPA, the Family Educational Rights and Privacy Act) have the right to see the education records of that child—but not those of other students. When in doubt as to what types of records a teacher may give out, he or she should consult the FERPA guidelines. The teacher must always secure his or her computer with passwords and be very mindful of clearing the screen of sensitive information being used when he or she has others around. The placement of the screen is also important if a teacher is working on sensitive data during the time that a class may be in the room.

Records can be easily lost with technology, so a teacher should ask what backup system a school district uses to be sure that grades and other important information will remain secure.

Technology Safety—An Ethical Issue

There are really two main issues that teachers must think about under the heading of safety—child safety and the "machine" safety. Teachers have the responsibility to protect expensive school equipment, which means that rules for use must be established so that the equipment is not severely damaged and can be used year after year. Teachers must also secure the equipment so that it does "not disappear." To avoid having viruses take over, the teacher must have students avoid going onto certain sites and/or accepting certain emails while on school equipment. If the teacher controls the password, he or she should make sure that it remains secure and that machines needing one are locked at the end of the day (if required).

Almost everyone who has used the computer or other devices has been in a situation that has caused physical discomfort. Teachers are also responsible for making sure that the technologies they have in their rooms for children are set up for comfortable physical use. This includes the height of the chair, the work surface, and a possible document holder. Obviously, students come in all sizes, so they should be taught to properly adjust (if possible) the seating and eye-to-screen length to their physical attributes. The lighting is another critical issue, particularly glare. Windows and/or overhead lights can quickly cause eyestrain, so the tilt of the screen and its placement is important. The brightness of a screen can be adjusted as well. Too long in any position can create painful situations, so teachers must consider time limitations of computer use in terms of age appropriateness.

Teaching proper posture can also help alleviate pain. Securing all cords and electrical hazards must be a consideration in classrooms.

Mental health is important for students as well. Many districts install firewalls that do not allow certain things to be viewed. A teacher must still check to see if that which he/she presents or that which students are viewing is safe and age appropriate. An appropriate part of ethical technology is addressing sending scams and viruses to others intentionally. Scams ("phishing") are a regular part of the Internet today, and people lose a considerable amount of money by being lured in. Cyber predators often target children of all ages as well. Teaching children to never give out personal information to those online who are unknown is a critical part of technology safety. If a child suspects that someone who is unknown is trying to "get too close," teachers should help children see how important it is to report it to an adult to have it checked out, particularly if someone wants to "meet up."

Hacking has also become a part of technology that can cause financial and informational loss. Some hackers do it for the challenge, while others (usually students) do it to change information such as grades or cause havoc to a school. Students should be taught that there are stiff penalties for those who are caught breaking into school systems, but schools may not often enforce them with young students. This, says Kassner (2013) in his article "Hackers: From Innocent Curiosity to Illegal Activity," is one of the prime reasons that students continue to the next level of hacking. Hacking for any reason should be considered as serious misconduct.

In one instance, a racially-charged item was placed on Jefferson High School's Facebook page. The district began at once to investigate who was responsible. The district network administrators suspected that the campus Facebook was hacked by a group who called themselves "the Jeff Electronic Army" or JEA. The district network administrators had experienced some previous incidents with hacking last year when some desperate students hacked into the district electronic grade book system to bump up their grades. When the current suspected hacking behaviors were detected, district network administrators used "packet sniffers," a program that can see all of the information passing over the network to which it is connected in order to monitor their networks and perform diagnostic tests or troubleshoot problems. With both experiences, the districts decide to take measures to prevent more incidents by assigning IT personnel to setup stronger firewalls, follow hacking forums to pick up on all the latest methods, encourage institute-wide users to change passwords frequently, install proper scanning software programs, and run attack and penetration tests to detect vulnerable points in the network that can be easily accessed from both external and internal users. The district encourages schools and teachers to make user-awareness campaigns to make all network users aware of the pitfalls of security and the necessary security practices to minimize hacking risks. They also want to send out the message to potential hackers that modern technology is so advanced that tools can be used to track "digital footprints" of hackers' online activities; therefore, it is better "not to even think about it!"

Keeping students and equipment safe is an ethical responsibility. Teachers must do all they can to maintain the safety of use.

The Web

The Web is a major component in today's classrooms. Reviewing some key concepts with regard to Web pages and Internet usage will be helpful. Materials or content on the Web are protected under the copyright law and cannot be freely used or modified without permission from the copyright holder. Web site content is protected under copyright law whether or not it carries a copyright notice. Permission from the copyright holder is required, in writing, if a work is being used beyond fair use.

What does it take to view a web page? Web pages (.html documents) can be read with a browser (examples: Internet Explorer®, Firefox®, Safari®). HTML documents can be read without Internet access. This means that a teacher can create Web pages for his/her students to use in the classroom without Internet access.

Each web page has a URL (Uniform Resource Locator) which is the address of documents and other resources on the World Wide Web and includes the following:

http://www.copyright.gov

1. http://—**http** stands for **hypertext transfer protocol** and defines how messages are formatted and transmitted (http://www.webopedia.com/TERM/H/HTTP.html accessed 3/11/14).
2. www—stands for World Wide Web is often not needed today when entering a URL into the address box of the browser
3. copyright—is the domain name which is used to identify an Internet protocol (IP) address
4. The domain suffix (.xxx) located at the end of a homepage (or main address) indicates which domain the Web page belongs to (Webopedia, 2014c) (see Figure 10.15):
   * gov—government agencies
   * edu—education
   * org—organizations (nonprofit)
   * mil—military
   * com—commercial business
   * net—network organizations
   * ca—Canada (e.g., as countries have two letters)

Figure 10.15 A few popular domain names are shown.

What should teachers consider before using a Web page with students? Whether teachers realize it or not, each time they visit a Web page they are evaluating it, depending on what one is looking for and how he/she will use the information provided (see Table 10.5). If one does this automatically when he/she is on the Web, it must be at a heightened level for each Web page students are to use in the classroom. All Web pages should be previewed before having students use them. Depending on the age of the audience, it is preferable to have students click on a link to go to a Web page rather than having them enter the URL and possibly entering it incorrectly—a URL incorrectly entered can sometimes direct a student to a Web site that is inappropriate! When using web resources the teacher should consider the following:

* Rich content
* Accuracy of the information
* Source of the information (reliable source or someone who just created a Web page for fun)
* Page design which includes colors scheme, fonts, page layout, and graphics
* Navigation
* Copyright date. Is the date current?
* A listed contact person or web master for the Web site
* Inappropriate elements: bias, inappropriate language, violence, and inappropriate graphics and advertisements
* Appropriateness for audience (Does content and the way it is presented work for your audience?)
  * Stimulation factor (on target to maintain interest level versus overly stimulating for the age group)
  * Readability for one's particular age group

Teachers may want to educate students to be flexible when they encounter broken links on Web pages. Due to the dynamic nature of the Web, outdated online materials and inaccessible links are almost unavoidable. Teachers can demonstrate to students how to self-help by finding substitute materials, access cached information, or apply advanced search techniques for other alternatives. At the same, teachers should also remind students to update Web page information and ensure accuracy of the information they have posted on the Web as a courtesy to viewers who visit the information they have posted.

Table 10.5 Web resource evaluation checklist

Criteria	
Rich content	☐
Accuracy of the information	☐
Sources of the information	☐
Page design	☐
Navigation	☐
Copyright date	☐
Contact person or web master information	☐
Free of inappropriate elements	☐

File Formats

A file format is how a document is saved, depending on the software being used to create the document. When doing a "save as" in any software, the program defaults to its native file format (e.g., Microsoft Word [.doc or .docx], Excel [.xls or .xlsx], and Windows Live Moviemaker project file [.wlmp]). Most software also gives the user additional file format options for saving the document. For example, Microsoft Word will allow a document to be saved in multiple file formats including RTF (rich text format) and PDF (portable document format). As a rule of thumb, one should always save the document being created in its native format and then do a "save as" and save in a different format if that is needed.

Audio, graphic, and video files are key components of many Web pages and multimedia documents. Files are saved in different formats and often the format chosen depends on how the file will be used. It is important to remember that when using someone else's work in any of these file formats, copyright/source information is required when using them in multimedia documents, and, depending on how they are being used (for education or for commercial), may require a royalty fee to owner of the document being used.

Some file formats use lossless or lossy compression when saving documents. Lossless compression (e.g., PC platform—WinZip) reorganizes a file so that the file size is smaller, but it can only reduce the size of a document a specific amount. Lossy compression methods, such as M4A for audio and JPG for graphics, remove file data from the document, which cannot be retrieved once deleted (see Figure 10.16). To insure that a document in its original form is not lost, one should always work on a copy of the original as a safeguard against disaster. Lossy compression is often used with graphic, audio, and video file formats. For instance, the popular photograph format, jpeg, is a lossy format. Photographs that are saved with .jpg extension will lose its sharp quality over extensive editing (Figure 10.16).

JOAT/Shutterstock, Inc.

Figure 10.16 A sharp JPG photograph may become grainy after extensive editing.

To reach a larger audience, proprietary video formats should be converted to popular formats such as MP4, WMV, and MOV. For instance, digital stories created with MS Photo Story or MS Movie Maker should be output to a common video format before distributing to students' families. In addition, electronic brochures or newsletters created with MS Publisher also need to be saved as a PDF document when sent through a long listserv of recipients. The PDF format conversion usually protects the contents from being changed and keeps the file sizes smaller. Documents can be accessed by almost everyone, and the format also keeps the contents in the right format during transmission.

Webopedia offers a comprehensive list of graphic formats (2014a) and file extensions (2014b). The Web site's search feature will also allow a search for a specific format. Table 10.6 is a partial list of more commonly used file formats.

Table 10.6 A list of commonly used file formats

BMP: Bitmap formatted graphics are most often clip art. This type of graphic is usually created using paint software.
EPS (Encapsulated postscript file): Generic vector/raster graphics file format.
GIF: A graphic file format that can have 256 colors.
HTML (hypertext markup language): Web page document.
JPG or JPEG (Joint Photographic Experts Group): Lossy compression graphic format used for photographic images that can support 16 million colors.
MIDI (.mid): MIDI stands for musical instrument digital interface.
MOV (.mov): QuickTime video clip.
MP3 (.mp3): Windows-compatible audio format.
MP4 (.mp4): Video file.
PDF (Portable document format): PDF documents can be read with Acrobat Reader® (free download from Adobe).
PICT: Graphic file format developed by Apple Computer and supports 8 colors. PICT2, a newer version of this file, supports 16 million colors. Both of these graphic file formats are supported by Apple Macintosh computers.
PNG (Portable Network Graphics): Lossless bitmapped graphics format that supports transparency and opacity. This file format does not support animation.
Real Audio (.ra, .ram, .rm): RealPlayer is required to play this type of streaming audio file.
RTF (Rich text format): Generic word processing file format that can be opened by any word processing software.
WAV (.wav): Windows-compatible audio file format. Uncompressed WAV files can be quite large.
WMV: Windows media video.

Teachers can convert individual media files such as M4A audio file output from iPad audio recording app to the popular MP3 format by going through free online media converter sites such as http://www.online-convert.com or http://media-converter.sourceforge.net.

It is a good practice for teachers to use the file formats recommended by their schools or districts or are the most common when creating tests, worksheets, hands-outs, and other course materials. A file that cannot be accessed by recipients, whether colleagues, students, or students' families, can cause teachers headaches. They can also be students' models in terms of *media literacy*. Knowledge about various media formats also help teachers to become more effective media users. For instance, digital sound files must be structured so that a media player can read them.

Conclusion

There also comes a tremendous amount of responsibility for the user using technology tools. The user needs to be concerned about using these tools legally and ethically. Doing this is important as a user, but it becomes even more important if one is the teacher in a classroom and is modeling technology and its usage for children.

As a classroom teacher, there is an ethical responsibility to use technology tools in a manner that conforms to the teachers' ethics code which many states enforce. There is also the responsibility to stay in compliance with federal, state, and school district laws and/or guidelines.

Technology is a tool to help facilitate student learning. Technology is evolving, and the rules and laws associated will also evolve. This means that teachers and students must stay current on the changes associated with any given technology and its associated components.

Additional Resources

Academic Integrity
http://www.ryerson.ca/academicintegrity/episodes/
This site has effective animated episodes on certain issues with academic integrity.

Cheating: Pressures, Choices and Values
http://www.hrmvideo.com/catalog/cheating-pressures-choices-and-values
This resource is about students' academic cheating.

Cheating—at school
http://www.cyh.com/HealthTopics/HealthTopicDetailsKids.aspx?p=335&np=286&id=1427
This Web site is very informative about the breakdown of examples of cheating.

References

American Library Association (ALA). (2014). Introduction to information literacy. Retrieved from http://www.ala.org/acrl/standards/informationliteracycompetency

American Psychological Association. (2014). APA style. Retrieved from http://www.apastyle.org

American Psychological Association. (2012). APA style guide, APA style guide to electronic references (6th ed.). [Kindle version]. Retrieved from http://www.amazon.com

Computer Ethics Institute. (n.d.). The ten commandments of computer ethics. Retrieved from http://computerethicsinstitute.org/home.html

Copyright Clearance Center. (2005). The TEACH Act: New roles, rules and responsibilities for academic institutions. Retrieved from www.copyright.com/media/pdfs/CR-Teach-Act.pdf

Cyberbullying Research Center. (2009). Cyberbullying warning signs. Retrieved from http://www.cyberbullying.us/cyberbullying_warning_signs.pdf

Daugherty, L., Dossani, R., Johnson, E., & Oguz, M. (2014). Using early childhood education to bridge the digital divide. Retrieved from Rand Corporation Web site: http://www.rand.org/content/dam/rand/pubs/perspectives/PE100/PE119/RAND_PE119.pdf

International Society for Technology in Education (ISTE). (2014). Retrieved from http://www.iste.org

International Society for Technology in Education. (2007). ISTE Student Standards. Retrieved from https://www.iste.org/standards/standards-for-students.

International Society for Technology in Education. (2008). ISTE Teacher Standards. Retrieved from https://www.iste.org/standards/standards-for-teachers

Kassner, M. (2013). Hackers: From innocent curiosity to illegal activity. Retrieved from www.techrepublic.com/blog/it-security/hackers-from-innocent-curiosity-to-illegal-activity/

McMahon, R. (2007). Everybody does it: Academic cheating is at an all-time high. Can anything be done to stop it? Retrieved from http://www.sfgate.com/education/article/Everybody-Does-It-2523376.php

Merriam-Webster. (2007). Ethics. Retrieved from http://wordcentral.com/cgi-bin/student?book=Student&va=ethics)

Nath, J. L., & Cohen, M. D. (Eds.) (2011). *Becoming an EC-6 teacher in Texas: A course of study for the Pedagogy and Professional Responsibilities (PPR) TExES*. Belmont, CA: Wadsworth/Cengage Learning.

National Telecommunications and Information Administration. (1999). Falling through the net: Defining the digital divide. Retrieved from http://www.ntia.doc.gov/report/1999/falling-through-net-defining-digital-divide

Rodrigues, A. (2011, June 10).Seniors cheating in high school sociology case study. [Blog post]. Retrieved from http://sociologyseniors.wordpress.com/2011/06/10/students-cheating-in-high-school-sociology-case-study-adriana-rodrigues

Texas Education Agency (TEA). (2012). TExES™ Pedagogy and Professional Responsibilities (PPR) EC-12 (160) Test at a glance. Retrieved from http://cms.texes-ets.org/files/9113/4193/1936/ppr_EC_12_160_TAAG.pdf

United States Copyright Office. (May 2012). Circular 1, copyright basics. Retrieved from http://www.copyright.gov/circs/circ1.pdf

United States Copyright Office. (June 2013). *Circular 40, Copyright Registration for Pictorial, Graphic and Sculptural Works*. Retrieved from http://www.copyright.gov/circs/circ40.pdf

United States Copyright Office. (December 1998). The Digital Millennium Copyright Act of 1998, U.S. Copyright Office Summary. Retrieved from http://www.copyright.gov/legislation/dmca.pdf

United States Copyright Office. (June 2012). Fair use. Retrieved from http://copyright.gov/fls/fl102.html

United States Patent and Trademark Office. (2013). Trademark, patent, or copyright? Retrieved from http://www.uspto.gov/trademarks/basics/definitions.jsp

Webopedia. (2014a). Graphics formats. Retrieved from http://www.webopedia.com/quick_ref/graphics_formats.asp

Webopedia. (2014b). File extensions. Retrieved from http://www.webopedia.com/quick_ref/fileextensionsfull.asp

Webopedia. (2014c). Domain name. http://www.webopedia.com/TERM/D/domain_name.html

Webopedia. (2014d). Freeware. Retrieved from http://www.webopedia.com/TERM/F/freeware.html

Webopedia. (2014e). Shareware. Retrieved from http://www.webopedia.com/TERM/S/shareware.html

Webopedia. (2014f). Public domain. Retrieved from http://www.webopedia.com/TERM/P/public_domain_software.html

Webopedia. (2014g). Open source software. Retrieved from http://www.webopedia.com/DidYouKnow/Computer_Science/open_source.asp

Chapter 11

Employing Technology to Facilitate Assessment of Student Learning

Ronald S. Beebe, Irene Chen, and Janice L. Nath
University of Houston-Downtown

Meet Mr. Johnston

Mr. Johnston uses peer editing in his high school English class to increase students' understanding of how to best create various genres of writing. His typical practice had students exchanging papers during part of the class, yet this did not afford enough time for many students to provide feedback to their peers. Generally, most students received editing comments from only one or two students, with little quality feedback provided. Frustrated by the amount of time in class needed to exchange papers and the lack of substantive comments among his students, Mr. Johnston looked for a technological tool that could both shorten the time to receive feedback as well as engage more students in the peer editing process. He decided to explore the use of Dropbox as a platform for students to upload their work but also gain access to the writing of classmates. Mr. Johnston thought exchanging edited documents through a shared cloud space such as Dropbox would allow students asynchronous access to writing assignments for peer editing as well as free up instructional time in class to focus on the essentials of writing and editing.

As part of the planning for implementing this idea, Mr. Johnston spent time with the students in class to develop good peer-editing skills. Because he would not be available to provide in-class guidance during the editing process and to insure consistency in the online peer editing comments, he developed a rubric clearly describing the editing requirements and intended focus of student comments. He also arranged for students to use the computer lab at school in case they had limited access to the Internet and to insure compatibility with the word processing program.

As a result of using this technological adaptation, Mr. Johnston found the number of thoughtful comments regarding the construction of a thesis, development of an argument, and consideration of an audience increased, as well as the number of students providing feedback on individual assignments. Students noted an appreciation for the additional time to carefully review peer's work, and the ability to extend their feedback beyond simple spelling and grammatical errors improved their own writing skills.

Beginning to Think About Assessing with Technology

Technology provides various opportunities to assess student learning and work that can provide both formative and summative outcomes. Blogs, wikis, shared workspaces (e.g., Dropbox, Google Docs, Smartsheet, and SharePoint), and other types of asynchronous discussions offer platforms on which to base new ways of assessment practices. Although much has been made of implementing technology for delivering content, it affords an excellent option for assessment of student work. While these options present students with engaging means of demonstrating knowledge and understanding of content, the use of these formats requires careful thought and planning to avoid becoming a set of "bells and whistles." Additionally, teachers need to plan for time to inform and instruct students on how to use the technology—for example, assisting students in navigating a wiki page in order for them to easily add or edit text, make comments, and post to the wiki page's discussion forum or how to access SharePoint files, upload documents, and so forth.

When employing technology in the classroom, teachers should first consider the purpose of its use. As Wiggins and McTighe (2006) note, the development of assessments should be driven by whatever knowledge and skills students are to demonstrate in the lesson's goals and objectives. By considering the nature of the information to be assessed, alignment of the assessment with the learning objectives should provide "a good fit" with the best format to be used. Asking reflective questions such as "Why am I using this as an assessment?" and "Can this set of concepts be adequately addressed through traditional forms of assessment (written tests, essays, etc.)," or "Is there a technology option that could be used to make the project/lesson more engaging for the learner and the teacher?" helps to insure that the evaluation of student learning outcomes remains of primary importance. As a well-developed tool, technology allows students multiple ways to exhibit knowledge and skills not easily replicated in the classroom in a single assessment.

The goal of thinking about the use of a technological platform should be to prevent using technology "just to use technology." Teachers must think carefully about their assessment of students, including both the assessment of technology knowledge and skills and the assessment of content using technology. This chapter focuses on guidelines that may help with the use of technology in assessment. We begin with a brief narrative on planning in order to establish the context for the examples provided. The next section will offer examples of those which are asynchronous (working/communicating at one's convenience) such as with discussion boards and shared workspaces. Other types of assessment with technology and their uses will also be discussed, including rubric generators, performance assessments, e-portfolios, and others.

The Assessment Cycle

Assessment does not occur in a vacuum—as noted, it should be closely aligned with the goals of instruction. In writing an effective lesson plan, teachers include an assessment section because they (and students) want to know if learners "got it" and to what degree (how much or how well). This will direct the next step in teaching. A helpful framework for understanding the place of assessment in classroom instruction is provided in Figure 11.1. In this perspective, assessment occurs in tandem with instruction and can provide either formative or summative feedback to students. The results of formative assessment may lead one back to review what had been taught and how, or it may even indicate that the level of the original objectives had not been established appropriately; that is, the objective may have been too advanced or even too easy. Reteaching may need to occur at that moment, or, if students overachieved, the teacher may need to consider moving to more difficult lessons.

The first figure (Figure 11.1) illustrates the place of assessment in the teaching/learning cycle. Traditionally, teachers start from the objectives or skills to be learned, develop a lesson plan based on those objectives, and create assessments (e.g., tests, essays, projects) to measure and evaluate student mastery of concepts taught (Figure 11.2). Whether objectives or outcomes are determined first, assessment serves to inform both teacher and student what has been learned and what still requires further instruction, as well as what has been retained. Subsequently, teaching and learning follows a process of instruction, assessment, and feedback, that, when repeated, should indicate the level of mastery of the learning outcomes.

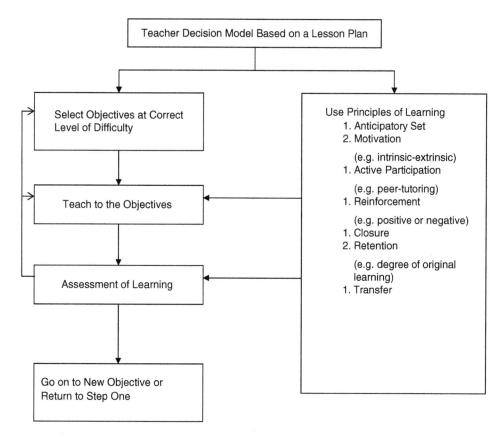

Figure 11.1 Model of the role of assessment in the instruction cycle. From Gentile, J. R. (1997) Educational Psychology.

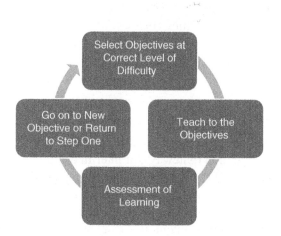

Figure 11.2 An abbreviated version of the assessment cycle.

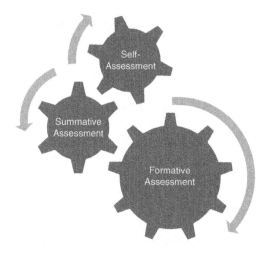

Figure 11.3 Three major types of assessment of children and adolescents.

Types of Assessment

We have already heard the terms formative and summative assessments. Assessment can be evaluated in both of these modes. **Formative assessment** provides an opportunity for students to attempt to demonstrate knowledge and understanding of learning objectives *during* the process of instruction and receive feedback (teacher or peer) as they work towards the mastery of the concepts. **Summative assessment** views student end products as representative of their level of mastery of the learning outcomes at the completion of instruction. **Self-assessment** is the process of examining one's own work carefully in order to evaluate aspects that are important to one's learning so that he or she can self-correct. Much learning can progress when all three work in tandem (Figure 11.3).

Planning and Teaching for Student Success

The Importance of Feedback

Students need and want good formative assessment so that they will know if they are progressing as expected or if they need to correct their knowledge and/or skills before a final summative assessment is made. Feedback, or determining how one is doing in an effort to reach a goal, is a major part of the successful learning process (Wiggins, 2012). Consider the following exchange between a student and her teacher:

> Carla received her PowerPoint presentation grade from Ms. Fortran. The only information Carla found was a C at the top of the page, but there were no other comments. Carla approached her teacher after class and asked, "What did I do wrong? I thought I had completed this with some good ideas. I really like what I presented. I was excited by this assignment!" Ms. Fortran replied, "Well, it just didn't have the information presented in the way I wanted it." "But I worked on it a couple of weeks during class time," Carla countered, "and you never said anything about what I was doing wrong. This isn't fair!"

When teachers assign larger projects or complicated tasks, it is important to schedule feedback that affords students the opportunity to submit work and receive information on what is correct and what still needs improvement before assigning a summative grade. As Wiggins (2012) notes, "Adjusting our performance depends on not only receiving feedback but also having opportunities to use it" (para. 26). In the scenario above, Carla was engaged in her project and invested the time in completing her lengthy PowerPoint presentation, thinking that all was going well. It would have been good practice for Ms. Fortran to have circulated among the students to offer informal feedback on their work in progress during class time, to have established some mini deadlines, and to have provided some formal feedback early in the project. In this case, timely feedback would have helped Carla redesign her work to receive a grade she felt was more reflective of her efforts.

In discussing feedback, there are several areas that are important to consider. One area of importance that we have seen above is the necessity of planning for and providing feedback early and often, particularly whenever assigning technology projects or other types of technology assessments. Many types of technology assessments are creative in nature and can be very subjective in grading. Planning for frequent feedback for corrections is crucial. Another area to be discussed later is how teachers can use technology to give feedback in much easier and timelier ways.

Interim Deadlines

Technology projects are becoming quite prevalent as assessments. Good planning can make a difference between student success and student failure. It can be quite helpful with many technology assessment projects to divide them up into logical units with a due date established for each section (gateways, or interim deadlines). This prevents students from receiving a low assessment for their inability to begin and maintain momentum (so that work is not started and completed on the night before a due date). Last minute work does not usually represent what a student knows or can do but what a student can throw together right before the final due date. Because technology projects often combine new technology skills with new content, this can end up as a disaster at the last moment, particularly when the student realizes that he or she may not have the technology expertise required of a project. Gateways assure that students are making progress and are given ample direction.

Helping Students Think at Higher Levels

A significant consideration in the design of assessments is determining the level of learning that is the target of both instruction and assessment. Bloom's taxonomy provides such a framework. Originally, the taxonomy was composed of six levels (knowledge, comprehension, application, analysis, synthesis, and evaluation); however, it has been revised (remembering, understanding, applying, analyzing, evaluating, and creating) to better reflect the process of learning (Anderson et al., 2001). Bloom's taxonomy provides a convenient means of determining the focus of an assessment relative to student learning outcomes (Miller, Linn, & Gronlund, 2013). Most types of traditional assessment position learners as recipients of knowledge where learning is measured and documented at the lowest levels of Bloom's taxonomy as knowledge and comprehension (Robles & Braathen, 2002). This type of assessment does not allow for higher-order thinking skills such as analyzing, evaluating, and creating (Speck, 2002). On the other hand, alternative forms of assessment assume the role of students as inquirers who are actively engaged in the learning process. In this case, assessment activates learning at higher-order thinking levels and embraces collaboration (Anderson, 1998). Although technology is often used as "an electronic worksheet," it is poised to take on a much greater role in producing higher-level thinking. Technology can be used to support student-centered activities, hands-on experiences, creation, and exploration. Technology can also provide a myriad of electronic resources. This makes it an effective teach-

Figure 11.4 Student filling out answers to a test with a pencil on a Scantron answer sheet.

ing and learning platform to encourage students' higher order-thinking. An important part of planning with technology is designing assessments which will help students reach those higher levels of thought.

Assessment strategies need to be diverse and provide multiple opportunities for learners and teachers to evaluate learning. The traditional Scantron® "fill in the bubble" tests (see Figure 11.4) tend to dominate our thinking about technology assessment practices, but there is a plethora of assessment practices with technology that provide useful alternatives—both for "quick checks" and for very deep and thoughtful assessment.

Thinking through Assessment Aids Student Success

Mr. Beaumont was teaching a unit on Texas history. Students were asked to design a multimedia project. Using jigsaw groups, each group was tasked to put together a plan of their design during the first phase of the project. Although some groups were on target, many were not at the level of his expectations regarding their technology skills. "Oh, my," he thought, "it's time to re-teach this material before the students are too far along in their project designs." He had set up mini-deadlines at several places throughout the duration of the project, and he was glad that he had required these formative measures so that students would be much more successful when the project was completed.

In the general guidelines that inform the use of technology when designing assessments, one of the first aspects to consider, as noted, is the purpose of the assessment: What is the knowledge and understanding students are to demonstrate through the assignment? Related to this is a determination of the type of assessment; that is, whether the task is to provide formative, summative, or self-assessment of specific learning outcomes. In the above example, Mr. Beaumont, based on information gathered through formative assessment, decided to re-teach the materials before the students were too far along in their project.

"Assessments become formative when the information is used to adapt teaching and learning to meet students' needs" (Boston, 2002, ¶ 2, as cited in Frey & Schmitt, 2007). While not exhaustive, guidelines for designing formative assessments include: (1) designing assessment activities that are relevant to students; (2) providing clear instructions for the assessment and its relationship to learning targets; (3) providing descriptive feedback to assist students in understanding where improvement is needed; (4) allowing students several opportunities to demonstrate learning; and (5) encouraging students to self-assess (Chappuis, 2005; Guskey, 2003).

Technology Strategies Resources

As previously mentioned, technology should not be used just for the sake of introducing a technology component into the lesson plan or classroom environment if that would not be the best choice for learners. Consideration of the goals for using technology in the assessment process will help in the development of clear guidelines, improvement of students' understanding of the role of the assessment in learning, and create a setting where instructive feedback can be provided. Effective assessment techniques can improve a teacher's understanding of student needs and help establish a more learner-centered classroom.

When incorporating technology into the assessment process, teachers should consider which specific types of technology tools (hardware, software, and peripherals) can be used to enhance student knowledge and understanding and inform instructional strategies. The next section will offer examples of technology tools that can be integrated for individualized instruction and formative, summative, and self-assessments. These include rubric generators, online discussion forums, shared workspaces, online test creators, online education/competition games, e-portfolios, interpretive exercises, performance assessment, storyboarding and prototype tools, and data analysis and presentation tools.

Rubric Generators

Creating expectations for work *prior* to an assessment creates a contract with learners that sets up an informative and fair system of grading. Constructing appropriate and useful rubrics is an essential process for many types of assessments, and there is a plethora of web and electronic resources that can be used to generate rubrics (see Table 11.1 for some of the more widely used Web sites). Generally, rubric-generating Web sites provide "ready-made" rubrics for a wide variety of subjects, including content areas, observation, peer appraisal, and so forth. To build a rubric using rubric generators, users will first choose a rubric template from a variety of categories, much like choosing an MS PowerPoint or MS Publisher template. For instance, if Mr. Jefferson, a U.S. history teacher, wanted to evaluate students' digital stories on the topic of the American Civil War, a "product rubric category" might be the best choice from a list of those which might include oral projects, work skills, art, writing, or science. He will then decide what criteria to use as row titles. Good rubric generators allow users to manipulate the computer mouse to pick and choose the row titles from a pull-down menu. In the case of Mr. Jefferson's digital stories, the following list of row titles was available for him to choose from:

- Point of View—Awareness of Audience
- Point of View—Purpose
- Dramatic Question
- Voice—Consistency
- Voice—Conversational Style
- Voice—Pacing
- Soundtrack—Originality
- Soundtrack—Emotion
- Images
- Duration of Presentation
- Grammar

Most teachers prioritize and list the most important criterion first. Once the rubric is being generated by the rubric generator and after the submit button is clicked, a rubric will be displayed on the screen. At this point, Mr. Jefferson can copy and paste to save the rubric to his word processor programs. After pasting the rubric to his word processor programs, Mr. Jefferson can further edit the rubric by making changes such as adding text, changing text, or deleting text. Additional rows and columns can be added to the rubric to provide more spaces to type up comments for each criterion or overall comments for the project. The creation of one's own rubric provides students with assessment that matches instruction actually given in the classroom. Teachers must be cautious about adopting pre-fabricated rubrics; for rubrics to be effective assessment tools, they need to reflect the specific learning goals and outcomes of the assignment.

Table 11.1 Some of the more widely used rubric generators

http://rubistar.4teachers.org
http://www.teach-nology.com/web_tools/rubrics
http://www.rcampus.com/indexrubric.cfm
https://docs.moodle.org/22/en/Rubrics

Whether Web-based templates or teacher-created rubrics are used, there are basic guidelines that should be considered when designing rubrics. First, it is important to consider the nature of the assignment or task to be evaluated; some factors to consider:

- What are the key learning outcomes related to the content which the student will need to demonstrate?
- What critical thinking skills should students be able to employ?
- What is the nature of the learning reflected in the assignment; that is, does it require assessing a product, a process, or both?

Next, the rubric needs to specifically address the learning outcomes to be assessed based on a clear definition of quality levels. This needs to reflect a continuum from low to high describing mastery of the outcomes being assessed. These are usually word descriptor phrases such as high quality/below expectations or excellent/marginal, or they can be numerical (5-1) or letter grades. Figure 11.5 (on the following page) provides an example of a rubric designed to assess a writing assignment. In this case, the assignment and associated rubric relate to a product of student work. The left hand column describes the learning goal to be evaluated (e.g., Focus, Organization, etc.) and includes a definition of that goal. Generally, it is advisable to limit the number of quality levels to three or four, as rubrics with fewer levels do not provide adequate feedback, and those with more become cumbersome to employ. Each of the levels needs to contain a concise description of the level of mastery demonstrated by the student's product. As mentioned, levels may reflect grade distributions (e.g., A, B, C, D) or descriptive terms (e.g., not evident, partial evidence, substantial evidence) and should be indicated in the top row of the rubric.

Because rubrics can be employed to assess both product and process, they are an excellent resource for evaluating projects that incorporate technology aspects. Oral communication is an increasingly important aspect of the curriculum, and one which may include the use of technology (e.g., MS PowerPoint, Prezi, and Vine) and generally requires assessment of both content and delivery.

Ms. Kohn wanted her chemistry students to present the results of their titration experiments as though they were at a research conference. She needed to assess both the product (in this case the results of the experiment) and the process (delivery of the results). Such presentations are often evaluated with a rubric that provides students with feedback on the correctness of the work and an evaluation of their presentation skills. Ms. Kohn also wants to include specific feedback regarding the organization and creativity of Prezi and other visual effects used in the presentation. Figure 11.6 provides an example of a presentation rubric which assesses both the product and process of an oral presentation assignment. Note that a new row and a new column are added through the word processing program to the rubric originally created by a rubric generator.

Online Discussion Forums

One area where technology provides a useful platform for assessment is group discussion activities. For example, whole class discussions are often difficult to assess strictly from an observational perspective. Further, engaging all students in class discussions is not always feasible, nor do all students interact in the same way. For example, extroverted learners are more likely to offer lengthy responses as they tend to think through the question verbally; on the other hand, introverted learners will ponder a response and often participate once the original discussion on the topic has ended. Some students are reluctant to participate at all, and, oftentimes, teachers do not realize that they do not call on everyone. In many thoughtful technology-related responses, it becomes clear whether or not all have responded.

In using a technology platform, students can demonstrate their knowledge and understanding of concepts as they engage in dialogue focused on the specific learning outcomes identified for the assessment. This can be done in a variety of ways. Online discussion boards, for example, afford an opportunity for all students to participate in a manner that is appropriate for their learning style and provide clear written data to inform assessment of student learning. In addition, the discussion board allows for interaction among students, which not only encourages students to learn from each other but also employs peer assessment skills.

What might such an assessment look like? Mr. Kator wants to assess the level of student understanding of a specific text in his high school government course and to engage the students in a dialogue about what

	Emergent (1)	Developed (2)	Mastered (3)	Exemplary (4)
Focus The single controlling argument is made with awareness of a specific thesis.	Thesis of the paper is unclear. The paper is poorly developed.	No apparent thesis but evidence of a specific argument. There is some evidence of development in the paper.	Thesis is clear; there is some evidence of a specific argument. The development of the paper is clear.	Thesis is distinct; the argument for the thesis is well defined. The development of the paper clearly supports the thesis and argument.
Content The presence of ideas developed through facts, examples, anecdotes, details, opinions, statistics, reasons, and/or explanations.	Superficial and/or minimal content provided.	Limited content with inadequate elaboration or explanation.	Sufficiently developed content with adequate elaboration or explanation.	Substantial, specific, and/or illustrative content demonstrating strong development and sophisticated ideas.
Voice and Audience Awareness The presentation clearly demonstrates a connection with the intended audience and communicates the author's interest.	Communicates lack of awareness of audience and lack of interest of the author in the topic.	Viewpoint is vague; does not seem to address a specific audience. Author's presentation is natural but lacks engagement with the topic.	Presentation is somewhat connected to an audience. Author shows some engagement with the topic.	Presentation clearly identifies and connects to a specific audience. Author shows clear interest and engagement with the topic.
Organization The order developed and sustained within and across paragraphs using transitional devices including introduction and conclusion. APA style is utilized correctly.	Minimal control of content arrangement. No evidence of APA style.	Confused or inconsistent arrangement of content with or without attempts at transition. Limited use of APA style.	Functional arrangement of content that sustains a logical order with some evidence of transitions. APA style is utilized with minor imperfections.	Sophisticated arrangement of content with evident and/or subtle transitions. APA style is utilized correctly throughout.
Style The choice, use of, arrangement of words and sentence structures that create tone and voice.	Minimal variety in word choice and minimal control of sentence structures.	Limited word choice and control of sentence structures that inhibit voice and tone.	Generic use of variety of words and sentence structures that may or may not create writer's voice and tone appropriate to audience.	Precise, illustrative use of a variety of words and sentence structures to create consistent writer's voice and tone appropriate to audience.
Conventions The use of grammar, mechanics, spelling, usage, and sentence formation.	Minimal control of grammar, mechanics, spelling, usage, and sentence formation.	Limited control of grammar, mechanics, spelling, usage, and sentence formation.	Sufficient control of grammar, mechanics, spelling, usage, and sentence formation.	Evident control of grammar, mechanics, spelling, usage, and sentence formation.

Figure 11.5   Example rubric for a writing assignment.

that text means. The first step is to develop clear instructions for engaging in the discussion forum (formative) (Figure 11.7) well as a specific rubric (summative) that will be used to assess student contributions.

Once the general guidelines and rubric for the discussion process are provided, the next step is to provide specific instructions to guide the students in terms of the assignment (see Figure 11.9).

	0	1	2	3	Score
Abstract	Not present	Does not provide a clear overview of the experiment; lacks reference to: purpose and method	Provides an overview of the experiment, but is missing reference to the one of the following: purpose or method	Clearly provides an overview of the experiment: states purpose, and describes method	
Problem Statement	Not present	Does not provide a rationale for the experiment	Provides a partial rationale for the experiment	Provides a complete rationale for the experiment	
Procedure	Not present	Presents clear procedural steps, but does not discuss instruments or data analysis	Presents clear procedural steps, discusses instruments, but does not describe data analysis	Presents clear procedural steps, discusses instruments and explains data analysis	
Findings	Not present	Presentation of results is not clear, missing complete discussion of the findings	Presentation of results is clear, but discussion of the findings is not presented logically	Presentation of results is clear; discussion of findings is logically presented	
Delivery	No eye contact with audience; reads from notes; low volume or monotone delivery	Minimal eye contact; mostly reads from notes; uneven volume, little inflection	Good use of eye contact but occasionally reads from notes; satisfactory delivery	Eye contact with entire audience; rarely looks at notes; delivery includes appropriate volume and inflection changes	
Presentation	Demonstrates no interest in experiment; does not inform audience	Demonstrates minimal interest in experiment; informs audience on some points	Demonstrates some interest in experiment; informs audience on most points	Demonstrates consistent interest in experiment; informs audience on all points	
Prezi and other visual effects	Either confusing or cluttered; Buttons or navigational tools are absent or confusing	Includes combinations of graphics and text, but buttons are difficult to navigate. Some buttons and navigational tools work.	Includes a variety of graphics, text, and animation. Adequate navigational tools and buttons	Includes a variety of graphics, text, and animation that exhibits a sense of wholeness. Creative use of navigational tools and buttons	
				Total	

Name of presenter _____

Comments:

Figure 11.6 Sample oral presentation rubric.

The design of this type of assessment lends itself readily to either a formative or summative approach to evaluation of student work. Teacher feedback in the discussion forum is one way to identify misconceptions and lack of understanding as well as indicate when students demonstrate mastery of the material. The discussion forum thread in Figure 11.10 is an example of how the thread engages students in dialogue about

Posting Guidelines

In order to be prepared for the class discussions, each week a discussion thread will be used to provide comments on the assigned reading(s) for the upcoming class. Each thread will have a specific prompt to guide reflection on the readings to allow for the expression of your perspective on the readings. These posts should be approximately 250–300 words in length, and do not require any reading outside of the assigned material for that week.

In addition, you will respond to two posts of your classmates. These posts should be approximately 75–100 words in length, and provide a substantive comment on the selected post. In other words, "Great ideas!,""I agree!," and "Ditto" are not insightful. Responses may compare or contrast the author's ideas with your posting or offer a comment on the insights the author provided you, and so forth.

Figure 11.7   Sample guidelines for a discussion forum.

Objectives	Low Performance	At or Below Average	At or Above Average	Earned Points
Knowledge of Topic	**0 points** —Answer does not display an understanding of the topic —Answer does not incorporate any aspect of the readings for the week	**1–2 points** —Answer displays a basic understanding of the topic —Answer incorporates personal experience, but makes no connection to readings, and/or video —Does not post response in a timely manner	**3–4 points** —Answer displays a good/ excellent understanding of the readings/topic for this week —Incorporates the readings, and/or video into answer —Posts response in a timely manner	
Responding to Classmates Questions and Comments	**0 points** —Does not respond to classmate responses for the week Or —Response is very vague and offers no real contribution to the discussion (i.e., I agree)	**1–2 points** —Responds to 1–2 classmate responses for the week —Response offers additional explanations or elaboration to classmates response —Does not respond to classmates in a timely manner	**3–4 points** —Responds to at least 3 classmate responses for the week —Response offers additional explanations or elaboration and incorporates personal experience and/or the readings into answers —Responds to classmates in a timely manner	
			Score:	

Figure 11.8   Sample rubric for assessment of discussion forum.

Haubenreich suggests at the end of his article that "the future of the debate over whether education belongs in the Constitution remains bright" (p. 453). Based on your reading of his argument, does the right to an education belong in the Constitution? What would such a "Constitutional right" guarantee and how would that be enforced? Or, do you believe education should be governed by states/localities? Provide support for your response from the article. Please follow the guidelines on Reflection Postings.

Figure 11.9   Sample discussion forum assignment.

a specific understanding of the assigned reading noted in Figure 11.9. In this thread, the teacher provides feedback confirming the correctness of the student's interpretation but also points to the contrary position. The interaction that follows extends the students' conversation on the topic. This "extended conversation" illustrates the way in which the technique of class discussion can be modified through the use of technology

Student 1: RE: The "right" to an education
I believe that the right to an education should belong in the constitution. This constitutional right will guarantee that everyone will have a fair chance at an education with no excuses. I don't think education should be governed by states or localities because everyone should all be on the same page. I don't think it's fair how some states laws are less lenient than others.
Instructor: RE: The "right" to an education (response to Student 1)
An interesting perspective, and valid. The issue, of course, is not only one of local control (which has been the historic rule) but also of funding. Those who believe that government is already too big may oppose more federal oversight. Nevertheless, there is something to be said for national standards for K-12 students.
Student 2: RE: The "right" to an education (response to Student 1)
I agree with you that it is unfair that standards differ from state to state. I also think that the every student has the right to have a good education regardless of where they are from.
Student 1: RE: The "right" to an education (response to Student 2)
Yes I feel that it is very unfair that the standards can differ from state to state. It shouldn't be harder for one state than the other so I don't think that makes sense in any way. . . . I feel like no matter anyone's culture or where they reside, it should be an equal opportunity for the right of an education.
Student 3: RE: The "right" to an education (response to thread)
I agree with both of you in that it is unfair that standards are different from state to state. This brings about the problem of disadvantagement on [sic] some states. I am also with you in that as students of the United States, it should be a right to have a good education regardless of where one is from, one's class, race, gender, religion, sexual preference, ethnicity, sex, intelligence, location etc.
Student 4: RE: The "right" to an education (response to thread)
I agree with what you said. If we get more teachers and staff in schools to feel that education is an important factor for life, I think there could be a major turnaround in the learning ability levels and graduating rates can increase.

Figure 11.10   Sample responses.

to enhance the teacher's insight on student learning. Note that this example provides the actual text posted; it has not been edited.

As can be seen in this example, providing specific guidelines describing the nature of the initial post of a student along with a clear presentation of the quality of responses, the students engaged in an informed discussion of the topic and indicated their areas of agreement and disagreement. Reviewing all the posts from a class thus gives the teacher an opportunity to determine the level of student comprehension of the assigned concepts (Figure 11.10). The teacher is now able to answer such questions as: (1) are there areas of knowledge that require additional emphasis, (2) have students demonstrated mastery of the concepts so that the next concepts can be addressed, (3) are there particular students who may need some individual attention, and so forth? Understanding student work both in terms of student mastery of concepts and effectiveness of instruction is an outcome of developing an appropriate rubric that allows for objective judgment of the product being assessed (refer to Figure 11.8).

Shared Workspaces

Another technology platform that is useful in assessing student knowledge and understanding are shared workplaces (e.g., Dropbox, Google Docs, and Wikispaces). Time constraints often impact the ability of students to engage in collaborative projects while in the classroom. Often, conversation and learning occur outside of the normal school day, and creative ideas cannot always arise within a forty-five minute class. Shared workspaces provide students an accessible platform to pursue work initiated during class when further thinking and planning around topics is required.

One option is to incorporate shared workspaces in the assessment process because these can provide a means for the development of student-generated texts focused on content, peer editing, and higher-order tasks involving evaluation skills. Developing authentic assessments which require students to demonstrate not only what they have learned but to evaluate that information in regards to important constructs and principles is essential in promoting critical thinking and deep learning (refer to Figure 11.11). As with discussion forums, shared workspaces can be used for both formative and summative assessment purposes separately or at the same time.

Figure 11.11   Students follow the process on shared workspaces.

For example, Mrs. Mathis wanted to develop an assessment that incorporated collaboration and demonstration of understanding algebraic principles of solving for an unknown. Rather than constructing a traditional test that identified what she saw as important concepts and specific paths for solutions, her idea was to have the students create a "text" for future students based on their understanding of the concepts and their application. She decided to use a wiki as the platform, as it permitted creation of separate pages and opportunities for student-generated text, tracked edits made, and a space for comments. Further, the wiki platform tracked the contributions, edits, and comments of each student, which allowed for a keener understanding of students' knowledge and assessment of the level of collaboration. Following guidelines similar to those for a discussion forum, Mrs. Mathis created a section on a wiki page that provided a clear rationale for the project and learning outcomes, her posting requirements, and tasks involved. In addition, to presenting a focus for the students, she created template sections with specific headings. The process would involve students creating problems, developing clear solutions, editing what other classmates presented in terms of accuracy, and providing comments supporting the created problem, solution process, and what was corrected or edited. The following example gives a snapshot of the students generating the text for the template.

The texts (see Figure 11.13) indicate additions made by three classmates (based on the different fonts) to the original author's contribution. As illustrated, the project provides the teacher with a clear indication of the students' understanding of the concept of solving for a single unknown. Additionally (refer to Figure 11.12), Mrs. Mathis is able to view the thinking processes of the student editors in terms of the nature of the added text. Here, the student editors extend the description of the steps needed to solve the problem as well as indicate the potential problems of one of the alternatives.

It should be noted that collaborative projects such as this one require a certain amount of scaffolding of student thoughts in order to fully complete the assignment; often the initial chapter drafts are not as detailed but, with appropriate feedback to provide guidance, students move beyond simple text and brief comments. In this case, Mrs. Mathis began each chapter with an outline of key tasks that required explanation. Starting with a clear presentation of the concepts to be mastered, each "chapter" in the text followed a specific outline requiring students to present solutions and support them with a narrative. In addition, a teacher can also provide a work sample to communicate his or her expectations. Creating a typical test allows for assessment of student knowledge and understanding of the learning goals focused on that particular lesson, but the process of peer-editing affords insight into students' higher-order thinking and ability to apply learning, synthesize new interpretations, and evaluate the "worth" of their peers' contributions to the text.

Chapter: Solving for an unknown

The purpose of this chapter is to provide a discussion of the various strategies that can be used to solve for an unknown. Each strategy should be clearly described, including procedural steps leading to a solution.

1. Create a problem that requires a solution for a single unknown, for example: $5x + 8 = 38$
2. Provide alternative means of solving the problem, including the steps required and an explanation of how the steps lead to the solution.
3. Write a brief narrative that explains the approaches used and how they are related.

Figure 11.12   Sample wiki page with a rationale section and a template.

Chapter: Solving for an unknown

The purpose of this chapter is to provide a discussion of the various strategies that can be used to solve for an unknown. Each strategy should be clearly described, including procedural steps leading to a solution. Be sure that x is a whole number.

1. Create a problem that requires a solution for a single unknown.

   $3x - 7 = 5$

2. Provide alternative means of solving the problem, including the steps required and an explanation of how the steps lead to the solution.

First, you need to make the equation simpler. To do that, add 7 to each side of the equal sign.

$3x - 7 + 7 = 5 + 7$

Then, the equation looks like this $3x - 0 = 12$, which is the same as $3x = 12$

Next, in order to solve for x divide each side of the equation by 3 like this $\frac{3x}{3} = \frac{12}{3}$

Now you know that $x = 4$

Another way to solve for x would be to divide each side of the equation by 3 first. This would look like

$\frac{3x}{3} - \frac{7}{3} = \frac{5}{3}$ which would then leave $x - \frac{7}{3} = \frac{5}{3}$

Then, add 7/3 to each side $x - \frac{7}{3} + \frac{7}{3} = \frac{5}{3} + \frac{7}{3}$ and then solve $x - 0 = \frac{12}{3}$ or $x = 4$

3. Write a brief narrative that explains the approaches used, and how they are related.

The first approach seems to be the simplest and does not require fractions. In the first example, $3x$ is isolated by adding seven to each side of the equation, since this still leaves each side equal. Once that is solved, then each side is divided by three so that the solution for x is found. In the second example, the division step is done first, then the step to isolate x. *The problem with this strategy is the inclusion of fractions.*

Figure 11.13   Sample wiki page entry for an algebra class.

Next, in order to solve for x divide each side of the equation by 3 like this $\frac{3x}{3} = \frac{12}{3}$

I think the steps are correct, but there does not seem to be a connection between the two equations. So I inserted this step to show how to get from $3x = 12$ to $x = 4$

and then solve $x - 0 = \frac{12}{3}$ or $x = 4$

This set of steps did not seem complete. I think you just forgot to add this, or you thought that we would know the answer from the previous strategy. Now, the entire solution is complete.

The problem with this strategy is the inclusion of fractions.

While I agree that both ways get the same answer, I think having to work with fractions is hard. I would just do it the first way.

Figure 11.14   Sample discussion posting.

The incorporation of wikis in the assessment process can be designed to meet most grade levels where text is appropriate and can incorporate all levels of Bloom's taxonomy. At higher grade levels, the use of student-generated text can address critical thinking, evaluation, and transfer of concepts to other areas. For example, in a social studies class, an "understanding the concept of freedom of speech" wiki could then support a debate regarding whether restrictions on cyberbullying violates an individual's freedom of speech and how that relates to slander or defamation of character. For their posts as well as any substantive editorial changes, conversations can be generated in the comments section that extended the material to the students' contexts. In this way, the assessment becomes relevant to the students, and the learning outcomes for the assignment are integrated into the students' experience.

Teachers can use the student-generated text (see Figure 11.15) to reflect on instruction in terms of addressing misconceptions, misunderstandings, and missing information. Feedback becomes an active, participatory

	0	1	2
Problem	No problem provided	Problem provided, but the equation does not use whole numbers for x	Problem provided is correct
Procedure	No procedure provided	Procedure is incomplete, does not address all steps	Procedure is complete, addresses all steps
Narrative	No narrative provided	Narrative does not completely describe the steps in the solution	Narrative completely describes the steps in the solution
Editing	No editorial changes or comments	Editorial changes are incorrect or do not add to the text	Editorial changes provide correct information and add to the text

Section	Score
Problem	/ 2
Procedure	/ 2
Narrative	/ 2
Editing	/ 2
Total Points	/

Comments:

Figure 11.15 A scoring rubric for the student-generated "wiki" project.

process that informs teaching and learning and provides a dialogue that works to close the assessment loop (instruction, demonstration of learning, feedback, and demonstration of mastery) (Hatzipanagos & Warburton, 2009).

In the case of Mrs. Mathis, in addition to a formative assessment standpoint, there was a summative aspect as well. Rather than administering a series of exams that may not accurately assess what students know because it is not in a format related to their learning style, this project was designed to provide an authentic assessment reflecting the students' ability to communicate their mastery of course concepts. Again, a simple rubric was employed as a means of communicating to each student his or her level of mastery (see Figure 11.15).

Online Test Creators

Technology affords several advantages when considering creating more traditionally designed tests. As with rubrics, most textbook publishers now provide electronic test banks focused on key concepts and learning outcomes, and, in some cases, these are aligned with state and/or national standards. While useful, it is important to be aware that some test bank items may narrow too specifically on memory/recall rather than concept understanding, so teachers should carefully read through items before using them in a test. Teachers must also be cautious to use an item only if it has been covered in class or as directed in a class assignment. Otherwise, students should not be held accountable for them.

Most learning management systems (LMS) offer test generator platforms that allow teachers to create a variety of test formats (e.g., multiple choice, short response, true/false, essay). Blackboard, for example, provides options for both tests and surveys, as well as an option to generate teacher-constructed pools of items for both options. Tests are designed to provide assessment feedback measuring student performance; surveys are not graded and provide anonymous feedback addressing such areas as student preferences, reflection on experiences, and so forth (refer to Figure 11.16).

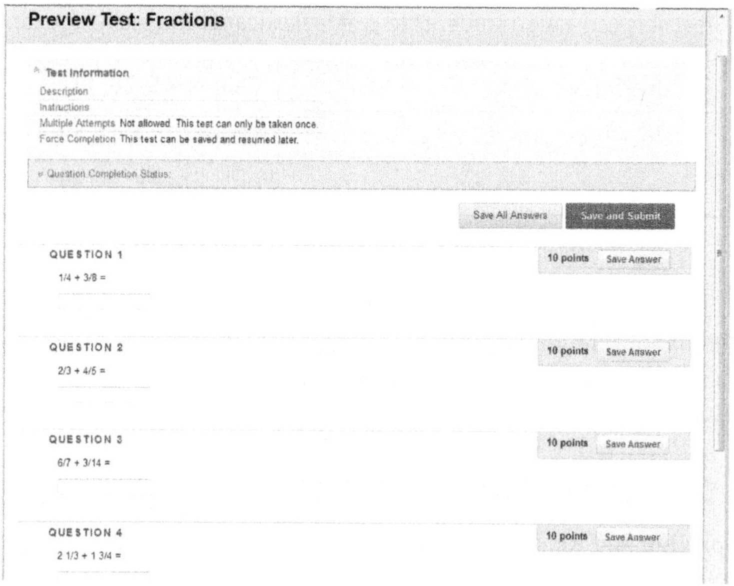

Figure 11.16   Screen shot of test in Blackboard.

Mr. Blackwell wanted to evaluate how well students understood mathematics concepts presented in class but did not want to use instruction time to give students exit tickets. Since his school had recently purchased a Blackboard license, he thought students could complete an exit ticket online. Using the test generator, he created a short quiz that focused on the key concepts presented during class. Students were then asked to complete the quiz online as part of their homework (or if computer access was a problem, after school or during their free period in the library). The test generator allowed Mr. Blackwell to provide the correct response as well as insert specific comments if the student gave an incorrect response. All of this could be entered into the test format in Blackboard so that students received immediate feedback when completing the quiz (see Figure 11.16). Additionally, he could review the quizzes in order to plan for the next day's instruction. Using this technology approach for formative assessment freed valuable class time, provided self-assessment information for students, and focused Mr. Blackwell's instruction. Besides, LMSs such as Blackboard immediately generate test reports that include the standard deviations, median, mean, highest score, lowest scores, and other relevant descriptive statistic data for the entire class. Mr. Blackwell can easily use these reports to re-teach topics on which students have not performed well.

It is important to experiment with online test formats in order to narrow the focus of the assessment. In some cases, it may be best to use multiple-choice items that employ carefully constructed distracters that inform the teacher of the conceptual mistakes students have. Mr. Blackwell could have created multiple choice test items for the exit ticket that used distracters which highlighted specific errors. For example, item two could have been constructed as:

$\frac{2}{3} + \frac{4}{5} =$ (a) $\frac{6}{8}$ (b) $\frac{6}{15}$ (c) $\frac{22}{15}$ (d) $\frac{8}{15}$ (e) $\frac{22}{8}$; which would indicate errors in the process of adding fractions (a. student added across numerator and denominator, b. student found the common denominator but added numerators, c. correct response, d. student multiplied across numerator and denominator, e. student cross-multiplied for numerator but added denominators).

On a lighter note, a new generation of online learning tools, or, as others might call it, memorization tools, was first introduced in 2007 to allow users to create "sets" of terms customized on the Web for their own needs. These sets of terms can then be studied under several study modes. Table 11.2 shows a list of online quizzes and accompanying interactive resources that can be created within minutes by teachers and students. When using these online learning tools such as Quizlet, Sporcle, Cram, and Flashcard Machine, students can choose to review the content in the formats of flashcards, tests, or other formats. Some quiz generators such as Cram and Quizlet have features to enhance studies such as shuffle, read, alphabetize, front first, integrating illustrations, and "read" with computer-synthesized voices. These online quizzes and interactive resources range from

Table 11.2   Teachers can assign students to create flashcards and exchange for unit review

Group 1	Use Quizlet.com	Chapters 9, 10, 11
Group 2	Use Cram.com	Chapters 12, 13, 14
Group 3	Use FlashcardMachine.com	Chapters 15, 16, 17
Group 4	Use Sporcle.com	Chapters 18, 19, 20

children's books, middle school foreign languages, and U.S. history to college calculus. For instance, a sixth-grade gifted teacher can assign students to create electronic flashcards and exchange them for the unit review of social studies. Adolescents often enjoy challenging their peers with activities such as this.

Online Education/Competition Games

Activities such as role-playing and Readers Theater easily lend themselves to using technology as an assessment tool. The incorporation of technology-based education games in the assessment process can be designed to meet all grade levels and can incorporate all levels of Bloom's taxonomy (refer to Table 11.3). In addition, there are numerous software and Web sites that offer students the opportunity to create game shows, board games, word searches (Figure 11.18), and puzzles (Figure 11.19), among other assessment options (refer to Figure 11.17). These types of platforms can be used in class or as projects—and for reviewing purpose. They provide students with an engaging and creative way to demonstrate concept understanding as well as instant feedback, either individually or in groups.

In addition to the activities above for early elementary grades, word recognition associated with pictures provides a video game style format to learning basic vocabulary (refer to Figure 11.20). In this example, students can click on the picture and the associated word is highlighted (or vice versa), which allows for students to self-assess their vocabulary knowledge. This type of drill is more exciting than a worksheet and engages the student with some "bells and whistles" for immediate feedback for the students and the teacher. There

Table 11.3   A sample list of online quizzes and interactive resources

Categories	Quiz Titles and URLs
Children's Books	Can you match the names of these Roald Dahl characters? http://www.sporcle.com/games/CatStarcatcher/dahlightful
Children's Books	Can you name the popular children's books based on their opening lines? http://www.sporcle.com/games/farishta/childrens_opening
Elementary Science	Fourth-Grade Science on Scientific Inquiry Vocabulary http://quizlet.com/13554243/hills-elementary-science-grade-4-flash-cards
Young Adults Books	Can you name the missing words from these titles of Young Adult books? http://www.sporcle.com/games/khands/missing-word-young-adult-books-a-z
Learn Spanish Language	Vocab 14A: La música y el baile http://www.flashcardmachine.com/machine/?topic_id=3103505&source=pub
Middle School Computer Literacy	Computer Literacy 101 http://quizlet.com/22756154/computer-literacy-101-chapter-8-flash-cards
High School Social Studies	Advance Placement (AP) U.S. History Review http://www.cram.com/flashcards/ap-us-history-review-4738708
Higher Education	College Educational Technology http://www.cram.com/flashcards/educational-technology-4677895

Students and teachers can create diagrams, games, and quizzes.

http://www.classtools.net

Students and teachers can generate their own e-learning quizzes, games, and applications with no coding.

http://www.contentgenerator.net

The site allows students to customize book covers, posters, play with prom make-over, and play with several other fun online activities.

http://www.glassgiant.com

Students and teachers can create several types of games online by using this Web site.

http://www.superteachertools.net

Students and teachers can create lesson puzzles, word searches, and other types of education games for presentations and print-outs.

http://puzzlemaker.discoveryeducation.com

Students and teachers can turn photos and video clips into interactive media and animations.

www.animoto.com

Figure 11.17 A sample of Web sites that allow users to create education puzzles and other types of games.

Darren Whittingham/Shutterstock, Inc.

Figure 11.18 Animal word search game that can be created using an online generator.

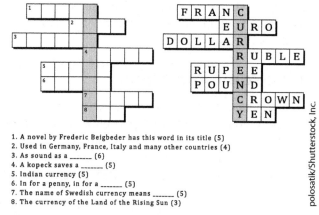

1. A novel by Frederic Beigbeder has this word in its title (5)
2. Used in Germany, France, Italy and many other countries (4)
3. As sound as a _____ (6)
4. A kopeck saves a _____ (5)
5. Indian currency (5)
6. In for a penny, in for a _____ (5)
7. The name of Swedish currency means _____ (5)
8. The currency of the Land of the Rising Sun (3)

polosatik/Shutterstock, Inc.

Figure 11.19 Online generators can create crossword for the world currency and related vocabulary words.

Jovanovic Dejan/Shutterstock, Inc.

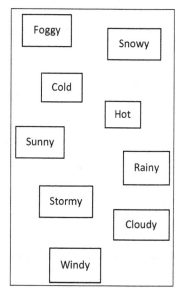

Figure 11.20 Sample picture vocabulary matching game.

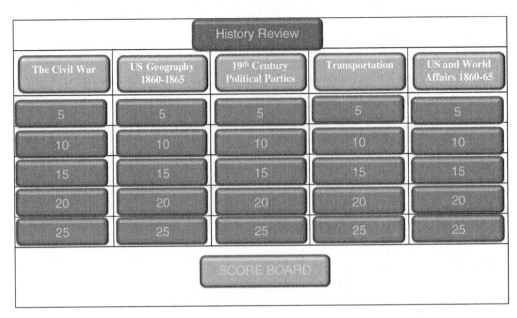

Figure 11.21 A "Jeopardy-style" review for History.

are times when immediate feedback such as this is useful on lower-level objectives, particularly in formative assessment, although the advantages of technological assessment can offer much higher levels of thought for students.

Electronic Portfolios

A teacher can also use portfolios to assess students' mastery of a certain content topic. Generally, there are four common types of portfolios, each with a specific purpose: (1) best work, (2) representative, (3) developmental-growth, and (4) summative (refer to Figure 11.22).

Consequently, it is important to determine the purpose of the portfolio, as that will indicate what types of artifacts should be selected. Additionally, clear guidelines for construction of the portfolio, its evaluation, and a determination of who will place artifacts in the portfolio should be decided before starting to build the portfolio. Using portfolios, students develop ownership of their work, especially if they are selecting the artifacts as well as reflecting on the quality or perspective the artifacts represent. A developmental-growth portfolio, for example, can provide opportunities for students to see how they have progressed in their mastery of concepts and typically incorporates student-selected work. Similarly, students and teachers can use a best work portfolio to showcase student work for both students and parents. A best work portfolio can also designate the student and the teacher to be contributors to the selection of artifacts. Portfolios also encourage student ownership of their learning and work through the process of identifying artifacts, evaluating their work, and reflecting on the learning demonstrated. A well-designed portfolio project should yield valid and reliable results, even

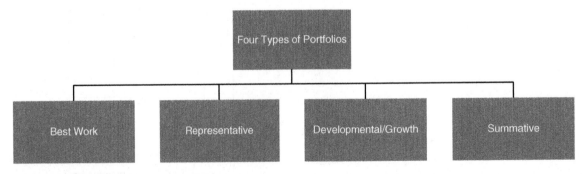

Figure 11.22 Four types of portfolios.

though no written test is conducted. How can this be done? A well-planned portfolio project guideline is the key. A portfolio is designed to last for a long period of time in order to demonstrate student progress overtime, so careful planning must occur.

According to Miller, Linn, and Gronlund (2013), "Portfolios also foster student skills in evaluating their own work. Self-evaluation is a critical skill in developing independent learning ability and one that is often emphasized and reinforced by asking students to include some form of self-evaluation and thoughtful reflection on each entry in their portfolios" (p. 284). In additional to self-assessment, portfolios can be an effective way of communicating with parents by showing concrete examples of what the students can do. Technology provides a convenient means of assembling student portfolios. There is a multitude of free Web sites offering e-portfolio platforms to meet a variety of needs (e.g., weebly.com, shownd.com, opresume.com, flavors.me, doyoubuzz.com/us).

Mrs. Green was looking for a way to have her seventh-grade students describe a variety of activities that they would complete during a unit on the environment focused on the theme "Reduce, Reuse, Recycle, Renew." She had previously required students to create posters or tri-fold presentations, and then they would participate in a gallery walk to observe the various work classmates had done. After one gallery walk, a student asked "How can we keep all of this information? There's just not a good way to store it, and some of the parts will get lost." Mrs. Green agreed that the posters and tri-folds were not the best method of creating a representation of the work in the unit. She spoke with her technology resource specialist who suggested using an electronic portfolio platform based on a Google app (https://sites.google.com/site/eportfolioapps/Home). This would allow her students to use a variety of Internet-capable devices to create, upload, and publish their work as well as serve as a convenient archive for later use. More about the applications of e-portfolios in teacher education will be addressed in Chapter 12, including many details that could also apply to school student portfolios.

Interpretive Exercises

Interpretive exercises, an innovative test question format, is considered an effective format to ask higher-order thinking skill (HOTS) questions. To help schools and parents better prepare students, most states published their released state mandated exams for public school students which were taken in previous years (such as the released exams published by the Texas Education Agency [TEA, 2014]). By reviewing the released exams, it is obvious that the percentages of interpretive exercise type of questions are increasing over the years. In examining the first ten questions in the 2014 fourth-grade TEA released STAAR mathematics test, one will find that all ten questions are asked in the formats of a clock (refer to Figure 11.24), a number line, a column chart (refer to Figure 11.26), a coin diagram (refer to Figure 11.27), a data table (refer to Figure 11.23), a fraction bar, or other types of graphic illustrations (refer to Figure 11.25 and Figure 11.28). Technology makes it particularly easy for teachers to generate many of these examples from photographs or clip art for understanding and practice.

Josh gives the same number of breadsticks on each plate in his restaurant. The table below shows the number of bread sticks in different numbers of plates.

Number of plates	15	30	45	60
Number of breadsticks	45	90	125	180

Which statement describes the relationship between the number of plates and the number of breadsticks?

A. The number of plates × 3 = the number of breadsticks
B. The number of plates + 30 = the number of breadsticks
C. The number of plates × 5 = the number of breadsticks
D. The number of plates × 60 = the number of breadsticks

Figure 11.23 A sample question for fourth-grade students using a data table.

Figure 11.24 A fourth-grade math question asks students to tell time by presenting a clock picture.

Figure 11.25 A fourth-grade question asks students interpret to a picture of math manipulatives.

Figure 11.26 A fourth-grade math question asks students to read a column graph.

An interpretive exercise consists of a series of objective items based on a common set of stimuli or introductory material. It is a special type of question in that the student is expected to answer by interpreting or understanding the presented visual materials. This type of questions typically ask for interpretation of graphs, poems, cartoons, diagrams, charts, stories, passages, pictures, or data tables. To answer the questions, students must comprehend, analyze, apply, or synthesize the information presented. Miller, Linn, and Gronlund (2013) note,

Figure 11.27 A fourth-grade math question asks students to answer a money question that is presented with coin graphics.

> The series of related test items may also take various forms but are most commonly multiple-choice or true-false items. Because all students are presented with a common set of data, it is possible to measure a variety of complex learning outcomes. Students can be asked to identify relationships in data, to recognize valid conclusions, to appraise assumptions and inferences, to detect proper applications of data, and the like. (p. 217) (Miller, Linn, and Gronlund (2013))

Here are five guidelines for interpretive exercise style questions:

- Relevance (or relevant to subjects)
- Similarity (or similar to what you are teaching in class)
- Brevity (or short)
- Answers not provided (or students have to think to get the answers)
- Multiple questions (or a series of objective items based on a common set of stimuli)

Thanks to modern desktop publishing programs such as MS Publisher, productivity tools such as MS Office Suite, and graphic editing utilities tools such as MS Paint, it has become easier for classroom teachers to create assessment items as interpretive exercises (refer to Figure 11.29, Figure 11.30, and Figure 11.31). When combined with graphic editing programs such as MS Paint, scanners, and digital cameras, teachers can be very resourceful when it comes to creating the introductory materials for interpretive

Figure 11.28 MS Excel is an effective tool for creating the data sets, tables, diagrams, and charts for the introductory materials of interpretive exercise.

Table 11.4   Technology tools are used to create the stimuli of interpretive exercises

Technology Tools	Types of stimuli for interpretive exercises
MS Word	Graphic organizers, poems, passages, data tables, stories, clip art, shapes, number lines
MS Excel	Graphs, data tables, pie graphs, column graphs, bar graphs, charts
WWW	Pictures, data sets, stories, cartoons, news, charts, maps, photographs
Other	Photographs taken by digital cameras, newspapers scanned by scanners, graphics edited with MS Paint

Figure 11.29   Newspaper articles can be used in the introductory materials of interpretive exercise.

"I see we're split between those who like my new tie, and those who welcome unemployment."

Figure 11.30   Newspaper cartoons can be used in the introductory materials of interpretive exercise.

Figure 11.31   Many types of graphics organizers can be used in the introductory materials of interpretive exercise.

exercises in the classroom in order to prepare students to become familiar with the formats of standardized tests such as commercial tests or state exams (refer to Table 11. 4).

In creating many of these assessments, however, educators must be wary of issues of plagiarism and copyright infringement in tests and other instructional materials they create for students and in class projects created by students. For the future generation of the Americans to become more aware of intellectual property at a young age, teachers need to demonstrate respects for property laws. More about the legal and ethical essentials of educational technology are addressed in Chapter 10.

Performance Assessment

Traditional assessment techniques are of two general forms: selection and supply. Multiple-choice, true-false, and matching items are called **selection test items**. When answering selection test items, students respond to each question by selecting an answer from choices provided. Essay questions, short answer, completion questions, or "fill-in-the-blank" questions are **supply test items** that require the student to construct a response. Both *supply test items* and *selection test items* are called **traditional assessment**.

On the other hand, extended supply items such as book reports, portfolios, experiments, and class projects are usually referred to as **performance assessment** (also **alternative assessment** or **nontraditional assessment**). Traditional assessment activities like fill-in-the-blanks and multiple-choice quizzes are quickly losing popularity and, in their place, learners are participating in more creative higher-level assessments that are more authentically testing the learners' knowledge, skills, and judgments. Performance assessment is gaining acceptance in K-12 classrooms (Miller, Linn, & Gronlund, 2013, p. 36). These researchers note:

> Performance-assessment tasks are intended to closely reflect long-term instructional goals and require students to solve problems of importance outside the confines of the classroom or to perform in ways that are valued in their own right. Written essays are one example of a complex-performance task that

reflects the instructional goal of effective communication more than a selected-response test could. Other examples include open-ended mathematics problems requiring extended responses, laboratory experiments in science, the creation of a piece of art, oral presentations, projects, and exhibitions of student work. (p. 36)

After several decades of computer application in schools, technology has infiltrated all aspects of education. Yet, teachers still talk about "doing a technology lesson," as though teaching with technology is somehow different from "everyday" lessons. Performance assessments require students to demonstrate specific abilities and, for most teachers, assigning technology-based performance assessment projects can be an easy way to integrate technology because students learn technical skills from each other and genuinely enjoy collaborating on the projects. Miller, Linn, and Gronlund believe that

Like essay questions, performance assessments should be used primarily to measure those learning outcomes that cannot be measured well by objective test items. . . . Performance assessments are better suited for applications with less structured problems where problem identification; collection, organization, integration, and evaluation of information and originality are emphasized (e.g., where is the best place to locate a restaurant?). They are also essential for learning outcomes that involve the creation of a product (e.g., painting) or an oral or physical performance (e.g., the presentation of a speech, the repair of an engine, or the use of a scientific instrument). (p. 285)

Technology, especially the Internet, can be a powerful tool to be incorporated into students' performance projects. Readers Theater, as mentioned, offers an entertaining and engaging means of improving fluency, enhancing comprehension of the text, building vocabulary, improving public speaking skills, increasing self-confidence, and exposing students to different genres. Reading teachers have used this strategy for decades to blend students' desire to perform with their need for oral reading practice. The strategy can be modified for all grade levels. What is Readers Theater for primary grade students? It's a way to involve students in reading aloud. Students "perform" by reading scripts created from age-appropriate books or stories. They can do so with or without costumes or props. With a technology "twist," students can record their own "theaters," edit with Audacity or other audio editing tools, post to and distribute through safe podcast sites such as Podbean or OUTMedia to have the audio sound and create audio effects as if they were radio broadcasts. When technology is used in support of projects such as this, it can, in turn, contribute to students' sense of authenticity and to the "real-life" quality of the task at hand. This is a technology-enhanced performance project.

Mrs. Lambert's elementary science class is broken into groups. Each group is responsible for one day's weather report per week. Each report rotates group members to serve as the reporter, the digital cameraman, data collector, the graphic arts director, and an "on the street" person who dresses appropriately for the weather, gives comments, etc. At the end of the week, the reports are merged and viewed, and predications for the weekend are given.

With the flexibility of student performance projects, teaching, learning, and assessment can be enmeshed in a single technology-based performance assessment activity. Technology makes it possible for students of performance assessment projects to aspire to produce inexpensive copies of multimedia materials with quality appearances. Table 11.5 describes technology-based performance projects ideas for elementary, middle, and high school levels.

Not everyone agrees that technology integration improves student learning. Some argue that research results have been mixed. Yet, overall, the evidence seems to support the belief that appropriate use of technology results in higher student achievement. The ease with which technology-based performance assessment projects can be integrated with instruction has made them particularly appealing to teachers and students. Thoughtfully planned, such performance assessment projects engage students to a much higher degree than in traditional assessment and lead to the development of twenty-first-century skills such as complex thinking, creative problem solving, and collaboration (Miller, Linn, & Gronlund, 2013, p. 36).

Storyboards and Prototypes

Increasingly, teachers are requiring students to create electronic products such as computer games, technology-based performance projects, electronic portfolios, animations, digital stories, coded objects, videos, 3-D

Table 11.5 Technology-based performance projects ideas (based on U.S. Department of Education, 1995)

Grade Level	Performance Assessment Project Ideas
Lower Elementary Grade Level	Students create multimedia reports that include not only text but also digitized photographs and sounds as well as artwork.
Higher Elementary School Grade Level	In a fifth-grade bilingual class, students engage in a semester-long project in which they develop multimedia documentaries of the lives of minority group members who had achieved prominence within the students' local community.
Middle School	Students can experience an increased sense of communication with external communities not only by obtaining information from external sources but also by creating documents describing school activities for their school homepage. Students must conduct and videotape interviews and compose written highlights from the interviews.
High School	Students in an architecture and design class use computer-aided design (or CAD) programs to plan and design a home for a hypothetical family with specified needs and financial resources.

designs, Web sites, electronic presentations, and many other complex and multifaceted projects for major course grades (refer to Table 11.5). The concepts of storyboards and prototypes that have a long-standing history in the industry can also be introduced as gateways to technology-based class projects as a part of formative assessment (before a complete project is turned in).

The digital storyboarding process was developed at Walt Disney Productions during the early 1930s and is still widely used by movie and animation studios (refer to Figure 11.32). A storyboard is similar to a comic strip—a series of rough sketches that show how a media sequence will look like. The user or viewer can visualize the layout and sequencing for the sake of planning and communication. In the storyboarding pro-

Figure 11.32 Original cartoon figures and pictures—drawn with black marker.

cess, technical details such as sound effects, dialogues, and captions can be described either in picture or in the note. The initial storyboard may be as simple as slide titles on yellow sticky notes, which are then replaced with illustrations and sketches by hands. Modern storyboarding tools, whether in the forms of Web 2.0 tools or apps, help to inspire students and organize thoughts (see Figure 11.33 for a list of storyboarding sites and apps). Teachers can distribute a storyboard template as seen below (refer to Figure 11.34) for students to illustrate and fill out, which can assist with project planning and communication among team members and team members to teachers. For instance, at the start of the project, teachers can ask the class to

---

ACMI (Australian Centre for the Moving Image) Online Storyboard Generator
http://generator.acmi.net.au/storyboard

Storyboard That Online Storyboard Generator
http://www.storyboardthat.com

Directr Storyboarding App
https://itunes.apple.com/US/app/id526717506?mt=8

Storyboards App
https://itunes.apple.com/us/app/storyboards/id392533504?mt=8

Figure 11.33 A list of storyboarding Web tools and apps.

Storyboard

Draw pictures for each important scene of your digital story. In the note area, add details about sounds, dialogues, captions for the scene.

Figure 11.34   A storyboard template that can assist with project planning and communication.

turn in a storyboard template to communicate initial digital project ideas with her. This should help students to receive useful feedback to start on the right track. Alternatively, students can draw stories by using MS PowerPoint to easily rearrange scenes when in the Slide Sorter View.

The idea of a prototype can also be introduced as gateways to technology-based class projects such as programming or other electronic projects. A prototype is an early sample, model, or release of a product built to test a concept or process or to act as a semi-completed product be replicated or finished. Creating a prototype is the step between the formalization of ideas and the final evaluation of a project (refer to Figure 11.35). While the project is under way, teachers can ask to see a prototype of the project, which can contain the major working structure of the project without full multimedia details.

With the visualization capabilities of technology tools such as storyboarding and prototype tools, project expectations can be communicated to guide students and formative assessment can be accomplished.

Data Analysis and Presentation Tools

Good formative assessments present useful data in in the form of feedback to students and teachers. With the increased use of smartphones, android tablets, laptops, and iPads in the classroom, an audience response system (e.g., iClickers) can offer teachers the opportunity to quickly assess student learning in the midst of instruction. Several of the more widely format compatible Web sites provide options for students to reply anonymously, support

Figure 11.35   The prototype diagram shows the phases of a mechanical project, sketch, project on a computer, prototype with a 3D printer, and the final product.

images and video prompts, give either typed or free-hand responses, and download a record of questions and responses (e.g., todaysmeet.com, padlet.com, socrative.com, infuselearning.com, getkahoot.com). These browser-based platforms provide quick, accurate assessment of student learning, opinions, and feedback to the class at large. Poll Everywhere is specifically designed for smartphones and tablets allowing for text messaging and integrates with various word cloud platforms to display responses (e.g., wordle.net, tagxedo.com, https://tagul.com). There are a vast number of graphic organizers for use that offer students and teachers assessment possibilities (both formative and summative). Interactive graphic organizers (my.hrw.com/nsmedia/intgos/html/igo.htm and www.vrml.k12.la.us/graphorgan) provide "type in" spider maps, main idea charts, conclusions charts, sequence chains, and many more. These types of assessment tools generate student engagement with the material while, at the same time, reflect their understanding of concepts; similarly, teachers receive immediate feedback on student comprehension of instruction.

In addition, teachers can use technology to monitor assessment results that inform instruction. Most districts use some form of electronic grade book that operates similar to an Excel® spreadsheet, which can be used to generate statistics on student achievement. Understanding trends among different learners, different classes, and across departments allows teachers to modify instructional strategies, confer with colleagues, and implement changes in teaching and assessment. Charts and graphs can also be generated to be used in the classroom with students to illustrate progress over a marking period or the school year. For some, this can be a motivational strategy to encourage high performance; however, each teacher will need to judge whether this is appropriate information for their particular class.

Summary

This chapter has addressed a number of ways in which technology can be used to improve and evaluate student learning outcomes. Assessment should be viewed as both a means of evaluating the students' knowledge and understanding as well as providing opportunities for higher-level, critical thinking activities. Additionally, the assessment tools employed provide feedback to the teacher regarding student misconceptions, confusion, or lack of mastery of requisite skills. This leads to potential changes and more effective instructional strategies. Technology platforms are varied, and it is important for the teacher to carefully consider the purpose of the assignment and whether using technology will enhance student mastery. Shared workspaces, such as Google Docs, Dropbox, blogs, and wikis offer creative and engaging opportunities for students to demonstrate mastery of learning outcomes. In addition, these platforms can be designed to deliver formative feedback, peer appraisal, self-assessment, and teacher response. Other technologies, such as game generators, e-portfolios, audience response systems, and word clouds provide exciting options for students to self-assess as well as provide feedback during class time that can be used to modify instruction. Finally, assessment results can be easily analyzed using electronic grade books (e.g., learnboost.com) and spreadsheet programs such as Excel® to modify instruction and track student achievement. Exploring the use of technology in conjunction with assessment opens doors for motivating improvement and learning.

References

Anderson, L. W. (Ed.), Krathwohl, D. R. (Ed.), Airasian, P. W., Cruikshank, K. A., Mayer, R. E., Pintrich, P. R., Raths, J., & Wittrock, M. C. (2001). *A taxonomy for learning, teaching, and assessing: A revision of Bloom's Taxonomy of Educational Objectives* (Complete edition). New York: Longman.

Anderson, R. S. (1998). Why talk about different ways to grade? The shift from traditional assessment to alternative assessment. In R. S. Anderson & B. W. Speck (Eds.), *Changing the way we grade student performance: Classroom assessment and the new learning paradigm.* New Directions for Teaching and Learning, No.74. San Francisco: Jossey-Bass.

Chappuis, J. (2005). Helping students understand assessment. *Educational Leadership, 63*(3), 39–43.

Frey, B. B., & Schmitt, V. L. (2007). Coming to terms with classroom assessment. *Journal of Advanced Academics, 18,* 402–423.

Gentile, J. R. (1997). *Educational psychology* (2nd ed.). Dubuque, IA: Kendall Hunt Publishing Company.

Guskey, T. R. (2003). How classroom assessments improve learning. *Educational Leadership, 60*(5), 6–11.

Hatzipanagos, S., & Warburton, S. (2009). Feedback as dialogue: Exploring the links between formative assessment and social software in distance learning. *Learning, Media and Technology, 34*(1), 45–59.

Miller, M. D., Linn, R. L., & Gronlund, N. E. (2013). *Measurement and assessment in teaching* (11th ed.). Upper Saddle River, NJ: Pearson Education, Inc.

Robles, M., & Braathen, S. (2002). Online assessment techniques. *Delta Pi Epsilon Journal, 44*(1), 39–49.

Speck, B. W. (2002). Learning-teaching-assessment paradigms and the online classroom. In R. S. Anderson, J. F. Bauer & B. W. Speck (Eds.), *Assessment strategies for the on-line class: From theory to practice* (pp. 5–18). New Directions for Teaching and Learning, No. 91. San Francisco: Jossey-Bass.

Texas Education Agency. (2014a). STAAR Released Test Questions. Retrieved from http://www.tea.state.tx.us/index4.aspx?id=25769814834&menu_id=793

U.S. Department of Education. (1995). Technology supports for project-based learning. Retrieved from http://www2.ed.gov/pubs/SER/Technology/ch8.html

Wiggin, G. (2012). Seven keys to effective feedback. Retrieved from www.ascd.org/publications/educational-leadership/sept12/vol70/num01/Seven-Keys-To-effective-feedback.aspx

Wiggins, G., & McTighe, J. (2006). *Understanding by design* (Expanded 2nd ed.). Upper Saddle River, NJ: Pearson Education.

Chapter 12

E-Portfolios for Teachers

Tina Nixon, Janice L. Nath
Technology Facilitator, University of Houston-Downtown

Meet Tanya

Tanya Gleason walked into her first interview for a teaching position. She remembered that her professors in her teacher preparation program had told her that having a portfolio was worthwhile for hiring purposes, so she even ran a hard copy of her portfolio (in case the technology at the interview site didn't interface well to open her e-portfolio). She also had a disk copy to leave when she finished the interview if there wasn't enough time to show everything she wanted the principal and/or the grade-level interviewing committee to see during her scheduled interview time. She felt very confident because her teacher education program had made their teacher candidates present their e-portfolios orally for the last three semesters before she graduated. This had given her much confidence in talking about her educational experiences and how they fit with best teaching practices. After the preliminary questions, the principal began with the serious questions. "I may have a third-grade reading/language arts position," Mr. Beck announced. "Can you tell me some ways that you might assess students in these areas?" Tanya quickly flipped to a running record she had completed in one of her methods classes. "Let me show you what I did in my field experience that I would like to continue to use," she told him, as she showed the principal on her iPad. "I am impressed," said the principal. "The last three candidates I interviewed didn't have portfolios." She got the job.

When Tanya was in her first year of teaching, there was so much to do that she wanted to put off keeping up with her professional portfolio. However, she did create a new folder and added a number of professional development certificates and activities for that year. She also photographed some of her students' best efforts and replaced some of her lesson plan examples with others that were even more exciting. When she was working on this, she thought of a few more ideas that would make these lessons even better, and she added those ideas to her reflections.

At the end of her first year, Tanya's husband was suddenly transferred to a new city. She found herself in a similar situation in another interview, but she was well prepared to "show and tell" about her teacher training and her experiences in her first year of teaching. She got the job (again).

A portfolio is often used as an assessment tool in both business and academic environments. In academia, a portfolio is defined as: "a selection of a student's work (such as papers and tests) compiled over a period of time and used for assessing performance or progress" (Merriam-Webster, 2014). To add to this, educational researchers (Avraamidou & Zembal-Saul, 2002) assert that it should be a *deliberate* collection of work rather than simply a scrapbook collection. At the collegiate level, portfolios have been used to assess the level of competence of students *and* as a road map to assist students academically (Gambrel & Jarrott, 2011). Chen and Light (2010) believed that as an assessment tool, the student portfolio is considered unique because, over time, it captures evidence of student learning. This may happen in multiple formats and contexts that can be captured in this type of documentation. In addition to an e-portfolio being used as a form of assessment, portfolios can also be used to highlight what those who have created them have learned, and this may also encourage them to integrate both their formal and informal learning (Chen & Light, 2010).

Most universities use teacher candidate portfolios in multiple ways. Teacher educators want to:

- monitor their potential teachers throughout a time period or throughout a program for progress;
- have an assessment tool at the end of various semesters (which often matches their state's certification requirements);
- have teacher candidates become reflective about their growth;
- have a way for preservice teachers to tangibly highlight their experiences in the job market upon graduation.

Wray (2008) found that shifting from a perspective of seeing portfolios only as tool for employment to a resource to evaluate professional growth was more beneficial to students. The reflective growth involved in this shift will be discussed in detail later in this chapter.

With the advancement of technology, the standard portfolio has now evolved into an electronic format. This electronic format has become known as the electronic portfolio, or e-portfolio. Compared to its hard copy predecessor, the e-portfolio is often seen as more accessible, capable of holding more information in various formats, and easier to update and modify. Many universities are requiring students to create an e-portfolio as a way to reflect on their work and to provide teacher candidates with a means of displaying their academic work to potential employers. Other researchers (Nath, Cohen, Hill, & Connell, 2012) also discovered that many teacher candidates found the process of creating a portfolio to be a valuable study tool for their state certification tests. Real life connections were realized as teacher candidates targeted, wrote about, and included personal examples from their field experiences and other assignments regarding the required state competencies. By the time future teachers had completed their portfolios, which were solidly based on the state competencies, teachers-to-be had worked so often with the competencies that they had been "well absorbed"—with very little formal study needed prior to taking state certification tests in professional development.

Research shows that while e-portfolios can be very beneficial to college students, concerns may also arise. Ali (2005) suggested that planning must take place before a university can begin to implement the e-portfolios and he provided nine steps to consider in overcoming these concerns. Students should be familiar with these concerns and address them within their portfolio without the expectation that their professor(s) should guide the process for them. Normally, professors will guide the process to some extent, but teacher candidates should also use the following points to better direct their own roles in their portfolio development and completion:

- define the aim(s) of one's portfolio (course grade, future hiring, professional development, etc.)
- consider the technology that is currently available to be used
- consider the type of technology that one would like to use and decide how to learn the necessary skills, if possible
- know and define one's audience when considering the creation of a portfolio
- become empowered to "show what you know"; do not be shy about showing your work and professional life to the best advantage (It might help somewhat to think of it as a tool to help "market" your knowledge and expertise.)

- plan for ongoing review and correction/revision of the portfolio
- incorporate a feedback mechanism into the portfolio from those who will view it (peers, experts, interviewers, etc.)

Prospective teachers should always begin by familiarizing themselves with their university's (or teacher preparation program's) expectations and work towards the process of building their portfolio as a responsibility to themselves. Thinking and planning ahead will make the portfolio more complete and certainly a less stressful, more reflective process. To start the process, e-portfolios for future educators should include (but not be limited to): a title page, table of contents, a short resume, samples of their work and of their students' work (from field experiences), reflections, a letter to viewers, and a comment box for individuals viewing the document (Ali, 2005).

While this information may be important, Gambrel and Jarrott (2011) show that e-portfolios should support evaluations and student learning similar to the traditional portfolio process. In a music classroom, Mills (2009), for example, observed that using e-portfolios provided a rewarding experience to students. Mills also found portfolios to be both formative and summative, depending on the learning environment. Mills describes the main strength of a learning portfolio as encouraging the students who created them to reflect on and assess the quality of their own individual work. The portfolio gives students wide boundaries to represent their own learning. This is beneficial to creators of portfolios because they also learn from the process of the work they put into their documents, which provides an additional set of skills (Ritzhaupt, Parker, & Ndoye, 2012).

Some teacher education programs have portfolio presentation days where teacher candidates participate in mock interviews using their portfolios. By seeing how their peers use many types of artifacts and design elements, the teacher candidates are able to critique their own work and see more clearly how they compare to others. More importantly, they may be better able to judge the quality and impact of their work on others. Sometimes a professor's evaluation of a student's work can be perceived as somewhat biased by that student, but when the student is able to contrast his or her portfolio presentation directly with excellent examples, mediocre examples, or poor examples, the understanding of these evaluations can become much clearer. An excellent factor regarding this type of product is that it is not based upon "one test" but that it can evolve over time and is easily modified with expert, peer, and self-feedback. Growth is the aim for teacher educators and their preservice teachers—rather than one-shot efforts such as final papers or exams.

Teacher candidates may also develop additional technology skills as they put together their portfolios. They may include an array of multimedia resources that support student-created material. These skills allow prospective teachers to showcase their work in different platforms for different audiences (Ritzhaupt et al., 2012). For most schools, technology is a needed skill, and teacher candidates can use their portfolios to their advantage over the job competition by demonstrating technology competence (and even superiority) in their portfolios to distance themselves above others in comparison for teaching positions. Although portfolios can be more time-consuming to develop and assess, they offer significant benefits for students and are, therefore, worth the investment of time and effort (Mills, 2009).

In another area associated with improvement during the process of portfolio development, teacher candidates should consider discussing the expectations of their portfolio with their instructors. Wray (2008) discovered in her study of university students that many of them found that discussion with their professors about their portfolios allowed them to make connections between the artifacts and their educational philosophy. Students also benefited when the instructor spent time discussing the different artifacts students could use within their portfolio (Wray, 2008). In one's education program, there may be a menu of suitable items and/or many student choices to include as headings or as artifacts to demonstrate mastery, but selecting the best can often be due to multiple conversations with professors (and peers). Artifacts are support for a heading. For example, under the heading of Classroom Management, Jon Martin, a

university senior, selected to demonstrate his knowledge and experiences by including the following artifacts: a classroom management plan which he had constructed, a picture of a workable management chart that he and his mentor used during his field experiences, a write-up of an interesting student management incident with a reflective resolution, and others.

Ritzhaupt et al. (2012) suggest that e-portfolios in both preservice and inservice teachers' perspectives serve them in three ways: representation, reflection, and revision. Representation refers to the work the student produces that documents his/her skills. Reflection is the student description that summarizes his/her perspective on the learning gained in producing the artifact. The last "r" is revision. This stage refers to students looking at their products to reassess what they have put together and to make changes as needed. For preservice teachers during the semester, it can seem difficult to keep up with revisions as new assignments become added, but the revision step is essential in having an excellent product without the pressure of having to complete revisions at the end and to incorporate improvements to new assignments along the way. One professor commented on this as a prospective teacher asked him for a reference. "I couldn't do it," he told a colleague. "She misspelled a very common educational term on her first assignment, the same word on the second assignment, and on the last one...and everywhere in between. If she would have revised the first couple of times, she would have seen this and corrected it. As it was, she never did, and I can't say as of now that she is going to be a reflective teacher who would represent our profession as a quality teacher."

E-portfolios are viewed by many as being a positive tool for prospective teachers in teacher education programs. Researchers (Strudler & Wetzler, 2005), however, discovered that the demands of creating an electronic portfolio have caused some students to shy away from taking this process to heart. They suggested streamlining the process and making the e-portfolio sustainable. In addition, some teacher educators see benefit from only requiring technology with which teacher candidates should be familiar and have used in the past, while other professors may want to use the portfolio experience to help their students learn new technology skills. Although it may require some extra individual time and effort, taking the extra step to learn new skills can be profitable in many ways to the prospective teacher.

In one study conducted by Wray (2008), some students enjoyed the process of creating an e-portfolio but wanted more direction as to what to include within the portfolio. An idea that seems to help this development is to create an "empty shell" at the beginning of the portfolio process with all of the required titles/slides but with no documents/artifacts yet. This can even be done in PowerPoint with a "slide shell" (refer to Figure 12.1).

As the timeline for completion progresses, documents/artifacts can be "slotted into" the shell and other slides added or deleted as needed to fill out the compete portfolio. This would be similar to creating a table of contents and adding pages/slides for each heading or filling in an outline at the beginning of a paper or other project.

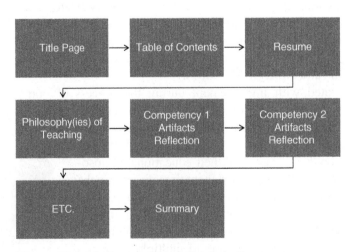

Figure 12.1   An "empty" PowerPoint shell.

Students' Ownership of Studies/Motivation for Self-Improvement

Stacey Barnes, a recent college graduate, was nervous about her upcoming interview for a fourth-grade teaching position. Stacey had worked hard throughout her years in college and wanted her academics as well as her positive student teaching experience to show in her interview. She knew it was important to dress appropriately and to answer each interview question both clearly and precisely. The job description stated specific qualifications for each candidate, and Stacey also wanted to ensure she addressed ways in which she met the requirements. Stacey prepared for her interview in some important ways; however, she did not take time to critically review her educational portfolio to ensure that it provided accurate examples and information that would support her as being the best candidate for the position. Her professors had given her feedback, but with student teaching and a host of graduation activities, she had not taken the time to go back and address their comments. When Stacey opened her portfolio to share examples with the interview panel, a few of her documents did not open, and she had to say weakly, "Well, this *was* a lesson plan I did". . . or "I *had* some examples of some student work here." In the interview, it became clear that a few of her documents didn't really support her interview responses, some of the documents were out of order, and not all of her reflections showed that she understood how to apply what she had learned in her undergraduate studies. One member of the grade-level team even asked her about a slide that did open, "Is that something you actually did, or you just copied and downloaded it?" (which she, unfortunately, had done). Stacey also saw how this "came over" to the panel when they asked about how she might incorporate various learning styles into her teaching and she just showed them a copy of Gardner's Multiple Intelligences chart. She had also neglected to label a few of the artifacts that she had included, so when one team member ask about a particular picture, Stacey became flustered and said, "Uh, I think this was something I did in my first semester field experience." She quickly realized that she needed to have prepared a better portfolio that showed her as a positive and organized teacher-to-be.

Andrey_Popov/Shutterstock, Inc.

Types of E-Portfolios

Several formats have been used to create e-portfolios (Ittleson & Lorenzo, 2005); these formats include Web-based, text-based, graphic, or multimedia elements. Additional formats may include electronic media such as CD-ROM or DVD (Ittleson & Lorenzo, 2005). Although CD-ROMs, DVDs, and flash drives are often used, many universities are using a more Web-based format. This format allows the students to easily share portfolios with potential employers and turn them in as an assignment. Unlike other formats, students no longer have to purchase discs or flash drives and make multiple copies of their portfolio. The concerns of scratching a disc or losing a flash drive are also eliminated because with the online format, students can provide a uniform resource locator, or URL. Students can also create quick response (QR) codes and attach to their business card or resume that will immediately direct users to their site. Some universities do require "hard copy" versions, so portfolio creators must always remember to back up their portfolio—no matter how it is created. This can be done on a different computer, on a flash drive(s), a cloud backup, emailing it to one's own or a second email, and so forth. A portfolio is a valuable document, and it is devastating to reach the end of a semester (or even several semesters of work) and have lost one's portfolio to an electronic glitch, loss, or theft of one's only copy on a disk or flash drive.

Bedrin/Shutterstock, Inc.

Figure 12.2   Back up portfolio files and artifacts on a cloud storage.

The University of Idaho uses a Web-based platform called Word-Press. WordPress is also commonly used at many colleges and universities. Using Web-based formats may eliminate the concern of who owns the e-portfolio. With newer cloud storage tools such as Google

Docs and Dropbox, which allow the inclusion of video, pictures, and texts, teacher candidates now have several ways to build an electronic portfolio (refer to Figure 12.2). Now, they cannot only build quality electronic portfolios, but they also have the opportunity to provide a clearer picture of what they have learned. However, some Web-based portfolios are not easily viewable from schools with strong firewalls to the Internet, and there is often information included that one would not necessarily want to be posted for public viewing (i.e., addresses, phone numbers, work addresses, pictures, and other information found on resumes/vitaes or other portfolio artifacts). It is always best to know for certain who will have access and how before posting on a Web site.

Some students may choose to use platforms that are more Web-based and provide them with the experience of creating a Website. Programs such as Weebly, MyFolio, and Silk, may offer this type of experience for students. Students may benefit from the ability to drag and drop photos and hyperlink material. If students want to include videos, it is important to understand how to embed or link the videos to their host platform. While searching for examples via Google, one of the authors of this chapter discovered that many of the links to student portfolios did not work. Students must check their links to ensure the material is up to date and working at all times.

A Principal's Reflections

I remember interviewing a few candidates for a third-grade teaching position I had at my campus. I'd gone through several candidates, and many of them did not meet our needs. What I remember the most is that one of the teachers presented a portfolio to provide examples of her teaching experience. She provided examples of lesson plans, rubrics, and evaluations from her previous teaching positions. I allowed her to guide us through the process and she did a great job until the very end. She was adamant of showing us an example of a teaching strategy we use here in the district. She asked if she could access the video from her Dropbox account via her laptop. As we all sat, waiting to see this video, the teacher struggled to get the video working for us. She cited problems with the network, so I asked if she would provide the link to her site so we could view it later. We really liked this candidate, so we didn't mind viewing it later. When we went to view the video later, the link still did not work and we received an error message saying: "The Page You Requested Was Not Found." I am not very knowledgeable in the area of technology, so I didn't push any further to see the video. The video was not the determining factor in our hiring decision, but it did play a major part in our decision.

Typical Items in an E-Portfolio

There are similarities and differences in e-portfolios, but, as mentioned earlier, many of the items within the portfolio may depend on the degree program. For example, an engineering portfolio may differ greatly from an educational portfolio. Although the artifacts within the portfolio may differ, the required material may be very similar. For example, a standard electronic portfolio may include the student's objective(s) and/or philosophies. A quick summary that clearly states future objectives is necessary to guide readers as they review the material included within the portfolio.

If the student is using the e-portfolio to pursue employment, it may be important to include (but not be limited to) the following items:

- title page
- table of content
- letter of interest in a particular position (if applicable)

- teaching philosophy(ies) (general and specific to content areas)
- a resume
- artifacts
  - s detailed lesson plans
  - s relevant work examples or meaningful assignments of the teacher candidate
  - s work samples of children (refer to Figure 12.3 and Figure 12.4)
  - s multimedia PowerPoints, technology games, and other items that one has created
  - s assessments
  - s pictures of relevant items (completed projects, bulletin boards, etc.) done by the teacher candidate
  - s pictures of meaningful school experiences (following district policies)
  - s observations/critiques by other professionals
  - s other examples of learning and/or mastery
- a list and short description (if needed) of appropriate organizations to which one belongs
- certificates for completing trainings or professional developments (refer to Figure 12.5)
- references (that are requested for permission *before* posting with each person's title, phones, and emails) and possible letters of recommendations (although most applications are now taken online rather than in letter format)
- summary and/or reflections.

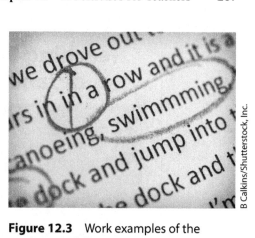

Figure 12.3   Work examples of the teacher candidate.

Figure 12.4   Work sample of the students.

Providing a resume provides an overview of what the student has accomplished, but the artifacts within the portfolio provides examples of that work for potential employers to review. It is important that one includes his/her most significant work in an e-portfolio (refer to Figure 12.6 for the title page for a social studies teacher's portfolio.). This may be assignments on which one received rave reviews, or it may, surprisingly, include one's best reflections about what was learned from a negative situation to show thoughtfulness and the ability to self-correct for growth. Running a spell/grammar check program (and/or having items reviewed for errors) is critical to being hired if using a portfolio. Principals will see glaring errors as a warning sign that a potential employee may not be able to teach school students proper grammar and spelling if he or she cannot present "clean" examples. They may also worry that, once hired, letters and notes sent home and to other colleagues and administrators may appear unprofessional.

Additional points to consider:

Figure 12.5   Certificate of training completion.

- Know that this portfolio not only shows one's knowledge about teaching but also one's technology skills. A principal can be impressed with the technology ability of the candidate by the examples that are selected, and technology expertise is valued in schools.
- Make sure that documentation is readable—font size, style, and so on.
- Keep page layouts the same rather than having some in PDF formats and others in Word formats
- Include detailed information/artifacts about one's classroom management. It can confidently be stated that there have been few interviews for teaching positions which have failed to ask about this area.
- Rich, detailed lesson plans as artifacts indicate a teacher who has the potential to produce excellent lessons. Shallow lesson plans show a teacher who is unqualified or uncaring about the details of the classroom.

Figure 12.6 A title page for a social studies teacher's portfolio.

- Include any appropriate volunteer projects, professional honors, and professional organizations of which one is a member. Outside (but appropriate) activities indicate a person who is well-rounded and who may go above and beyond to interact with the community.
- Title page pictures and pictures working in various field experiences can present a compelling addition to a portfolio. It shows that "I have been in schools. . . . I have some experience with students/children," or it may show someone's interest and commitment to a content area. The title page for a social studies position below shows a teacher's experience and interest in other lands.
- If choosing to include photos in the body of the portfolio, consider capturing how one works collaboratively with teachers and students. Also, select photos carefully in terms of one's clothing and grooming. Prom pictures, glamour shots, or those with low necklines, low pants, or very short skirts for women do not often have that everyday look that will be recognizable or connect with a school atmosphere. Including pictures of one's family and children may lead a principal to think in two opposing ways: "Oh, this person has children so he/she will understand students and parents well," or, on the other hand, a principal may think, "Oh, no! Small children mean lots of outside activities . . . and the teacher may be absent a lot when those children are sick!" There is no need to give away one's family situation one way or another, and the main objective of a title page picture is reconnect a face to a name positively when a principal has many interviewees. In addition, one must take into account other issues or concerns that may arise. For example, posting a title page with recent pictures taken with a fiancée may lead to a principal's thoughts of too many impeding wedding plans, and so forth. Some districts may have hair or beard restrictions for males, so men would want to consider a picture that matches those restrictions. Appearing ready to walk into a classroom in the district where one applies is the best choice for photographs. As one can see, each part of the portfolio sends a message to the viewer. Much thought must be put into each addition.
- A short, concise resume (or curriculum vitae [CV] as it is known in academia) is important for principals in a portfolio (refer to Figure 12.7 for a sample resume). They will want to clearly see a teacher candidate's qualifications. There are many formats (and professors may add different requirements to which students should adhere), but "simple" is best.
- Putting careful thought into one's philosophy must also be considered. One way to direct this is to examine a school's "mission plan" (their philosophy) for the school where one will interview. This is usually available on the district or school Web site. If both philosophies agree, all is well. If not, there could be problems and discomforts in working there. This can also happen in an interview. For example, if a principal clearly states that frequent testing and high test scores will be required for children

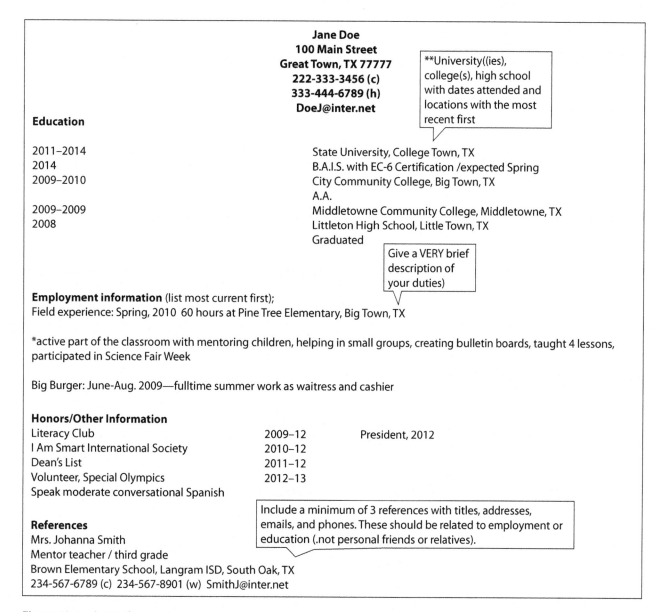

Figure 12.7   A sample resume.

starting the young childhood program at this school and the teacher candidate realizes that this may not necessarily agree with his or her own philosophy for this age group, it could be predicted that it may not bode for a good working relationship. How one feels about children, the basic purposes of schools, what students should be able to do when they finish their schooling, how teachers go about their work to accomplish goals, and so forth are essential to know about one's own philosophy. These thoughts will guide one's practice, and a portfolio can be used to set these down so that a teacher candidate can speak well to them and find a good "school match." A statement regarding the candidate's philosophy should be no more than about a 1 ½ pages, because principals will not have time in an interview to read through several pages. The philosophy statement should come to the point in a powerful way to make a clear impression.

• Plan to keep this portfolio as a way of life—there are many unhappy stories of teachers who have lost all their records of past experiences and professional development, excellent student examples, and so forth during weather disasters and other situations; therefore, backing up data and keeping multiple copies may serve to be beneficial throughout one's career.

Concerns with E-Portfolios

Some first-year teachers may have concerns with "negotiating their identity" through their electronic portfolio (Hallman, 2007). These students will add additions or make modification to their portfolio after it is turned in for a grade in order to make themselves more marketable during their job search with K-12 schools. One student stated:

> "You know that the professor wants us to be all reflective and represent ourselves as inquirers. But you know what? I don't really think that's what schools want. You know, I want to look confident, not like I'm questioning everything." (Hallman, 2007, p. 474)

The above thought is interesting because an aspiring teacher recognizes there are two different objectives he/she must accomplish. The first objective is to meet the academic requirements of courses and of a program, and the second objective is to obtain a teaching position. Preservice teachers should understand that universities have an ethical responsibility to ensure that their students work to meet the learning objectives for each course and that they must often demonstrate this to accreditation entities. While the expectations may appear extraneous to students, it is important to adhere to those expectations in order to meet the course requirements. Many educators, including those in schools, highly value those who can reflect critically and well in order to grow, but some may see too many negative examples as a detriment. However, if students want to make themselves more marketable in different ways for a specific opportunity, then they can modify their portfolio, as needed, after they have met the academic requirements.

Hallman (2007) also found that students should consider their target audience and how they can best portray themselves when writing for multiple and, perhaps, conflicting audiences. Again, a future educator can be challenged with this and must determine if he or she wants to be considered as more of a reflective, inquisitive student or an already completely competent student. The answer is that a principal will want to see both. Knowing this information may be a challenge because, as Hallman (2007) showed through her research, it may be difficult to see how the content of the e-portfolio could move smoothly from coursework for a university to a K-12 hiring tool. It is, perhaps, wise to see the portfolio process as "never ending." Very similar to a high fashion model's portfolio (where photos are constantly replaced with those of higher quality or those which are more relevant to a particular job [sportswear, evening attire, jewelry, the hands, etc.]), a teacher's portfolio will grow and change with added experiences and different audiences. Technology offers this option at the touch of a button. One can save a particular version (clearly labeled) and create a copy with revisions quickly and easily.

As mentioned earlier, students also want more direction as to what should be included within their portfolio. For example, in the study conducted by Wray (2008), it was found that students wanted their professors to provide an outline of everything that should be included within their portfolio. Students stated this would give them a clear direction on what to include so that they could work on that rather than compiling unsubstantial miscellaneous material. Providing an outline may be both beneficial and harmful, depending on one's perspective. Having a set outline may provide a guide to students who struggle with what to share. It may force students to consider resources and materials that are common at other major universities, which can then be used to level the playing field when competing against students from other universities for the same job. Although the benefits may help students, they may also hinder students from thinking outside the box, which may impact how they present themselves to potential employers (Hallman, 2007). Teacher candidates may be less inclined to look for opportunities to be creative and take risk to produce the best portfolio because they may want to show they are meeting all predetermined guidelines for their college or university. It may be of help in courses that do not necessarily require a portfolio as an end-of-course assignment to ask if the professor could still cue students as to if his/her major assignments could be used later on for a teacher education program portfolio. Future teachers should certainly ask.

Tension surrounding time and worth, validity and reliability, and autonomy and compliance are a concern for some who are creating a portfolio (Reis & Villaume, 2002). Many university students and professors may feel that there is not quite enough time allowed between the beginning of the course and the end for students to deliver. It may be felt, too, that this short interlude does not provide a reasonable amount of time for teachers/

professors to provide quality feedback to preservice teachers who may need to improve their work. Be that as it may, a good guideline to professors *and* students is to establish many intermediate deadlines throughout a course to ensure that a portfolio will not be completed a few days before (or worse, the night before) the end of class and that a prospective teacher has been able to use feedback along the way to adjust the product over the semester (or the program). It is also the future teacher's responsibility to meet these deadlines and to make modifications as directed for the grade and for the interview. A prime concern of educational programs is having their students obtain positions, but, in the end, it is the teacher candidates as individuals who are responsible for making sure they have a good product that demonstrates their own worth.

Some education students may find that the increased options of technology may be overwhelming. With a variety of applications, Web tools, and media outlets at their fingertips, determining which one(s) to choose may prove difficult if the students do not know how to use them to present their work in the best light. Peer and program support should be sought in order to grow. Additionally, students may not know what operating systems their evaluators will use to review their material. If a student uses a Mac operating system to create documents in the Pages software, a reviewer using a PC that operates the Microsoft Office Suite (Word, Excel, PowerPoint, etc.) may not have access to open a document because it is not supported by that system. This is part of the formative process that teacher candidates must check as university students. If a portfolio is to be presented in a course(s) on university equipment, the student should check early to see if his/her computer will interface with that system (even checking the equipment in the presentation room itself). Not being able to open documents, for example, creates stress for all parties because it may mean the teacher candidate does not receive an oral grade and must go back to quickly fix the portfolio, and the professor may have to hold up class grades to wait.

Matching a school district format is not as controllable. Many districts have extensive firewalls, so all files and documents should be on a disk or flash drive instead of connecting to the Web to open. Connections to these documents and navigation must be designed and tested with clear indicators of where to "click on" to navigate to the document or go back "home" to the table of contents. Not knowing if one's technology will be "a match" at a school is another reason for running a hard copy to back up the electronic copy for interviews. If the technology does not interface, the interviewee still has access to the information, and the interviewer can still see much of a candidate's skill. The portfolio (electronic or hard copy) can act as a safety net or prompter in an interview for candidates who momentarily forget an answer they want to give.

Another issue in portfolio creation is showing one's own work. Education students must always be ethical and never use other students' examples, replicating them as their own work (unless, of course, there was a group assignment/project; in which case, that should be made clear). Portfolio creators can use viewable portfolios as a means to compare one's own work with someone else's or as an example to spur one's thinking process—but they should never represent the work of others as their own. Many universities use plagiarism tools which search for these issues, and, if found, plagiarism can be grounds for removing someone from a teacher preparation program. Clearly referencing other's work is acceptable, but presenting someone else's efforts as their own is an unethical decision that can cost a grade and, possibly, as career.

Periodically checking that the links and attachments included in e-portfolios are working properly will help to ensure that it is ready for anyone at any time to view. Having a portfolio current and ready avoids the considerable stress of interviewing or being evaluated.

Mrs. Graza moved due to her military husband's orders in August—one week before school started. Because of the timing and not knowing necessarily where they would be living, she felt that obtaining a teaching position at this late date would be impossible. As luck would have it, however, the superintendent of the district was a new neighbor who greeted her in front of her new house during the moving in process. "What do you do?" he asked. "Well, I am a teacher, but I'm probably not going to be able to work this year. I'll have to fill out all of my records for this district." "What kind of documentation do you have?" he asked. "I have my portfolio with all my information handy," she told him. "Go get it," he told her, and after looking through it on his computer, he came back out and asked, "Can you start in three days? We can work with this! I have just the perfect match for you still open at one of my schools!"

e-Portfolios

Campus-Wide Portfolio Platforms

Campus-wide portfolio platforms such as TaskStream and TK20 play an integral role in the way universities assess and receive accreditation. TK20, as an assessment tool, provides information that assists units at all levels in: measuring and improving student learning outcomes; facilitating continuous improvement of academic and support services; and accumulating, generating, communicating, and disseminating institutional information to support assessment of student learning (TK20 Assessment Solutions at Work, 2014).

The percentage of teacher education programs in the United States who use portfolios to assess students is at least 90% (Ritzhaupt et al., 2012). While the assessment is necessary for student growth, it is also important for universities to receive and maintain accreditation. Banister, Vannatta, and Ross (2006) conducted a study on the best e-portfolio system and integrated three systems into the university setting. When considering the three types of platforms, they found it is very important for any university considering a portfolio system to consider:

- What are the critical functions and how do they relate to their college?
- What types of reports need to be generated?
- What type of storage environment do students need?
- How and when will students be introduced to the portfolio? (Banister, Vannatta, & Ross, 2006)

In comparing the three programs, the strengths and weaknesses of each were compared. Some strengths and weaknesses include:

Strengths	Weaknesses
LiveText (lesson plan template, unlimited storage space) TaskStream (ease of uploading artifacts and excellent customer support) Epsilen (easy interface and unlimited storage)	Difficulty downloading files, problems with the Mac OS, and limited storage space were the common concerns across the three platforms.

Another concern with using LiveText and TaskStream was the difficulty they posed to teachers. "While the LiveText and TaskStream certainly had the robust interfaces to support thousands of students uploading hundreds of documents, the data tied to these artifacts was difficult for faculty to input, retrieve, and aggregate" (Banister et al., 2006, p. 86). This especially raised concern because one of the primary reasons for a university to use an e-portfolio system is to enable the collection of data for its national accrediting body.

As mentioned, the security of student data can also be of concern with the electronic portfolio (Ali, 2005). If a portfolio creator makes the work accessible to anyone via the Internet, he or she can sometimes run the risk of losing control over who has viewing rights. Teacher candidates may not have the option to make their information completely private; therefore, it is very important to use a system that will allow him or her to provide more personal information to reviewers only.

Using E-Portfolios for University Accreditation

As noted, one major use of e-portfolios by universities is to share information and receive reaccreditation from their states or professional organizations (Ittelson & Lorenzo, 2005); therefore, student portfolios have become even more important to the university. The student e-portfolio provides a variety of documentation that supports student success and achievement to accrediting agencies. Portland State University, for example, requires each student to create an electronic portfolio. This document links student learning outcomes to its institutional portfolio, which is then publicized for internal and external audiences to display the students' educational experiences (Ittleson & Lorenzo, 2005). This is one way for a state (or national accrediting agency) to assure that a teacher education entity is providing a solid program for its students. Universities, therefore, may ask students to provide a copy of their portfolios (or provide access) for this purpose.

Examples of How Inservice Teachers Use E-portfolios

It is important to make note that teacher portfolios should not stop after students graduate from their undergraduate studies. As a reflective tool, it provides a substantive and concrete way to document growth. In addition, many graduate programs for educational leadership or other degrees require their students to produce a portfolio of some type during their last course of study. Before the popularity of the e-portfolio, the student would compile materials such as coursework and a practicum log.

An Internet search using Google by the authors resulted in several examples of e-portfolios created by teachers who were seeking a different teaching position or a different type of teaching position (such as an instructional specialist). Many of the electronic portfolios included examples of:

- Certifications
- Resumes
- Recommendations and evaluations
- Classroom management plans
- Specifically targeted lesson plans and/or teaching experiences

Many teaching assistants at the collegiate level also use electronic portfolios for promotion or placement into teaching positions. Among the many artifacts that may be used in an inservice teaching portfolio include:

- Student work samples (may include video footage)
- An overall philosophy of teaching
- A short philosophy of teaching various contents such as mathematics, reading, social studies, science, and so forth and/or should be inclusive of age levels ranges (early childhood, elementary, middle school, high school) that one may teach (This should answer the interview question of "How do you plan to teach _____ (content) in your classroom if you have a ___-grade class and why?")
- Observations
- Reflections
- Critiques/evaluations
- Unsolicited letters from students, parents, or colleagues
- References (with titles and current emails and phones numbers, *after* obtaining permission to use them as a reference)
- Other evidence of strengths that one might bring to the position

Carlos had really wanted a fifth-grade classroom his first year, but there was not one available. However, in his third year of teaching, he heard about a position in a neighboring school. In his interviews, the principal made it clear that mathematics was going to be a focus for the particular classroom fifth-grade class she had open. "How, in general, do you plan to set up your mathematics classroom, and what might I see on a typical day if I slipped into the back of the room?" Carl pointed out that he had a formal philosophy statement on teaching mathematics in his portfolio that she could read later on, but since he had already thought about it and written it in professional wording, he was easily able to talk about his belief in the use of manipulatives, student-centered activities, real-world problems, and other areas that he felt were necessary for children's understanding of mathematics. He spoke of allowing for exploration time and the need for cooperative group support in mathematics, and then clearly described a "typical math lesson" based on one that he had placed in his portfolio. He also told the principal, "I did note on your Website that there is a high percentage of English language learners here. If you look at my resume in my portfolio, you will see that I speak conversational Spanish. There are notes from three of my colleagues about different situations where that was really helpful to them with parents and a few notes from parents and children, although they are in Spanish."

Preservice teachers in education programs should select a tool that will be easy to access and update. While *easy* is the key, students should not settle on the quality of the tool they use because hiring committees may miss the quality of their work—based on the restrictions and/or the representations of their electronic portfolio. A simple Google search will produce several examples of student-created electronic portfolios. It will be beneficial to review what others have created and to note if the formats seem limiting or not. Another option is agencies that provide courses for students who need to learn how to select programs and create a competitive e-portfolio. Students may benefit from taking these courses.

Most district applications also require references, and, as noted above, a portfolio is the place to maintain a current list. The best references are those from someone who has seen a teacher candidate with children in the classroom (field supervisors, mentors, principals, and so forth) or in other situations (coaching, tutoring, etc.). A school district wants to know information about how a potential teacher interacts with students and as a team member in a school with others, and many people (including most professors who do not teach in field-based courses) cannot answer all of those types of questions, although they may be able to say that a particular teacher-to-be is a wonderful person and was a fabulous student. A reference cannot be a family member or peer/friend. This negates the validity of the reference.

A portfolio is also an excellent place to store information for filling out a job application. Most of this information is tedious to keep up with (particularly after a number of years [e.g., years and addresses of former professors, employers, references, and/or supervisors; professional development workshops completed; awards or professional organizations in college or elsewhere; and so forth]). Maintaining this type of information in a portfolio from the beginning (in college) and keeping it current later on guarantees that one will not need to spend hours locating it when it comes time to fill out applications.

Formatting the Final Products

The visual presentation of a portfolio makes a statement to the viewer. It may say, "I really care about the work I do, I am aware of technology design and its impact, and I pay attention to detail…and I will probably do so with instruction for my students," or it may indicate the opposite. In current times where there are many "slick" Websites, the overall design of a portfolio becomes important, particularly when there a competitive teaching market. Below are some hints that may help to make a good presentation.

- Use a simple color scheme without too many clashing colors.
- Use one basic background theme or template consistently throughout (there are many that relate to classrooms that can be downloaded free or purchased). A school theme can be very attractive but is not necessary; however, a common template helps to unify the portfolio. Making sure that titles are in the same place on each slide helps the reader to see organization, for example. Selecting a style that fits one's own personality will also send a message to the viewer.
- Use titles or subtitles on *each* slide so that it is easy to identify each when modifying or searching for the right examples to show. If a document is continued onto the next slide, indicate that in its title (e.g., Competency 3, continued).
- Use title fonts that are not too big (over 40, for example); 36 or 32 are big enough to not overpower the slide). Do not use font that is so small that it is difficult to read.
- Select a font style that is easily read. Ornate script can be hard to read in a formal document. Also, select a font that "matches" one's desired grade level. For example, Comic Sans is good for teachers of the younger grades but may appear too elementary for future high school teachers.
- Do not run typing into template borders or margins.
- Use dark type on a light background. Light type on a dark background is often difficult to read when the lighting conditions are not good.
- Using some sound and special effects in opening or closing slides may be fine, but an "overdose" is distracting for the viewer, especially when sound and blinking text is used in a school area.
- Take a camera/phone camera everywhere during field experiences or other relevant activities to snap shots that show your work with children or work within school settings. A picture really is worth a 1,000 words, and these types of artifacts confirm that a teacher candidate clearly has child-related or school experiences (but do be cautious to follow district policy in taking photos or videos of children).

Label any pictures to explain why they are part of the portfolio (Under one photo taken with girls doing crafts, a teacher candidate wrote, "I was a Girl Scout leader for three years, during which time I prepared craft and badge projects and lessons for 15 young girls each week. I also organized successful three-day campouts each summer with the girls and parent volunteers.")

- Think ahead about filming video clips when there is an exciting lesson activity or lesson coming in order up to arrange for videotaping. Be sure that the video is stable (not jerky) and the sound is at a level that can be understood well by viewers.
- The name of the teacher should be the main focus on the title page.
- If a meaningful quotation is used on the title page to sum up one's views on education, citing this quote is mandatory if it was written or spoken by someone else.

> Education is the most powerful weapon which you can use to change the world.
>
> *Nelson Mandela*

- Use formal English and formal phrasing (use "children" or "students" rather than "kids," etc.).
- Run Spell/Grammar check each time the portfolio is modified.
- Check navigation on each page to make sure the user can get back to the Table of Contents page easily and that each linked document opens.
- Have a second (or third set of eyes) go through the portfolio.
- Make it "one's own" so that it will be a pleasure to work on it and can be seen as a true picture of one's own personality.

Evaluating the E-Portfolio

Rubrics

Rubrics should not only be used to grade a student's e-portfolio but should also be used to guide its process of development. Following a rubric set by a professor, for example, can initiate a document that teachers-to-be may use to create a timeline that will allow them to complete their portfolio in a timely manner. The rubric should be written thoroughly without much room for the students' own interpretation—if it is to be graded objectively by the professor. Teacher candidates may want to examine their portfolio rubrics given by a professor carefully (and early) *and* ask questions up front about documentation as they go through the process—rather than wait until the end to ask if particular assignments/documents will match the criteria for specific areas (refer to Figure 12.8 for a nonexample of a teaching portfolio title page). Again, scrambling for

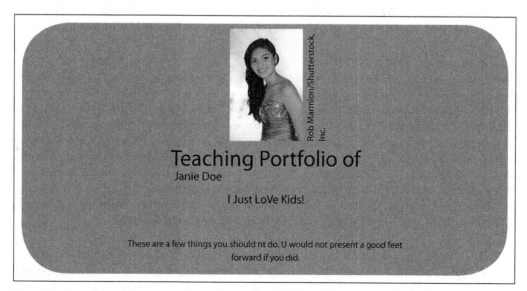

Figure 12.8   A nonexample of a teaching portfolio title page.

documentation is stressful and often produces a substandard portfolio that one will not want to put into use for professional purposes. Collecting and saving work to go towards possible use in the portfolio throughout the semester (and even throughout one's teacher education program) can be a valuable way to obtain quality artifacts in the end. Barrett (2003) suggests: (1) determining levels of performance in the rubric; (2) determining the criteria by addressing the components/elements that will be assessed individually; and (3) determining the content descriptions.

Peer Grading

Involving one's peers in the assessment of their work has been seen to be beneficial (Ali, 2005). Not only will the teacher candidates learn from the feedback of their peers, but they may also learn from the feedback they provide to others. This research also calls for peer review to be an essential part of the process of the development of the portfolio. Peer assessment should be ongoing throughout the development of the portfolio. Oral presentation of portfolios in class can also provide value when peers are required to rate or list comments on their fellow students' presentations. As they view others' portfolios, new ideas for their own portfolios are generated, and these comments can act to improve what the presenter may not have seen when originally constructing the work. If done orally, an opportunity to vocalize views and to "practice an interview" is provided—as previously mentioned. This also gives practice time in locating important examples/artifacts very quickly that one may want to show in a real interview. A principal or a grade-level team will not want to wait for a teacher candidate to flip through numerous slides to try to locate a specific one about which he or she wants to talk in the short time scheduled for the interview.

auremar/Shutterstock, Inc.

Self-assessment

It is also crucial for education students to self-assess their work, especially if there is a supplied rubric. If the material that a student is presenting in his or her portfolio does not meet the required objectives/goals (of a particular course, an interview, etc.), the material should be removed, or the teacher candidate can ask professors if it is acceptable to include. There may be additional artifacts or material that could bring an additional level of understanding or simply make the portfolio stronger. Seeking approval and guidance from professors (or one's teacher education program) *ahead* of deadlines is always the safest path. Turning a rubric into a checklist is also recommended. This allows one to quickly assess whether or not each required item is included.

> Claudia Gomez, as she began her portfolio in her junior year, thought of the process much like a grocery list or a school supply list that she might take to the store. When at the store, each item on the list was of some importance, so she would spend time "walking up and down each aisle" until she found the item. As she found the item, she might draw a line through it or put a check beside it to show that she could move on to the next item on the list. If she didn't find the item right away, she might skip it and come back to it. If the store did not carry the item, she might draw a circle around it to say she needed to look for this item later in another store. This helped her mindset in making sure she completed all the requirements of her portfolio. She also knew that, as when one goes to the store, there are always some extras that end up as treats in the basket. She wanted to make sure that even those these items might not have been on "the list," they were special enough to include, so she would save them as well. Whenever she did an assignment that could be used in her portfolio in her education classes, she mentally and physically cross-checked her portfolio list.

This method might be a good one to begin assessing one's own portfolio. A rubric is a good checks and balances system. Taking the time to really understand what is being asked within each section of one's portfolio will help to create a valuable document—both for a grade, for further professional development, and for the hiring process.

As a note, quality is of foremost importance. If one is asked to supply a lesson plan, he or she should not supply a short lesson plan template but should make sure to have detailed plans listed for each subject that will be required to be taught. One must be sure that each artifact included within the portfolio is labeled and is introduced with a title and header. An evaluator needs to know why the item is relevant, so one must take the time to explain where the item was obtained. For example, Jayme Chang included this as a description for one of her artifacts:

> I taught this math lesson in a fourth-grade class during my student teaching at Lee Elementary. I began with a mini lesson on number talks and then led the class in a lesson on long division. I was also evaluated on this lesson by my student teacher mentor on January 23, 2014, and I have included my observation scores (click here to see my evaluation). The best part of this lesson came after I carefully divided students into groups to use manipulatives because they had great discussion and were all successful at their task.

When using a portfolio for an interview, one should remember that it is valuable look at the Web site of the school/district and add something that shows one can relate to the particular students/staff/demographics/area there.

As a reminder, each link in the electronic portfolio must be working, and the material (audio and/or video) should also be clear and easy to view and hear. Visual design is important in the overall message, and attention to details is always noted by assessors in the teacher education program and by hiring administrators. First impressions through the portfolio do matter.

One of the chapter's authors recently met with a principal at an elementary school, and the administrator stated, "I welcome candidates who want to show samples of their work during an interview. I do caution them to be mindful of the time and try not to provide *too* much information at once [a good reason to have a disk or flash drive to leave with them for later viewing]. Strategically, they should work the information from their portfolio into their answer for the interview question."

Some additional hints for the portfolio process are included below:

1. Save all artifacts from one's teacher education program. This will eliminate the need to reproduce or recreate them if they become useful or needed at a later date.
2. Ensure that the artifacts represent you and the work you have completed. Do not include generic material that is standard for the course and will be well known to all educators unless you can meaningfully tie it to your own personal application in some way. Ask, "Have I shown that I have actually applied this concept in some way?" A downloaded picture or clip art image is not enough, as well, unless accompanied by one's own thoughts on why it is an applicable artifact. It is also critical not to use examples provided by your academic program as your own. Remember to be ethical when compiling artifacts for your portfolio. Ensure the work you compile is your own.
3. Include your name and dates on material. This will provide some validity and ownership to your artifacts. This may reduce/eliminate the reproduction/use of your work by other students, too.
4. If choosing to use picture(s), make sure that they are "professionally related" and are not snapshots from a party, date, or something that does not represent school professionalism. If the picture includes students, be sure that permission is granted to use it. During your work in schools, try to take many pictures of artifacts that may make an impact (bulletin boards you may have created, student work, involvement in a field day or special project, etc.). Try to take a few pictures where your face is seen, but students' backs are to the camera in case a district would not allow students' faces to be in photographs.
5. Including some student notes will be of interest, but they need to be more than just "I love you, Ms. Jones."

One way to bring all of this altogether in a successful portfolio is to establish deadlines on a calendar for tentative dates on which you want to complete each stage of your portfolio. Some

pikcha/Shutterstock, Inc.

professors may include this for you with interim deadlines, but others may leave this open to the student.

David is a fourth-grade elementary teacher with many years of experience, who understands the importance of collecting student work samples to show parents their child's academic achievement throughout the school year. David has worked in the elementary environment and has witnessed the influx of technology into his classroom. His work examples often include both formative and summative assessments. Some of his assessments may derive from online collaborative transcripts through Web tools such as Google Docs, backchannel applications, or Web sites. David also has the opportunity to provide audio and video examples of student assessments to parents during parent conferences and/or open houses. David wishes that he had the same technology resources available when he was in his undergraduate teacher education program to collect work samples for his own records as he has now. He feels that is a powerful statement to show a child's work at the beginning and at the end when they leave his instruction. He also noted that having audio and video available helps others understand clearly when a child is not making progress so that other professionals or parents, for example, can step in quickly. He also uses examples that would include student work via a mobile device, such as a Galaxy tab or an iPad. David originally looked at creating a portfolio as a means to collect data on his students. Now that he is pursuing an advanced degree in teacher education, he has found the material he has collected through the years will serve to be beneficial when he applies for an instructional specialist position with his current employer.

Final Thoughts

A portfolio can be a valuable asset during and after one's academic career. Understanding how to create a portfolio and what to include in a portfolio can make a huge difference. Not only do the artifacts paint a picture of the teacher candidate or teacher, but also the reflections and critiques reveal whether he or she has met the established learning and performance outcomes. One's portfolio can be used not only for evaluation and self-evaluation "along the way", but also for growth and improvement throughout a teacher's career.

References

Ali, S. (2005). An introduction to electronic portfolios in the language classroom. *The Internet in Support of Learning to Teach TESL Journal, 11*(8). Retrieved from http://iteslj.org/Techniques/Ali-Portfolios.html

Avraamidou, L., & Zembal-Saul, C. (2002). Making the case for the use of web-based portfolios in support of learning to teach. *The Journal of Interactive Online Teaching, 1*(2). Retrieved from www.presentationmullingar.ie/wordpress/wp-content/uploads/2013/07/Making-the-case-for-the-use-of-Web-Based-Portfolios.pdf

Banister, S., Vannatta, R. A., & Ross, C. (2006). Testing electronic portfolio systems in a teacher education: Finding the right fit. *Action in Teacher Education, 27*(4), 81–90.

Barrett, H. C. (2003). Evaluating electronic portfolios. Retrieved from http://electronicportfolios.com/ALI/rubrics.html

Chen, H. L., & Light, T. (2010). *Electronic portfolios and student success: Effectiveness, efficiency, and learning.* Washington, DC: AAC&U Association.

Gambrel, L. E., & Jarrott, S. (2011). The bottomless file box: Electronic portfolios for learning and evaluation purposes. *International Journal of ePortfolio, 1*(1), 85–94.

Hallman, H. L. (2007). Negotiating teacher identity: Exploring the use of electronic teaching portfolios with preservice English teachers. *Journal of Adolescent and Adult Literacy, 50*(6), 474–485.

Ittleson, J., & Lorenzo, G. C. (2005). An overview of eportfolios. *Educause Learning Initiative*, 1–27. Retrieved from http://net.educause.edu/ir/library/pdf/ELI3001.pdf

Merriam Webster Online. (2014). Portfolio [Def. 5]. Retrieved from http://www.merriam-webster.com/dictionary/portfolio

Mills, M. (2009). Capturing student progress via portfolios in the music classroom. *Music Educators Journal, 96*(2) 1–8.

Nath, J. L., Cohen, M. D., Hill, L., & Connell, M. (2012, Feb.). *WE think they work: What do students really think about electronic portfolios?* Paper presented at the annual conference of the Association of Teacher Educators (ATE), San Antonio, TX.

Reis, N. K., & Villaume, S. (2002). The benefits, tensions, and visions of portfolios as a wide-scale assessment for teacher education. *Action in Teacher Education, 23*(4), 10–17.

Ritzhaupt, A. D., Parker, M. A., & Ndoye, A. (2012). Qualitative analysis of student perceptions of eportfolios in a teacher education program. *Journal of Digital Learning in Teacher Education, 28*(3), 99–107.

Strudler, N., & Wetzel, K. (2005). The diffusion of electronic portfolios in teacher education: Issues of initiation and implementation. *Journal of Research on Technology in Education, 37*, 411–433.

TK20. (2014). Assessment solutions at work. Retrieved from http://www.tk20.com/

Wray, S. (2008). Swimming upstream: Shifting the purpose of an existing teaching portfolio requirement. *Professional Educator, 32*(1), 1–16. Retrieved http://files.eric.ed.gov/fulltext/EJ802013.pdf

Chapter 13

Using Technology to Study for Certification Exams

Jane Thielemann-Downs
University of Houston-Downtown

Meet Jessie

Born as a member of the Millennial Generation, Jessie takes the Internet for granted, accepting the utility of services such as smart phones, Google apps, online chatting, online shopping, Wikipedia, FaceTime, Facebook, and streaming videos. He prefers frequent and quick interactions with digital content and is constantly multitasking. Educator preparation programs nationwide are facing a new youth culture of digital natives like Jessie.

This semester, Jessie is student teaching in a middle school while, at the same time, preparing for his state certification exams. He knows how critical it is for him to pass his certification exams before the end of the semester because many school districts will not even interview (much less hire) a teacher candidate who has not passed the tests. It is important for Jessie to become familiar with all of the available technological resources to accomplish his goal of becoming a certified teacher, including the myriad of resources available to study electronically.

The typical college student of today is a digital native, so it is important to take advantage of the wide variety of technology tools available for preparing teacher candidates for state certification examinations. Digital natives, fluent in acquiring and using technological tools and learning this technology quickly with an intuitive understanding, seem to use technology tools as an extension of their brains (Black, 2010). When researching and learning a topic, they easily handle multiple streams of information. Digital natives prefer frequent and quick interactions with content, and they display exceptional visual-literacy skills. These are essential skills when navigating the digital technology used today (Black, 2010). Nontraditional students who may not have grown

PlusONE/Shutterstock, Inc.

up with technology in the same ways will find it to their advantage to "jump in," both in terms of resources for studying now and for when they are in classrooms with technological test prep packages for their own students.

It is upon these characteristics that this chapter was developed—as numerous resources are available to assist and support today's preservice teachers in preparing for certification examinations. Specifically, this chapter describes (a) the reason why adding technology is useful in preparing for certification exams; (b) the effective approaches for using technology to study, and (c) an overview and description of national and state online resources available for study, including: videos, preparation manuals/textbooks, test-at-a-glance overviews, tutorials/test simulations, interactive practice exams, and general guides/tips for test-taking. The TExES (Texas Examinations of Educator Standards) are discussed in details, and this chapter also describes information about the PRAXIS, the national teacher certification exam used for licensure in many states. In addition, the national trends and statistics concerning teacher certification are presented.

Using Technology-Based Sources

Most technology-based source materials described within this chapter can be accessed any time—during evenings, weekends, or daily breaks (refer to Figure 13.1). These materials can be viewed repeatedly as needed and cover a wide range of subject content, best teaching practices, and practice questions. The user's ability to control the learning media is important to success. Therefore, in order to take advantage of this material, teacher candidates must become familiar with these technology-based resources and use them to meet individual test preparation needs.

Figure 13.1   Most technology-based source materials described within this chapter can be accessed any time—during evenings, weekends, or daily breaks.

Effective Approaches to Study

Effective learning does not just "happen." In order to make the most of preparation for certification exams, preservice teachers must create a specific plan for successful examination completion. First, teacher candidates should determine when their educator preparation program will allow them to take a specific exam. When cleared, the teacher candidate should then register for that examination several weeks or months in advance, choosing a test date that allows plenty of time for review and study of the material (refer to Figure 13.2). If teacher candidates have just completed course work on a particular exam, they should not wait too long—as important information may not be as fresh on their minds later on. Registration bulletins can be downloaded free of charge for the TExES examinations (Texas Education Agency, 2014e).

Second, teacher candidates should become familiar with the content for each of their required tests by reviewing the online test preparation manual carefully. The manual will give a "test-at-a-glance" summary of the content divided into major subject areas and competencies. Test-takers should then gather and organize various study resources that meet each individual's own learning style. Finally, a study schedule should be created that distributes test preparation and practice into multiple study sessions over a specific time period.

Teacher candidates may choose to work within online media to interact with peers to discuss ideas, share strategies, voice concerns, provide mentoring, and support one another (Sternberg, Kaplan, & Borck, 2007). Forming a study group in order to share test tips and discuss the exam's content is an effective test preparation tactic. Different online technology applications can be used to support the varied models of learning. For example, members of the study group may choose to use asynchronous (not at the same time)

Figure 13.2   Digital natives use electronic devices and Web-based calendars to plan for exam study and registration deadlines months in advance.

Table 13.1 Synchronous communication tools for group meetings

Google Hangouts
GoToMeeting
WebEX
Skype
FaceTime
UberConference

communication tools (e.g., e-mail, threaded discussion boards, newsgroups), which would allow each member of a study group to contribute at his or her own convenience. Group members may alternatively choose to use synchronous technologies (e.g., webcasting, chat rooms, and desktop audio/video technology) in order to approximate face-to-face learning within the study group (refer to Table 13.1). If constant discussions and exchange of information is needed, synchronous platforms will be more effective than asynchronous platforms. However, if each member has to wait, think, or work on individual tasks before forwarding to the next person, the asynchronous platform will work better. Some groups may choose to schedule a meeting with Doodle scheduling or meet at a central location with an electronic whiteboard (such as a school or university) in order to discuss the material together.

Study groups work well for a number of reasons. First, they create a responsibility to participate, so they assure that some studying will occur. They also require members to actively participate through teaching and explaining the material to other members of the group. When one must teach, the material is more likely to be retained. More minds working together come up with more ideas to help remember the materials that may, in turn, resonate better with a learner (Sternberg, Kaplan, & Borck, 2007).

Preparing for Computer-Administered Testing

In past years, there has been increased movement toward computerized testing. The move towards adaptive assessments was designed to produce the most precise estimate of student achievement and growth and greater detail in diagnostic feedback. **Computer-administered testing** is an assessment model in which candidates answer questions (multiple-choice questions) that are part of a computer program. In most cases, individuals who take these exams can often receive their scores immediately or very quickly after testing. While there are clearly advantages to administering tests via computer, there are also possible drawbacks in that a certain level of technological literacy and comfort is required (Stone & Davey, 2011; http://cms.texes-ets.org/cat/).

versus

Online Resources: Videos

Since almost all certification exams in Texas and many other states are now administered using a **CAT (Computer-Administered Testing)** system, successful candidates must be familiar with this system of testing, although there are still alternative testing methods using pencil and paper and other methods, especially for those with special needs. An effective way to become familiar with computer-administered testing is to use a similar technology-based system for preparation; future test takers can begin the familiarization process by first viewing a video which explains the computerized testing experience (Texas Education Agency, 2014d) (refer to Figure 13.3).

The video presents important information specific to the CAT experience including:

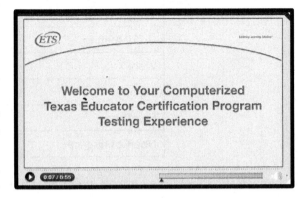

Figure 13.3   A video to introduce the TExES CAT presented by TEA and ETS.

- The first screen contains the examinee's personal data and photo. If this information is correct click "continue."
- Several information screens are shown culminating with a confidentiality statement. Clicking "continue" signifies agreement to the terms.
- The examination clock will begin when the examinee starts the actual test. The clock will appear in the upper right-hand corner of the screen. If it is distracting, it can be clicked off.
- The test has no tutorial; however, basic navigation instructions and question type information is available by clicking "help."
- There are directions at the beginning of each section of the test. Some additional resource information, such as the periodic table and mathematics reference materials, is also available during sections of some tests.

It is also important to note that additional tutorial videos are available from Educational Testing Service (ETS) concerning alternate character toolbars for certification exams in Languages Other Than English (LOTE) EC-12—French (610), German (611) and Spanish (613) (http://cms.texes-ets.org/texes/acttutorial/#altchar). Tutorial videos are also available from ETS concerning the use of graphing or scientific calculators since an online calculator is now part of the testing software for some of the TExES tests (Texas Education Agency, 2014a).

Online Tesources: Test Preparation Manuals

Education Testing Service (ETS), a national testing company, is currently contracted to create and administer teacher certification exams for dozens of states in the USA. In Texas, ETS develops and administers Texas Educator Certification Exams (TExES™) to individuals seeking educator licensure/certification. ETS has developed a preparation manual for each TExES certification exam (Texas Education Agency, 2014b). For a complete listing of preparation manuals visit: http://cms.texes-ets.org/texes/prepmaterials/texes-preparation-manuals

The test preparation manuals (refer to Figure 13.4) are available free for download from ETS. These manuals are designed to help examinees become familiar with the test competencies, the test question formats, and appropriate study resources. Each preparation manual gives an outline of the test, a list of the domains and competencies that will be tested, strategies for answering multiple-choice questions, sample test questions, and an answer key with rationales. In addition, ETS also provides

Figure 13.4   TEA TExES Preparation Manual.

Supplemental Guides for the **Bilingual Target Language Proficiency Test** (BTLPT) Spanish and LOTE French, German, Latin, and Spanish EC-12 tests. These supplemental guides provide a preview of the actual test screens used in the computerized tasks encountered in these tests. The guides provide information about the introductory log-in screens, general regulations and policies and general directions. However, it is important to note that only a limited number of sample questions are provided in the ETS preparation manuals; therefore, teacher candidates should seek further practice with additional questions from other resources.

Figure 13.5   A podcast device.

The BTLPT is a special type of certification test that presents some challenges for teacher candidates who want to teach in bilingual education classrooms. There are four domains in the test: listening, reading, oral, and written. This Spanish oral test assesses teacher candidates' knowledge by combining content, best practices, language, and culture. For oral expression type of questions, test takers are typically asked questions such as: "What could you do to develop critical thinking in students?" and are given one minute to prepare and one minute to record the answer. To practice delivering the answers orally, teacher candidates in the past have used stop watches to keep the time. However, some Millennials like Jessie may resort to simple and free podcast sites such as Yodio and PodBean to rehearse their time-measured answers (refer to Figure 13.5).

Online Resources: Test-At-A-Glance

Each of the **test preparation manuals** includes a **Test-At-A-Glance** chart which provides a quick overview and description of the test's content. The Test-At-A-Glance charts outline the areas of content (domains) to be tested, the number and types of questions, and the weight percentage of each. Each of the domains is further defined by a set of competencies or standards which detail the knowledge and skills needed by the teacher candidate. The approximate percentage of the test allotted to each domain is usually shown in table or pie chart form.

Online Resources: Test Preparation Textbooks

Many commercially-made test preparation textbooks and manuals are available to preservice teachers (i.e., Barron's, Research & Education Association, Mometrix Test Preparation). These textbooks can be easily obtained online through Web sites such as Amazon.com, and they typically provide an outline of the domains and competencies to be tested as well as sample practice questions. Most test preparation textbooks focus exclusively on practice questions, usually providing a complete practice exam experience to the reader. However, a few of the test preparation textbooks focus on content as well as practice questions.

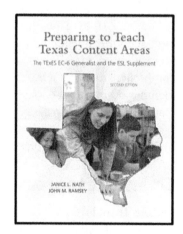

Figure 13.6   *Preparing to Teach Texas Content Areas: The TExES EC-6 Generalist and the ESL Supplement (2nd ed.).*

Content area test preparation guides differ from most preparation manuals in that they provided an overall summary of the content knowledge tested on the exam. This information, drawn from a wide range of teacher preparation textbooks, research articles, and education documents, offers the examinee a review of the material typically taught during professional development courses. For example, Nath and Ramsey's (2011) TExES E-C 6 Generalist preparation text, *Preparing to Teach Texas Content Areas,* (refer to Figure 13.6) offers a comprehensive review of the eight content areas taught from early childhood through the sixth grade: language arts and reading, mathematics, social studies, science, art, music, health / physical education, theatre arts, and ESL. Each content area section contains a content summary, sample lesson plans, and prompts, as well as practice questions. This comprehensive test preparation textbook also helps students understand many of the basic theories and methodologies behind best practices typically applied to each content area. The

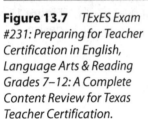

Figure 13.7   *TExES Exam #231: Preparing for Teacher Certification in English, Language Arts & Reading Grades 7–12: A Complete Content Review for Texas Teacher Certification.*

Figure 13.8   The BTLPT Webinar presented by TEA and ETS.

book concludes with preparatory information and a content summary of material for the ESL supplemental certification.

A **content book** for preparing for the Pedagogical and Professional Responsibilities (PPR) exam edited by Nath and Cohen (2011) is also available. This text, *Becoming an EC-6 Teacher in Texas: A Course of Study for the Pedagogy and Professional Responsibilities (PPR) TExES*, offers a complete course of study for the PPR exam that is specifically built around the Texas standards for teacher certification including: human growth and development, student diversity, planning and instruction, learning theory, classroom environment and management, communication, student engagement, technology, assessment, home/school relationships, and laws, ethics and structure of education in Texas. Each chapter, devoted to a specific competency, provides detailed pedagogical and theoretical background, best teaching practices, and practice questions. Many preparations books like this one are available as ebooks as well.

There are some preparation books for upper-level content as well. A **content-based book** for high school English teachers is also available on Amazon.com. This textbook, *English, Language Arts and Reading 7–12 for Exam 231* by Thielemann-Downs (2014) (refer to Figure 13.7) offers a complete review of the current high-school English curriculum in the areas of American, British, Multicultural, and Young Adult literature, literary and poetic elements, basic grammar and spelling rules, methods and strategies for teaching reading comprehension, literature interpretation, and writing as well as speech and business communication. This text includes 90 multiple-choice practice exam questions and four practice essay response prompts. Helpful information with regard to essay development, length, and scoring is also provided.

Other books are available from online searches, depending on one's content area. University or department libraries may also have practice books to use.

Online Resources: Tutorials/Test Simulations

Online Tutorials are more interactive and specific than a textbook. A tutorial seeks to teach by example and to supply information to complete a certain task. ETS provides video tutorials to orient students to the test and to practice using specific tools before test day (Texas Education Agency, 2014c). ETS also provides tutorial Webinars for specific tests. A tutorial presented by the Texas Education Agency (TEA) and ETS is available for the Bilingual Target Language Proficiency Test Spanish (BTLPT) (http://cms.texes-ets.org/texes/acttutorial) (refer to Figure 13.8).

Tutorials and interactive exams are also available from commercial companies to help prepare preservice teachers for certification exams.

For example, **240Tutoring** (refer to Figure 13.9) is an online resource (2011) for teachers preparing for their certification exams. 240Tutoring offers instructional content developed to address the specific knowledge of each test area. The instructional content is an in-depth, comprehensive review of the subject knowledge tested. 240Tutoring also offers practice questions as well as an assessment feature that provides feedback about a test taker's strengths and weaknesses (http://www.240tutoring.com).

Figure 13.9   240Tutoring is an online resource for teachers preparing for their certification exams.

Online Resources: Study Tips Booklets

ETS and the TEA also offer test strategy and tips booklets that contain general information about preparing for and taking Texas educator certification exams. These booklets are in PDF format and can be downloaded at no cost. http://cms.texes-ets.org/texes/prepmaterials/strategy-and-tips.

The booklet, *Study Tips: Preparing for the Texas Educator Certification Tests*, (refer to Figure 13.10) contains useful information on preparing for multiple-choice tests and constructed-response tests. The instruction, tips, and suggestions contained here can help the teacher candidate become a better prepared test taker. Most teacher candidates already know from their own experiences in taking tests that good preparation is an important component of success.

Figure 13.10   *TEA Study Tips: Preparing for the Texas Educator Certification Tests*

The **Reducing Test Anxiety** booklet (refer to Figure 13.11) provides practical help for people who suffer from test anxiety. Although designed specifically for Texas Educator Certification test takers, it is useful for anyone who has to take a test. This guide reviews the major causes of test anxiety and offers practical advice on how to counter each one (www.ets.org/s/praxis/pdf/reducing_test_anxiety.pdf).

Online Resources for Content (STAAR)

There are a number of state tests for various grade levels that have been released in Texas for teachers to use in terms of content. Some of these are under the old testing system in Texas (the TAKS [Texas Assessment of Knowledge and Skills]). Teachers can take these test themselves to see if they know the content that they are

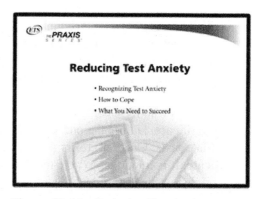

Figure 13.11   Reducing Test Anxiety presented by ETS.

tasked to teach and to practice for their own content tests. One only needs to type in "TAKS test released" and/or "STAAR tests released" for a number of grade levels and content area tests choices to be displayed.

The State of Texas Assessments of Academic Readiness (*STAAR*™) EOC (End-of-Course) tests mastery of the Texas Essential Knowledge and Skills (TEKS) by high school students for a given course and determines college and career readiness. Even though students entering the ninth grade must pass all five exams to graduate from high school, these EOC assessments are helpful to teacher candidates who may be preparing for a specific content exam as a way to self-assess weaknesses and strengths for the high school content that they hope to teach. The level for the state certification tests may be higher than the released tests, but these will aid in practice for each subject area listed.

Required high school STAAR End-of-Course (EOC) assessments include the following subjects:

- Algebra I
- Biology
- English I (combined reading/writing)
- English II (combined reading/writing)
- U.S. History

As mentioned, sample released tests from past years are available online, and immediate online scoring is available for some tests that are digitally interactive. Sample booklets containing released test questions are also available for downloading in PDF format. These tests are easily accessed through the Texas Education Agency (TEA) Web site and some school district Web sites. To obtain the STAAR test booklets from the Houston Independent School District, visit the (HISD) Web site (http://www.houstonisd.org/domain/21201), click on "STAAR," then scroll down to click on "High School".

A number of various companies also have online ordering for practice STAAR tests. Those who are taking the EC-6 Generalist test, for example, may want to order the sixth-grade tests (for students) to practice questions that they may see on their own EC-6 Generalist test for content in mathematics and reading.

Out of State Certified Educators

Many states have reciprocity with other states; that is, they recognize other states' teaching credentials. However, teacher candidates may also have to make application and may need to retest if grade level certifications are different. Educators certified in other states who are seeking certification in Texas, for example, must apply for a review of credentials. To obtain information about this process, educators need to visit the Texas Education Agency homepage and click on Educator Certification. The application process involves several steps described below:

- Create a TEA Online Account
- Complete application and pay a nonrefundable fee
- Submit official transcripts from all universities and colleges one has attended
- Submit copies of all certificates, front and back

Educators who have completed the review of credentials and are found to be eligible may be issued a **One Year Certificate**. During the one-year period of this nonrenewable certificate, the educator must complete all appropriate tests. Once all Texas requirements are completed, educators may apply online for a **Standard Certificate.** It is important to note that educators who have completed a certification exam that is found to be comparable to a Texas test may request an exemption from the Texas exams.

PRAXIS Series Tests

*The **Praxis Series** tests are currently required for teacher licensure in approximately 40 states and U.S. territories (refer to Figure 13.12). These tests are also used by several professional licensing agencies and by several hundred colleges and universities. Since *The Praxis Series* tests are used to license teachers in many states, teacher candidates can test in one state and submit their scores for licensure in any other *Praxis*™ user state.

The official **Praxis** (test preparation) guide is published by ETS, the company that actually makes the tests. These preparation texts are available in three formats: eBook only, eBook with downloadable interactive practice tests, and paperback with CD containing interactive practice tests. The eBook/paperback text includes hundreds of authentic Principals of

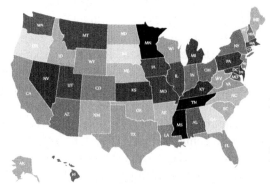

Figure 13.12   The Praxis Series tests are currently required for teacher licensure in approximately 40 states.

Hamik/Shutterstock, Inc.

Learning and Teaching scenarios (PLT) and Praxis II® questions, so the practice experience: simulates the real exam; gives sample Praxis I (PPST) essays with actual scorers' comments; offers comprehensive outlines of PLT study topics; and presents sample case studies. The test preparation guide also provides detailed coverage of the Praxis II Elementary Education Content Knowledge (0014) and Curriculum, Instruction, and Assessment (0011) tests. Moreover, the interactive practice tests (in downloadable or CD format) provide three full-length practice Praxis I® (PPST) exams (http://www.amazon.com/Praxis-Official-Guide-Second-Pre-Professional-ebook) (refer to Figure 13.13).

Figure 13.13 The Praxis Series Official Guide published by ETS.

Future Trends in Teaching, Learning, and Teacher Certification

Currently, the three major trends in teaching and learning involve **collaborative learning**, an ever-increasing use of **technology**, and **blended learning**. These trends, in turn, have resulted in a change in focus in how to train and prepare future teachers.

Today's Internet users are exposed to a global society that requires cooperation and information exchange. In progressive schools across the country, students and teachers are sharing information and connecting with others through social media. Collaborative learning has become a powerful tool in education. Each day students and teachers test out ideas and theories, learn facts, and gauge the opinions of others. Students learn to explore their own kid-specific social networking sites on their blogs, on schools' sites, and of course on Facebook and Twitter. Educators have discovered that they can attract students' attention where they naturally live outside the classroom—the online social world (Barseghian, 2011).

Figure 13.14 The growing dependency on technology has great impact upon the classroom and teacher certification.

Sites like *Classroom 2.0, TeacherTube, PBS Teachers, Edmodo, Edutopia,* and countless others are comprised of teachers' sharing success stories, asking for advice, and providing support to others. In response to this trend, future teachers can expect: (1) the U.S. Department of Education to be working on establishing a one-stop shop for teacher networks, and (2) the development of commonly accepted guidelines for using *YouTube, Facebook,* and other social media in schools (Barseghian, 2011).

This growing use and dependency on technology, the second of the three major trends in teaching and learning, has great impact upon the classroom (refer to Figure 13.14). Pens and pencils are far from obsolete, but forward-thinking educators use interactive tools to attract students' attention. Teachers are using *Guitar Hero* to teach music, *Geo-Caching* for high-tech scavenger hunts, Google Maps for teaching literature, *Wii* in lieu of P.E., *VoiceThread* to communicate, *ePals* and *LiveMocha* to learn global languages with native speakers, *Voki* to create avatars of characters in stories, and *Skype* to communicate with peers from all over the world. Moreover, programs like *Digital Youth Network* focus on teaching students to create podcasts, videos, and record music; and *Adobe Youth Voices* teaches kids how to make and edit films and connects them to documentary filmmakers (Barseghian, 2011). Tech-savvy teachers are threading media-making tools into the curriculum with free or inexpensive tools like comic strip-creation site *ToonDoo, Microsoft Photo Story 3* for slide shows, *Soundslides* for audio slide shows, *Microsoft Movie Maker*, and *VoiceThread* to string together images, videos, and documents, to name just a few.

Students in high schools and colleges are using digital e-portfolios (the tech-form of resumes) to showcase their work on storage devices or Web sites that link to their assignments, achievements, and course of study using photos, graphics, spreadsheets, and Web pages. This explosive trend has resulted in an unprecedented growth of high-tech companies and venture capitalists investing evermore capital in the education market (Barseghian, 2011). See more about using e-portfolios in Chapter 12 of this text.

A third trend in teaching and learning is combining computers with traditional teaching (blended learning). Knowing that today's learners are "wired" at all times, teachers are directing students' natural online proclivity towards schoolwork. One type of reconfiguration is referred to in newly created terms—reverse teaching, flipped classrooms, backwards classroom, or reverse instruction (Barseghian, 2011)—in which students hear lectures at home and use class time to do the follow-up work. This movement is growing quickly; the Department of Education plans to spend $30 million over the next three years to bring blended learning to 400 schools around the country (Martinez, 2010, para. 4).

Changing Student Demographics

Another growing trend is the changing demographics in America's public schools (refer to Figure 13.15). Latino children represent a particularly urgent call to action in early childhood education. Comprising more than 20% of U.S. kindergartners (U.S. Census, 2010)—a statistic that is rapidly growing—many Latinos start school with limited English-language skills. Latino children enter kindergarten about six months behind their non-Latino peers academically (Bridges & Dagys, 2012). The achievement gap persists as children advance through school, often culminating in low academic outcomes: nationwide, 45% of Latinos drop out of high school (Bridges & Dagys, 2012).

Figure 13.15 The changing demographics in America's public schools.

As classrooms across the country become increasingly culturally and linguistically diverse, teacher preparation and training programs must respond to these changes. The demand for ESL and bilingual certified teachers is growing each year, and many educator preparation programs in Texas and California have changed their program's focus in response to the demands (Bridges & Dagys, 2012). Currently, most districts in many states require that their teachers test for ESL certification either before being hired or at least by the second year of employment. A number of test preparations (both online and in hard copy) for this area also exist (as noted earlier in the chapter), and many programs highly recommend that teachers take the test for this as soon as possible to make themselves more eligible for employment.

Summary

In sum, today's college students, unlike their counterparts forty years ago, are from diverse cultural, economic, and geographic backgrounds. The changing nature of college students and their needs in an increasingly global-oriented society are the primary impetuses for providing a wide variety of technology-based tools for learning. Digital natives like Jessie have been surrounded by computer technology since birth, use it constantly, and expect to use it when learning and studying. These students learn and study through active participation (Black, 2010). This chapter has provided information about the multiple streams of information that future teachers can use to prepare for teacher certification exams. Most of these materials are easily accessed any time—evenings, weekends, during daily breaks. These materials can be viewed repeatedly as needed and cover a wide range of content, best practice sessions, and practice questions (http://cms.texes-ets.org/registration bulletin). Finally, an important fact for teacher candidates like Jessie to consider is the changing job market for certified teachers. As classrooms across the country become increasingly culturally and linguistically diverse, teacher preparation and training programs have responded to these changes (Bridges & Dagys, 2012). Changing ways of teaching and learning, changing student demographics, and changing job market trends have all merged to create a demand for teacher candidates who have obtained up-to-date technological skills along with a depth of knowledge and understanding in best pedagogical practices.

References

240Tutoring. (2011). 240 Tutoring. Retrieved from http://www.240tutoring.com

Barseghian, T. (2011). Three trends that define the future of teaching and learning. Retrieved from http://blogs.kqed.org/mindshift/2011/02/three-trends-that-define-the-future-of-teaching-and-learning

Black, A. (2010). Gen Y: Who they are and how they learn. *Educational Horizons*, Winter, 92–100.

Bridges, M., & Dagys, N. (2012). Who will teach our children? Building a qualified early childhood workforce to teach English-Language Learners. *New Journalism on Latino Children*. Institute of Human Development (NJI). Retrieved from http://latinoedbeat.files.wordpress.com/2012/09/njlc-brief-092412_pages.pdf

Houston Independent School District. (n.d.). STAAR. Retrieved from http://www.houstonisd.org/domain/21201

Mann, D., Reardon, R., Becker, J., Shakeshaft, C., & Bacon, N. (2011). Immersive, interactive, web-enabled computer simulation as a trigger for learning: The next generation of problem-based learning in educational leadership. *Journal of Research on Leadership Education, 6*(5). Retrieved from http://files.eric.ed.gov/fulltext/EJ958891.pdf

Martinez, B. (2010, October 18). Blending computers into classrooms. *Wall Street Journal.* Retrieved from http://online.wsj.com/articles/SB10001424052702304772804575558383085638118

Nath, J. L., & Ramsey, J. (2011). *Preparing to teach Texas content areas: The TExES EC-6 Generalist and the ESL Supplement* (2nd ed.). Boston, MA: Pearson.

Nath, J. L., & Cohen, M. D. (2011). *Becoming an EC-6 Teacher in Texas: A Course of Study for the Pedagogy and Professional Responsibilities (PPR) TExES* (2nd ed.). Belmont, CA: Wadsworth Cengage Learning.

Sternberg, B., Kaplan, K., & Borck, J. (2007). Enhancing adolescent literacy achievement through integration of technology in the classroom. *Reading Research Quarterly*, International Reading Association, *42*(3), summer. Retrieved from http://reading.org/downloads/publications/RRQ-42-3-NDR.pdf

Stone, E., & Davey, T. (2011). Computer-adaptive testing for students with disabilities: A review of the literature. ETS: Princeton. Retrieved from http://www.ets.org/Media/Research/pdf/RR-11-32.pdf

Texas Education Agency. (2014a). TEC home. Retrieved from http://cms.texes-ets.org

Texas Education Agency. (2014b). TExES test preparation manuals. Retrieved from http://cms.texes-ets.org/texes/prepmaterials/texes-preparation-manuals

Texas Education Agency. (2014c). Test preparation tutorials. Retrieved from http://cms.texes-ets.org/texes/acttutorial

Texas Education Agency. (2014d). TExES CAT. Retrieved from http://cms.texes-ets.org/texes/acttutorial

Texas Education Agency. (2014e). Registration bulletins. Retrieved from http://cms.texes-ets.org/texes/acttutorial

Thielemann-Downs, J. (2014) *TExES Exam #231: Preparing for Teacher Certification in English, language arts & reading grades 7–12, a complete content review*. Createspace: Amazon.

Chapter 14

Transformative Learning: Preservice Teachers Becoming Reflective Practitioners through the Utilization of Technology Tools

Christal G. Burnett and Laura A. Mitchell
University of Houston-Downtown

Meet Ms. Tijerina

Ms. Tijerina, a new teacher in fifth grade, noticed that her students' scores on their last mathematics benchmark test were not as high as she had hoped. She knew that she had been going through the material more rapidly, which meant that she had been "ditching" the use of manipulatives (see Figure 14.1) so she could use more pencil-and-paper activities. As she was reflecting on the students' test scores, she asked her teammates, who also taught mathematics, about what they were doing. Through this reflective conversation, Ms. Tijerina realized that she should not have omitted the step of working with the manipulatives. She decided to create a lesson with the students using manipulatives and video record the students. She would review the video recording to see how the students were interacting with the manipulatives and with their teammates to understand how they were learning the math concepts. After observing how the students worked with the manipulatives and their teammates, she created some new lessons that better taught the objectives. Once she felt that they had mastered the concepts, she gave them a pencil-and-paper test to see if they mastered the mathematics benchmarks.

Introduction

Throughout a teacher preparation program, preservice teachers receive guidance as they consider curricular, management, and assessment decisions based on educational theory and best practices. During field experiences and student teaching, teacher candidates are shown how and why they must purposefully think about the decisions they will make in the classroom as they prepare to assume their roles as certified teachers of record. In the teacher preparation classroom, preservice teachers review related theories, develop skills, and gain an understanding of how such information should influence their practice—often encouraged by their program's assignments to reflect on lesson plans, teaching incidents, assessment results, and so forth.

During this time, some preservice teachers begin to develop their own reflective practices, which they will hopefully implement in their future classrooms. Reflective teaching requires that constructive criticism come not only from support personnel (e.g., mentors, university supervisors, principals) but from oneself as well.

The term "induction" is used to refer to a period during which a new teacher completes an introductory period, which is normally equivalent to one's first year as a teacher. In order to assist new teachers during their induction year in transitioning into a new role, some districts (and even some universities or other teacher preparation programs) assign them induction mentors. The purpose of these mentors is to serve as a support system and to provide peer evaluation to help new teachers.

Beyond the induction year, in the early years of the teaching career, teachers must develop the practice of automatically assessing the quality of the educational practices they use and the educational experiences they provide their students. The inservice teacher cannot simply rely on trained personnel to initiate dialogue regarding his/her strengths or weaknesses of teaching in the classroom; rather this must begin to occur internally. For teachers of record, there is no longer a university professor, field supervisor, or mentor teacher in the back of the classroom to observe and offer suggestions for improvement. Even a principal is only there a very limited amount of time during the year, so the teacher must be his/her own assessor for all educational interactions that go on during each day.

One of the most difficult aspects of the teaching profession is the professional isolation from colleagues that it imposes on its practitioners (Danielson & McGreal, 2000). Teachers spend most of their days alone in their own classrooms with their own students. Few opportunities are available to casually observe, discuss with, and learn from other teachers or other educators such as specialists or professors. Little time is available to consult with one's colleagues about a difficult dilemma. As Danielson and McGreal state,

Figure 14.1 Students use cubes as manipulatives to solve math problems.

> The isolation of teachers has been well documented. On their evaluation forms after a workshop, many teachers will write that the opportunity to discuss issues with their colleagues was the most beneficial aspect of the day. Teaching is highly complex, and most teachers have scant opportunity to explore common problems and possible solutions, or share new pedagogical approaches with their colleagues. (p. 24)

The awareness of who we are, what we bring to the classroom, who we teach, and the most appropriate practices needed to provide an excellent and equitable educational experience to students must be much more heightened. Nonetheless, the task of reflecting on each and every decision made, the action that was taken (or was intended to be taken), and the words uttered—and the consequences of such practices—is vital in knowing how to teach the content which students must acquire and to address the whole child and his/her development in all areas. In other words, teachers must not only be their own toughest critics but must also become knowledgeable in ways to address the issues that are uncovered through their own intentional reflective teaching practices.

Background

Reflective Practice: Definitions and Perspectives

Thinking is a natural process of the human psyche. Thinking is also what makes people, in general, human. Everyone is always thinking about something. Even when one says, "I don't want to think about it," thinking is happening. Some people do their best thinking in the shower, driving to work, or right before they wake up from a deep sleep. Dewey (1933) described the differences between random thought and reflective thought as "a consecutive ordering in such a way that determines the next thought as its proper outcome" (p. 13). Reflective thoughts are consecutive and with consequences. They grow from one another and support one another through consecutive thought pattern. This might be termed the "If . . . then" process of thought for teachers. When thoughts are connected, they become reflective thoughts. For example, Mr. Gaston thought to himself, "Karla has been acting upset all day. *IF* I call on her today, *THEN* she is likely to withdraw completely. . . ."

Mrs. Salinas was in a conference with parents, and she perceived that they were becoming very defensive. "*IF* I will just listen a moment," she told herself, "*THEN* I will give them a chance to vent their frustrations with the situation, and we can go on from there."

In order to manage reflective thought, people often write in a journal, discuss their thoughts with others, contribute to a weblog (blog), record their audio reflections, and so forth. Through journaling and other reflection activities, they become observers of their own learning environments.

Schön (1983) described reflective thinking as a process of using prior knowledge, expertise, and experience to reframe a problem. When reflective practitioners find patterns or view actions from different perspectives, they may arrive at a new idea or a different solution. Many people, for example, may accept a particular practice as tradition that has been established by an authority. They accept the everyday reality as "that's how it should be because (most often) that is the way it has always been done." Schön, however, described how *reflective* practitioners experience a disequilibrium or difficulty in the everyday practice under question. They begin to ask: "Why did this not work? Why do we do it this way? Could there be an even better way?" The traditional practice that once seemed effective and efficient is now a problem that needs a solution. Schön suggested that approaching such situations requires a process that involves action that is persistent and with careful consideration. This reflective process necessitates intuition, emotion, and passion to follow through with necessary changes that will cause the reflective practitioner to approach the problem with new perspectives.

Argyris and Schön (1974) believed that reflective practitioners must integrate thought with action. The traditional way of doing things becomes what is termed the "Theory in Use" (p. 3). They found that when reflective practitioners integrated knowledge or expertise with competence and rigor, the reflective practitioner moves from solving problems from Theory in Use ("what is") to Theory in Action ("what can be"). Reflective practitioners become competent in taking action to learn from the situation and then take action to solve the problem. Zeichner and Liston (1996) applied this theory to teachers. They found that when teachers think about their teaching, they look at problems in the classroom (or even everyday practices that may not be as effective as they could be) from different perspectives or angles, ask themselves and others questions about their own teaching practices and actions, and examine their motives and attitudes within the context in which they work. Table 14.1 lists 22 common themes found in teacher candidates' weekly reflective journals (Doyran, 2013).

Table 14.1   Common themes found in teacher candidates' reflective journals (Doyran, 2013)

1. Self-awareness
2. Awareness related to students
3. Awareness related to teaching profession
4. Awareness related to schools
5. Methodological issues/theory
6. Preparing and grading exams
7. Positive and negative factors affecting the pre-service teachers' performance while teaching
8. Motivational factors
9. Personality factors which influence the teaching-learning process
10. Professional factors related to teachers
11. Classroom management and how difficult it can be
12. Teacher roles/characteristics in the classroom and while teaching
13. Different roles mentor teacher should have
14. The importance of time management
15. Peer pressure while teaching
16. Peer motivation while teaching
17. Mentor teacher pressure (as they are observing and giving feedback and grades)
18. Feedback received from peers
19. Feedback received from the mentor teachers
20. Feedback received from the supervisor at the university
21. Rules and regulations at school
22. Effective blackboard use

The surge of interactive technology in recent time opens doors for preservice and inservice teachers to find useful technology tools to support their engagement in reflective practices throughout their teaching process (see Figure 14.2). By utilizing electronic journals, blogs, and social media, reflective practitioners can evaluate the teaching events they experience. They use the technology tools to document the problems they encounter throughout the teaching process, identify the problems that evolve from the event, and determine solutions to the problems. Using tools such as blogs and interactive journals (synchronous, or real time, and asynchronous, or "any time") provide computer mediated communication for teacher reflection with teams on the problems they experience. Teachers collaborate together by writing about or recording the event, sharing the reflections with each other, and developing solutions to the problems with colleagues as a team.

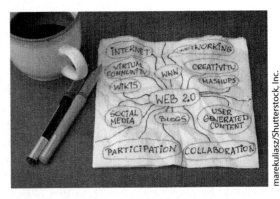

Figure 14.2   A concept web shows a variety of ways and technology tools to facilitate reflective practices.

Technology tools allow effective practitioners to move from a technical, traditional format to an intuitive, conscious choice of being. Greene (1978) described this process as being "wide awake" or conscious and noted that a teacher's decision making must be based on research, knowledge of the youth in the classroom, and self-awareness. Greene summarized the transformative process that teachers experience when they are examining their practice in the following way: the teacher facilitates the teaching process with students, reflects about what worked or did not work, and adjusts the process to meet the needs of the students (see Figure 14.3). When Ms. Tijerina, for example, realized that her students did not do well on the mathematics benchmark tests, she reflected on what she had done during the teaching process. She collaborated with her colleagues to discover what might be missing from her lesson and used technology tools to capture the data. This reflective

Figure 14.3   The teacher facilitates the teaching process, reflects, and changes the process to meet the needs of learners.

process moves teachers from thinking about what *they* are doing in the teaching process to reflecting about what works for the *students* in the classroom.

As noted, teachers break from the traditional or mechanical ways of teaching by asking questions—particularly "why" questions (see Figure 14.4). This questioning process requires teachers to attend more fully to their own professional lives and to question *what is* to *what could be* in the *ideal* teaching and learning process (refer to Figure 14.4). Technology tools create a space for the teachers to shift from their regular thinking processes in teaching and move to a more collaborative space with a team of teachers. This creates the transformative teaching process where the teacher actually becomes the learner by closely examining data from an educational incident.

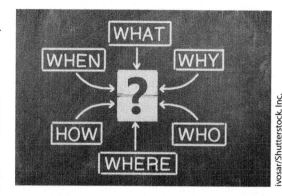

Figure 14.4   Teachers break from the traditional or mechanical ways of teaching by asking questions.

Intentional inquiry is an important part of the reflective process. Teachers will begin to self-question by realizing a situation or a problem is not working or is not right for students in some way. This could occur in any area of their practice—with a child's learning or management, with a parent, colleague, or administrator, and so forth. They experience disequilibrium or dissonance and deliberately ask, "Why didn't this work?" Then, they begin asking, "What could I have done differently in this situation?" Schön (1983) called this **reframing the problem** or situation. Once reflective practitioners can reframe the problem, they **question the existing framework**, see patterns within the framework, and look for new ideas. This inquiry process leads the practitioners to **possible changes or solutions**. They **test their new solution** to see if it works, and, if it does not, they **repeat the questioning cycle** for other solutions.

Reflective practitioners reframe the problem or conflict in a way that may create a surprise or even illicit an "aha" for the problem or solution (Schön, 1983). Reflective teachers also want to see if the new solution is an ethically sound practice by knowing best practices and researching, if needed. The solution needs to be compared with their own values and perspectives to see if they now have a new perspective through which to view the situation. They need to know if it "feels right" for their personality and teaching styles and *is* right for learners. If it is, the reflective practitioners will adapt their situation to a new framework of knowledge.

Figure 14.5   Reflective practitioners question their perspectives, beliefs, teaching practices, and actions.

Teachers who are reflective practitioners follow this process while also exploring their own personal motives and context in which they work. They question their perspectives and beliefs about the students they teach (see Figure 14.5). They examine their own personal assumptions and biases to know what and why they believe. This personal reflection leads teachers to look into their own stories so they can understand who they are and why they respond as they do in different situations. This personal introspection allows teachers to take ownership of their own teaching practices so they keep what is important to them while making needed changes. They are able to use inquiry on their own teaching practices and actions to make their practice better for students, colleagues, parents, administrators, and themselves. Teacher candidates may begin to follow this process, too. A level of self-doubt is common when teachers (or teacher candidates) ask themselves some of the following questions:

- Am I really a good teacher (or going to be a good teacher)? Why or why not? What can I do about it if the answer is negative in any way?
- How does my teaching style compare to the styles of colleagues?
- Are my lessons engaging, and are they increasing academic performance?
- Are my classroom management skills as effective as those of other teachers in my school? Are they good for children?
- Can I communicate effectively with parents?

- Can I address the needs of *all* learners and students with various learning styles?
- Do I have biases which become oblivious to students in the classroom? Is my classroom a positive place for all students?

Although difficult at first (especially when one is totally honest with oneself), this type of questioning can become a way of life with practice. Some have likened it to performing on stage, while at the same time, sitting in the audience at a play judging how that performance is progressing (Osterman & Kottkamp, 1993). Teacher education programs encourage this practice to become automatic through adding reflection components to many assignments during courses of study to self-evaluate.

When coupled with technology integration, a teacher must ask introspective questions such as these and many more:

- Are students really different learners than when I was in school, and must I use technology in different ways to reach them?
- Am I not using technology (or not using it to its full potential) because I don't know how, don't feel comfortable, and/or need more training?
- Am I making good choices in the technology I use, or am I just using technology as an electronic overhead projector or for drill games?
- Am I assuming that all children and their families have (or have had) access to technology?
- Have I made technology use safe in my classroom?
- Would I know if there were cyberbullying incidents occurring with my students?
- Am I aware of the latest technology integration strategies?

Obtaining proficiency in technology and reflective teaching practices is as important for the preservice teacher as acquiring content area knowledge and classroom management skills (see Figure 14.6). Proficiency in the use of technology is no longer preferred, but required. Today's teacher must be able to manage administrative tasks such as taking attendance and submitting lesson plans electronically, using the educational hardware and software available on campus for instruction and resources, and becoming familiar with possible educational opportunities of social media and common electronic devices such as cell phones and tablets. For example, Ms. Long, knows that best teaching practices includes grouping, so she uses a search engine on her computer to type in "cooperative learning groups methodology YouTube", which resulted in numerous pages of ideas and videos of these models. Not only does the integration of technology enhance the students' acquisition of content and increase their development of the twenty-first century skills required for the workforce, it also facilitates the process of reflective teaching for teachers who engage in reflective practices on a regular basis to enhance the educational experiences of their students.

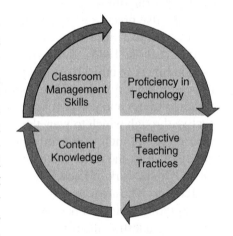

Figure 14.6 Professionalism in teaching has many facets, including obtaining proficiency in technology and reflective teaching practice.

Preservice teachers can utilize electronic devices such as cell phones, digital cameras, and tablets by carrying them into the classrooms. Connectivity with the Internet gives them the flexibility to upload data, take pictures, or create documents within the real time of teaching. They can send this information to colleagues, students, and/or parents for feedback. The preservice teacher learns how to transfer personal knowledge of electronic devices, social media, and media to use in their teaching process. Data is the subject of reflection and more easily captured, reviewed, and analyzed when teachers use electronic devices to facilitate reflection on their teaching practices. Tasks that once took weeks to organize and complete, such as scoring and analyzing certain types of assessment or videotaping a teaching episode, can now be done instantaneously. For example, by using apps and some online services such as Google Docs (with the Flubarro extension), teachers can easily create assignments and auto grade them without having to always take stacks of papers home. Preservice teachers can not only observe their mentor teachers with whom they work, they can also observe their own teaching practices through digital recordings.

Figure 14.7   Preservice teachers utilize cell phones, digital cameras, tablets, and other devices to observe their mentor teachers and/or their own teaching practices.

Preservice teachers by definition are novices who should show sufficient growth in the areas of critical thinking and "effective reflection" on their paths towards becoming autonomous teachers during their teacher preparation programs (Loughran, 2002). A number of educational researchers have studied this area. Rodman's (2010) study showed that preservice teachers' reflections demonstrated a better understanding of how to apply good theory and strategies to create stronger educational opportunities for students. They shifted from an egocentric perspective to being able to consider how their actions impacted the students; their reflection, in general, exhibited a more student-centered perspective. This shift in perspective should be a natural growth progression. For example, Malek, a senior education major, had just finished his last student teaching lesson. He and three other student teachers at the school were sitting in the lounge reminiscing about how scared they had been in the beginning. In regards to management, they had, at first, not noticed half of what was occurring in the classroom. "My mentor sat down with me almost every day, and we 'went over it.'" Malek said. "Now, my class can't get away with anything! I see every trick. In the beginning I was just so focused on getting the information out that I couldn't even think of anything else. Now, if you search multi-tasker in the dictionary, you'll see a picture of me!" Participating in reflective practices with supportive educators such as mentors and supervisors during the preservice years helps future educators develop professionally and personally so they can move into self-sufficient reflective practice. As well, their familiarity and deeper understanding of the importance of reflective teaching carries over to their appointment as inservice teachers (Ward & McCotter, 2004). Using electronic modes to reflect on one's teaching, interactions, and beliefs helps to facilitate the reflection process and broaden the scope of information acquired through such a process.

When preservice teachers learn about and practice reflective teaching during their field assignments, they carry that experience with them into the classroom as novice teachers. For example, they find ways to utilize electronic devices in a manner that others who may be less technically experienced may not have used. The energy that novice teachers bring into the classroom is invaluable because they can remind many experienced teachers of the importance of reflective practice while using electronic devices. The preservice teachers develop skills by reflecting about their teaching experiences, observing their mentor teachers, and observing students *with intentionality* in the classroom (see Figure 14.7). Preservice educators begin the transformative practice of teaching by developing the practice of reflecting; these skills are then utilized as they enter their own classroom as a teacher of record.

Seeing Through Others' Eyes

In order to make such discoveries about one's self, an educator must engage in the practice of "withitness." First coined by Kounin in 1970, the term "withitness" refers to a teacher's awareness of what is happening in the classroom at all times (Gettinger & Kohler, 2011). Originally used in the context of classroom management, the implications of "withitness" touch nearly every aspect of teaching. Extending the idea of "withitness" to teachers purposefully monitoring and analyzing their own practices and beliefs about education is not a stretch but rather a first step towards incorporating reflective practices in teaching.

Becoming a reflective educator involves intense introspection on the part of the individual, and, therefore, some may mistake reflective teaching for an isolated undertaking rather than a continuous "loop" (or loops) of inquiry (refer to Figure 14.8). However, there is much more of a collaborative nature required to partake in reflective teaching practices. In fact, there may be (and should be) many of these loops occurring at the same time about multiple areas of teaching (e.g., instructional methods, management, efficiency, working with parents, technology integration, and many more). Effectively reflecting on one's beliefs, teaching, and classroom practices requires not only one's own teaching but gaining an understanding of how others perceive the educational practices as well.

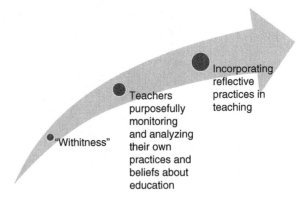

Figure 14.8   A teacher moves from idea of "withitness" and reflective practices to incorporating more effective practices into teaching.

Brookfield (2002) argues that critical reflection must incorporate the perspectives and experiences of others. He states that teachers must consider four lenses when examining their own teaching: (1) the autobiographical lens, (2) the students' perspectives, (3) colleagues' experiences, and (4) theoretical literature (refer to Figure 14.9). The information gleaned from critical reflection based on the use of these four lenses not only allows educators to make more informed judgments about their teaching practices, but teachers gain confidence and a new found engagement in their teaching practices through consulting other sources as a part of reflection.

As a preservice teacher, the teacher candidate learns about and is encouraged to participate in reflection as a requirement of a university course or program requisite, usually as part of the fieldwork experience. Teacher candidates, as part of the teacher preparation process, normally have at their disposal their peers, cooperating teacher, and university supervisor who will encourage and remind them to use reflective practices. Once certification is obtained, however, the inservice teacher must provide a personal impetus and seek out feedback from students, colleagues, administrators, and students' families for information regarding the instructional practices. This requires the preservice teacher to follow the training and experiences he or she learned during their teacher preparation program and to recognize the confidence in teaching that he or she now has. According to Rodman (2010), preservice teachers who receive the opportunity to witness and develop reflective teaching practices are more likely to apply good theory to their practices and move away from teacher-centered reflection towards student-centered reflection. They develop the confidence and the efficacy in themselves to make decisions for the benefit of their students. The preservice teacher discovers the responsibility of being the teacher with open-mindedness and wide-awakeness as described by Greene (1995). Greene believed that when teachers began the reflective process, they were expected to make good choices and decisions for children. These are based upon their own training and experiences and that of other respected experts in the educational system.

kiri1/Shutterstock, Inc.

Figure 14.9   Brookfield's (2002) four lenses of self-examination.

Figure 14.10 In addition to Brookfield's (2002) four lenses, the family lens should also be considered.

Autobiographical lens

Perhaps the most obvious piece of being a reflective teacher is that of consciously thinking about one's own teaching and practice through one's past experiences from "the self" perspective (Figure 14.11). Although no singular definition of reflection exists, all descriptions incorporate the act of self-reflection and problem posing (Loughram, 2002). The most basic type of reflection requires educators to consciously think back on their teaching or other educational interactions, identify ways that facilitate and impede student learning, and make changes to improve the educational interaction in the class and better meet students' needs. Davis (2006) warns that self-reflection must be productive reflection, requiring the practitioner to move beyond mere description of what occurs in the classroom to an analysis

Figure 14.11 Teachers use conscious introspection to improve teaching.

of teaching and learning and then to action. Productive self-reflection, according to Davis, includes two indicators: knowledge integration and analysis. Teachers demonstrate knowledge integration during reflection when they notice and reflect on four aspects of teaching: (1) instruction, (2) learners and learning, (3) content area knowledge, and (4) assessment. She also holds that reflection must not be teacher-centered but must include a student-centered focus aimed at understanding how students learn and how the instruction addresses those needs.

Apart from reflecting on different aspects of teaching, the ideas of time and purpose must also be considered to practice effective reflection. Although reflection means analyzing past actions, it is important to engage in meaningful reflection at different stages throughout the process. Reflection-on-action includes analyzing the practice *after* it occurs, while reflection-in-action occurs *during* practice (Schön, 1983), usually during a moment when realization occurs that a change in midstream could be more fruitful. Reflection-on to-future action occurs when teachers practice thinking ahead about what *will* or *could* happen, and they try to change it before mistakes are made. Loughran (2002) notes that the type of information one can collect differs as a result of anticipatory, retrospective, and contemporaneous reflection. Although the teacher reflects on the same situation, the change of time, perspective, experience, and framing yield different sets of information that enhances understanding and allows for effective change in practice to occur. Participating in video self-analysis, for example, can help verify one's recollection of a lesson or interaction and make a more accurate assessment of classroom management, identify mannerisms, and improve overall teaching. Dye (2007) as cited in Snoeyink (2010) notes that analyzing video of oneself helps teachers "revise their internal representations of their own performance, thus more accurately identifying their own performance gap" (p. 102). In today's world, digital video recording devices make this extremely easy.

The Student Lens

The basis of all reflection in teaching is to enhance the educational experiences of the students in the classroom. If students are not learning, it makes no difference how well the teacher believes he or she is doing—it is not enough. An observant and reflective teacher can make educated decisions in planning and conclusions regarding the success of a lesson, particular classroom practices, or interactions; nonetheless, the most accurate information about the students' perception of the success of an educational experience comes from the student. Teachers should evaluate the success of their actions not based solely on student achievement on assessments or the students' perceived level of engagement but also include opportunities to solicit information from students about their educational experiences.

One aspect that should also be included is the socio-emotional environment in the classroom. If students are to provide full attention to the learning activities, their affective filter must be minimally triggered. Although the affective filter hypothesis was proposed by Krashen (1984) and was specific to second language acquisition, the idea that the learning environment will affect a student's level of anxiety, motivation, and self-confidence transfers across all learning environments. Teachers must constantly reflect on the environment they create and address issues that may arise. Creating opportunities for students to submit feedback on how enjoyable, comprehensible, or relatable a lesson or activity was can help the teacher modify or design future learning experiences.

Again, technology in today's classrooms can make this easy. Younger children can complete an end of day online survey where they choose the appropriate "face" or "emoticon" (emotional icons) which describes how they feel and tell the teacher (through an automatic recording) why they feel that way. The teacher can also set up an anonymous and/or confidential messaging option in the online classroom workspace to allow students to provide feedback about the lessons, activities, or student interactions which they may not feel comfortable stating to the teacher face to face.

Figure 14.12 Expressions teachers can use for feedback with younger children.

Essential to obtaining accurate, honest feedback from students is to build a trusting rapport with them. If the teacher shows interest and fairness and explains how the feedback is used to enhance the classroom experience, students will tend to provide useful comments. Some suggestions for eliciting student feedback include using interviews or student focus groups to receive whole class feedback in a face-to-face fashion. These arrangements can easily be adapted to online or electronic collection through a survey tool such as SurveyMonkey, Socrative, Google Forms, or learning management software similar to Blackboard Learn or Moodle. Teachers can solicit student feedback through the use of response forms such as the Critical Incident Questionnaire (CIQ) which requires students to comment on the strong, weak, and unique moments in the classroom (Brookfield, 1995). Students provide the teacher with insight into their perspectives about the learning experiences on a weekly basis through a CIQ which allows them to share their opinions freely and maintain anonymity (see Figure 14.13).

Brookfield's Critical Incident Questionnaire

Please respond to the following questions about this week's classes:

1. At what moment did you feel most engaged with what was happening?
2. At what moment were you most distanced from what was happening?
3. What action, taken by anyone (teacher or student), did you find most helpful?
4. What action, taken by anyone (teacher or student), did you find most puzzling or confusing?
5. What about the class surprised you the most? (This could be about your own reactions to what went on, something that someone did, or anything else that occurs).

Adapted from Brookfield, S.D. (1995). *Becoming a critically reflective teacher.* San Francisco: Jossey Bass.

Figure 14.13   Critical Incident Questionnaires (CIQs) solicit student feedback about strong and weak areas of a lesson.

Figure 14.14 Students use a classroom response system to provide instantaneous feedback to the teacher.

Classroom Response Systems (CRS) solicit responses from students through the use of clickers that allow educators to poll their students on questions of their choice given a multiple choice format (see Figure 14.14). If the campus does not have a CRS, a software-based audience response tool may be used as an alternative. Web-based audience response and polling tools function in a similar manner, but the information is transmitted through the Internet, and students can use their cellular or smart phones, tablets, or laptops to submit their answers. The results are tabulated synchronously and can be discussed immediately, if desired. There are several free Web-based audience response tools as well as options that include a monthly charge for the service.

The Peer Lens

As mentioned earlier, the teaching profession can, at times, seem like an isolated and lonely profession. Throughout the school day, teachers are involved in instruction in their classroom, with the exception of planning and lunch. There are very few opportunities during the school day to communicate with colleagues—and even fewer opportunities to have a colleague observe one's teaching practices or vice versa. Nonetheless, having the input of a colleague who has a familiarity with the campus culture, student body, and common habits of teaching, can be invaluable. Apart from receiving a different perspective on teaching and learning issues, communication with a colleague helps to build support—a major factor in teacher retention. In order to gain information through the peer lens, a teacher must be willing to initiate dialogue with colleagues in the field; this dialogue can occur in face to face or virtual forums.

The idea is to open lines of communication and collaboration with other educators. First-year, and occasionally teachers who are new to a school, are usually assigned a mentor who provides an instant opportunity to discuss ideas or dilemmas related to improving one's educational practices. Another collaborative space, a professional learning community (PLC), is a group of educators working collaboratively to seek answers to their questions, share what they discover, and act upon their new knowledge to enhance a school's effectiveness in the education of its students (Hord, 1997). If educators reflect on the "big ideas" of a PLC (e.g.,

Web-based Audience Response Tools	Free Web-based Audience Response Tools
ClickerSchool: www. clickerschool.com	Infuse Learning: www.infuselearning.com
LectureTools: www. lecturetools.com	Kahoot: www.getkahoot.com
Poll Everywhere: www. polleverywhere.com	Verso: www.versoapp.com
QuestionPress: www.questionpress.com	Mentimeter: www.mentimeter.com/
Socrative: www.socrative.com	Google Forms: www.google.com/forms/about/
Top Hat: www.tophat.com	

Figure 14.15 Web-based audience response systems can be used with personal electronic devices such as laptops, cell phones, and tables.

ensuring that students learn, creating a culture of collaboration, and focusing on the results), then teachers will be more reflective in their practices to evaluate the effectiveness of learning in their classroom (DuFour, 2004). Peer coaching, Critical Friends Groups, and structured group problem solving, along with intentional investigative improvement, collaborative dialogue, and structured communities of practice construct ways for teachers to interact with peers for the sake of improving education. Partner or group collaboration such as peer coaching, even as a preservice teacher, can foster the development of reflective practices, which, in turn, can produce an inservice teacher who enters the first years of teaching understanding the importance of reflection and actively seeking support from peers (Kurtts & Levin, 2000). Collegial feedback and collaboration can be easily facilitated through electronic means by creating online communities of practice (CoP). These can be particularly effective when group members are not in close physical proximity with one another or to allow for asynchronous communication which allows for different schedules. Lave and Wenger (1991) proposed the idea of a CoP as a group of people sharing a common interest and a desire to engage in and contribute to practices of their community (as cited in Lee & Brett, 2013). The rapidly growing networking platforms and spaces easily provide for virtual communities of practitioners. Blogging, wikis, discussion boards, and social networking spaces allow for the formation of CoP and PLCs where educators can discuss topics of interest and concern with the goal of finding solutions to implement and improve the education of their students in classrooms around the world (Salazar, Aguirre-Muñoz, Fox, & Nuanez-Lucas, 2010). Just as with face-to-face group dialogue, it is important to join online collaborative communities that provide for a safe space to discuss questions and concerns as well as contribute to the development of others. It may be to one's benefit to join an online community where information can be shared with a broader audience as well as maintain a semblance of anonymity. Remaining anonymous allows a teacher to speak freely without having to censor the posting to avoid judgment or identification by coworkers or to worry about being connected to controversial topics occurring on their particular campus.

Like professional learning communities, peer coaching, and communities of practice, anonymous online platforms for educators give teachers opportunities to bring their questions, concerns, and ideas to a group of educators who will provide insight through the peer lens. In online discussion forums such as the Teacher Chatboards section of Teachers.net (http://teachers.net/) and the Communities section of Edutopia (http://www.edutopia.org/community), educators connect on an anonymous platform while staying connected with a large network of educators. For instance, as of November 2014, some topics that are relevant to new teachers or teacher candidates in the Communities section of Edutopia are:

- 5 Quick Classroom-Management Tips for Novice Teachers
- What I Wish I'd Known as a New Teacher
- Avoiding New Teacher Burnout

The initial post of the discussion topic titled "Avoiding New Teacher Burnout" was dated October 7, 2014. Within three weeks, over 1,300 people reviewed this Edutopia online discussion thread created by a new teacher with the question, "Daily, I see teachers that are in the 'burnout' stage of teaching . . . I see students suffering due to the fact that their teachers have given up. I am asking for advice on how to avoid the 'burnout' stage. Any advice?" (Gadawg 01, 2014).

One English teacher responded by stating that this is a time of changing attitudes in education and suggested that the new teacher embrace "teacher moments" by finding one positive moment every day. She continued to advise that students react to teachers' positive energy which will, in turn, lead to more of those teacher moments. The English teacher wouldn't go so far as suggesting that new teachers avoid "teacher spaces" where she might pick up "negative vibes", however (LDee, 2014). Another teacher suggested that the new teacher might have heard frustration vents from teachers who have been at it for a long time but felt that those teachers are still good teachers and may have just needed to talk it out (OffBeatTeach, 2014). Then the forum facilitator suggested that the new teacher may want to find a new community of people with whom she could laugh (people from outside of the educational community) because non-teacher friends might help teachers gain perspective (Thomas, 2014).

When facing "professional burnout", "becoming overwhelmed", or needing to talk about other common or confidential issues, new teachers sometimes can be embarrassed, may not feel safe talking to other teachers on their campus, or simply may not be able to find an understanding adult with whom to have a discussion.

Anonymous online forums such as the above provide a safe channel for novice and mentor teachers to share experiences. Regardless of the space used, a teacher must remember, however, to always remain professional with any dialogue.

The Theoretical Lens

Although Schön's (1983) book, *The Reflective Practitioner*, was in a way a reaction to the contemporary focus on book knowledge, there is relevance to being abreast of current research and literature when reflecting on one's teaching practices. University educators, administrators, psychologists, classroom teachers, and others seek to inform others about their studies and findings on a myriad of topics about teaching and learning. More informed, accurate decision making occurs when a teacher incorporates researched-based practices in the classroom. Whether the concern relates to lesson planning, strategies to use with students with exceptionalities, how to provide a comprehensible education to an English language learner, or ways to strengthen classroom management, information from strong educational research should be incorporated into the decision making process.

One of the most obvious ways to build knowledge about the field is to subscribe to journals related to education and particular fields within education. As students, preservice teachers typically have access to their university library's electronic journals and books. Using databases such as Education Resources Information Center (ERIC) (http://eric.ed.gov/) or Educational Full Text (http://www.ebscohost.com/academic/education-full-text) puts a wealth of knowledge at one's fingertips. Professional organizations or societies such as the National Council of Teachers of English (www.ncte.org) (*Voices from the Middle*), the National Association for Bilingual Education (www.nabe.org) (*Bilingual Research Journal*), or Kappa Delta Pi (*New Teacher Advocate*) may also maintain associated journals, and many organizations offer a membership discount for students. Many of these journals are electronic. Even without joining the organization, there is often information available to the public on the website. Most organizations now have additional ways to stay connected by following them on Facebook, Twitter, LinkedIn, Google+, Pintrest, or YouTube. A number of organizations have annual conferences as well, and many now have electronic connections to papers, presentations, or addresses by experts at these conferences for members.

Additional ways to stay informed about current research and trends in the field include participating in professional development, joining e-mail listservs or discussion boards, and subscribing to e-newsletters. Many educational organizations and leaders now offer webinars that can serve as professional development opportunities and, occasionally, as mentioned, keynote presentations from conferences are available on the Web as well. Subscribing to really simple syndication or rich site summary (RSS) feeds allows a teacher to have data from favorite websites monitored automatically without the need to visit the sites individually. By checking favorite Web sites with educational information, a teacher can get an aggregator (feed reader) such as FeedReader or ReadKit (which can read the feeds) and subscribe to the RSS feeds of one's choice. See Table 14.2 for a small sample of sites with RSS feeds that inform about current research in the field

RSS feeds list the most recent additions to the Web site's content in reverse chronological order and include the title and the first line of text. By clicking on the title, the reader is immediately connected to the content. To identify sites with RSS feeds, look for the RSS symbol, typically an orange square with white radio waves, on the Web page (see Figure 14.16).

Table 14.2 A list of sites with RSS feeds that inform about current research in the field

Institutes	Web Addresses
Institute of Education Sciences-What Works Clearinghouse	http://www.ies.ed.gov/ncee/wwc
National Association for Multicultural Education	http://www.nameorg.org
Autism Speaks	http://www.autismspeaks.org
U.S. Department of Education	http://www.ed.gov
National Science Teachers Association	http://www.nsta.org

The Family Lens (refer to Figure 14.10)

Introspection, peers, and theory from communities of educators are not the only areas that should be considered as part of reflective practice. Families of students have specific goals, needs, or desires for their children, and each can provided feedback to the teacher regarding the family's perception on how the teacher is meeting their needs. Families can also provide important information about their child which can be taken into account by the reflective teacher. Ideally, the family member(s) and teacher will meet, and this process can be facilitated by online scheduling tools such as SignUpGenius or Doodle. However, engaging in electronic communication can aid family-teacher interaction as well. Surveys or questionnaires, which solicit information about the child, can be disseminated through electronic mail, the teacher's Web page, or social learning platforms like Edmodo. Educators can encourage feedback from families by engaging them in classroom activities and posting information online. Parent-teacher conferences can have an optional electronic option for family members who are unable to visit the campus. Such conferences can occur through Skype, FaceTime, or online collaboration software like

Figure 14.16   RSS feeds provide links to the most recently updated content on the organization's website. Sites with RSS feeds insert the RSS symbol on their webpage.

Blackboard Collaborate. Although a teacher may choose to engage families in electronic communication, it is important to note that the same amount of professionalism and caution is required in any communication between the school and the family—electronic or otherwise. Additionally, each educator must check with his or her district to see which of these video sites, if any, are blocked by school firewalls. By opening the lines of communication between the family and the teacher and by explicitly asking for feedback from family members of the students teachers can incorporate the familial lens into their reflection as well, always keeping in mind that teachers cannot automatically assume that all families have digital access (the Digital Divide).

Reflective Practices to Consider

As with many aspects of being a strong, effective teacher, becoming a reflective practitioner requires preparation and practice. Although many educators may engage in a reflective teaching practice "here and there", for the most part reflective teachers are not born but created through their own sense of responsibility for themselves, their students, their profession, and for society. Reflective teaching is an ongoing, continual process which one develops and modifies overtime. Incorporating reflective teaching practices allows educators to strengthen the education provided to students by maintaining a heightened level of awareness of their interactions with students, peers, and families. Simply reflecting on the day's events is not the totality of reflective teaching. Zeichner and Liston (1996) propose five features of a reflective teacher which include:

- attempting to solve a problem in their practice,
- acknowledging and questioning the assumptions and values they bring to the class,
- recognizing the cultural and institutional environments in which they teach,
- participating in curriculum development and school change, and
- being responsible for furthering their professional development.

By participating in a variety of reflective teaching practices, the teacher increases the possibility of properly modifying their lesson and other teaching practices.

Dewey (1933) also added the ideas of open-mindedness, responsibility, and wholeheartedness to reflective teaching. Accordingly, a teacher must take responsibility for reflecting and for the consequences of one's actions. Teachers must do this wholeheartedly to maintain focus on what is best for the learner, considering all possibilities with an open mind—even the possibility that they themselves could be wrong.

As noted, engaging in reflective practice takes time and requires a collaborative environment. Educators must reflect within themselves, collect feedback from students and families, identify colleagues who are willing to participate in the ongoing collaborative effort, and stay well-read in current educational research. One way to facilitate the process is to incorporate multimedia technologies in the reflective process. In the following section, we present a description of common reflective teaching practices along with more examples of ways to facilitate such practices through the use of technology.

Journaling

There is an emerging body of literature that addresses the use of multimedia tools, computer-supported collaborative learning, and other Web-based products as options for reflective practice for teachers. Studies such as Kajder & Parkes (2012) and Killeavy & Moloney (2010) explore the use of Weblogs and videologs as tools for reflective practice. The blog is a Web site, or the contents of the Web site, that contains personal commentary, or reflections, while a vlog is a blog that has video content. Both studies found that these forums can be used to reflect on one's own teaching as well as solicit feedback in a peer-review setting. While Killeavy and Moloney's study was less definitive regarding the benefits of Weblogs, they suggest that establishing a sense of community is important to promote contributors' willingness to share. As well, they suggest that using blogs instead of print journals is beneficial for individuals or communities in rural or distant areas. Stronger support for the use of blogs and vlogs was found by Kajder and Parkes (2012) who also identified the benefit of electronic journaling in creating online communities of practice that were vast and had a broader physical range. It was noted that Web 2.0 tools captured more raw, "thinking in the moment" entries than printed reflection. As a contributor to a blog or vlog, a teacher has access to a larger community of practice, allowing for the possibility or varying points of view, constructive critique, and viable solutions to enhance the students' learning experiences. Electronic journaling is available through e-mails, blogs, vlogs, word processing, and Webpages; all allow for electronic journaling to occur. Some options also allow the teacher to include images, audio and video, and links to additional content. Again, confidentiality is paramount when sharing, and professional guidelines must always be followed. When considering the type of medium to use, teachers may want to consider their comfort level with the tool, the expectations or guidelines they view of a particular medium, and their willingness to explore technology that may enhance their own reflections.

Shoffner (2009) discovered that her students had certain beliefs about the capacity and/or expectations of different electronic resources. For example, does a particular tool require an entry of a specific length? Is this forum more (or less) confidential than another? Who will be reading this entry, and is it okay to use less formal language and structure in one forum versus another? Kadjer and Parkes' (2012) study revealed that blogged reflections were more "surface" in nature, while vlogged reflections were more "pedagogical" in nature. Sample surface level reflections include more logistical comments: "I started class by calling them 'to order,' taking role, and speaking a couple of minutes on business matters. I reminded them of homework due the following day and went over the plan for today's class" (p. 237). Pedagogical level reflections such as "I knew that they were learning because when we would do the criticism part of it—after listening—they knew what they needed to do next" (p. 239) focus more on how students are learning. Although the preservice or inservice teacher may consider these factors, the best tool to use is the one that will yield the most feedback to make changes to enhance the students' education. See Table 14.3 for a list of sample reflection blogs.

Table 14.3 A list of sample teaching reflection blogs

Jenn Reed's Teaching Reflection Blog	http://jennreed1220.wordpress.com/2012/01/27/classroom-management-ups-and-downs
Newteachersblog: Reflecting on teacher professionalism	http://newteachersblog.wordpress.com
Reflections on teaching by Ms. Mercer	http://mizmercer.edublogs.org
The Blog Adventures of a Substitute Teacher....	http://kauaimark.blogspot.com
"In for Good" by Ms. Stewart	http://inforgood.wordpress.com
Teacher reflection blog by Dr. Beyer	http://morrill.cps.edu/teacher-reflection-blog
Reflections of a science teacher	http://sanmccarron.blogspot.com

Video Recordings

One of the hardest tasks of reflection is to step out of the role of teacher and observe oneself from a third person perspective. Video recording of the classroom permits the teacher, and perhaps, a colleague(s) to see how teaching and learning transpires during the school day. Peer video analysis, as described by Harford, MacRuaire, and McCarten (2010), shows the peer-videoing analysis as a transformative process during which pairs of teachers record, then view each other's practices in a way that promotes dialogue and a shared learning experience. An alternative to peer recording is to set up a camera in one's own classroom and provide the video to colleagues or upload it to a limited access site where individuals in a community of practice can view it and provide feedback. In both cases, the colleague can provide feedback electronically or face to face, and the teacher can view him- or herself to analyze the captured teaching practices. The two sets of feedback can be discussed and positive changes made. In Peer Coaching communities, peers are trained to become trusted colleagues who build professional relationships without the fear of evaluation from superiors. Also, in videoing, one must remember to follow district rules for filming students, although filming for professional development is often allowed for self-evaluation.

Some teacher candidates choose to set up password on their reflective e-journals, vlogs (see Figure 14.17), or blogs to allow access to a selected few, while others share reflective contents to the general public through YouTube and other social network. This can be accomplished on monologue, documentary, dramatization, or interview formats. See Table 14.4 for a list of representative reflective vlogs of student teachers or new teachers.

For instance, "JennReed", while a student teacher, kept a blog at http://jennreed1220.wordpress.com as a "platform" to organize her journals in text as well as URLs to her reflection videos posted on YouTube. "JennReed" created a YouTube channel titled "JenniferReed1220's channel" as well. In the **monologue** format, she reflected about differentiation, classroom management, adjusting lessons, the purpose of homework, and other topics relevant to student teachers.

The **documentary** of a student teacher's reflection is a nonfictional video intended to document some aspect of a student teacher's life to honestly record for the purposes of instruction or maintaining a historical record. The line blurs between documentary and **dramatization**, in that with dramatization, the video is *organized to center on the reflection of a teacher.* With the **interview** format, the student teacher has a conversation with a second person about his or her experiences.

Often in the preservice teaching experience, prospective teachers have missed or lost opportunities to reflect on an event because they did not see it or observe it due to their main focus being on themselves. Being aware of everything going on in the classroom ("withitness") comes with experience. When they review teaching experiences through technology tools such as video recordings, however, they may see the body language or the faces of the students. They may then begin to understand that the teaching process is not just about how they teach the lesson but how the interactions between themselves and the students create the learning process. The

Figure 14.17 A vlog can be posted to password protected blog sites

Table 14.4 A list of representative reflective vlogs of student teachers or new teachers

Vlog Formats	Titles	URLs
Monologue	JenniferReed1220's channel	https://www.youtube.com/watch?v=6bK3mmT6J3E&feature=youtu.be
Documentary	Bonnie Wagner High School English	https://www.youtube.com/watch?v=vp-qOlf6tc4
Documentary	Year-long Teaching Documentary of Jennifer McNickle	https://www.youtube.com/watch?v=e6wAMC41ZXQ

reflective process, through the use of technology tools, leads to development in the teaching process and will provide teachers with opportunities to participate in the transformative process of growing as teachers. The Teachthought staff (2013) suggests that students can become a part of this as teachers appoint as one of their classroom jobs a "videographer of the day" to take a few minutes of footage of learning. This provides the students and the teacher with highly insightful feedback.

Besides asking students to be "videographer of the day," video recording can go high-tech as well with a new generation of technology that consists of mobile, wireless video and audio recordings that work together to record components of the classroom.

Teachers have used screen capture (also called screenshot, or screen-cap) images taken by the computer user to record the visible items displayed on the monitor. Screen captures display still images, while a step above and beyond are lecture captures, which refers to the process of recording the content of a procedure, lecture, conference, or seminar in video format for viewers to remotely access, either in real time or asynchronously. The lecture capture may use any combination of microphones, cameras, screen captures, slideshows, and/or document cameras. Products such as Camtasia, Screencast-O-Matic, and Jing are used to create lecture captures.

With the increasing demands of video contents for flipped classes and tutorials, teachers who provide lecture captures to students routinely had to set up generic mobile multimedia carts loaded with videotaping equipment to move around from class to class. Lately, self-capture possible products such as Swivl combine robotic mobile accessories, apps, and cloud solutions for making video capture in class more professional. The recording robot automatically follows a speaker and provides wireless audio. The app and cloud options provide a storage and sharing solution. If you have not seen a product like this, simply visualize the robot wireless vacuum cleaners in TV commercials that roam around the house to clean the floors.

Know Your Students

Another step in the reflective process for teachers is to know their students well. Often, teachers need to know their students' personal lives in order to make connections to the students and the learning process. When the teacher makes personal connections to the students in the classroom, students become more engaged in the learning process. An exciting tool that teachers can use to learn more about their students is digital storytelling or digital narratives. Students and teachers can use software programs such as MS Photo Story, MS Movie Maker, and iMovie to make a video or movie. These digital processing tools help the students create an action movie with personal photos, home movies, and a written script to describe personal events. The students develop their narrative by telling their autobiographical story. The teacher who assists their students in creating their stories learns about the students in the process. What begins as an introspective process for students easily transforms into a reflective process for the teacher as consideration for how one's teaching meets the needs of each student and as the teacher gathers information about the students to incorporate into future lessons and educational activities.

Teachers also find the discussion tools in programs such as Edmodo, Weebly, Blackboard Learn, and Classroom 2.0 as a way to participate in the reflective process when students complete their reading reflections. Students can respond and read their classmates' responses to questions about the content that the teacher is presenting in the classroom. Through discussions, the teacher can begin to see how to create a better understanding of the content for each student. The students respond to the discussions by describing their current knowledge about the topic, providing examples of what they have learned, and, finally, stating whether or not they agree with the content or the question that was presented to them. By sharing these reflective thoughts in discussion boards, the students have opportunities to organize and publish their thoughts in a more formal way. They have an audience of their peers who will read and respond to their thoughts.

Peer Coaching and Technology

As noted, interpersonal interactions with peers, such as through peer coaching, have been found to help beginning teachers develop as reflective practitioners and encourage feedback from peers. Additionally, new teachers develop reflective practices that are more focused on how their practices affect their students' learning than more self-centered concerns (Kurtts & Levin, 2000).

Peer coaching is another collaboration tool for the preservice or novice teacher whereby the teacher finds another teacher as a partner to meet with on a regular basis. This can be on a formal schedule with professional development training, or it can be in an informal setting such as friend or colleague. Many preservice teachers develop a network with classmates in their teacher preparation program which leads to the development of trusting relationships among a smaller cohort of their peers. These relationships last beyond the teacher preparation program and become the basis of support and collaboration as they graduate from preservice teacher to novice teacher.

Peer coaching allows for teachers to meet together and talk about their teaching practices, issues with students, and evaluation of their curriculum. As we have seen, peer coaching sessions can be face to face, virtual, or online. Coaching sessions give the teacher an opportunity to reflect with a colleague in a safe manner without the anxiety of being observed, scored, or evaluated by an administrator or supervisor. Rather, they can honestly share concerns they may have with a trusted colleague who watches, listens, provides data, and supports them to enhance problem solving. This format works well because the teacher him- or herself selects an area for examination (e.g., Am I calling on *all* my students or just some? Am I asking higher-level just lower-level questions? What is my "travel pattern" around the room, and am I near all students at some point during the lesson? What type of oral feedback am I delivering to students?). The teacher also selects the method of data collection by the peer, and the two colleagues plan and talk through the objective(s) of the lesson and the observation. The colleague views the lesson (face to face or electronically), collects the data only as specified by the teacher, and presents it to him/her without judgment, and then they reverse roles. Using technology, the teacher and the observer can view lesson multiple times, even reviewing them together to focus on critical areas. Because the last step of feedback without judgment can be difficult, special development training can be obtained. Both partners must see the process as an honest, trusting, open-minded, self-searching way to improve one's practice. As a professional development activity for a teacher or an entire school, this is an exceptional reflective tool.

Video Conferencing

Video conferencing is an important collaboration tool. Teachers can use video conferencing to share with colleagues in other schools or in other cities. They can talk about the teaching practices that they are doing in their classrooms, describe problems that they may have encountered with students, and find solutions with other teachers. Teachers can use Skype, WhatsApp, or HangOuts from Google+ as free connectivity tools. These tools allow teachers to call in or connect through computers in one place for a video conference and share with each other. These moments of sharing are invaluable to novice teachers as they discover that others are there to support them and that they can collaborate together to solve problems in the classrooms.

Mind Mapping

Whether one terms it semantic mapping, concept mapping, or mind mapping, these representations provide visual relationships and connections between a set of ideas and concepts (refer to Figure 14.18). Placing one's thoughts or ideas in a visual form has been shown to aid in developing a deeper understanding of a lesson one plans to teach as well as to aid in cultivating reflective practices regarding pedagogical instructional decisions (Blackwell & Pepper, 2008). These researchers found a significant difference in the amount of reflection that occurred as related to decisions about instruction between preservice teachers who used concept mapping during lesson planning and those who did not. An analysis of kindergarten teachers' semantic maps by Lim, Cheng, Lam, and Ngan (2003) revealed evidence of reflective thinking as demonstrated through a change in perspective and attitude, as shown through connections and links in their maps, towards the content and teaching curriculum.

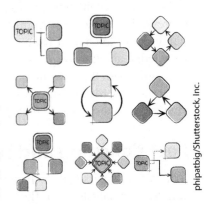

Although these studies in particular focused on the use of mind maps to facilitate lesson planning, the use of such maps can be used in various aspects of teaching such as classroom management and assessment. Plotting out a behavior management plan or designing a lesson is more easily accomplished through the use of a Web-based concept map tool or software. Electronic mind mapping allows for the addition, subtraction, revision, and/or saving of ideas and topics related to the teaching task at hand. Creating and

Figure 14.18 A sample mind map. Additional examples can be found in Fig. 14.2, Fig. 14.4, and Fig. 14.19.

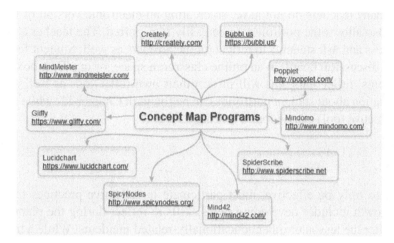

Figure 14.19   Web-based concept map tools

analyzing one's own sematic map will facilitate reflective practices as the teacher rearranges the map to reveal new understanding. Some mind mapping tools such as Inspiration and Kidspiration can be purchased while other programs provide free services with the opportunity to purchase packages with more features. Concept maps can also be created using a graphic organizer with MS Word. Figure 14.19, created with SpiderScribe, lists 10 free mind mapping programs available online.

Using Reflection to Assess and Analyze the Data

In this day and time, in order to prove, support, or request anything such as additional resources for students, a teacher must include in his/her rationale the appropriate data. Collecting data about one's teaching or students' progress is important to gain the big picture about curriculum, assessment, and the quality of the educational experiences of the students. Often, teachers are responsible for collecting important data, submitting reports, and discussing those reports with parents. Since the push is to show the quantitative (the hard numerical) data, many times the qualitative (descriptive) data and the reflective process of understanding how the data can inform the teacher about his/her own teaching practices is omitted. In the beginning case study when Ms. Tijerina realized that her students did not do well on the mathematical benchmark test, she had some choices to make about her own teaching practices. She could have responded to her students' failures as if it were their fault. Perhaps the students had not studied well or were not listening. Maybe they did not complete the homework assigned the night before. She could have even thrown her hands up and said that her students could not learn the material. Instead, she looked at the test scores to understand exactly where they were failing. When she saw that most of the class failed to answer the questions correctly, she realized that it was her teaching process rather than the students' learning process that needed correcting. She then went to her colleagues (possibly in peer coaching sessions) to discover how she could improve the teaching process. Once she reflected with her colleagues about the lesson (which she could easily do online), she found what was missing and learned what she could do to improve the lesson. Returning to her math class with new plans and ideas about how to reteach the materials, Mrs. Tijerina made a second attempt to create a learning environment where her students would be successful. Once she retaught the materials, she gave them the test again to assess their progress. This reflective practice puts the assessment and evaluation on the teaching and learning process rather than on the individuals. By collecting the data and reflecting on the lesson, Ms. Tijerina was able to pinpoint where the problems were in the learning process.

Teachers can also use reflection on assessments to understand why students are not progressing in the learning process. When teachers meet with content specialists to discuss the progress of their students, they must take into account the stories behind the numerical data. What have they learned about themselves as well as about their students that play a role in the educational process? Assessment in the classroom should encompass formal and informal, formative, and summative assessment. Teachers must reflect on the performance of their students as well as their own performance (from the autobiographical lens as well as from the student lens). An additional assessment at the heart of reflective practices is the student portfolio. Physical portfolios often take space that many teachers do not have, so creating an electronic version of the students' work not only saves space but also allows the portfolios to be easily transported. The teacher can review the portfolio to gauge student progress and ask students to reflect on the artifacts as well. Student feedback can be submitted electronically (in a discussion board, in an online classroom space, or in a Dropbox) or as a hard copy. As teachers read the students' reflections, this will inform their own reflections as well about the learning that occurred. Other information about student portfolios can be found in Chapter 11, while information on teacher portfolios (another reflective tool) can be found in Chapter 12.

Conclusion

All teachers, in order to truly be effective, must participate in reflective practices throughout their career. Part of professional growth includes developing one's skills to reflect during the planning phase, during the implementation, and after the lesson or other educationally-related incidents. While a main focus of reflective teaching is the lesson, all professional educational interactions and activities should be included in a teacher's reflective practice.

A common misconception is that reflective practice is an individual, isolated task. As we know, teachers spend the greater majority of the school day in isolation of their colleagues; however, a more collaborative nature for reflection is necessary. It is important for teachers, both preservice and inservice, to take into account reflection from various points of view which include: the autobiographical, peer, student, theoretical, and family lenses (see Figure 14.10). Consulting and incorporating feedback from these entities allows for a more thorough reflection; however, collecting such data can be difficult to facilitate. The advent of technological tools such as online classroom spaces, social learning platforms, electronic survey tools, social media sites, and classroom response systems adds a level of ease to soliciting and collecting data from different entities. Additionally, there is ample accurate information available via the Internet from reputable educational sites that allow preservice and inservice teachers to apply stronger teaching strategies as a result of their reflective practice.

These electronic tools and processes allow the teachers the time and venues to develop reflection. Reflective practice is an ongoing practice that teachers need to develop. When teacher candidates initially practice reflection in the preservice stages of teaching, they begin to learn the transformative process of their own teaching practice. By utilizing technology tools such as blogs, journaling, or videos, they capture the teaching experience immediately and accurately. These teachers can then review the experience by themselves or with others to make adjustments or improve the teaching experience through reflective practices.

If teachers truly want to educate the generations of students who will pass through their classroom, they must incorporate reflective practices as a part of their daily activity. The information gained as a result should inform future action which should in turn create stronger educational experiences for students and more confidence for the teacher. The reflective cycle continues endlessly until the teacher steps out of the classroom for the final time with the assurance that he or she has always resolutely sought the best for students.

References

Argyris, C., & Schön, D. (1974). *Theory in practice: Increasing professional effectiveness.* San Francisco: Jossey-Bass.

Blackwell, S., & Pepper, K. (2008). The effect of concept mapping on preservice teachers' reflective practices when making pedagogical decisions. *The Journal of Effective Teaching, 8*(2), 77–93.

Brookfield, S. D. (2002). Using the lenses of critically reflective teaching in the community college classroom. *New Directions for Community Colleges,* 118, 31–38.

Brookfield, S. D. (1995). *Becoming a critically reflective teacher.* San Francisco: Jossey-Bass.

Danielson C, & McGreal T. (2000). *Teacher evaluation to enhance professional practice* [e-book]. Alexandria, VA: Association for Supervision and Curriculum Development. Retrieved from http://www.ascd.org/publications/books/100219/chapters/A-Blueprint-for-Teacher-Evaluation.aspx

Davis, E. A. (2006). Characterizing productive reflection among preservice elementary teachers: Seeing what matter. *Teaching and Teacher Education,* 22, 281–301.

Dewey, J. (1933). *How we think.* Chicago: Henry Regnery.

Doyran, F. (2013). Reflective journal writing on the way to becoming teachers. *Cypriot Journal of Educational Sciences, 8*(1), 160–168. Retrieved from http://www.world-education-center.org/index.php/cjes/article/view/8.1.12/pdf_149

DuFour, R. (2004). What is a professional learning community? *Educational Leadership, 61*(8), 6–11.

Edutopia. (2014). Avoiding new teacher burnout. Retrieved from http://www.edutopia.org/discussion/avoiding-new-teacher-burnout

Gadawg01. (2014, October 7). Re: Avoiding new teacher burnout [Online forum comment]. Retrieved from http://www.edutopia.org/discussion/avoiding-new-teacher-burnout

Gettinger, M., & Kohler, K. M. (2011). Process-outcome approaches to classroom management and effective teaching. In C. M. Everston & C. S. Weinstein (Eds.), *Handbook of classroom management: Research, practice, and contemporary issues* (73–95). New York: Routledge.

Greene, M. (1978). *Landscapes of learning.* New York: Teachers College Press.

Greene, M. (1995). *Releasing the imagination: Essays on education, the arts, and social change.* San Francisco: Jossey-Bass.

Harford, J., MacRuaire, G., & McCartan, D. (2010). 'Lights, camera, reflection': Using peer video to promote reflective dialogue among student teachers. *Teacher Development, 14*(1), 57–68.

Hord, S. (1997). Professional learning communities: What are they and why are they important? *Issues... about Change, 6*(1), 1–8. Retrieved from http://www.sedl.org/change/issues/issues61/Issues_Vol6_No1_1997.pdf

Kajder, S. B., & Parkes, K. A. (2012). Examining preservice teachers' reflective practice within and across multimodal writing environments. *Journal of Technology and Teacher Education, 20*(3), 229–249.

Killeavy, M., & Moloney, A. (2010). Reflection in a social space: Can blogging support reflective practice for beginning teachers? *Teaching and Teacher Education, 26,* 1070–1076.

Krashen, S. D. (1984). Bilingual education and second language acquisition theory. In California State Department of Education, Office of Bilingual Bicultural Education (Ed.), *Schooling and language minority students: A theoretical framework* (pp. 63–91). Los Angeles: Evaluation, Dissemination and Assessment Center California State University. (ERIC Document Reproduction Service No. ED249773)

Kurtts, S. A., & Levin, B. B. (2000). Using peer coaching with preservice teachers to develop reflective practice and collegial support. *Teaching Education, 11*(3), 297–310.

LDee. (2014, October 26). Re: Avoiding New Teacher Burnout [Online forum comment]. Retrieved from http://www.edutopia.org/discussion/avoiding-new-teacher-burnout

Lee. K., & Bret, C. (2013). What are student inservice teachers talking about in their online communities of practice? Investigating student inservice teachers' experiences in a double-layered CoP. *Journal of Technology and Teacher Education, 21*(1), 89–118.

Lim, S. E., Cheng, P. W. C., Lam, M. S., & Ngan, S. F. (2003). Developing reflective and thinking skills by means of semantic mapping strategies in kindergarten teacher education. *Early Child Development and Care, 173*(1), 55–72.

Loughran, J. J. (2002). Effective reflective practice: In search of meaning in learning about teaching. *Journal of Teacher Education, 53*(1), 33–43.

OffBeatTeach. (2014, October 27). Re: Avoiding new teacher burnout [Online forum comment]. Retrieved from http://www.edutopia.org/discussion/avoiding-new-teacher-burnout

Osterman, K. F., & Kottkamp, R. B. (1993). *Reflective practice for educators: Improving schooling through professional development.* Newbury Park, CA: Corwin Press, Inc.

Rodman, G. J. (2010). Maximizing the learning experiences of pre-service teachers through reflective engagement. *Academic Exchange Extra.* Retrieved from http://www.unco.edu/ae-extra/2010/3/rodman.html.

Salazar, D., Aguirre-Muñoz, Z., Fox, K., & Nuanez-Lucas, L. (2010). On-line professional learning communities: Increasing teacher learning and productivity in isolated rural communities. *Systematics, Cybernetics and Informatics, 8*(4), 1–7.

Schön, D. A. (1983). *The reflective practitioner: How professionals think in action.* New York: Basic Books.

Shoffner, M. (2009). "Because I know how to use it": Integrating technology into preservice English teacher reflective practice. *Contemporary Issues in Technology and Teacher Education, 9*(4), 371–391.

Snoeyink, R. (2010). Using video self-analysis to improve the "withitness" of student teachers. *Journal of Digital Learning in Teacher Education, 26*(3), 101–110.

Teachthought Staff. (2013). 20 things you can do in (about) 10 minutes for a smoother running classroom. Retrieved from www.teachthought.com/teaching/20-things-you-can-do-in-about-10-minutes-for-a-smoother-running-classroom

Thomas, L. (2014, October 27). Re: Avoiding new teacher burnout [Online forum comment]. Retrieved from http://www.edutopia.org/discussion/avoiding-new-teacher-burnout

Ward, J. R., & McCotter, S. S. (2004). Reflection as a visible outcome for preservice teachers. *Teaching and Teacher Education, 20*(3), 243–257.

Zeichner, K. M., & Liston, D. P. (1996). *Reflective teaching: An introduction.* Mahwah, NJ: Lawrence Erlbaum Associates.

Chapter 15

Governance and Administration of Technology Use in Schools

Viola M. Garcia
University of Houston-Downtown

Meet Mr. Vela

Mr. Vela asked his fourth-grade social studies students to work on a group project. One group approached him about bringing their own technology devices to school to investigate and identify the contributions of people of various racial, ethnic, and religious groups to Texas. The teacher is unsure whether the school policy allows this. Further, he does not know if all devices are acceptable or if there is a ban on specific types of devices or Web sites. He is puzzled as to how to respond to the students and how to proceed with the unit of instruction.

Governance and Administration of Technology Use in Schools

Technology use in the schools is advancing faster than could ever have been imagined--even a decade ago. In order to address the needs of students in an ever changing school environment, it is important that teachers are familiar with and comply with policies, procedures, and administrative decisions related to technology use in schools. Teachers must understand and be assured that policies and procedures have been developed to help them and their students (especially with safety issues) (Figure 15.1). Policies also help students and parents know the rules and processes, and they help teachers successfully integrate instructional technology and implementation opportunities for students in their classrooms.

Figure 15.1 Beginning teachers must learn about technology governance and policy decisions.

jurgenfr/Shutterstock, Inc.

Decision Makers and Decision-Making for District Information Technology

There are a number of issues with which school districts must deal when making decisions about technology: budgeting, needs, piloting, training, safety, repairing/upgrading equipment, and many more (refer to Figure 15.3). In order to effectively support teaching and learning, one overarching responsibility of school boards, superintendents, and administrative leaders regarding technology integration in schools is to set the expectations for daily implementation and use of technology in schools. All of these are under the umbrella term "technology governance issues". Districts may rely on administrators to deal with many issues or appoint a school technology governance team. Some overreaching questions among many then become: how do superintendents and, school board members determine what to purchase, why, and, at what point and how might some districts determine that the latest "bring your own device" is the most suitable solution? (Figure 15.2)

Figure 15.2   Policies guide teachers when considering "bring your own device" options.

School leaders should engage administrators, teachers, and content area and technology experts in decisions such as these and many more regarding technology. In this collective process, assessment of needs can be conducted in school districts to review existing technologies and to determine plans for relevant and future technology implementation. It will be every teacher's responsibility to participate during the collection of data and/or, at times, to serve on committees to ensure that good decisions are made about technology. Every student will be using technology in the future, and the equipment and training are an extensive investment in that future.

After analyses are conducted (Figure 15.3), collective recommendations and multiyear action plans can be developed. It is important that they be aligned with instructional needs, strategic plans, and goals and expected learner outcomes that enable teachers to work collaboratively to accomplish the end goal(s). An action plan can then be developed to motivate and promote creativity and cultivate high levels of engagement and commitment to meet the goals of the plan that will lead to teacher and student success.

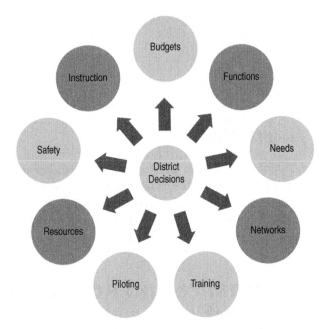

Figure 15.3   Multiple factors are considered in making decisions about technology in a school district.

A teacher's awareness and knowledge about the decision making processes and the district's technology plan help frame his or her decisions about technology use in the classroom.

Information Networks for Decision Makers

Will every teacher be a decision maker for technology use and implementation? At first, perhaps, the beginning teacher will only be responsible for decisions in his or her own classroom. However, there will be a growing responsibility for teachers to become part of school, district, state, and even national efforts to help students attain technology literacy and skills. How will teachers know what decisions must be made and how to judge if the decisions are good ones? District policies and procedures provide guidance to teachers along with state and national standards and those developed by national content area organizations (see Chapter 9 for more).

The Technology Leadership Network (TLN) was founded by the National School Boards Association in 1987 to provide an innovative way for school board members, district administrators, and technology specialists to investigate and have access to best practices shared by school districts across the country so as to make well informed decisions (Technology Leadership Network, 2014). As might be expected, a number of information networks have been created over the last ten years to provide similar resources for decision makers. One such resource is Project RED (2013).

With the belief that technology can make a substantial impact on schools and students, three research organizations - The Greaves Group, The Hayes Connection and One-to-One Institute - established Project RED: Revolutionizing Education. Initially these organizations conducted a national survey of technology programs in 1,000 schools, which is the first and only national research focusing on academic results and the financial implication of education technology. The findings showed that if effectively implemented, technology programs can lead to improved student achievement and significant return on investment. (Introducing Project RED, http://www.projectred.org)

In 2013 alone, Project RED provided and archived a number of webinars. These serve superintendents, finance directors, curriculum directors, technology directors, principals, and educators. Some of these include: *Financial Implications & Impact of Technology-Transformed Schools, Transformational School Leadership for the Digital Age, Teaching and Learning in the 1:1 Environment, Standards and Curriculum, Device Selection for 1:1,* and *Creating the Appropriate Infrastructure for 1:1.* In addition, these are resources created to help district leaders make decisions about technology integration and use in schools: (a) the International Society for Technology in Education (ISTE), which serves educators and leaders throughout the world, (b) *Discovery Education* (http://www.discoveryeducation.com) which offers a variety of lesson plans and teacher resources, and (c) printable worksheets by grade level and subject (U. S. Department of Education, Office of Planning, Evaluation, and Policy Development [US DOE, 2003]). One of the main purposes of ISTE is to describe the use of technology in classroom settings, regardless of the funding source. Surveys were conducted to determine the availability of computers, the use of technology for instructional and professional activities, and perceived barriers to the use of technology. New resources continue to be developed to provide guidance on technology use to new and practicing educators in schools. These information resources are invaluable to teacher candidates and beginning teachers. When investigating acceptable use policies and related information about the use of technology tools, these resources and many others provide the foundation for teachers' technology integration in instructional planning.

Policies on the Use of Technology Tools

School policies address a number of technology issues that are reviewed periodically and are clearly outlined in faculty, student, and parent handbooks. New teachers should note that such policies are normally accessible to all (often via the district Web site). Initial considerations are given to such topics as digital citizenship and responsible use policies by all users, including students, teachers, and administrators. Policies are quite often developed to level the playing field for students with limited exposure or experience (the Digital Divide) with any of the technology devices used in the district. Students' limited familiarity with technology could otherwise be a major stumbling block in technology integration (Figure 15.4). There is also a need to address homebound students and/or student assignments given for after school because some students may not have access to the technology in their home and are put at a great disadvantage when they are not able to complete required assignments. Homework assignments that require Internet research, flipped classroom modes of instruction, and the use of e-textbooks force administrators and teachers to consider issues of equity in a new digital environment. In an effort to equalize opportunities, school districts have forged new relationships with broadband and other Internet service providers. These are critical components in providing cost-effective access for such needs. Teachers can be reassured that conversations and collaborations among school district administrators, municipal, county, and state agencies seek to provide technology resources to more students and families. They want to assure: (a) that contractual arrangements and specifications are met, (b) that installation of hardware or connectivity is not disruptive of instructional processes, and (c) that hardware and software technologies are:

- intuitive
- user-friendly
- supported structurally
- supported administratively, and

Marynchenko Oleksandr/
Shutterstock, Inc.

Figure 15.4 Limited familiarity with technology may be a stumbling block in technology integration.

- supported technologically and:
  - are not cost prohibitive,
  - provide a seamless process for implementation, and
  - have transitions which include plans for impending iterations of upgrades and changes.

Each one of these areas involves important policy considerations with which new teachers must become familiar and which are intended to guide technology related decisions they make in the classroom such as the one faced by Mr. Vela in the scenario at the beginning of the chapter.

Policies That Link Technology to School Budgets

Many large districts have grant writing offices which support teachers by investigating, organizing, and disseminating information about grants or funds available for different initiatives, including technology purchases and implementation. Teachers may work with the grant writing expert(s) to submit a funding proposal to acquire monies to support their work. It is not unusual for teachers to write small grant proposals to obtain technology necessary to achieve their class goals using such devices as iPads, scientific calculators, projectors, probeware (for science) and so forth. Inasmuch as teachers participate in such initiatives, there are basic technology requirements that the school district must provide. Budgeting and the economics of providing the necessary hardware, software, staff development, and contracts for Internet safety (such as protecting students from cyberbullies, pedophiles, scams, and identify theft) are major costs. These costs need to be considered when planning for teachers and students to access the Web while at school or away from school. Smart budgeting includes contractual assurances that upgrades and technical support are provided and that upgrades are seamlessly integrated. This also includes apps purchases, updates and access to licensing agreements, software purchases, and considerations for recurring or replacement costs. These are all expensive matters, as are plans for new costs, contingency costs, and pilot costs, which should be reflected in the budget functions of a school district regardless of the size of the district (Figure 15.5).

Figure 15.5   The initial costs, recurring costs, contingency costs, and pilot costs of computer hardware and software are reflected in school budgets.

Then, of course, there is teacher training to enable effective usage that must be folded into the budget. With the initial interest in technology implementation in the United States, the federal role in supporting technology has been relatively consistent to date (US DOE, 2003).

> The vast majority of direct federal funding for educational technology comes from two sources, the E-Rate program and a state formula grant program operated by ED that is dedicated to educational technology. From fiscal years 1997 through 2001, the state formula grant program was known as the Technology Literacy Challenge Fund (TLCF) program; No Child Left Behind, the 2001 reauthorization of the Elementary and Secondary Education Act, replaced the TLCF with the new Educational Technology State Grants (also known as the Enhancing Education through Technology or EETT) program. (p. 3)

Knowledge about sources of funding helps teachers plan for grant writing opportunities. A great deal of money for educational technology initially came from the Title I program, as many local districts and schools chose to use their Title I allocations for technology-related expenditures. Analyses of the TLCF program revealed that the percentage of funds to high-poverty districts declined between 1997 and 2000. An analysis of all E-Rate applications and discount approvals through January 2000 indicated that public schools were the primary recipients of the program, receiving 84 % of the discounts. *Federal Funding for Educational Technology and How It Is Used in the Classroom: A Summary of Findings from the Integrated Studies of Educational Technology* (US DOE, 2003) summarizes the three final reports produced by the Integrated Studies of Educational Technology (ISET).

The ISET findings revealed that "Technology is now considered by most educators and parents to be an integral part of providing a high-quality education. There is concern, however, that not all students, particularly students in rural schools or schools with a high percentage of minority or poor students, have equal access to educational technology, both in terms of the availability of equipment and the successful integration of technology into the classroom" (p. 3). Even though the federal government continues to support technology integration in schools, it is wise for new and experienced teachers to know and learn how to access various available funds and to seek grants to support technology initiatives. These technology resources are highly motivating to students who have grown up using technological devices and who expect to learn via virtual and electronic sources.

Teacher candidates should know about investigating grant and funding opportunities for technology resources so they are prepared as beginning teachers to tap into those resources. This proactive approach gives new teachers the advantage of providing innovative ways to engage students in instructional technology approaches.

Policies on Administrative Needs and Functions

There are many other parts of a teaching position that a teacher must carry out besides day-to-day instruction. Some college students may remember that their teachers kept class grades in a spiral or bound grade book which was highly guarded. However, very few teachers today rely on the trusted traditional grade book or attendance rosters. Teachers today rely on electronic management systems to enter grades, attendance, anecdotal records, reports, and many other forms of data. What assurances can teachers expect regarding the integrity of data systems they rely on for every day work? The security and back up of Web-based portals for data access, data management, and use have generated sophisticated off-site and cloud based resources for fail safe systems and necessary data retrieval. These systems include student data management systems, teacher evaluation portals, parent portals, finance management data sharing systems, energy conservation systems, child nutrition services, transportation services, building maintenance, heating and cooling, and scheduling systems. These are just a few examples of the dependence and sensitivity to complex systems that are electronically managed and, if jeopardized, provide serious limitations to safe and secure settings for the administrative functions required of educators.

Figure 15.6 Safe and secure settings for the administrative and technology functions are essential.

arka38/Shutterstock, Inc.

Instructional technology integration can best be accomplished and used effectively if student data systems and resources are available to teachers and administrators. These resources include but are not limited to hardware, software, and technical support (Figure 15.6). In addition, technology solutions are used to prepare for a variety of administrative and emergency situations. These allow for employees, students, parents, the community, and local law enforcement officials to be notified of emergency situations. These events, including violence that place schools in a lockdown mode (such as with an active shooter), also cover weather or other types of disasters, requiring district preparedness that extends well beyond evacuation charts and emergency drills. Good, effective communication and timely response to such emergencies is of paramount importance to minimize the potential danger and to ensure the safety of the faculty, staff, students, and the surrounding community. While current modes of texting or email notifications are used, vigilance about future needs and real-time responses are ongoing endeavors for school district administrators and technology specialists and teams to consider. These are but a few examples of the structural and administrative support that teachers receive in an attempt to create a secure environment to do the necessary and important non-instructional requirements of their job. Teacher candidates and beginning teachers can be assured that these safe and secure support systems are continually being reviewed and upgraded by their districts.

Supporting the Professional Development of Teachers

Imagine being a first-year teacher, or even an experienced teacher, and having your principal announce that teachers are expected to use iPads for all instruction. Or, imagine that students will not be issued textbooks, and they will have to now use eBooks. This could be very exciting, but do you know what instructional technology training is available in your district to prepare for such initiatives? How would you find the quickest way to learn to use iPads for instruction? Are there workshops, webinars, one-to-one sessions, or other forms of support? Providing teachers with opportunities to work one-on-one with technology and professional development specialists, master teachers, and support staff is critical in order to meet new technology integration requirements. This helps teachers improve their craft in order to best plan for student learning opportunities.

Instead of a one-size-fits-all workshop model, professional development should encourage teachers to create structures where they participate in developing professional activities that address their own needs and interests (refer to Figure 15.8). It is best if teachers do this in collaboration with school leaders. This type of professional development is most productive and beneficial. Pilot programs are a critical part of setting up successful implementation of technology that allows teachers in school districts to pretest processes, products, software programs, and strategies before their full implementation in schools. This provides for glitches to be resolved and for both teacher and student focus groups to give critical feedback for continuous improvement to meet instructional objectives. Professional development policies must provide teachers time for planning, implementation, assessment, and review of goals, instructional frameworks, and best practices.

A layered approach to technology initiatives not only considers teachers' professional development and school integration but also administrative training (Figure 15.7). Principals, assistant principals, and instructional leaders need to understand the new technology's intended use, the time frames for implementation, and the expected learner outcomes. With this preparation, they can support and guide teachers in these new initiatives. In this way, principals can tap into existing talent at the district level and among teachers to increase support and confidence among reluctant users and to encourage calculated risk taking among the teacher leaders in their schools to support new initiatives. Bringing employees together at all levels in this training process further supports common goals and their successful implementation.

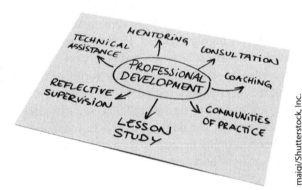

Figure 15.7   A layered approach to professional development.

A vital aspect of professional development for teachers to successfully incorporate technology into instruction requires adequate time for production and preparation. Some of the techniques, strategies, or resources may take several hours for even an experienced teacher to program in order to identify links, to bookmark, practice, upload to the Internet, and so forth. Often, even installing and setting up some software is tedious and time consuming, leading many teachers to avoid technology integration completely. The issue of allowing for time cannot be overstated in having teachers feel prepared and confident. A good integration plan will schedule for this time.

Ultimately, when talented teachers effectively execute the intended strategic instructional goals and objectives, there can be higher likelihood of student success. When a school district makes the decision to equip students, generally seventh grade and up, with iPads or similar devices (where every student gets his/her own device), the implementation plan must include the preparation of teachers to (a) understand the goals and objectives of the initiative, (b) become familiar and experienced with the tools, and (c) prepare for the intentional, organized, deliberate and focused use of those tools for the instructional and academic growth of students. Faculty development and support of the technology integration plan, as mentioned, should include individualized opportunities for the professional development of teachers. An important component of the successful integration of new initiatives is that an informed, collective workforce (who practices personalized training) promotes successful and supportive student-centered, instructional services.

When a new teacher is presented with innovative technology initiatives by a principal, the teacher should be informed as to where to access the training, how to prepare to implement the new initiative, and what additional training is available to support the students. In addition to training for new initiatives, prospective and new teachers should become familiar with data

Figure 15.8   Professional development promotes personal development.

systems to support effective instructional practices. There are often teachers in each school who are known to be "tech savvey" and to whom others can consult above and beyond the technology specialist. Informal or formal technology committees where teachers are helping and teaching others are very productive for schools. Teachers can also take it on themselves to "learn by doing" or simply self-teaching themselves, but resources should always be available when needed.

Connecting Data Systems to the Best Instructional Practices

A strong professional development plan and a technology integration plan must be appropriately aligned with the district's strategic plan and instructional goals and objectives that guide teaching and learning. Alignment produces an environment by which all levels of the school district are strategically parallel with its instructional initiatives and provide support before, during, and after implementation of the new or ongoing plans. Even with the best laid plans, adequate resources must be made available. When they are not, teachers' lessons must be adapted accordingly or technology integration must be reconsidered. Future teachers who practice connecting data systems to instructional practices are prepared to teach because they can systematically link data about their students' strengths and needs to appropriate instructional approaches in a systematic, coherent fashion.

Teacher Training for Use of Student Data Systems

> Students primarily use technology to gather, organize, analyze, and report information, but this has not dramatically improved student performance on standardized tests. These findings lead to the conclusion that future efforts should focus on providing students and teachers with increased access to technology along with training in pedagogically sound best practices, including more advanced approaches for technology-based assessment and adaptive instruction" (Davies & West, 2014, p. 841).

How does a teacher know how well students are learning? Luckily, as mentioned above, technology can often help easily collect various types of data through data systems that teachers and districts can use to make good instructional decisions, but teachers must know how to collect and use that data. One area in which training and support is most beneficial is in building collaboration and structural designs to support teachers' understanding and use of student progress measures through data collection and data management reviews. A variety of structures that include overarching data management committees, team meetings, and training opportunities help teachers in this regard (Figure 15.9). In these group structures, teachers can refine their knowledge, skills, and/or strategies to approach data gathering, information seeking, and alternate solutions to challenging scenarios. Implementing professional opportunities in collaborative environments builds participation and inclusion at all levels to support student success.

Utilizing a management system by which course materials, resources, links, management tools, and content are systematically organized for ease of the teacher's management and the students' use is imperative for implementing best instructional practices. Improving and supporting teaching and teachers' use of instructional technology gives more students informed, adaptable teachers who, in turn, support students to their utmost potential. Measures of effective teaching now include aspects of technology integration and use that include comprehensive measures to support student growth. Many school districts have taken steps to methodically plan, implement, review, reassess, and redesign or redirect important aspects of such data systems initiatives and processes that engage teachers at the district and campus levels.

Teachers can be confident that improvements in these management systems continue to occur and to be investigated. A series of reports (US DOE, 2009, 2010, 2011) by the U. S. Department of Education over the years describes attempts to connect student data management systems and instructional practices. The *Teachers' Ability to Use Data to Inform Instruction: Challenges and Supports* (US DOE, 2011) describes teachers' thinking about data that could guide districts' efforts to provide appropriate initiatives to prepare and support teachers in their expected use of student data as a basis for improving their effectiveness. Findings reveal that while teachers were adept at finding information in a table or graph, corresponding written text provided minor challenges. Difficulties in evaluating written statements about data that required basic mathematical calculations, for example, suggest that teachers may have misconceptions about their students' performance. A promising aspect of the report indicates that the teachers "appeared quite sensitive to the fact that students will do better on a test if they have received instruction on the covered content and had their learning assessed in the same way (e.g., same item format) in the past" (p. x). The *Use of Education Data at the Local Level: From Accountability to Instructional Improvement* (US DOE, 2010) documented a dramatic increase in the proportion of teachers with access to a student data system between 2005 and 2007 and provides a picture of increased local practices in implementing data-driven decision making provided in the earlier reports.

Important findings in the report include the assertion that data-driven decision making is an ongoing process. This process is not a one-time event centered on the acquisition of a data system. This supports the thinking about system-wide innovations and long-term strategies as part of a continuous improvement process. Other findings reveal that teachers need data from recently given assessments and diagnostic information on students' learning needs and that the use of this type of data should be a regular part of teachers' practice. This

Figure 15.9   Teachers can receive guidance on technology use and practices via video conferencing.

requires that schools provide time for teachers to meet with colleagues to discuss and use data according to the *Use of Education Data at the Local Level: From Accountability to Instructional Improvement* (US DOE, 2010). It is suggested that there be positions that are funded for instructional coaches who help teachers connect data to alternative instructional approaches. Further, the coaches provide modeling of data-driven decision making for continuous improvement in their own operations.

> Mrs. Lee teaches eighth-grade mathematics. She has an average of 25 students in each of her classes, so it seems an overwhelming task at times to know where each of these students are. She does know that just teaching lessons "to the middle" or based on how her textbook chapters are arranged is not effective teaching for many students in her classes. Two years ago, her district invested in a data management system that is starting to pay off in helping her to target individual areas of need. District math committees have designed benchmark tests to be given at designated intervals, and the data management system allows teachers to have the scores of each student and each concept quickly in her hands. During the first year, the district provided training on how to use the system, and this year she is able to run her data and understand it. From the beginning of the year, she was able to see the progress of each of her students. She and her grade-level colleagues meet after each benchmark test to generate new strategies to help students who are struggling on the concepts tested. The grade-level committee also asked the district for some blog space so that math teachers throughout the district could communicate and share ideas for improvement. At the semester break, she compares students' scores from last year and is clearly able to see that she is more effective in reaching students with individual needs—because she now has a way to see what those needs are.

The development of models of how to connect student data to instructional practices and to enhance teachers' assessment interpretation and data use skills also require time and support. The US DOE 2007 and 2008 reports on *Teachers' Use of Student Data Systems to Improve Instruction* provide evidence of increased teachers' access to and use of data from student data systems through a secondary analysis of data from teachers and district technology coordinators as part of the US DOE National Educational Technology Trends Study (US DOE, 2008). This allows teachers to use these systems to provide information to parents and to track individual student test scores and monitor student progress. The *Implementing Data-Informed Decision Making in Schools: Teacher Access, Supports and Use* (US DOE, 2009) report from the US Department of Education draws on case study findings resulting from interviewed district staff members as well as principals, whereby teachers were given a set of scenarios involving hypothetical student data to probe teachers' understanding of student data taken from the U.S. Department of Education's National Educational Technology Trends Study. Findings revealed that even though data systems were used in school improvement efforts, they were having little effect on teachers' daily instructional decisions at times. This was because neither teachers nor administrators were able to see a comprehensive record of students' longitudinal and up-to-date educational experiences and performances. Another important finding is that few of the data systems incorporated resources (such as instructional materials, model lesson plans, and formative assessment results) linked to frameworks and curriculum guides that could provide teachers a more comprehensive process by which to operate. These reports illustrate the progress that continues to be made and the initiatives yet to be incorporated to build more effective and efficient use of data systems intended to improve instruction. Nevertheless, beginning teachers must include time in their busy schedules to understand and receive training on the use of these complex data management systems. Once they learn how to use these systems, they can link data about their students to instructional practices that are most appropriate to their needs.

Instructional Technology Resources

The members of the graduating class of 2027 are mere toddlers today; however, current technology trends which have accelerated since their birth reveal that they will rely only on an address and GPS for directions rather than on maps. They will buy and sell on sites similar to eBay as frequently if not more often than through shops and stores. Their "books," newspapers, classified ads, photo albums, or need for cash will be replaced with personal devices and a variety of online options. In the core areas of English language arts and reading, mathematics, science, and social studies, there are tools and resources already available to expand students' knowledge, skills, and approaches to learning and knowledge-seeking. In the future, these will have expanded in ways that we are not able to articulate today.

Figure 15.10   Today, we do not know technological advances that will be available to the class of 2027.

A brief summary of existing resources in the core instructional areas provides a hint of what these young learners will encounter in classrooms of the future. Teacher candidates can refer to chapters in this text focused on technology for each of the content areas and for other areas such as ESL (Figure 15.11), early childhood, and special education for more details. The next sections of this chapter provide a general overview of instructional technology resources currently available in the core content areas. Future teachers should know the instructional technology resources available in the different content areas so that they can engage students in new and creative ways. Future students and their families will have used multiple electronic devices at home, and new teachers need to respond to these changing environments because there will be an expectation from parents and students to do so.

Figure 15.11   Instructional technology resources are available in all content areas.

Science Resources

In the area of science, electronic opportunities abound to engage students in self-initiated inquiries and discoveries (Figure 15.12). "I'm more interested in arousing enthusiasm in kids than in teaching the facts. The facts may change, but that enthusiasm for exploring the world will remain with them the rest of their lives" are passionate comments made by Seymour Simon (2014). (http://www.seymoursimon .com). Simon, author of more than 250 highly acclaimed science books, provides sciences resources and a Web site which includes free downloads of materials for educators to use as well as multiple resources for students. Monthly newsletters, blogs, books, and electronic resources provide the latest materials.

Figure 15.12   Interactive science resources are readily available for use in today's classrooms.

General science technology tools, tools for instruction in chemistry, biology, physics, environmental and earth science, space astronomy and astrophysics, and medicine and nano science are bountiful (refer to Figure 15.13 for an example). These go beyond YouTube channels and apps which already provide virtual labs, simulations, digital libraries, short films, and scientific lectures. There are many other resources via iPads and Chrome books on topics from science, technology, engineering, mathematics (STEM) to gaming (http://edtechteacher.org/tools/science).

Figure 15.13 Thermometers for science experiments can be pre-programmed.

Social Studies Resources

Even though WebQuests are currently popular resources (as are virtual trips to countries and historical sites students are studying), using the Internet to research a country and historical sites is common place in the area of social studies. The explosion of online search engines and data bases, such as The Library of Congress and the National Archives (which have databases that center around American history and culture), are but limited Web-based resources. Provisions for expanded communication options for teachers and students include the use of podcasts by which students could use iPods to create radio casts of information they research. They could use blogs to host online discussions to respond to other teachers or students and their discussion questions. Pen Pals is a hallmark social studies tool long used to help students understand and engage with other cultures. Reliance on a postal service and communication via letters has long since been replaced with the use of email with students in a country, region, or area that students are studying (refer to Figure 15.14 for an example of how communicating via email and social network sites, social studies students could render aid to people recovering from natural disasters). This traditional mode of exploration and understanding is likely to be replaced by video and virtual experiences. These methods allow students to ask questions first hand and to 'experience' the culture through someone their own age. Videoconferencing that allows students to talk with experts or a guest speaker provides real learning opportunities. Teachers can facilitate and plan for these rich activities. They should check school policies or with the principal about enabling the use of necessary technologies, planning for the experiences, and supporting students with additional resources they may need. This happens during exciting lessons but also far prior to that in technology planning committees, training, and so forth to support today's teachers with these types of technological capabilities.

Figure 15.14 Social studies students could render aid to people recovering from Hurricane Sandy.

English Language Arts and Reading Resources

In the area of English language arts and reading, opportunities via e-textbooks, adaptive reading sites which provide leveled books, and so forth promote student development and grow into more difficult texts as they become better readers and writers. These tools which often contain graphics, video, sound, and animation allow teachers to provide differentiated instruction to an ever changing population of students with more diverse needs and interests. Other resources include the use of text-reading software. Teachers with students who have special needs and English language learners will want to provide opportunities for students to "hear" the written word or to use the translation options to optimize language acquisition for non-English speakers. These tools are also beneficial for students who may experience a lag in language development. Other helpful tools allow for creations of story boards, the use of interactive libraries, dictionaries, word play and phonics-based games, opportunities for read alouds, online language arts games, grammar and letter writing resources, vocabulary development games and activities, and fluency and comprehension resources. Technology resources in this content area can be used to accommodate students with learning disabilities, English language learners, different learning styles, and variations in student interests and academic performance. The teachers who interact with colleagues, attend training, and commit to staying current technologically will be able to provide such resources for their students.

Mathematics Resources

The National Council of Teachers of Mathematics (NCTM) includes in its strategic priorities that NCTM will "Promote strategic use of technology to advance mathematical reasoning, sense making, problem solving, and communication" (http://www.nctm.org/uploadedFiles/About_NCTM/Mission/NCTMStrategicPlan2013.pdf). The organization highlights the increasing importance of statistics, modeling, and discrete mathematics and the need to update curriculum pathways to prepare students mathematically for their futures. There are many mathematics resources for teachers, students, and parents. A site such as "Ask Jeeves for Kids-SquirelNet" is an example of the tutoring and support system that provides students fast and easy ways to find answers to questions. From the elementary assistance provided by such Web sites as *Learn Your Tables* to the more sophisticated free online scientific calculators for complex calculations, technology resources are plentiful in the area of mathematics. Online magazines and publications provide mathematics-related news articles, podcasts, and mathematics puzzles designed along "real-life" scenarios (Figure 15.17). There are numerous interactive Web sites that allow students to practice and find solutions to difficult problems (Figure 15.15). These Web sites provide step-by-step solutions that help students learn and understand how to solve mathematical problems. Some include PBS (*http://www.pbslearningmedia.org*) mathematics lessons online, *All About Fractions, Math is Fun, FunBrain Math Practice and Challenges, JAVA Flash Cards, Money Sense Problems,* and videos to name a few. Students' ability to learn on demand or as needed will be greatly enhanced by enriched resources that are illustrated and already available.

Figure 15.15 Student engagement and curiosity is increased with technology resources.

Many content areas or general teaching organizations have conferences and newsletters that almost always include ideas for technology integration (refer to Figure 15.16). There are also conferences strictly for teaching with technology that are often geared for both classroom and university teachers. Some districts will fund membership fees and travel to these regional, state, national, and international conferences. New teachers should take full advantage of these opportunities.

Figure 15.16 Networking meetings and conferences allow teachers to share ideas about technology integration.

Online Learning

New teachers should be aware of the possibility that they may either be required to use online management systems or teach online classes in the future. These initiatives, when supported by district administrators, provide exciting opportunities for teachers to expand their reach to students outside their own classroom. Auyeung (2004) explains that both students and teachers benefit from a virtual environment in which they exchange ideas, views, and comments. Blackboard Learn technology, for example, uses communication tools such as Discussion, Email, Course Portfolios, Wikis, and Chat facilities. These provide a variety of options for the organizational needs and internal and external communication within a school or within a school system. The Blackboard tracking tools assess whether the tools and content are used and how they are used. Teacher can see the frequency and entry points by which particular resources are used by students. The teacher can then use this analysis for future development of coursework in targeted and strategic ways that promote and facilitate communication and collaboration. Teachers, schools, and school systems can establish an online presence: (a) to post critical information, (b) to conduct online surveys and dialogues, (c) to elicit critical information from the teachers and students about how the programs are going, and (d) to share educational insights and strategies to improve programs and collaborative relationships. This existing management technology has the capacity to transform every aspect of a school's mission, goals and objectives. As an example, opportunities for online professional development abound, as do educational applications to improve programmatic initiatives.

While Web-based instruction has been more ubiquitous in higher education institutions than in public education, states have initiated online or virtual networks and classrooms to meet the varied needs of small, rural, and financially-challenged school districts or homebound students. While public schools can learn from the work in higher education, caution is required in generalizing to the K-12 population because the results are, for the most part, based on studies in other settings (e.g., medical training, higher education). Regarding virtual networks, the *National Educational Technology Trends Study State Strategies Report: Vol. 1* (US DOE, 2007) reveals that the Enhancing Education Through Technology program is among the largest federal programs seeking to improve student achievement through the use of technology. This program is funded by the federal government, and this report supports the relationship between state educational technology program activities and the overarching goals and purposes of the No Child Left Behind Act of 2001. Findings in the report indicate that many states have technology standards for teachers to specify the knowledge and skills that teachers need to use technology for both administrative and instructional purposes. Both teacher and student preparedness to use technology cannot be minimized in future endeavors to expand virtual or online options for teaching and learning.

Figure 15.17   Teacher candidates should subscribe to educator resources on the use of technology.

Implications for Future Practice

To keep up with the quickly changing needs and requirements of technological innovations in schools, teacher preparation programs and school districts need to support teachers in new initiatives. Students in future classrooms will be no less inquisitive or creative than students in former years; however, technological tools will allow administrators and teachers to inspire and motivate student learning through creative uses of technology resources. Teachers will continue to blend content knowledge and pedagogical knowledge, but they will have access to electronic forms of assessment and record keeping to design and create learning experiences to maximize learning, skills, attitudes and knowledge creation. It will be important for teachers to model and demonstrate confidence in the use of digital age tools that support research and learning. An understanding of district policies will guide teachers and students in the use of digital resources in such a way that they are used appropriately and that they promote learning and collaboration. All educators should aspire to grow professionally in the use of digital tools

Figure 15.18   Teachers participate in communities of learning to develop their own technology skills.

and resources and participate in communities of learning to develop their own technology skills (refer to 15.18 to see that participating in a Webinar is a way to participate in a community of learning). Our future, and the future of young people, depends on the enthusiasm of educators to embrace educational technology in its many facets to inspire connected learners.

References

Auyeung, L. H., (2004). Building a collaborative online learning community: A case study in Hong Kong. *Journal of Educational Computing Research, 3*(2), 119–136.

Davies, R. S., & West, R. E. (2014). Technology integration in schools. In J. M. Spector, M. D. Merrill, J. Elen, & M. J. Bishop (Eds.), *Handbook of research on educational communications and technology* (pp. 841–853). New York: Springer.

Discovery Education. (n.d.). Retrieved from http://www.discoveryeducation.com

Edtechteacher (n.d.). General science tools. Retrieved from http://edtechteacher.org/tools/science

Integrated Studies of Educational Technology (ISET) as cited in U.S. Department of Education, Office of the Under Secretary, Policy and Program Studies Service. (2003). *Federal funding for educational technology and how it is used in the Classroom: A summary of findings from the integrated studies of educational technology*, Washington, D.C.)

National Council of Teachers of Mathematics. (2014). Lessons and resources. Retrieved from http://www.nctm.org/uploadedFiles/About_NCTM/Mission/NCTMStrategicPlan2013.pdf

No Child Left Behind Act of 2001. The No Child Left Behind Act of 2001. Retrieved from http://www2.ed.gov/nclb/overview/intro/execsumm.pdf

Project Red: Revolutionizing Education. (2013). The Greaves Group, The Hayes Connection, One-to-One Institute Web site. Retrieved from http://www.projectred.org

PBS Learning Media. (2014). PBS & WGBH Educational Foundation Web site. Retrieved from http://www.pbslearningmedia.org

Simon, S. (2014). Seymour Simon Web site. Retrieved from http://www.seymoursimon.com/ http://schoolcomputing.wikia.com/wiki/Technology_in_Social_Studies?action=history

Technology Leadership Network. (2014). http://www.nsba.org/services/technology-leadership-network Reproduced with permission. Copyright © 2014, National School Boards Association.

U.S. Department of Education, Office of the Under Secretary, Policy and Program Studies Service. (2003). *Federal funding for educational technology and how it is used in the Classroom: A summary of findings from the integrated studies of educational technology*, Washington, D.C.

U.S. Department of Education; Office of Planning, Evaluation and Policy Development; Policy and Program Studies Service. (2007). *State strategies and practices for educational technology: Volume I—Examining the enhancing education through technology program.* Washington, D.C.

U.S. Department of Education, Office of Planning, Evaluation and Policy Development. (2009). *Implementing data-informed decision making in schools: Teacher access, supports and use.* Washington, D.C.

U.S. Department of Education, Office of Planning, Evaluation, and Policy Development. (2010). *Use of education data at the local level from accountability to instructional improvement.* Washington, D.C.

U.S. Department of Education, Office of Planning, Evaluation and Policy Development. (2011). *Teachers' ability to use data to inform instruction: Challenges and supports.* Washington, D.C.

U.S. Department of Education, Office of Planning, Evaluation and Policy Development, Policy and Program Studies Service. (2008). *National educational technology trends study: Local-level data summary.* Washington, D.C.

CPSIA information can be obtained at www.ICGtesting.com
Printed in the USA
LVOW02s2127040915

452268LV00003B/19/P

9 781465 266583